An Introduction to
Asian Politics

An Introduction to Asian Politics

C. I. EUGENE KIM
Western Michigan University

LAWRENCE ZIRING
Western Michigan University

PRENTICE-HALL, INC., ENGLEWOOD CLIFFS, NEW JERSEY 07632

773381

Library of Congress Cataloging in Publication Data

Kim, Chong Ik Eugene (date).
    An introduction to Asian politics.

    Includes bibliographies.
    1. Asia—Politics and government. I. Ziring, Lawrence (date), joint author. II. Title.
DS33.K55   320.9'5'042   76-28342
ISBN 0-13-478081-7

©1977 by Prentice-Hall, Inc., Englewood Cliffs, New Jersey 07632

Printed in the United States of America

10 9 8 7 6 5 4 3 2 1

PRENTICE-HALL INTERNATIONAL, INC., *London*
PRENTICE-HALL OF AUSTRALIA PTY. LIMITED, *Sydney*
PRENTICE-HALL OF CANADA, LTD., *Toronto*
PRENTICE-HALL OF INDIA PRIVATE LIMITED, *New Delhi*
PRENTICE-HALL OF JAPAN, INC., *Tokyo*
PRENTICE-HALL OF SOUTHEAST ASIA PTE. LTD., *Singapore*
WHITEHALL BOOKS LIMITED, *Wellington, New Zealand*

For
Adlai, Leona, Margaret, and Sarah.
Their enlightened generation will show us a new path.

Photo Acknowledgements

Page 106   Heron Casle, Himeji, Japan, *Courtesy of Blackhawk Films, Inc.*
            Geisha Girl Serving Sake, Japan. *Courtesy of Blackhawk Films, Inc.*

Page 107   Chinese Children at Play, PRC. *Courtesy of Alfred Ho.*
            A Busy Port Scene, PRC. *Courtesy of Alfred Ho.*
            A Chinese Commune, PRC. *Courtesy of Alfred Ho.*
            Celebrating the Chinese Communist Revolution, PRC. *Courtesy of Alfred Ho.*

Page 108   Rural Scene near New Delhi, India. *Courtesy of Blackhawk Films, Inc.*
            2000 Year-Old Sri Chamunduswari Temple on top of Chamundi Hill, Mysore City, India. *Courtesy of Blackhawk Films, Inc.*
            Street Scene, Calcutta, India. *Courtesy of Blackhawk Films, Inc.*

Page 306   A Village in Laos. *Courtesy of Prentice-Hall Media, Inc.*
            A Cambodian Market. *Courtesy of Prentice-Hall Media, Inc.*

Page 308   Classic Thai Dancers, Thailand. *Courtesy of Blackhawk Films, Inc.*
            Manila by the Sea, The Philippines. *Courtesy of Prentice-Hall Media, Inc.*

Page 309   Household Chores in the Rural Philippines. *Courtesy of Prentice-Hall Media, Inc.*
            A Family Dwelling in the Philippines. *Courtesy of Prentice-Hall Media, Inc.*

Page 374   A Glimpse of Seoul, Korea. *Courtesy of Prentice-Hall Media, Inc.*

Contents

Chapter Five

Chapter Six

Chapter Seven

Chapter Eight

Preface

Every page of this book has been written with the student in mind. As teachers of undergraduates, we are sympathetic with student complaints that they are often confronted with textual materials that deaden rather than enliven their interest. As Asian specialistists who have taught general survey courses over many years, we are particularly sensitive to the needs of those young people whose only link with Asia is the dinner hour television account, the abstract newspaper headline, or the brother, cousin, or father who served in Vietnam. Student consciousness does not always translate into informed awareness. Moreover, in the great majority of American universities and colleges it is seldom possible to offer more than one course that focuses exclusively on Asian politics. Students taking this course want to know more about the Asia that they hear mentioned so frequently. But having attracted the student, it is necessary to hold his or her attention.

In our classes we have concluded that students are too often confronted with reading matter that overwhelms and discourages rather than excites and satisfies the reader. If students feel they cannot cope with the reading they will not labor—and even if they do—they will not necessarily understand what they have read. We feel our experience is not unique, that our colleagues in other institutions share our concern. This concern explains the motivation for the present volume.

An Introduction to Asian Politics has few footnotes, tables, and charts. Only a minimum of emphasis has been given technical or theoretical constructs. There is hopefully little jargon in it. It has been our quest to make *An Introduction to Asian Politics* a readable, concise, and interesting *first* book on Asian politics. In a sense we would like it to be read as the first word on the subject. The book will have served its purpose if students react favorably toward it and develop a positive attitude in their study of Asia.

For students, *An Introduction to Asian Politics* should be preparatory to more sophisticated presentations. Those who are provoked by the book (and of course by their classroom experience) will want to know more about Asia. It is our wish that this volume will make it easier for teachers to expose their students to materials of a more specialized nature. If the curious student can develop the confidence to handle advanced texts, this book will have more than served its purpose.

Asia has affected the course of American history, and it will continue to influence our lives. Our young people need to know a great deal about the vast continent and its turbulent populations. This book acknowledges the responsibility that we have as teachers to present another part of the world to our students.

Although we have avoided using numerous citations for the above stated reasons, we nonetheless recognize the enormous debt we owe the small army of scholars who have tried to inform us about Asia and its significance. At the end of each chapter are recommended readings, which not only assist the teacher and student in identifying relevant publications but also represent the sources utilized in producing this work. To the many unidentified authors whose publications we have consulted, we offer our heartfelt thanks.

While we are in the process of expressing our gratitude, it is most appropriate that we mention our wives: Raye M. Ziring who typed repeated drafts and offered advice and encouragement, and Hiroko Kim for her patience and understanding. We are also indebted to Christine Redman, Joan Lim and Brian Borlas for their secretarial and bibliographic assistance; to Shirley Swenson, Kenneth Rocco, Judith Matousek, and Judith Younkman Clevey, our students, who took the time to read and comment on portions of the manuscript; to those secretaries and colleagues in the Department of Political Science at Western Michigan University whose good humor enabled us to expedite the finished manuscript; and finally we wish to express our warm appreciation to Prentice-Hall, Inc. for their amiable cooperation.

As is customary, we humbly note here that we alone are responsible for any errors that have inadvertently crept into the text.

C. I. EUGENE KIM
LAWRENCE ZIRING

An Introduction to Asian Politics

Chapter One

An Introductory Note

The western world views its advanced technology in an ethnocentric way, often forgetting a few startling facts about the other half of the globe. For example, Asia covers one-third the land mass of the earth, contains two-thirds of the world's people, and possesses more cultural variety than the remaining continents combined. The East also has witnessed dramatic socio-political change more persistently than any other region of the globe. Asia of the post-World War II decades must be approached with these facts in mind. The student is *not* stumbling upon a semiconscious or primitive hinterland. The Asian continent has been and continues to be a dynamic, resource-laden region, and it is not coincidence that so much world attention has been focused upon it. (See Tables 1-1 and 1-2.)

The rekindling of ancient civilizations and the formation of independent states have been a part of the story of Asia since 1945. It is a story of old discoveries and new quests, of old relationships and new leadership, of passive masses and active minorities. In political perspective, Asians are struggling to find the meaning of government and the purpose of politics. Asia and the word *orientalism* have long been associated with systems of total power. Asia's masses may not possess decision-making responsibilities, but they have not remained immobilized in the political history of their respective countries. Their political participation follows lines in keeping with durable practices that focus on survival, i.e. unconditional grants of authority, infallibility, and personalized offices, in contrast to the ideals of western political philosophy, with its emphasis on limited government and political competition and choice.

Japan is the foremost example of an Asian country that has successfully modernized itself. Yet no one disputes the perpetuation of traditional Japanese norms and values. Communist China espouses an alien ideology, but despite its much publicized Cultural Revolution, China cannot conceal

1

MANY FACES OF ASIA

TABLE 1-1
Statistical Profiles

Country	Population°°	Annual Rate of Increase††	Surface Area°	Density†
Japan	109.67	1.3	372,313	291
China	824.96	1.7%	9,596,961	85
India	586.27	2.1	3,280,483	175
Pakistan	68.21	3.6	803,943	83
Bangladesh	74.99	2.8°°°	143,998	497
North Vietnam	23.24	2.0	158,750	142
South Vietnam	19.95@	1.8	173,809	111
Cambodia	7.89	2.2°°°	181,035	42
Laos	3.26	2.4	236,800	13
Thailand	41.02	3.2	514,000	77
Indonesia	127.59	2.3°°°	1,491,564	84
Philippines	41.46	3.0	300,000	134
North Korea	15.44	2.8	120,538	125
South Korea	33.46	1.7	98,484	334

°   Square Kilometers (one kilometer equals 0.621 mile)
°°   1974 estimates in millions
°°° estimated
†   population per square kilometer
@   1973 estimate in millions
††   1970-73 estimates

Source: Table compiled from *Statistical Year Book 1974* (New York: United Nations, 1975), pp. 70-71, and *Monthly Bulletin of Statistics,* Vol. XXX, No. 2 (New York: United Nations, February 1976.)

the influence of an ancient past. Similarly, the two Koreas seem poised between a turbulent past and an uncertain future. The countries of Southeast Asia are relative newcomers to the political scene: Indonesia, Thailand, Vietnam, Laos and Cambodia reveal more about their past than their present status. Even the Philippines, which avoided the turmoil experienced by its neighbors in the immediate post-World War II period, has succumbed to the relentless forces of its history. In South Asia, the picture is no different. India continues to struggle with its British-influenced parliamentary experiment, while traditional socio-political characteristics take on increasing importance. Pakistan, now separated from its eastern province, looks for a new beginning in a controlled parliamentary setting and shows little inclination to dispense with its original objective of creating an Islamic state. The new nation of Bangladesh, which rose from the ashes of the 1971 Indo-Pakistan War, intends to follow the dictates of secularism and socialism, but conventional Bengali culture is an obstacle to this plan.

TABLE 1-2
Population Distribution

Country	Year	Urban	Rural
Japan	1970	68.1	31.9
China	1971°	25.0%°	75.0%°
India	1971	19.9	80.1
Pakistan	1971	13.1	86.9
Bangladesh	1971°	12.0°	88.0°
North Vietnam	1970	9.5	90.5
South Vietnam	1970°	20.0°	80.0°
Cambodia	1970	10.3	89.7
Laos	1970	15.0	85.0
Thailand	1970	18.2	81.8
Indonesia	1971	17.4	82.6
Philippines	1970	31.7	68.3
North Korea	1971°	30.0°	70.0°
South Korea	1971°	40.0°	60.0°

° Estimated

Source: Compiled and modified from Lucian W. Pye, *Southeast Asia's Political Systems,* Second Edition (Englewood Cliffs, N.J.: Prentice-Hall, Inc., 1974), p. 98.

Democracy is no longer the rule. The euphoria created by the destruction of the Axis powers (Germany, Japan, and Italy) in World War II and the subsequent emergence of numerous sovereign states has been replaced with a cynicism that reflects the realities of a world gripped by conflict. In the immediate post-World War II period, it was taken for granted that democratic institutions and systems would flourish. The nations of war time alliance were expected to assist one another in their economic development. The world's resources, it was believed, could be utilized for programs of maximum human utility, and general prosperity was a convincing prospect. Economic stability promised to limit, if not eliminate, class conflict, and middle-class values were assumed easy to assimilate. Where Asia is concerned, few, if any, of these expectations were realized.

It is necessary to understand the impact of World War II on Asia in order to explain the current malaise. First, the countries of Asia show uneven development. All the nations described here were grossly affected by the war and its aftermath. Many were still struggling to achieve independence, while others engaged in violent campaigns to determine who would succeed to power. Democratic systems may have been germane for the United States and certain countries of western Europe, but they were not the most important concerns for the peoples of Asia. There was no significant middle class to bolster into a democratic role. Substantial segments of Asia's population were mobilized for national ends, but broadened political participation also increased the demands on government. Thus the newly independent Asian governments were under pressure to satisfy the aspirations of their populations, especially by the youths who, in cooperation with the professional classes, insisted on harvesting the "fruits" of statehood. As time passed, it became obvious that the leadership could not cope with the problems of scarcity, greed, and corruption. Daily life could not be sustained without resorting to authoritarian tactics. Conflict not cooperation, arbitrary actions not compromise, established the patterns of political life.

Authoritarian political systems have always been more prevalent throughout history, their durability attesting to their ability to function as agents of stability. They appear in many forms and are reinforced by a variety of myths and rituals. From the primitive headman to ruler-priests, on through to divine monarchs and contemporary popular dictatorships, the authoritarian model is an adaptable institution. All are responses to necessity. This elitism, however, reflects basic weaknesses of human society. Thomas Hobbes remarked that

> Covenants without the sword, are but words, and of no strength to secure a man at all.
> The bonds of words are too weak to bridle men's ambition, avarice, anger, and other passions, without fear of some coercive power.[1]

Such philosophy links government with physical power, and is based on the willingness of people to sacrifice their personal freedom for security. By implication then, human society has meaning only when it is subordinate to strong leaders. For many Asians, it is a matter of absolute power on the one side, or anarchy on the other. In modern Asia there is no claim to legitimacy without physical power, and any government is deemed better than disorder and chaos. What limits Asia's authoritarian rulers are not legal enactments and constraints, but countervailing power.

Bureaucracies are prevalent in Asian states. They reinforce the authoritarian model and are vital to political effectiveness. Moreover, Asian bureaucracies are older and more closely tied to the political process than their western counterparts. Whereas the American bureaucracy became prominent only in this century, Asians have experienced the heavy hand of civil administration from time immemorial. Traditional bureaucracies were designed to serve the state's interests rather than the individual, long before the idea of popular government was introduced. In the West, representative government preceded the expansion of bureaucracy. Be-

[1]Thomas Hobbes, *Leviathan*, in George H. Sabine, *A History of Political Theory*, revised edition (New York: Henry Holt and Company, 1956), p. 468.

cause the United States was endowed with a climate and soil conducive to abundant agriculture, there was little need for bureaucracy in its early years, or for that matter in pre-industrial Europe. In Asia, however, where massive public works projects, such as canals, irrigation systems, and fortifications were considered vital for the survival of the state and its subjects, bureaucracy was essential for social mobilization. By contrast, aristocracies were more a feature of European tradition. The European feudal system spawned a multitude of basically autonomous, self-sufficient principalities. Hence a fragmented aristocracy, not a centralized bureaucracy, formed the first representative institutions. Aristocracies declined when a growing middle class demanded political power, and when advances in science and technology made them antiquated nonentities. In the absence of a significant middle class, the Russian czarist aristocracy gave way to a more disciplined party-bureaucracy. In non-communist Asia, rulers have only recently and reluctantly displayed signs (usually under pressure from external sources) of sharing authority with incipient representative institutions.

Asian nations require broad-based cooperative ventures if they are to make material progress. Bureaucracy must therefore insist on almost complete conformism. This is believed imperative in projects requiring social mobilization. Given the emphasis on collective action, administrative behavior must affect national performance, as in the case of communist bureaucracies. When cooperation and conformism are twin features, populations submit to authoritarian techniques of governing. The gravity of the problems facing Asian nations dictates the use of relatively harsh methods. The submerging of personal ambition is a *sine qua non*, and self-aggrandizement is a serious crime. Nevertheless, in some Asian states the pursuit of personal gain is undiminished despite the existence of legal penalties. Bureaucratic corruption is a significant problem, but the weakness of democratically controlled institutions is no less significant.

AN APPROACH TO THE STUDY OF ASIA

Asian countries, with the possible exception of Japan, have often been classified as *transitional* societies. Considerable emphasis has been given their quest for modernity through industrialization. This is one way of studying Asian polities, and it is not rejected in this volume. However, it might be more rewarding to view the states and peoples of Asia as they are politically, rather than what they may become economically. In this context, Japan is no exception. The Asian continent is indeed in transition, but this suggests a multidimensional condition, with special stress on the political forces influencing a variety of life-styles. Our perspective does not encourage the discarding of the traditional for the modern. We prefer the notion that tradition is being modernized, particularly in a political sense. Asian tradition is not on the wane. On the contrary, it is at the core of the change process, establishing patterns and fashioning the destiny of the nations involved. Asian states are moved by the rhythm of their experiences, and it is these aspects that we examine in this text.

Our approach in this volume places heavy emphasis on historical developments. This decision was made deliberately, only after considerable thought. Since World War II events in Asia have moved with a suddenness that leaves even the specialist confused. Personalities, systems, ideas are in constant flux, and theorizing is difficult and often faulty. Students of contemporary Asia first need to develop an awareness of the past forces and patterns shaping the Asian landscape. This can best be accomplished with a thorough overview. Our purpose, however, is not that of the historian. We are concerned with on-going events. In each chapter the past is examined in order to comprehend the present. Broadly speaking, we are concerned with political problems and issues, and how the countries of Asia try to solve them.

RECOMMENDED READINGS

Almond, Gabriel, and James S. Coleman, eds., *The Politics of the Developing Areas*. Princeton, N.J.: Princeton University Press, 1960.

——————, and G. B., Powell, Jr., *Comparative Politics: A Developmental Approach*. Boston: Little, Brown, 1966.

Apter, David E., *Choice and the Politics of Allocation*. New Haven, Conn: Yale University Press, 1971.

——————, *The Politics of Modernization*. Chicago: University of Chicago Press, 1965.

Binder, Leonard, et al., *Crises and Sequences in Political Development*. Princeton, N.J.: Princeton University Press, 1971.

Black, Cyril E., *The Dynamics of Modernization*. New York: Harper & Row, 1966.

Coleman, James S., ed., *Education and Political Development*. Princeton, N.J.: Princeton University Press, 1965.

Dalby, M. T., and M. S. Werthman, eds., *Bureaucracy in Historical Perspective*. Glenview, Ill.: Scott, Foresman, 1971.

Deutsch, Karl, *Nationalism and Social Communication: An Enquiry into the Foundations of Nationality*. Cambridge, Mass.: MIT Press, 1953.

Eisenstadt, S. N., *Modernization: Protest and Change*. Englewood Cliffs, N.J.: Prentice-Hall, 1966.

——————, *The Political Systems of Empire: The Rise and Fall of the Historical Bureaucratic Societies*. Glencoe, Illinois: Free Press, 1963.

Emerson, Rupert, *From Empire to Nation*. Cambridge, Mass.: Harvard University Press, 1960.

Finkle, Jason L. and Richard W. Gable, eds., *Political Development and Social Change*. New York: Wiley, 1966.

Geertz, Clifford, ed., *Old Societies and New States*. Glencoe, Ill.: Free Press, 1963.

Huntington, Samuel P., *Political Order in Changing Societies*. New Haven, Conn.: Yale University Press, 1968.

Janowitz, Morris, *The Military in the Political Development of New Nations*. Chicago: Chicago University Press, 1964.

Kautsky, John H., *Communism and the Politics of Development*. New York: Wiley, 1968.

——————, *The Political Consequences of Modernization*. New York: Wiley, 1972.

Lapalombara, Joseph, ed., *Bureaucracy and Political Development*. Princeton, N.Y.: Princeton University Press, 1963.

——————, and Myron Weiner, eds., *Political Parties and Political Development*. Princeton, N.J.: Princeton University Press, 1966.

Lerner, Daniel, *The Passing of Traditional Society*. Glencoe, Illinois: Free Press, 1963.

Moore, Barrington, Jr., *Social Origins of Dictatorship and Democracy*. Boston: Beacon Press, 1966.

Myrdal, Gunnar. *Asian Drama: An Inquiry into the Poverty of Nations*, three volumes. New York: Pantheon, 1968. Abridged one-volume ed., New York: Vintage, 1972.

Pye, Lucian W., ed., *Communications and Political Development*. Princeton, N.J.: Princeton University Press, 1963.

——————, and Sidney Verba, eds., *Political Culture and Political Development*. Princeton, N.J.: Princeton University Press, 1965.

Riggs, F. W., *Administration in Developing Countries: A Theory of Prismatic Society*. Boston: Houghton Mifflin, 1964.

Rustow, Dankwart A., *A World of Nations: Problems of Political Modernization*. Washington D.C.: Brookings Institution, 1967.

Shils, Edward, *Political Development in the New States*. The Hague: Mouton, 1962.

Wittfogel, Karl A., *Oriental Despotism: A Comparative Study of Total Power*. New Haven, Conn.: Yale University Press, 1957.

Chapter Two

Japan:
Asian Achievement

A *land of paradoxes!* One hears many exclamatory remarks of this sort by western visitors to Japan. Examples are plentiful: modern super-highways soar over rutted and dusty country roads; multi-story skyscrapers stand next to two-story shacks; the imperial palace remains a serene oasis in Tokyo, a city of more than ten million people. Japan's Gross National Product, third only to that of the United States and the USSR, has grown at a record-breaking rate, but per capita income is still relatively low. The democratic order of the country, instituted during the allied occupation following defeat in World War II, is operative, but is merged with Japan's unique tradition and culture.

THE OLD AND NEW

The old and new are intricately inter-mixed in the Japanese political process. Outwardly, many Japanese political structures are modern, but internally, traditional Japanese informal orientations govern decision-making. Traditionally, the Japanese emphasize function rather than form. Substantive decisions and efforts to achieve consensus are more important than procedural questions. Japanese decision-makers talk together informally—*hanashiai*—for many hours and often in a casual atmosphere to arrive at a unanimous decision. Drastic decisions are unlikely in this situation, and even if such a decision is made, it is made under the guise of outward calm.

Tradition and conformity are strong elements in the Japanese political culture. In victory and defeat, the Japanese people are proud of their tradition. As a nation they are sentimental and highly permissive of their own wrongdoings and occasional variations from the norms. The individ-

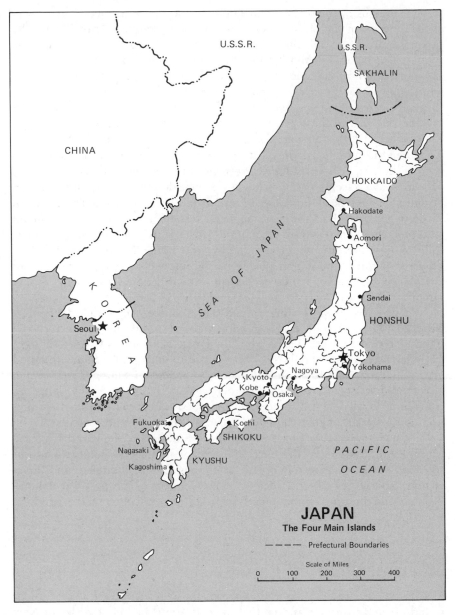

Source: Robert E. Ward and Roy C. Macridis, *Modern Political Systems: Asia* (Englewood Cliffs: Prentice-Hall, Inc., 1963). Reprinted by permission Prentice-Hall, Inc., Englewood Cliffs, N.J.

ual alone must be responsible for his or her wrong-doings or deviations from accepted behavior. From childhood, the Japanese people are taught to be conscious of the social implications of their personal acts. There is no clear concept of sin in Japanese culture as is found in the West. The Japanese substitute for this concept, however, is the sense of guilt and shame. The Japanese child is constantly admonished not to bring shame to the family. One's behavior is governed by a sense of guilt. But, then, a wrong-doing, in the eyes of some, could be to others the pursuit of a righteous cause. One can be brave and admired, but wrong. As a matter of fact, one of the most popular literary and dramatic themes in Japan is the conflict of different senses of guilt and shame and divided loyalties.

For the most part, the Japanese people are trustful of their government. They have been taught to respect authority, even though their top officials have recently been subject to considerable public scrutiny and criticism. The typical Japanese informal and affectionate relationship, in business and politics, however, depends less on a hierarchical command situation than on a sense of mutual trust. It is a paternalistic leader-follower relationship. As in the family, the father figure is politically a benevolent but authoritarian person. In family decisions, the father's word is final, but the father is not necessarily a fearful figure within the family circle.

There is a strong feeling among the Japanese people that debts must be paid. The Japanese are a generous people, and no gift is received without a due return. "Thank you" in Japanese means, "I never thought such an occasion would arise," or "I am so indebted." Some thankful occasions carry with them one's life-long, unending loyalty. This tradition is reflected in the leader-follower relationship. It implies a life-long pa-tronage in loyalty. One's teachers also deserve unending loyalty. Learning and education are highly valued in Japan as the keys to achievement.

These patterns in Japanese culture are not static, however. Changes are inherent, although the direction they will take is not certain. For instance, the socializing role of the family has gradually eroded, and Japan is now rapidly becoming a society of mass culture. The post-war generations of Japan are a new breed, very often critical of their age-long traditions.

THE LAND AND THE PEOPLE

Stripped of its pre-war imperial expanse, Japan is composed of four major islands. The northern island of Hokkaido is approximately the size of New England, and the southern island of Kyushu is the size of the state of Georgia. Lying between these islands are Shikoku and the main island of Honshu. The depression between the southern part of Honshu and the northern portion of Shikoku has resulted in the creation of a shallow inland sea. The Japanese islands form a great arc along the coast of East Asia and are comparable to the east coast of the United States in latitude and general range of climate.

Japan is a small country (143,000 square miles) when contrasted with geographical giants like the United States, Russia, and China, but is only slightly smaller than France or pre-World War II Germany.

The great stretches of towering mountains and hills are interspersed with rapid streams and small valleys, creating a scenically beautiful land. The coastline is rugged, and no place in Japan is far from the sea. Fishing, therefore, has been a major Japanese industry. Most of the people live in the lowlands facing the sea, and communication was, until recently, easier by sea than by land.

The insular position of Japan has contributed greatly to the shaping of Japanese history. The island country of Japan is set apart from the nearest continental land, the Korean peninsula, by a strait that is one hundred miles in width. Five hundred miles of open sea lie between Japan and China. Historically, this island kingdom has been an isolated land. Even in the days of China's domination of East Asia, Japan was never subjected to direct Chinese influence and was able to develop a more unique culture than, for example, Korea.

Ethnically, the Japanese people are Mongoloid like their neighbors in Korea and China. Archaeological evidence indicates that early Mongoloids came to the isles by way of Korea. When they arrived, the area was inhabited by the Ainu people. The Ainu may have been a group that became separated from Caucasian stock at an early stage in their development. They are fair-skinned with some surface hair and possess the physical characteristics of the Caucasian people. However, they were soon pushed north by the arrival of Mongoloid peoples and their more advanced culture. Many Ainu have intermarried with the Mongoloid peoples and as a result they have decreased in number and live in primitive settlements in the remote sections of the northern island of Hokkaido and in the smaller islands farther north.

Although Korea was the major contributor in the Mongoloid migration to the Japanese islands, others came from more distant regions such as northeast Asia and the coastal areas of south China. Close ethnic parallels exist between the present Japanese people and the people of Southeast Asia, and the earlier cultures of the people in these two areas are similar. The coastal area of south China may have been the bridge linking the Japanese people with the people of Southeast Asia.

The Mongoloid settlers in Southwest Japan, organized in closely knit clans, pushed northward. One of the clans from Kyushu moved up a natural highway skirting the inland sea between Honshu and Shikoku and finally settled in the small plain adjacent to the eastern end of the inland sea. This group took the name Yamato. The Yamato clan gradually spread its suzerainty over other clans and became the first unifying influence in the country. The people of this clan worshipped the sun goddess (*Amaterasu Omikami*), the founder of their clan, and organized themselves as a theocracy. Their leader served as both the secular and the religious chief. The unbroken line of the Japanese imperial family is believed to have stemmed from the first priest-chief of the Yamato clan.

HISTORICAL FOUNDATION

Much of the history of Japan in the Yamato period and the periods preceding it is known to us through the earliest written records of the Japanese people, the *Kojiki* (Record of Ancient Matters, A.D. 712) and the *Nihonshoki* (Record of Japan, A.D. 720), which were primarily the mythological justifications for Yamato dominance over other clans.

In the fifth century A.D., Japan was increasingly influenced by the highly advanced civilization of T'ang China, and a wholesale cultural borrowing from China, including Chinese characters, took place. Buddhism, with its rich cultural expressions, was also introduced in Japan, first via Korea and later through direct contact with China. Moreover, Japan attempted, after the Chinese fashion, to implement a centralized political system with supreme power vested in the Emperor. A permanent capital was set up in Nara in A.D. 710. In 794, the capital was moved from Nara to Heian, the present-day Kyoto. This remained the imperial capital for more than a thousand years until its transfer to Edo, today's Tokyo.

Gradually, the Yamato imperial family lost effective power. It was never replaced and there has never been another imperial family. But, even at the height of its power and sway during the Nara and Heian period the imperial government was never in full control of the numerous territorially-based clans, each with its own government. The Chinese system of government—a centralized bureaucracy with a national examination system for the recruitment of officials—never worked effectively in traditional Japan. Each clan was too powerful to submit to centrally-appointed officials.

Japanese feudalism evolved from the practice of landowning clan chiefs recruiting armed retainers to protect their domains. These retainers eventually constituted the *samurai*, a warrior caste. The samurai were the most privileged class in feudal Japan, and they were emulated, but also feared, by the general populace. Their strict code of behavior emphasized loyalty to their lords. Their ascendency to power coincided with the decline of Chinese influence in Japan. Given their place in Japanese society, the samurai made Japan unique in the history of East Asia.

The *bushido* is the way of life of the samurai. The code itself has never been written, but consists of maxims handed down by word of mouth or found in the writings of well-known warriors. Bushido stands for honor, justice, and all things that make one proud to be a warrior. To follow bushido is to serve; virtue lies in faithfulness to one's lord.

In feudal Japan, the test of dominance among the various feuding clans was waged on the battlefield. The victor ruled the country as a military governor duly sanctioned by imperial prerogative, and this precedent established by the Minamoto family in the twelfth century, was followed by successive military governors. Minamoto Yoritomo, the founder of Minamoto military rule, came to command the strongest military contingent in Japan. Acting in the name of the Emperor, he established the only effective central government. The seat of his headquarters, Kamakura, was the true political capital. Yoritomo never attempted to usurp imperial power. Instead he maintained the constitutional fiction that the imperial family was the ultimate source of power in the land.

The sixteenth century was a period of widespread unrest, political disintegration, and civil war involving the feuding samurai lords. Finally, Oda Nobunaga (1534-1582) established rule over the country, but his reign was short-lived. He was succeeded, however, by one of his generals, Toyotomi Hideyoshi (1536-1598), who ruled the country from his opulent Osaka castle. One of his ambitions was to conquer China. As a first step toward this end, he sent expeditionary forces to Korea on two separate occasions, in 1592 and 1597. When China (during the Ming dynasty) came to the aid of Korea, a stalemate resulted and Hideyoshi's expeditionary force never achieved its objective. Hideyoshi died in 1598, his dream unrealized. His contingents were withdrawn from the Asian mainland, and in the end the exercise had proved a costly venture for Japan.

When Hideyoshi died, his only son, Hideyori, was too young to assume leadership. A struggle for power ensued among Hideyoshi's powerful vassals and commanders. The final victory in this period was won by Tokugawa Ieyasu (1542-1616) in a decisive battle at Sekigahara (1601), a village lying half-way between Kyoto and Edo (Tokyo).

Tokugawa Ieyasu succeeded where his two predecessors had failed. He effected the lasting unification of the country. The government he established, which lasted 250 years, was a feudal system. The country was divided into feudal territories with the *daimyo* (feudal lords) in control. It was kept isolated from foreign influence. The Confucian ideas associated with the Chinese Sung dynasty philsopher, Chu Hsi, were carefully nurtured by the Tokugawa government to condition people to believe in the ethical state, benevolent rulers, and obedient subjects. There was no place for individuality in Tokugawa society, and to form political factions was tantamount to treason. The daimyo were closely watched and isolated from one another as much as possible, with political communication existing between the Tokugawa ruler and the daimyo, but not from daimyo to daimyo. The responsibilities of high officials in the Tokugawa's central administrative structure were rotated occasionally or divided in such a way as to avoid monopoly of power by any one person.

In the Tokugawa political system, the sacred and nominal position of the Emperor was kept intact at the court capital of Kyoto, while the Tokugawa established their government in Edo. The Tokugawa were the largest and most powerful lords, holding the largest estates and wielding the greatest wealth. About one-half of the country was ruled by branch families of the Tokugawa ruler or his allies. The remainder of the country, especially the large fiefs of Satsuma and Choshu in the south and southwest, was dominated by daimyo who had been Tokugawa's defeated enemies. They were required to live in Edo for a period of time, every other year. Their families, however, were left behind in Edo when they left the city to ensure their loyalty. These daimyo, who were called the "outer lords," were among those who later helped overthrow Tokugawa rule.

Within Tokugawa Japan, every effort was made to preserve the formal feudal status quo. A culture, however, is never completely static, no matter how isolated, and enough changes occurred within Japanese society to eventually render feudal controls unworkable. After two centuries of peace, the merchants gained power, while the samurai and feudal lords lost it. Many towns and cities developed. Confucianism and the relative peace that the Tokugawa regime was able to engineer encouraged samurai scholarship. Some samurai scholars, who engaged in the study of the Japanese way of the gods started questioning the legitimacy of Tokugawa rule and feared the spread of Buddhism as a popular religion. There was also a growing interest in European culture, despite Tokugawa's longstanding policy of isolation. There emerged a small, but intellectually vigorous group of students informed in the European sciences, particularly in southwestern Japan. These scholars worked through the medium of the Dutch language, which they learned from the Dutch at Nagasaki, the only open Japanese port at that time. They became keenly aware of the technological prowess of the West.

THE MEIJI RESTORATION

On July 8, 1853, Commodore Perry's squadron of black steam ships of the United States anchored off Uraga near Edo, causing consternation among the Japanese people. The United States was not interested in the territorial conquest of Japan. Perry had been sent to secure a treaty with

Japan, which would open Shimoda and Hakodate as ports of refuge where ships could obtain coal and stores. It would assure castaways of good treatment. The United States also wanted to set up a consulate. The Japanese council surrounding the Tokugawa government was divided on the question of accepting the treaty. To refuse the treaty could mean war and certain defeat. At last, the Emperor was consulted, an unprecedented practice for the Tokugawa rulers.

The treaty, as it was finally signed in 1854, exposed the weakness of the Tokugawa regime. The long, traditional policy of isolation was ended. The Tokugawa regime was financially bankrupt and even its legitimacy was in question. Externally, it was in no position to defend the country against Perry. Internally, the forces arguing against continued Tokugawa rule were too strong to be successfully counteracted militarily. Sensing this, the opponents of the Tokugawa regime coalesced around the double slogan, "Honor the Emperor; expel the barbarians," and pressed their attacks as they made military preparations. Submission to the restoration of imperial rule, not another feudal military regime, could be also the most face-saving device for the Tokugawa family, given the imperial myth as the ultimate source of power in the land. In point of fact, the last Tokugawa ruler voluntarily surrendered his political power to the Meiji Emperor and the samurai restoration leaders. Only die-hard Tokugawa followers made a last, bitter military stand against the restoration forces.

The forces that opposed the Tokugawa regime and rallied around the Meiji Emperor came primarily from the traditional anti-Tokugawa clans in south and southwest Japan. They consisted of young samurai from the Satsuma, Choushu, Hizen, and Tosa clans. Their common cause was to restore the Emperor to power, and this popular objective legitimized their actions.

As forces opposing the Tokugawa regime, the samurai restoration leaders rallied behind the Emperor, but also argued for the expulsion of the Western "barbarians" and against the Tokugawa policy of accommodating western demands for an "open door." As leaders of the new Meiji government of Japan, however, they were committed to Japanese modernization, and they openly imitated the West in order to make Japan militarily strong and prosperous, even if it was at the expense of the feudal social and political system, which had endowed them with privileged status.

As early as the winter of 1872-1873, the new Meiji government introduced compulsory military service, eliminating the need for the aristocrat-warrior. The loss of this cherished samurai position was radical enough, but even more serious was the loss of their privileged economic status. At first the government paid the samurai pensions, but this proved too expensive and was soon discontinued. In 1876, the samurai were prohibited from wearing their traditional two swords and were reduced to the status of ordinary subjects. Most adjusted to the situation and capitalized on their experience by taking positions in the army, navy, bureaucracy, or business. The Satsuma rebellion of 1877 was the last gasp of the fast-dying Tokugawa feudal society. A new peasant army, well-armed and drilled in the western manner, defeated this group of samurai rebels opposing the new restoration government. Thus passed into history the era of "the way of warriors" in Japan.

The restoration leaders were a remarkable group of men: young, ambitious, and highly capable. The small circle of leading figures in Meiji Japan, often referred to as the Meiji oligarchs, all came from the south and southwestern regions of the country, particularly the Satsuma and the Choshu clans, and enjoyed similar samurai backgrounds. In feudal Japan, they were born to lead; now they were determined to lead in the creation of a modern Japan. There were no mass rebellions. The feudal relationship between leaders and followers remained. The masses followed the leadership which the government provided and they bore the brunt of expenses for the modernization of the country. Various reforms were planned and carried out. These reforms spread over a wide area of political and socioeconomic life. They included: (1) abolition of the feudal political structure; (2) abolition of hereditary servitude and restraints on travel and choice of occupation; (3) the consolidation of local, provincial, and national governments and their monetary functions; and (4) establishment of universal education, and military conscription. The government also provided leadership in business and industry. Model factories were built with public funds, and generous government subsidies were given to businessmen and industrialists. Public railroads were constructed, and the government set up telegraph and telephone systems.

Provisions of the Meiji Constitution

With the Meiji restoration, the Emperor was once more reinstated in the ultimate position of power, but the Meiji oligarchy took actual control of the government. The political scene was fluid. Many ex-samurai clamored for participation in the government, and some organized their own support groups to exert pressure. The constitution was yet to be devised. Meantime, the Meiji oligarchs relied on old, familiar practices.

On April 6, 1868, the Emperor gave a Charter Oath and made the following pronouncement before an assemblage of court nobles, daimyo, and samurai who were gathered for that purpose. The brief but significant document ran as follows:

1. We will call councils and rule the nation according to public opinion.
2. Men of the upper and lower classes shall, without distinction, be united in all enterprises.

3. Civil officials and military officials shall be in one accord, and all the common people shall be so treated that they can attain their aims and feel no discontent.
4. Old unworthy ways and customs shall be destroyed, and everything shall be based upon the just and equitable principles of nature.
5. Knowledge shall be sought among the nations of the world and thus the welfare of the empire will be promoted.

The Charter Oath was a remarkable document calling for a modern Japan eager to learn from the West. The first provision of the Oath, "We will call councils and rule the nation according to public opinion," was most controversial with many political groups clamoring for a parliamentary system of government. The Meiji constitution of 1889 was to climax a long series of debates on the nature of constitutional government for Japan.

The constitution, which was superceded only by the present post-World War II constitution, reflected the political concepts of the ruling clique within the Meiji government. The constitution, drafted secretly, strengthened oligarchic rather than representative rule. It also strengthened the myth of imperial absolutism. Because it was promulgated as a gift from the Emperor to the people, no criticism of it was tolerated. Its chief architect was Ito Hirobumi, a young samurai restoration leader from Choshu who was a confidant of the Meiji Emperor and served several times as Prime Minister. His search for a constitutional model led him to Europe and finally to Germany, where German advisors helped in drafting the constitution.

The constitution provided a strong, centralized unitary state for Japan and made the Emperor the ultimate source of power. All appointive, executive, administrative, legislative, and judicial powers were vested in his person. The constitution made it clear that the Emperor, the successor of an unbroken line of divine ancestors, was a sacred personage. He was to rule the people through his chosen councilors.

The constitution also established a two-house Diet, or legislative assembly, consisting of an appointive House of Peers and an elective House of Representatives. The powers of the House of Representatives, the only area in which political parties could exert a controlling influence, were essentially negative. Legislation could be initiated by either House only with the approval of a cabinet minister. This immediately hobbled the parties in the area of reform legislation, because for many years cabinet posts were held by members of the conservative ruling oligarchy. Only with the establishment of party cabinets in the 1920s was this difficulty reduced. The cabinets were responsible only to the Emperor, and the Emperor constitutionally owed no one an explanation for the exercise of his appointive power. This situation prevented the Diet parties from easily toppling cabinets. Even the Diet's control of the purse strings was undermined. In case the Diet refused to pass a budget, the budget of the previous year automatically went into effect.

The aim of party government is to control government personnel and policy. The structure of government under the Meiji constitution made both of these goals difficult to attain. Only the limited power of the House of Representatives could be achieved by political parties. The power of appointment to the cabinet, or to the centralized bureaucracy, lay with the Emperor, who acted through a handful of powerful advisors. A small group of men who advised the Emperor on the choice of Prime Minister became *Genro* or elder statesmen, and in their capacity as councilors to the throne, the members of the Genro wielded imperial decision-making powers. The Genro was a unique institution in Japanese political development. The five initial members were all restoration samurai leaders active in the restoration government. They were never replaced, and a power vacuum created by the departure of the aging Genro from the political arena was never successfully filled within the framework of the Meiji constitution.

The Meiji constitution was never a well-synthesized document. It created several centers of power that were not properly checked and balanced. For instance, the Emperor was sovereign, but he was too sacred to direct the day-to-day work of government. The constitution provided a cabinet system of government, but the cabinet was responsible only to the Emperor. The Diet was given a weak and negative role in the government and was unable to exercise positive influence in the decision-making process.

The military and the Privy Council constituted the other centers of power. The Privy Council advised the Emperor on matters concerning the Constitution, emergency decrees and martial law, treaties, and international law. As military advisors, the Chief of the Army General Staff, the Chief of the Naval General Staff, the Army Minister, and the Navy Minister also reported directly to the Emperor. Military leaders wielded an unfair amount of power. This was due to the practice of selecting Army and Navy ministers directly from officers on the active duty list, a practice that dated from pre-constitutional times. Because of this practice, the military could disrupt the government by recalling an Army or Navy minister to active military duty, or by refusing to fill the position. Between 1915 and 1936, Army and Navy ministers were also drawn from the retired officers, but the military remained a dominant influence in the Japanese government.

The Emperor Meiji died in 1912 and was succeeded by his only son, the Emperor Taisho (1912-1925). However, Emperor Taisho became insane toward the end of his short reign. His son, Hirohito who was to become the Emperor Showa was appointed regent.

   The cumulative effects of the Meiji reforms and many basic social changes were making an impact on the country. Compulsory education increased the literacy rate. Mass communications media developed, and Japan made impressive progress in other areas of development, such as urbanization and industrialization. The Gross National Product increased from 1,997 million yen in 1900, to 11,845 million yen in 1920. The electorate was larger and more politically vigorous. Universal manhood suffrage was put into effect in 1925. Internationally, Japan had extricated itself from an unfavorable position in dealings with the West and had managed to rise to the status of an imperial power. Japan was the victor in wars with China in 1894-1895, and with Russia in 1904-1905. Territorial possessions by 1912 included the islands of Taiwan, the Pescadores, Sakhalin south of the 50th parallel, and the Korean peninsula. Japan also enjoyed "most favored nation" status with China (see Chapter Three, p. 64). During World War I, Japan fought on the side of the western allies and became inseparably related to these powers. This period coincided with the spread of liberal ideals for liberty, equality and democracy throughout the world following the peace settlement at Versailles.

   Japan was governed by the "Taisho Democracy" between 1918-1922 and 1924-1932, when the cabinets were headed by leaders of the majority party or majority coalitions in the Diet. Prime Minister Hara, a major party leader, was the first non-samurai commoner to assume the position of premier. Similar to other party leaders of the day, he lacked effective control of government. Various power groups in the government were beyond the control of the party cabinet. Each group was strong enough in its own right to topple the cabinet and government. Political parties achieved power only through the acquiescence of other competing power groups. The military eventually replaced the political parties and assumed the dominant decision-making role in the government.

THE MILITARY RISE TO POWER

In 1931, the famed "Manchurian incident" occurred. The Japanese army had been stationed in Manchuria during the Russo-Japanese War (1904-1905), remaining there to protect the Japanese South Manchurian Railroad system, which had been set up in 1906. Japan's presence in Manchuria had never been secure, however. In fact, the Chinese Nationalist government started "rights recovery" campaigns and challenged the Japanese position in Manchuria in the 1920s. Negotiations soon stalemated, and the two governments were unable to come to terms over Manchuria. The Japanese Manchurian Kwantung army took matters into their own hands and settled the question by forcing Japanese occupation of Manchuria.

The Tokyo government had not been consulted beforehand, but was forced to acquiesce to the *fait accompli*.

The 1920s and the 1930s saw the emergence of an increasing number of ultra-nationalistic organizations of young military officers and civilians, who refused to accept the second power status accorded Japan at the Washington and London disarmament conferences (1922, 1930). These groups advocated an expansionist foreign policy. They also insisted on business reforms (particularly giant family corporations called *zaibatsu*), and political reorganization. These ultra-nationalistic organizations were responsible for the assassination of some leading party leaders. The most daring anti-government nationalistic provocation came in February, 1936. A group of young officers in the First Division, stationed in Tokyo, revolted and assassinated the army Inspector-General, the Finance Minister, and Admiral Saito, who was Lord Privy Seal. Tokyo was seized by the rebels and held for three days. Civilian control over the military had never been institutionalized in Japan. Young officers reacted with nationalistic fervor against economically depressed conditions. They were supported by influential and vocal civilian leaders, as well as elements of the general populace who viewed territorial expansion as paramount to Japanese security. They called for *Lebensraum* (living space) and looked to the military to press Japan's national interests against China and other powers.

Within the military, there were two main factions. The young officers dominated the Imperial Way Faction (*kodoha*) and their conservative senior officers led the Control Faction (*Toseiha*). In order to control the radical young officers, party politicians were forced to support the moderate senior officers group.

If the Japanese government had created a military structure that was responsible to the command structure, the desire for war, which was prevalent in the officer corps, probably would have been controlled. Instead, the lines of influence in decision-making began at the lower levels of the command structure. The two main groups that controlled the military power structure during this period were the radical young officers' group, composed primarily of company and junior field grade officers, and the *chuken shoko*, the so-called "nucleus group," composed largely of field grade and junior general officers.

The chuken shoko played a particularly significant decision-making role in the military because of their positions within the Army General Staff and within the Military Affairs Bureau, the policy-forming organ of the War Ministry. Because these were positions that controlled the drafting of plans and policies, the chuken shoko were able to transform their own views into official military policy. Moreover, their policy drafts were virtually never questioned by those who were supposedly their superiors.

By the mid-1930s the ambitions of the young officers and the chuken shoko could only have been thwarted by a strong cabinet opposed to their expansionist views. Such a cabinet did not exist. After 1936, Japan lacked a center of political power responsible for national decision-making, and the nation was rapidly drifting into a world war due to the ambitions of ultra-nationalistic elements.

Under military leadership, Japan set out to control China and expand its empire. Domestically, the Japanese people experienced growing regimentation and expanding governmental control over business and politics. Internationally, and in violation of the League of Nations Covenant, the Japanese government had already consolidated its position in Manchuria in 1932, by creating the puppet state of Manchukuo. Charged with aggression, Japan withdrew from the League in 1933. From Manchuria, Japan began penetration of China, and in the mid-1930s created a series of so-called "autonomous" regions in north China as a step toward the establishment of Japanese dominance over East Asia.

The Japanese military occupation of north China and the second Sino-Japanese war began in the summer of 1937, and quickly spread to central and south China. Japan never won a clear-cut victory, however. As the war dragged on, Japan found itself drawn into a larger struggle than had been anticipated. China would not capitulate as long as it was morally and materially supported by the Allied powers. The natural resources of Southeast Asia became an important issue. Japanese industry required these materials to sustain the war effort, but the entire area was in the hands of European powers and American interests. Japan began its invasion of Southeast Asia early in 1941, and later that year provoked a war with the United States by attacking Pearl Harbor. Japan plunged into a global war, eventually suffering defeat and ruin. American occupation of Japan occurred from 1945 to 1952.

POST-WAR GOVERNMENTAL STRUCTURE AND OPERATION

American Interlude

Although in theory the occupation of Japan was an Allied responsibility, in practice it was almost exclusively an American operation. An American general, Douglas MacArthur, was appointed Supreme Commander for the Allied Powers (SCAP), and the two primary objectives of the occupation of Japan were intially set forth by the American State-War-Navy Coordinating Committee as:

> 1. To ensure that Japan will not again become a menace to the U.S. or to the peace and security of the world. . .

2. To bring about the eventual establishment of a peaceful and responsible government which . . . should conform as closely as may be to principles of democratic self-government . . .[1]

Steps were quickly taken to achieve the first objective, to demilitarize Japan. Demilitarization included liquidating Japanese imperial spheres and limiting Japanese sovereignty to the four main islands. It also included the destruction of Japan's military hardware and war potential. The Army and Navy ministries were abolished, and all military forces at home and abroad were disarmed and disbanded. Furthermore, the International Military Tribunal for the Far East was set up to try suspected war criminals. Japan was to renounce war for any purpose as stated in Article 9 of the new constitution,

the Japanese people forever renounce war as a sovereign right of the nation and the threat or use of force as means of settling international disputes.[2]

Japan was never to maintain land, sea, and air forces, or any other war potential.

SCAP undertook its second objective: to form a new democratic government in Japan. This would entail a gigantic social, economic, and political revolution. It was a subtle and difficult problem, however, because Japanese cooperation was essential for its success. Administratively, SCAP worked through the Japanese bureaucracy. SCAP supervised and directed policy decisions, but was not responsible for day-to-day working arrangements in the government. Despite defeat and the subsequent purge of pre-war personnel, Japan still managed an efficient government administration. Working alongside the Japanese, SCAP had an effective staff under the strong leadership of General MacArthur.

The steps that SCAP took to politically remake Japan may be summarized in the following broad action programs:

1. Remove hindrances to democratic growth.
2. Encourage changes conducive to democratic growth.
3. Remedy the Meiji constitution to provide proper checks and balances and a clear locus of political responsibility among the governmental powers.

---

[1]See "United States Initial Post-Surrender Policy for Japan," Appendix II in Edwin O. Reischauer, *The United States and Japan* (Harvard University Press, 1965). For a collection of documents for the period, see also Supreme Commander for the Allied Powers, Government Section, *Political Reorientation of Japan*, September 1945-September 1948 (U.S. Government Printing Office, 1949).

[2]Article 9 of the Constitution.

No political or social reforms could endure without the support of the people. The necessary support was generated by reforms that served the interests of a broad spectrum of society and created new alliances.

One of the first acts of SCAP was to release all pre-war political prisoners and dissolve all pre-war nationalist organizations. All known ultra-nationalists in designated public and private offices (approximately 200,000) were replaced by new personnel. The concepts of personal equality, individual independence, and freedom were applied throughout Japanese society, affecting the traditional interpersonal relationships in the family and in the society, as a whole.

SCAP also readjusted the balance of power in Japanese society through economic and political reforms. The zaibatsu (giant family corporations) and their leading executives were purged, and their financial activities were restricted. In this way, the political influence of the big industrialists was reduced. At the same time, a labor movement and collective bargaining were encouraged. Under a program of land reform, land was redistributed largely at the expense of absentee owners. Ownership of land was restricted to two and one-half acres, and no one could hold land in absentia. SCAP also carried out the decentralization of the police and educational systems and encouraged and promoted local autonomy.

The 1947 constitution sought to institutionalize these reforms on a permanent basis. It was drafted within SCAP's Government Section and presented to the Japanese government on February 13, 1946. The Japanese government, after some persuasion and pressure, adopted it without substantive change, and an Imperial proclamation to that effect was made on November 3. This constitution, which was finally put into effect on May 3, 1947, is Anglo-American in spirit and includes some of the most democratic features to be found anywhere.

The Occupation lasted until April 28, 1952, when a peace treaty was signed restoring national sovereignty to the Japanese people. During the six years and eight months of occupation, however, SCAP policies experienced major shifts in orientation. Initial zeal for the reform of a militaristic, authoritarian enemy nation was modified, and Japan came to be regarded as an important ally of the United States in East Asia. Major efforts shifted from retribution and punishment to the maintenance of friendly relations. Many of the old leaders were permitted to revive their activities. Restraints were eventually imposed on the labor movements and clandestine Communist party activities. Some costly reform measures were also curtailed for reasons of economy.

The occupation administration focused increased attention on economic recovery, sometimes neglecting other earlier reform considerations. New business leaders emerged with a heavy concentration of wealth and influence reminiscent of the pre-war zaibatsu leaders. SCAP reasoned that Japanese economic recovery and growth were necessary for political stability and the success of political and social reforms. The United States also wanted to extricate itself from the responsibility and expense of feeding the Japanese people. For years after the surrender, American aid to Japan in foodstuffs and other goods amounted to one-half billion dollars per year.

The willingness of the Japanese people to cooperate with the occupation convinced the occupation forces of a future friendly relationship between the United States and Japan. A few other considerations also contributed to the change in SCAP policy. Soon after the war, the United States experienced a cooling of its wartime alliance with the Soviet Union. Both countries differed widely over post-war solutions to problems. Furthermore, the balance of power in East Asia shifted drastically as the scales in China's civil war turned in favor of the Chinese Communists.

Constitutional Framework

Japan's 1947 constitution is based on the principle of popular sovereignty, and it states in its preamble:

> We, the Japanese people, acting through our duly elected representatives in the National Diet, determined that we shall secure for ourselves and our posterity the fruits of peaceful cooperation with all nations and the blessings of liberty throughout this land, and resolved that never again shall we be visited with the horrors of war through the action of government, do proclaim that sovereign power resides with the people and do firmly establish this constitution.

Another outstanding feature of the new constitution is its controversial Article 9. It stipulates that the Japanese people are "forever" to renounce "war as a sovereign right of the nation and the threat of use of force as means of settling international disputes." To this end, the Japanese people are forbidden to maintain "land, sea, and air forces, as well as other war potential." As subsequently interpreted, the maintenance of a self-defense force is not in violation of the provision.

Emphasizing the importance of fundamental human rights in a democratic Japan, the constitution also devotes one-third of its content to such guarantees. Thus guaranteed are:

> freedom of thought, conscience, assembly, association, religion, choice of occupation and residence;
> academic freedom;
> equality under the law;
> universal adult suffrage;

the right of workers to organize, to bargain, and act collectively;

freedom from any discrimination because of race, creed, sex, social status, or family origin;

marriage based on mutual consent of the partners;

equality between the sexes in such civil matters as property rights, inheritance, and divorce;

the right to minimum standards of wholesome and cultural living;

equal educational opportunities;

and the right of the accused to receive just treatment and to defend himself.

Within the national government, the legislature (called *Diet*) was made the highest organ of state power. The executive and judicial branches of government are responsible to the Diet. The post-war Japanese constitution has preserved the format of the Meiji constitution, but the Emperor is stripped of political authority, and the Diet, as representative of the people, is made an effective, governing body.

The Prime Minister is the head of the cabinet. He must be a member of the Diet. He is elected by the Diet members. The role of the Emperor in the appointment of Prime Minister is merely ceremonial. The Prime Minister designates the Chief Justice of the Supreme Court and the Emperor appoints him. The fourteen associate justices of the Supreme Court are appointed by the Prime Minister and "attested" by the Emperor.

The appointed judges must be approved by the electorate in the first general election following their appointments. Furthermore, every ten years their appointments are reviewed by a similar electoral process. The constitution decrees that judicial power is vested in a Supreme Court and in such inferior courts as are established by law. The Supreme Court is the highest court in the country and administers a single, uniform national court system throughout the country. It has the power to interpret the constitution and decides on the constitutionality of any law, order, regulation, or official act. The judges of the inferior courts are nominated by the Supreme Court and appointed by the cabinet for a term of ten years.

Under the constitution, all local units of government are created by the national government and exercise only those powers that are delegated to them. To encourage local autonomy within this unitary framework, the constitution stipulates the direct popular election of all local public officials and authorizes each local unit to manage its own affairs. National legislation that affects one locality must have approval by a majority of voters in that locality.

The constitution can be amended on the initiative of the Diet, whereas under the Meiji constitution, the sole power of amendment resided in the Emperor. A two-thirds vote of all the members of each House is required to initiate an amendment. Once initiated by the Diet, an

THE ORGANIZATION OF JAPAN'S NATIONAL GOVERNMENT

- - - - - Indicates semi-autonomous status or indirect control

The Japanese People

Emperor

Legislative Organs

National Diet
- House of Councilors
- House of Representatives

Elects

Administrative Organs

Prime Minister / Cabinet

Prime Minister's Office

Board of Audit

National Personnel Authority

Constitutional Research Council

National Defense Council

Legislation Bureau

Cabinet Secretariat

Ministries of

- Justice
- Foreign Affairs
- Finance
- Education
- Science and Technology Agency
- Welfare
- Agriculture and Forestry
- International Trade and Industry
- Transportation
- Postal Services
- National Defense Agency
- Construction
- Labor
- Home Affairs

Juridical Organs

Supreme Court

High Courts

- Family Courts
- District Courts
- Summary Courts

amendment proposal must be ratified by a majority of the votes cast at a special referendum and if so ratified the Emperor "immediately" promulgates it.

Governmental Organs in Operation

As "the highest organ of state power" and "the sole law-making body," the National Diet is directly responsible to the people (see Figure 2-1). It is composed of two houses: the House of Representatives (Lower House) and the House of Councilors (Upper House).

The House of Representatives consists of 511 members, who are elected from 123 electoral districts, plus Okinawa, for a term of four years.[3] The House is usually dissolved before the expiration of its term, however, and a new election is held. The organization of the House of Representatives includes a Speaker who normally is elected by the majority party in the House. He presides over its deliberations and maintains order. A vice-Speaker, who frequently comes from the opposition party, is also elected by the membership. The House of Representatives meets in full sessions, but increasingly the standing committees of the House perform the major deliberative functions.

The internal organization of the House of Councilors is much like that of the Lower House. It consists of 252 members elected by the electorates organized in two different constituencies. The local constituencies consist of 47 electoral districts (each prefecture constituting a district); 152 councilors are elected in these districts, with between 2 to 8 councilors representing the same district. The remaining 100 councilors are elected from the nation as a whole and represent the national constituency. The people vote separately for these two different constituencies. Unlike the House of Representatives, the House of Councilors cannot be dissolved. The members serve a term of six years, with elections staggered at three year intervals.

Although legislative supremacy is one of the distinct features of a parliamentary system of government, an institutional arrangement for close cooperation between the executive and the legislative branches is an important feature. Such cooperation has increasingly resulted in executive dominance in the legislative process. The executive branch, with its ever expanding national bureaucracy, has become better equipped for complex decision-making. The Japanese constitution bestows many legislative

[3]Japan, Office of Prime Minister, Bureau of Statistics, *Japan Statistical Yearbook, 1973-74* (Tokyo, 1975), "Composition of Members of the Diet, Local Government Assemblies and Local Heads (1973, 1974)," p. 596. The membership size of the House of Representatives was increased from 491 to 511 with the passage of a new election law in 1975.

powers on the executive branch of government. Growing executive dominance in the legislative process had made the cabinet the originator of all
important legislation, and the cabinet's Bureau of Legislation either drafts
or reviews all public bills.

Since 1955, the Liberal-Democratic Party (LDP) has been dominant
in the Diet. Because of strict application of party loyalty in the legislative
process, the LDP cabinet-sponsored bills are passed by the LDP members
in the Diet. In actuality, it is more likely that any legislative proposal is a
work of delicate compromise among various factions within the LDP.
Once a bill is presented to the Diet, the LDP has to answer to opposition
in and out of the Diet and to the electorate, whose support the LDP
cannot afford to lose.

The executive branch of government has enumerated powers exclusively within its jurisdiction. It has the power to submit bills to the Diet,
to supervise the administration of the state, to administer the law, to
conduct the civil service, to enact cabinet orders, to manage foreign affairs
and conclude treaties, and to administer national finances and expend
money from the reserve fund.

In the administrative process, the cabinet heads the civil service. The
cabinet ministers are political appointees and they are shuffled at about
one year intervals in a balancing act of various factions within the ruling
party. The stabilizing influence of various ministries is a huge bureaucracy
of some two million civilian employees. These employees are divided into
two groups: regular and special employees. The regular service employees
are clerical and administrative employees of the national government. The
special government service includes the cabinet posts, all positions requiring Diet approval for appointment, high officials in the Imperial court,
judges, ambassadors and ministers, Diet employees, common laborers, and
employees of government corporations (including Japan National Railways, Japan Monopoly Corporation, and Japan Telegraph and Telephone
Public Corporation).

In Japan, a strong Confucian tradition of high social status for public
officials still prevails. This tradition originated in the days when public
officials were regarded as chosen servants of the Emperor. Thus even
today young people seek positions in government service. The post-war
constitution, however, states that a government bureaucrat is a public
servant, who is a politically neutral professional and who performs his
duties and responsibilities in the interest of the people. The National
Public Service Law, enacted in 1947, made the national government
bureaucracy subordinate to the elected representatives of the people to
foster an efficient and democratic administration. The National Personnel
Authority was established to administer this law. Fashioned after the
United States Civil Service Commission, this authority is an independent

agency, consisting of three commissioners appointed by the cabinet and approved by the Diet.

One of the democratic features of the post-war Japanese constitution is the decentralization of governmental power giving local governments and administrative departments autonomy in personnel matters. A local public service law, which passed the Diet in 1950, governs these local personnel departments. Each local government has its own civil service personnel commission, which corresponds to the National Personnel Authority in organization and function.

In post-war Japan, the independent and impartial status of the courts as the sole organ of judging rules and regulations was established. The Court of Administrative Litigation, which had existed as a separate court in pre-war Japan, was abolished with the establishment of the new constitution. There is now only one unified court system headed by the Supreme Court. The Japanese court system constitutes a single, unified hierarchy and does not have a federal-state court structure as in the United States. There is, however, limited use of litigation: lawyers play a very minor role, while the prosecutor has great importance. For this reason the courts have not gained much independence under the new constitution. What happens outside the court system is as important as what occurs within. Many disputes are settled informally without a judicial decision, although greater use is made of the court system in commercial matters. There are no juries in the system.

Local Autonomy

The Local Autonomy Law of 1947 was designed to codify the constitutional principle of local autonomy. There are now many additional statutes dealing with the local civil services, local finance and taxation, local elections, and police, firemen, and education.

Prior to 1945, the local governments were merely administrative units of the national government, and practically all local officials were centrally appointed. After the enactment of the Local Autonomy Law, the Home Ministry was abolished. Governors of prefectures and mayors of municipalities now are elected by the voters in their respective areas for terms of four years. There are forty-seven prefectures (*ken*) including the metropolitan prefecture of Tokyo (tokyo-*to*), a district of Hokkaido and two urban prefectures (*fu*) of Osaka and Kyoto. Each prefecture is divided into municipalities, which include cities, towns, and villages. Each unit has a legislature, or consultative body, but there is no local judiciary.

Despite these provisions for local autonomy, Japan is still a unitary state. The local governmental units are created by the national Diet, and what powers the local governments exercise are delegated to them by the national government. Their functions include the enforcement of many national laws under the direction and supervision of the appropriate ministries. Recently, the power of the national government to manage local affairs has increased. This has happened for a number of reasons.

One reason for this transition is that by tradition and experience the Japanese people lack expertise in the management of their own community affairs. The national government still occupies the center of the stage in political activities. It makes all important decisions and has the financial and personnel resources to provide a leadership and direction the local communities need. It prescribes, under the present tax structure, all taxes— except insignificant extralegal ordinary taxes— available to local entities. It also collects about 70 percent of the total tax revenue. Many local problems such as social security, unemployment, and economic planning are indeed national problems, and the national government is in a better position to coordinate local efforts to solve them.

Thus far, this *reverse course*, as the trend toward centralization is called, has caused controversy in two particular areas: education and the police system. In 1956, school boards were made appointive rather than elective in order to end election politicking among school board officials and to overcome strong leftist influence within the school system. In 1958, the ethics course was restored to the curriculum against bitter opposition by liberals. They feared that such a course, as in the pre-war days, would be exploited to promote anti-democratic, militaristic features.

Centralization within the police system has resulted primarily from two considerations: (1) awareness on the part of locally autonomous units that the expense and inefficiency of their police administrations were a drain on their budgets, and (2) the volatile nature of Japanese society and politics in the midst of post-war recovery. In 1954, the Diet passed a new police law that instituted a unified police system in each prefecture. A Public Safety Commission was placed in operational control of the police in each prefecture. Commissioners are appointed by the governor, subject to approval by the prefectural assembly. The Chief of the local police headquarters is appointed by the National Public Safety Commission, with the consent of the prefectural commission.

Usually, the National Public Safety Commission is headed by the Autonomy or Home Affairs Minister and five other commissioners, who are appointed by the Prime Minister with the consent of the Diet. This commission is charged with the administration of police affairs related to state security and the overall coordination of police administration. Its functions include general control over such matters as police education, communication, criminal identification, and criminal statistics. Also under its jurisdiction is the National Police Agency, concerned with crime investigation and detection and police communications on the national level.

MAJOR POLITICAL FORCES

Interest Groups

The Japanese people prefer to act through the channels of a group. Traditionally, to act anonymously for the good of the entire group is a highly virtuous act. To seek individual distinction or self-aggrandizement is considered rash and immature behavior. "Individualistic" is a pejorative term to the Japanese.

The manner in which political demands are made through groups can be divided into two categories. One is through traditional cliques and factions that are tightly knit and based on face-to-face communications; the other is through modern forms of organization, such as trade unions and business and professional associations. The latter are more open in membership, more specific in purpose, and based less on personal loyalty between leaders and followers. What really has taken place in Japan is the mixing of traditional and modern types of organizations, so that personal cliques and factions, common to the traditional organizations, are found within modern associations.

The most important of the business associations is the Federation of Economic Organizations (*Keidanren*). This federation consists of large corporations and trade associations in such fields as steel production, banking, insurance, foreign trade, retail sales, amusements, warehousing, and real estate. Other major business associations are the Federation of Employers' Organization, the Japanese Chamber of Commerce, the Kansai Economic Federation of the major firms in the vicinity of Osaka, Kobe, and Kyoto, the Economic Federation of Tokyo, and the Medium and Small Enterprise Central Associations. These are the major business associations; many others of varying sizes also exist.

Japanese businesses have traditionally enjoyed the benefits of state support. No business, particularly the giants in industry and commerce, has been successful without the help of state grants and easy loans. In turn, the government has relied heavily on select business corporations for rapid industrialization following the Meiji restoration and during post-war economic recovery. Business organizations have also supported conservative political parties financially and through other means.

Close cooperation between government and business has not been matched by a similar relationship between government and labor. Historically, the Japanese labor movement can be traced to the turn of the century. It never became a major force in either economic or political affairs in pre-war Japan. Strongly socialistic in orientation, trade union membership in the 1936 peak year of the pre-war labor movement stood at 420,000, representing only 6.9 percent of the non-agricultural workers.

This weakness of Japanese organized labor is attributed to many causes. First, the political environment was hostile toward labor move-ments. The pre-war Imperial Japanese government was opposed to them. Labor unions were hounded by the police, and their leaders were often put into jail. Labor activity was regarded as subversive, and people with conservative political dispositions shied away from it. Second, labor was in a weak bargaining position within the Japanese economic structure. The supply of labor in pre-war Japan almost always exceeded demand because of the existence of surplus labor in the countryside. The "dual" structure of Japanese industry meant that industries were either too large or too small for labor to organize effectively. Labor relations in Japanese industry were paternalistic. The employer-employee relationship was like that of father and son in the Confucian familial relationship. It was not a contrac-tual and impersonal relationship, but a highly personal and affectionate one.

The post-war development of the labor movement in Japan owes much to the occupation, which favored, at least in the beginning, a strong and healthy labor movement. In the occupation reforms, labor at last found a favorable political climate, and unions mushroomed. By 1946 there were 23,323 labor unions with 5,692,179 members, representing 46.8 percent of the non-agricultural workers.

The General Council of Japanese Trade Unions (*Sohyo*) is the most powerful and politically active of the labor unions. This federation of national and local unions represents about 45 percent of all the unionized workers in Japan. It is a huge combination of many different unions with differing political orientations and many leadership factions. Mainly, it serves as the mainstay of the Japanese Socialist party. The two other important labor federations are the Japanese Federation of Trade Unions (*Domei*) and the Congress of Industrial Unions of Japan (*Sanbetsu*).

Agriculture is another major sector of the Japanese economy that has played an important political role. Farmers were regarded as a down-trodden lot in feudal Japan. However, Japan was primarily an agrarian country before becoming an industrial state, and the agricultural mode of life has shaped much of its culture.

Traditionally, agrarian interest groups have been interested in main-taining the prices of agricultural commodities on a par with the general price index.[4] The agricultural sector of the population, however, represents many differing interests. Landholders, owner-cultivators, and tenant farmers vie with one another for influence. The occupation-enforced land reforms alleviated this problem by reducing tenancy and the influence of landlords in the rural community.

---

[4]*General price index* refers to the relative market value of goods and services in a society.

Presently, 99 percent of the six million farm families belong to various agricultural cooperative societies. Many of these societies trace their origin to pre-war organizations. For instance, the Agricultural Cooperative Association (*Nokyo*) was organized in 1947 as the successor to the Agricultural Association (*Nogyokai*), which the government helped organize in 1943 to amalgamate all existing farm organizations. The Agricultural Cooperative Association claims to represent all class interests in the rural areas and has traditionally supported the conservative government. The Japan Farmers Union (*Nichino*) was organized to promote the interests of the poorer farmers. Since its inception, it has been dominated by socialists. The Union soon split into two factions, and the right wing socialist elements organized a separate organization in 1947 called the All-Japan Farmers Union (*Zenkoku Nomin Kumiai*).

A list of other important interest associations includes groups representing medical professions, women, and youths. The Japanese Doctors Association and the Japanese Dentists Association are supported by a majority of the practicing physicians and dentists. The Associations have sought to influence the government regarding excessive bureaucracy in regulating fees and health programs. The women's associations include the All-Japanese Federation of Local Women's Organizations, the Housewives Federation, the Japanese League of Women Voters, and many conferences sponsored by the political parties. A major youth association is the All-Japanese Federation of Students Self-Governing Organizations or *Zengakuren*. This is a national organization of university students, which includes many ideologically divergent groups. Many youth organizations are sponsored by political parties, religious groups, and others. There are also various organizations of the veterans of World War II, local governmental units, and religious associations. Foremost among these is the Value Creation Society (*Soka Gakkai*), a Buddhist sect, which has shown a phenomenal growth in membership from some 6,000 households in 1951 to 6,500,000 households in 1970. It has become a forceful religious and political movement in Japan, catering to the interests of the urban poor and politically alienated.

Political Parties and Programs

Party politics in Japan are not post-war phenomena. Following the surrender, many old-line party politicians became active again, regrouping themselves as political parties proliferated. Out of these parties, there eventually emerged Japan's present major political parties: the Liberal-Democratic party, the Japan Socialist party, the Japan Communist party, and the Democratic-Socialist party. The Clean Government party was organized in 1964.

The Liberal-Democratic Party (LDP) is the dominant party in Japan. It was formed in 1955, by the merging of the post-war conservative Liberal and Democratic parties. It has controlled the personnel and policy-making of the central government.

The LDP maintains headquarters in Tokyo, with local branches for basic administrative units (such as city, county, town, and village) and various voluntary associations. Its Central Academy of Politics is an auxiliary institution designed for the systematic training of party cadres (workers) and activists. The great number of councils and committees within the LDP organization, however, has tended to fragment the organizational structure of the party. The formal system of decision-making consists of the Party Conference, the Assembly of the Members of Both Houses of the Diet, and the Executive Council. Other important organs of the party include the Policy Affairs Research Council, Organization Committee, Party Discipline Committee, and Election Policy Committee. The Secretary-General is the chief administrator of party affairs, whereas the Party President, elected by the Party Conference for a two-year term, is the highest executive officer.

The Executive Council together with the Policy Affairs Research Council are the most important policy-making organs of the party. Appointed by the party President, their membership includes most of the influential figures in the party, representing various factional interests. The Policy Affairs Research Council usually makes major policy recommendations to the Executive Council. Once approved by the Executive Council, the recommendations by the Policy Affairs Research Council usually become party policies.

The national organization of the LDP includes the prefectural federations and local branches, which claim one and one-half million members. Attempts have often been made to transform the LDP into a mass-based party without much success. The LDP remains a cadre party. Its strength is not in its mass organization, but in the success of the individual conservative candidates in the elections and the generally conservative orientation of the Japanese people, particularly in rural areas. Political appeals are usually made not in terms of mass organizations, but rather on the local orientations of support groups and personal relationships.

As explained earlier, the LDP is closely allied with the Japanese business community, drawing most of its funds from it. Additional donations are received from individual groups, enterprises, and organizations. Ideologically, the Liberal-Democratic Party is anti-Marxist and anti-Communist. It publicly upholds democratic principles, advocates a sound capitalistic economy, and represents close alliance with the United States. As the enduring ruling party in Japan, however, it has a strongly pragmatic orientation. It is a conservative party by Japanese, not American, standards. The government of the Liberal-Democratic party has promoted legislation of various social welfare measures.

The Japanese Socialist Party (JSP), the second largest party in the Diet, was organized in its present form in October, 1955. Theoretically, the Party Congress, representing all branch and affiliated organizations and ideological right and left factions of the party, is the governing body. When it meets, members debate on a wide variety of issues (much more so than their conservative counterparts) and adopt a party platform. The Congress elects members of the Central Committee, the Central Executive Committee and its Chairman, and a General-Secretary of the party. The real decision-making power of the party, however, resides with the top executive officials headed by the Chairman of the Central Executive Committee. The chief administrative officer of the party is the General-Secretary.

The General Council of Japanese Labor Unions (*Sohyo*) is most influential in the JSP council. The General Council plays the dominant role in financing the elections for the party, and approximately one-half of all contributions come from it. For the socialist party candidates, endorsement by the General Council means a greater chance of winning in the election.

The most controversial aspect of the socialist platform has been their foreign policy. The Socialists are opposed to the pro-American attitude of the LDP. They have strongly opposed Japan's Security Treaty with the United States, insisting on the withdrawal of American troops and installations from Japan.

Domestically, in the face of economic prosperity under continued conservative rule, few in Japan have chosen the socialists' formula for economic prosperity. This formula tends to be expressed in utopian or apocalyptic terms, drawing primarily upon social grievances from traditional ideological sources. The party though factionally divided is committed to opposition to "American imperialism" and "peaceful revolution" to a socialist Japan.

The Japanese Democratic Socialist Party (DSP) parallels the Japanese Socialist Party in organization. In 1960, the perennial controversies between the ideological left and right factions within the Japenese Socialist Party resulted in the establishment of a separate socialist party by the rightist elements. It has only a small following, however. Its representation is the smallest of the five major parties in the Diet, which was elected in 1972. Its electoral strength, as a matter of fact, has been declining and it won only nineteen Diet seats in 1972, a decline of ten seats from the previous twenty-nine.

DSP espouses a middle-of-the-road policy within the Japanese political spectrum. It is associated with the Japanese Federation of Trade Unions (*Domei*), a politically moderate labor federation, as compared with the General Council of Japanese Trade Unions (*Sohyo*). The party's leadership is largely composed of a slightly older socialist generation, and includes a higher percentage of local politicians.

The moderate programs of the party include the rejection of the policy of neutralism for Japan, promotion of cooperation with the free world through the United Nations, and a strong anti-Communist stand. It also espouses a parliamentary democracy for Japan. The party has advocated the gradual modification of Japan's Security Treaty with the United States and the eventual withdrawal of American troops from Japan. It has also sought a cautious and gradual improvement of Japan's relationship with the People's Republic of China.

The Japan Communist Party (JCP) has enjoyed legitimate status since October, 1945. Soon after Japan's surrender, its leaders were released from prison and the party was reorganized (its formal organization dates back to 1922). Although the Communist Party has never enjoyed a popular appeal, in the 1972 general elections it registered a remarkable showing. The Communists polled slightly over 10 percent of the popular vote and gained thirty-eight seats, almost tripling their strength in the Diet. The JCP thus recaptured its high point of power. Their previous high point of power occurred in the 1949 general elections, when they polled 10 percent of the votes and became the fourth largest party in the Lower House of the Diet with thirty-five seats.

Since the open estrangement of relations between the Soviet Union and the People's Republic of China, an intense, factional struggle for dominance has developed between the Chinese and the Soviet parties. Under the leadership of Miyamoto Kenji, the party now insists on an independent course of action vis-a-vis the USSR and China and hopes to capitalize on its 1972 electoral success to increase mass appeal through further moderation of its policy positions.

In contrast to its earlier militancy, at the 1970 Congress the JCP called for a united, anti-imperialist front dedicated to peace, neutrality, and democracy. It seeks to control the Diet in cooperation with other "democratic forces," such as the JSP, through parliamentary means. It opposes violence and radical leftist groups such as the *Sekigun* (Red Army) and the *Rengo Sekigun* (United Red Army).

The JCP is the third largest party in the Diet following the 1972 elections. Its reformist appeals have had an impact on the electorate. Not only has it made an impressive showing in urban strongholds, particularly against the Komeito challenge, but also it has capitalized on a growing disenchantment against LDP dominance in the rural regions.

The Komeito (Clean Government Party) was initially organized as a political arm of the Value Creation Society (Soka Gakkai). Known as the Clean Government League at that time, it was active in local elections. Its members were elected to various local assemblies, finally polling some two million votes in the 1962 election for the House of Councilors, the first national election in which it had ever participated. The party designation was adopted in 1964 as the League planned active campaigning for its members in the upcoming 1965 councilors election. In that election, the party polled about seven million votes, becoming the third largest party in the House of Councilors with twenty members.

Not until 1967 did the Komeito compete in an election for the House of Representatives. In that year, the party ran a successful campaign and polled more than 5 percent of the votes cast, winning twenty-five of the thirty-two seats, which the party contested. The campaign was waged on the grounds of corruption within the conservative leadership. The Komeito candidates won against not only the conservative candidates, but also against the socialist candidates. The surprising fact about the Komeito, in the 1067 election, was the high rate of success of its candidates. In the 1969 election, the party won forty-seven seats in the House of Representatives, an increase of twenty-two seats over the previous election. Seventy-six Komeito candidates competed in 1969, but their electoral success was not as impressive. In the 1972 general elections, the Komeito experienced a great setback: the number of Diet seats won by its candidates declined from forty-seven to twenty-nine, the greatest defeat suffered by any party.

In 1972, the Komeito ran independent of its parent organization, the Value Creation Society. Their ties were officially severed in May, 1970. The Komeito was accused of having intimidated the writers and publishers of anti-Society books, and the Society felt damaged by its ties with the Komeito. The Komeito proved inept without support from the Society.

Other than members of the Society, the party draws its support mainly from alienated or unsuccessful segments of the rapidly changing Japanese society. It has its strongest support in the urban centers where the Communist party is also strong.

In the ideological spectrum of Japanese political parties, the Komeito is much like the conservative-moderate socialist parties, but it insists on ideological purity. It advocates a democratic polity for Japan and a capitalistic economy. It campaigns for the doubling of welfare payments for the people in need. It also opposes the rearmament of Japan, atomic testing, and the docking of American nuclear submarines in Japan. It insists on an end to corruption in government.

Parties in Operation

Due to the conservative dominance of the LDP, Japan's government has been dubbed a "one-and-one half party system."[5] Opposition parties in Japan have been relatively weak and unable to organize a viable coalition alternative. Their ideologies have been too divergent for compromise, appealing to different constituencies and support groups.

A curious situation emerging from this continued conservative dominance of the political scene in Japan is that the conservatives have become as progressive in domestic legislation as the socialists, who have argued for a wide range of welfare legislation. In order to stay in power, the conservatives must make concessions and adjustments to meet the demands of the increasingly articulate populace.

Another situation, characteristic of their advantage, is the tendency of the conservatives to dictate decisions to the other parties in the Diet. Inter-party communication and compromises have been difficult. The opposition parties, however, have used extra-legal techniques to gain concessions, including fist fights in the Diet between conservative and opposition Diet members, boycotts, agitation for strikes, and demonstrations for public sympathy.

Factionalism in the LDP and in contemporary Japanese politics, at large, refers to stable intra-party grouping on the basis of the traditional patron-client relationship. Factions and cliques are almost universal organizational phenomena, but in Japan's case they are characteristically stable and institutionalized.

Each faction, particularly within the ruling, conservative LDP, has its own financial support bases outside the party. Each experiences different influences, forming unique policies. Each faction has its own headquarters and does its own fund raising. Its membership is fairly stable and the leader-follower relationship is maintained as long as the leader returns to the Diet following each election. The members of the faction meet regularly as a club or study group.

The factions are really parties within a party, and they have added variety to the continuous conservative one-party dominance in the country. Factional leaders are usually longstanding Diet members who are influential in the party circle and who have many business and other outside contacts. Factional leaders are able to assist their followers in

[5]Robert A. Scalapino and Junnosuke Masumi, *Parties and Politics in Contemporary Japan (Berkeley and Los Angeles: University of California Press, 1967), particularly p. 53.*

getting elected to the Diet and deliver what their supporters expect in monetary and other rewards. In return, they expect a loyal following in a neo-feudalistic leader-follower relationship.

Understandably, a factional leader tends to draw a certain type of follower. This observation may be true more among the minority factional leaders and among the ideologically leftist-oriented than among majority leaders and pragmatic conservative parties. The LDP factions are seldom ideological factions, and their internal struggles usually pivot around the presidency of the party and for greater influence in party decision-making.

The LDP presidency is a hotly contested office, and a winning coalition is achieved through intensive negotiation among the various factions. The presidency of the party means the nation's premiership. By achieving a winning coalition, the candidate is in a position to promise positions in the government and political and financial favors to the factions.

Party factionalism has been variously assailed because of its divisive tendency and its obstructionist impact. Some efforts have been made to remedy it. Factional politics are here to stay in the Japanese political process, however, as long as they serve useful purposes and are integral to Japanese political style and culture. These groups articulate various interests in the one-party-dominant situation, and factional leaders provide access for the masses who otherwise are outside the closed party circle. Moreover, no Prime Minister can act alone, inasmuch as he is a product of an alliance of the factions and all major decisions reflect a compromise among factional interests. It is through this process of compromise that LDP factionalism has greatly contributed to the party's flexibility and receptivity to change. At the same time, however, too much factionalism may immobilize the party when united action is needed. It may also fragment responsibility for decisions, causing the party to become less responsive to the interests of the masses.

POLITICAL DYNAMICS

The Electoral System

In the Imperial government before 1945, the electorate chose only the members of the House of Representatives. The House of Peers was appointive. The legislative body was never a center of decision-making. Party politics were not popular, and though sometimes regarded as a necessary concomitant to a modern polity, they were generally regarded as disruptive of national unity.

In the first election, held in 1890, the electorate numbered only

450,000 (about one percent of the total population). This number gradually increased as the tax qualification was reduced, but the electorate was still only 1,000,000 in 1902, and 1,500,000 in 1912. The greatest increases in size of the electorate followed the 1925 legislation of universal manhood suffrage (about 12 million in the 1928 election), and the post-war introduction of universal suffrage (about 37 million in the 1946 election). The occupation also introduced a new electoral system. Elections are held in a different political environment and have come to have different meanings than they did in pre-war Japan. The Diet, particularly the House of Representatives, is truly a center of decision-making in post-war Japan, and electoral positions carry much more prestige and power than before. The electoral contest is no longer carried out in a subdued atmosphere. In contrast to pre-1945 elections, campaigns are much noisier. Japanese voters presently number approximately sixty-five million men and women, out of a total population of 107 million. The basic election law, the Public Offices Election Law of April, 1950, has occasionally been subjected to political in-fighting and amendment, but the right to vote (those twenty years old or older, who have established residency in the district for three months or more) remains its fundamental feature.

For the election of the House of Representatives, the country is divided into 123 districts (since the 1967 general elections) plus Okinawa, each electing from three to five representatives. One exception to this general rule is the district of Amami Oshima, which was created in 1955, with only one House seat assigned to it. Theoretically, the larger the population, the more representatives elected in the district.

Regardless of the number of representatives chosen from each district, however, the people vote for only one candidate. Thus, the individual votes for fewer candidates than the total number of seats distributed to his or her district. This single-vote system within the multi-member constituency encourages minor party representation in the Diet. At the same time, however, more than one candidate from the same party, often with different factional allegiance, could be elected from the same district. The post-war era has seen a general decline in the number of candidates running for election and an increase in the role of political parties in the nomination of candidates. Though independent candidates are still elected in Japan, party nomination and endorsement have been increasingly sought by candidates to aid in their election.

In Japan, the legal requirements for candidacy to the House of Representatives are minimal. There is no residency requirement, and all qualified Japanese voters twenty-five years of age or older can run in any district by filing their candidacies with local Election Management Commissions. Certain public officials, however, must resign from their positions before they become candidates, and no one may simultaneously be a member of both Houses of the Diet. The application for candidacy must accompany a deposit of 150,000 yen (about 500 dollars), and if candidates fail to poll a certain percentage of the votes, they forfeit the deposit fee.

The above minimal candidacy requirements are matched by stringent regulation of the electioneering process. When the House of Representatives is dissolved, the cabinet must call a general election within forty days. The coming of an election must be announced at least twenty days in advance. The candidacy registration must be filed within four days following the official notification of the election. Formal electioneering is carried on only after the registration of candidates is completed. The amount of money candidates are permitted to spend on a campaign is specified by law by dividing the number of registered voters by the number of representatives for that district, and multiplying by a fixed amount. Candidates are required to report their campaign fund expenditures to the proper authority and to publish them; they are subject to the formal accounting of such expenditures.

Regulations, though somewhat ineffectively enforced, cover practically all other aspects of campaigning, including personnel, campaign offices, speeches, advertising, and publicity in general. Canvassing from house to house is strictly prohibited; no petition campaign is allowed; no food and refreshments may be served as part of a campaign; no leaflets, buttons, or handbills may be distributed; no campaign parades are allowed; the distribution of written materials is limited to a specific number of campaign postcards; the use of cars for campaigns is restricted; a limited number of campaign posters are allowed; and a limited number of speeches may be given. Thus far no television, radio, or newspaper ads are permitted.

The Election Law was designed to protect the public from corruption and to guarantee a fair election. However, these regulations tend to favor incumbents in the election. New faces in Japanese politics find it hard to gain the necessary publicity. Short and restricted campaigning cannot overcome a long, subtle, and informally cultivated exposure to the voters.

Voting in Japan is not compulsory. It is, however, regarded more as a duty than a right, particularly in the rural areas. The government takes positive steps to register voters and to encourage electoral participation. The Election Management Commission of each city, town, and village is held responsible for the preparation of a basic list of voters each year, and the list is made public. Generally, voter participation is greater, and the rate of turnout is more stable in Japan, about 75 percent, than in the United States. The electoral turnout also is greater in rural areas than in urban areas and greater in local elections than in national elections. The Japanese rural voters are still bound by tradition, and they may still be

TABLE 2-1
Party Preference and Socio-Economic Characteristics of the Voters*

	Liberal-Democrat	Socialist	No Party
National average	43%	22%	22%
Sex			
Male	47	22	19
Female	40	21	25
Age			
20-24	27	32	29
25-29	38	30	29
30-39	39	25	24
40-49	48	20	19
50-59	52	16	24
60-	53	8	21
Education			
Elementary	42	14	25
Middle school	44	23	21
High school	43	25	23
College	42	26	20
Occupation			
Professional	33	37	21
Managerial	42	13	35
White-collar, big business	34	32	23
White-collar, small, medium business	42	30	20
Family enterprise	48	17	26
Small business owner	62	10	19
Agricultural-fishing	59	12	16
Blue-collar, big business	19	51	15
Blue-collar, small, medium business	30	26	30
Day labor	35	28	17
Umemployed	40	20	26
Voting rate			
Always vote	47	24	16
As often as possible	41	20	29
Don't vote	27	15	40
Population classification			
6 largest cities	41	23	25
200,000 and more	37	27	21
100,000-200,000	46	15	31
50,000-100,000	36	22	25
To 50,000	45	18	25
Towns-villages	47	22	17

* "Don't Know" respondents and minor party supporters (13 percent) excluded.

Source: Warren M. Tsuneishi, *Japanese Political Style* (New York: Harper & Row, 1966), pp. 160-61. See also Tokei Suri Kenkyujo, *Kokuminsei no Kenkyu Dai 3-ji Chosa, 1963 Chosa* [Japanese National Character: Third Survey of 1963], p. 77. Adapted by permission of Harper and Row, New York.

persuaded by group norms and by a sense of duty and group loyalty. They are easily mobilized to participate in elections, whereas urban voters suffer from political alienation and cynicism.

Some other characteristics of the Japanese voters are identified in the previous table (see Table 2-1). Among the variables examined in these tables, differences in age and occupation seem most significant in the support for the LDP and the Socialist party candidates. Only younger people, professional people, and big business blue-collar workers are more likely to support the socialist parties than the LDP. In all other aspects, the LDP shows greater appeal among the electorate than do the Socialist parties. The particular stronghold of the LDP votes has been traditionally with older people, farmers, fishermen, and small business owners, not with the new generation Japanese, who are urban, educated, and politically articulate. Concomitantly with Japan's rapid post-war development, however, the latter group has been increasing in number and political strength and has been posing a serious threat to the LDP's dominant political position.

The 1972 Election

In a nation as compact and crowded as Japan, information and opinions circulate rapidly and even small changes produce national repercussions. At present, it would seem that the Japanese people are satisfied with the unprecedented economic prosperity engineered by the conservative LDP. However, periodic government surveys of public opinion reveal a significant increase in the level of expectations and attendant frustrations, particularly among poor farmers and the expanding urban white collar and labor work force. These groups constituted approximately 60 percent of the Japanese work force in 1970 and are expected to exert a significant influence upon the political arena in the future. This changing political millieu provided the atmosphere for the 1972 House of Representatives general election, an election that may prove to be a landmark in Japanese electoral politics.

The resignation of the 71-year-old Prime Minister Sato due to ill health ended the eight year rule of the aging politician. Although there were more powerful factional leaders aspiring to the succession, 54-year-old Kakuei Tanaka was chosen rather unexpectedly. Tanaka was a break with the traditional image of the successfuly LDP politician. He was not a member of the powerful Tokyo University clique within the LDP and his education was primarily of a vocational nature. A millionaire businessman before entering politics, Tanaka was a young, unorthodox, and outspoken self-made man. He was to represent a fresh outlook for the LDP establishment.

Once in office, Tanaka pressed forward dynamic policies of

internal and international development. He announced with much fanfare
a grand design for remodeling the Japanese islands in order to cope with
the problems of urban overcrowding and congestion. Recovering swiftly
from the shock of the surprise Nixon detente with China in early 1972,
Tanaka hurriedly concluded a normalization treaty with the Peking government. Likewise, the stalemated negotiations for a formal peace treaty
with the Soviet Union were resumed as well as opening the possibility of
Japan's cooperation in joint enterprises in Siberia. In order to capitalize
upon the "Tanaka boom", a December election was called and Tanaka
campaigned actively. In spite of the lavish expenditures and vigorous
politicking of the LDP, the election results proved to be a disappointment
for the LDP. Although the LDP managed to retain a slim majority in the
Diet, it lost sixteen seats and received only 49.9 percent of the votes cast.
The Komeito and the Democratic Socialist Party (DSP) suffered as well,
losing their Diet seats to the Japan Socialist Party (JSP) and the Japan
Communist Party (JCP). The JSP rebounded strongly from its 1969 setback. The JCP was, however, the real winner, increasing its strength from
fourteen seats to thirty-eight seats (see Table 2-2).

The JCP has steadily increased its electoral strength in recent years.

TABLE 2-2
Results of the 1972 Lower House Election

	Number of Seats Won	Pre-election Strength	Percent Total Vote	Percent in 1969
LDP	271 (277)°	297	46.9	47.3
JSP	118 (114)	87	21.9	21.4
JCP	38 (39)	14	10.5	6.8
Komeito	29 (30)	47	8.5	10.9
DSP	19 (20)	29	7.0	7.7
Other groups	2	0	0.3	0.2
Independents	14 (1)	3	5.1	5.3
Total	491 (10 vacancies)	477 (14 vacancies)	100.0	100.0

°   Redistribution of party strength at the opening of the 74th Diet session in January, 1975.

Source: See Japan Institute of International Affairs, *White Papers of Japan, 1971-72* (Tokyo,
1973), p. 297.

In the 1972 elections, the JCP's strong showing was largely at the expense of the Komeito and the DSP, but what most concerns LDP leaders is the growing popularity of the JCP in rural areas. The Japanese voters who are getting more and more disenchanted with the establishment seem to be turning to the JCP as a reformist party. The LDP's long dominance has had a stifling effect on the increasingly articulate populace, and the people are searching for an alternative. Economic recovery and amazing development under the conservative leadership have produced some un-pleasant by-products that now concern the people. These include corrup-tion, high prices, social welfare, urban living, pollution, and energy short-ages. The LDP is strongly identified with old timers; and the people of Japan appear to be in search of a new political atmosphere.

Coupled with the changing demands of the electorate are the reori-entation and reorganization of the JSP and JCP. The two parties were able to prepare for the 1972 election more effectively than ever before. Not only were they able to minimize their factional disputes but they also modified their heretofore ideological approach in favor of an increasingly pragmatic one, concentrating more on electable candidates rather than party men. The possibility of a coalition opposition to the LDP arose during the election with the JCP Central Committee Chairman Nosaka declaring, " We want the Japan Socialist Party to make great advances. The Japan Communist Party would like to exert sincere efforts to move closer to the Japan Socialist Party."[6] After the election, the JSP Chairman Narita triumphantly predicted the realization of an anti-LDP coalition by 1975.[7] The obstacles in the path of this coalition, however, remained fairly serious. The divergent ideologies of the opposition parties, as well as the competition between the JSP and JCP for a leadership role in any coali-tion, served to make the prospect of a unified opposition somewhat tentative.

The Aftermath of the 1972 Election

The 1974 House of Councilors election served to further the steady decline of the LDP's political fortunes. The 252 members of this second Diet chamber are elected in staggered terms, and in 1974 some 130 seats were contested. The LDP launched an all-out drive in order to protect its tenuous eight-seat majority and the Tanaka forces were confident of success. Tanaka predicted winning 80 seats out of the total contested. However, those problems cited above combined with a 39 percent increase

[6]Quoted in "LDP's 'Evils' attacked by Nosaka in Hokkaido," *Asahi Evening News*, November 23, 1972.

[7]Ikeda Hajime, "JSP Aims at All-Opposition Group," *Japan Times*, December 18, 1972.

TABLE 2-3
House of Councilors Election (July 7, 1974)

	Elected	*Hold-over*	*Total*
LDP	62	64	126 (128)°
JSP	28	34	62 (61)
Komeito	14	10	24 (24)
JCP	13	7	20 (20)
DSP	5	5	10 (10)
Independent and others	8	2	10 (7)
Total			(250—2 vacancies)

°   Redistribution of party strength at the opening of the 74th Diet session in January, 1975.
Source: Asahi Shinbun, July 8, 1974.

in the cost of living index under Tanaka served to work against the LDP. Tanaka's unrealistic optimism was perhaps based upon a recent increase in opposition factionalism as well as a significant replenishment of the LDP war chest for the 1974 election.[8]

The major source of funding for the LDP was the *Kokumin Kyokai* (National Association), a political fund raising arm of the Federation of Economic Organizations (Keidanren). Each member business paid dues to the organization rather than contributions. In 1974 these dues were increased to support the LDP against the rising tide of opposition parties unsavory to business interests. Although the 1974 election turned out to be one of the most expensive elections in Japanese history, the LDP nevertheless lost its eight seat majority in the House of Councilors (see Table 2-3). Perhaps the most serious consequence of the LDP decline is its

[8]The *Asahi Shinbun* reported the following increases in the revenues of major parties in preparation for the 1974 election.

Revenues of Major Parties (in millions of yen)

	Jan-June '74	*Jan-June 1973*
LDP	14709	9061
JCP	4484	1738
JSP	2339	488
Komeito	645	381
DSP	599	339

Source: Adapted from the *Asahi Shinbun*, December 25, 1974.

inability to continue to dictate its will in the Diet. The danger of an evenly opposed party system might lead to immobilization of the legislative process especially in controversial areas such as defense, education, and trade liberalization.

As in 1972, the JCP gained the most from the 1974 election. It increased its popular vote by only 1.4 percent, but managed to gain nine seats through extremely effective allocation of voting support for specific candidates through the complex of electoral districts and multiple candidacies. Evidence of the weakening of Tanaka's party control was evidenced in an outbreak of LDP factionalism, resulting in some districts splitting the vote between competing LDP candidates.

Following the election, the *Asahi Shinbun* responding in part to public anger against excessive business involvement in the election published secret *Kokumin Kyokai* documents revealing its fund raising practices. Public protest began to batter the business-LDP nexus. Some businesses announced withdrawal from the association. Even within the LDP, Deputy Prime Minister Takeo Miki (who was later to succeed Tanaka as Prime Minister) resigned on July 12, saying he would work to reform the party and "money-power-politics."

In the end, the leadership of Kokumin Kyokai was forced to resign and its name was changed to *Kokumin Seiji Kyokai* (National Political Association), but nothing much has been done to the reality of corporate giving to the LDP and the enormous influence which the Japanese business community exercises in the LDP council. Meantime, Tanaka was charged with conflict of interest, having profited personally from his political career and having been implicated in a huge land scandal. Even the legitimacy of his plan for remolding the Japanese islands came under attack. Tanaka resigned his premiership on November 26, 1974 after only about two years in office. Miki, known as "Mr. Clean," was then named by the LDP leadership to succeed Tanaka. The new prime minister planned to reform the LDP, as well as party and election financing practices. He wanted to return morality to party politics. But he could not act alone. He had to depend on a delicate factional coalition within the LDP in order to stay in power. Ironically, Miki's administration was also shaken by alleged links with the American Lockheed Corporation. LDP leaders have been accused of accepting financial gifts in return for promoting Lockheed sales in Japan.

Political Activists

If politics is a game, then the players are the political activists. This group does more than simply vote at election time or join political groups. They play various leadership roles in the political process as members of the Diet and as high government officials. As leaders of political parties and special interest groups, they have an influential role in decision-making. They are local political bosses, and radical student group leaders as well.

Political activists in Japan have been classified as government and non-government leaders. They could also be called formal and informal leaders. Little can be said about the informal political activists. They are difficult to identify. Few efforts have been made to study them, despite the fact that much political activity surrounding decision-making occurs outside the confines of the formal governmental structure. The Japanese political process emphasizes consensus rather than actual head-count decisions, and there have been few charismatic leaders in Japanese political history. Leading political figures often have bureaucratic backgrounds. They are manipulators of small groups, rather than figures with mass appeal. They prefer anonymity to popular acclaim. Often the real wielder of power is a former, rather than a current, office holder.

Formal political activists generally are former bureaucrats, local politicians, or business leaders. Political activists in Japan tend to be older, more experienced people. Most successful, for instance, those who become Prime Minister or a cabinet member, have been those with bureaucratic backgrounds. They are graduates from top Japanese universities, such as the Tokyo University Law School, and ex-official figures who have successfully served the national bureaucracy.

Successful politicians have their own geographical bases (*Jiban*), the so-called "hard vote" areas, which they have cultivated carefully, usually in their home districts. In Japan, a politician wins a seat in the Diet more for his personal and affectionate relationship with his constituents than because of party label and policy stands. Politics are played on a very personal, informal basis, sometimes to the extent of being invisible to outsiders.

More formally, each candidate has a support organization in his or her district, *Koenkai* (literally meaning "public speech meeting"), which has become vogue in post-war Japanese political and electoral processes. Periodically, "public speech meetings" are held. Supporters consist of several divisions—a women's group, a youth group, and so on—and each group organizes many activities on a regular basis and for special occasions.

If a Diet member is an influential political boss, he has many local leaders working for him. They are often officials of local groups and organizations, such as the Red Cross Service Organization, the Federation of Housewives, or the League of War Widows. Local political bosses are long-time residents of their respective localities. They know many families on an intimate basis and are always willing to aid a family in distress, or to congratulate them on a happy occasion. In many ways, the Japanese political process reflects unique qualities, bred in the long history and tradition of the people. Traditions change but are never completely eradicated in developing nations.

The informal, affable Japanese interpersonal relations and decision-making style tend to preclude radical changes. But the Japanese political process has not been immune from occasional violence. It has also had its share of radical and reactionary movements. Professional radical and reactionary activists intend to subvert the status quo through the use of force. More notable, however, have been student organizations.

Japanese students have been known for their political activism and leftist leanings. In 1960 Japanese students joined others in waging massive demonstrations in Tokyo and other cities against Japan's ratification of the U.S.-Japan Security Treaty. The government of Prime Minister Kishi was shaken by this so-called *Ampo* crisis and was finally forced to resign. The planned visit of President Eisenhower to Japan was also cancelled because of the protests. Likewise, many colleges and universities were closed down during 1968-1969 because of widespread campus disputes and student strikes.

In many ways Japanese students constitute a special class by themselves, reacting strongly against discrepancies between their youthful hopes and aspirations and the realities they find surrounding them. In rapid social change and economic development the universalistic values of the society at large very often conflict with the particularistic nature of the family. Many Japanese students find themselves politically alienated and cynical toward their government and politics in general.

Zengakuren, a nation-wide federation of student self-government associations, is well known for its leftist leaning. Its radical elements were catalysts at key points in the Ampo struggle. Perhaps most extreme among its factions is *Rengo Sekigun* (United Red Army), which has become widely known because of sensational exploits by its members, such as the April 1970 hijacking of a Japan Air Lines to Pyongyang (North Korea) and the Tel Aviv airport bloodbath on May 30, 1972. Student organizations on the right of the Japanese political spectrum include various nationalist (*minzoku-ha*) groups of which *nichigakudo* (Japan Student Alliance) is most representative. It purports to: overthrow *Zengakuren*; destroy the Potsdam system and discard the present constitution for a new Japanese-made constitution; establish a self-reliant defense system; and spread Mishima's spirit.[9]

---

[9]Mishima Yukio was a famous writer and nationalist who committed traditional Japanese harakiri suicide on November 25, 1970 in apparent protest against the weakness of the Japanese Self-Defense Forces.

PROBLEMS AND PROSPECTS

Japan's most remarkable post-war success has been effective economic development. Japan's development has made it not only the most industrialized and wealthiest nation of Asia, but has achieved a technological status comparable to such twentieth century super-powers as the United States and USSR. Japan has achieved this status despite defeat in World War II and a lack of most of the raw materials needed for industrial development.

Defeat in the war forced Japan to limit its geographical base to the four main historical islands, small in size and densely populated. Japan's post-war allies and partners in trade remember well this country's former militarism and urge for imperial expansion. Aggressive Japanese overseas economic expansion has recently encounted strong opposition.

Trade is essential to the Japanese economy and prosperity. Most raw materials needed for industry must be imported, and manufactured goods must be exported. The smooth flow of raw materials is critical to the Japanese economy. The energy crisis resulting from the Arab oil embargo has proven much more severe in Japan than in the United States. A favorable international atmosphere for trade is, therefore, essential, but Japan is powerless to sustain such an atmosphere. Japan's military establishment is constitutionally limited to a self-defense force, and though modern and sophisticated in equipment and growing in strength, it is still small. Japan's political influence is also too limited to protect its trade advantages against unfavorable international political developments. These are serious frustrations for Japan as a trading nation and may create unstable situations in this nation's economic and political future.

Thus far Japan has been able to maintain a pragmatic posture, as characterized by her relations with the United States. The policy of the conservative government is to sustain a delicate balance between political and economic necessities. For trade and national security, Japan has been closely allied with the United States. The United States has been an invaluable trade partner of Japan and the sponsor of much of Japan's post-war economic recovery. The U.S.-Japanese Security Treaty of 1952 (revised in 1960 and again in 1970) was concluded in the spirit of mutual trust and conciliation. It stipulates a mutual dependency for national security, as well as the willingness of the United States to come to the defense of Japan in case of external threat. The United States, as a victor in World War II, disavowed any territorial ambition in Japan and returned Okinawa, once a mighty American military bastion, to Japan in 1972. The Japanese government was, however, mildly critical of American involvement in Vietnam, and would like to have a freer hand in dealings with Communist and other bloc nations.

Internally, Japan's unprecedented prosperity has created many problems. Improvement in agricultural technology and rice production has led to over-production, with consequent need for government protection from falling prices and farm impoverishment. Also, Japan no longer has an abundant, industrious, and cheap labor force. The composition of the labor force and its style of living have changed. Workers are now better educated and more organized. More of them are white-collar workers. Their expectations have risen greatly. When expectations are not met, frustrations also rise. Prosperity seldom is evenly distributed. For most of the people in Japan good housing is too expensive. Prices on the whole have risen too fast, and per capita income is not commensurate with growth in Gross National Product.

General prosperity has pacified the public and the ruling Liberal-Democratic party, in power since 1955, has received credit for it. The Japanese parliamentary system of government is still a one-party dominant system. The opposition forces, supported by a majority of labor unions, intellectuals, youth, and urbanites, have been articulate in airing their disenchantment with the government, but they have not been able to gain controlling power.

The Japanese opposition forces are often dogmatic, and a great ideological gap exists between the government and anti-government forces, leaving little room for compromise. Should the ruling LDP, factionally divided as it is, fail to produce a winning combination and become unsuccessful at the polls, Japan may be faced with political paralysis.

The rise of the military in pre-World War II Japan is a great lesson in this connection. Nationalism is still a potent political force in Japan. Political parties have failed to induce genuine popular participation in the country's political process. Politicians are often regarded as corrupt. The failure of civilian government in the 1930s was, in large measure, responsible for bringing the Japanese military into the political forefront. However, military ascendency to power in post-war Japan is unlikely, at least in the foreseeable future. There is a growing concern in Japan for the protection of international interests; but most of the Japanese people do not feel that another international war will occur involving Japan. The strongly pacifist, neutralist orientation of post-war Japanese, particularly among the intellectuals and youth, is against rearmament.

Internationally, despite a basic western orientation, Japan must assume a course of action independent from that of the United States to protect its security and continued economic growth. Overall, the Japanese relationship with the United States has been one of subservience, at times to the point of enduring unexpected "shocks." What the Japanese press called "Nixon Shock" was the announcement in July, 1971, of his impending visit to the People's Republic of China. The "Dollar Shock" refers to the forced revaluation of the yen when the United States floated the dollar in August, 1971, and levied a 10 percent surcharge on imports.

The direction Japan will take to resolve these problems should have a significant bearing on future U.S.-Japanese relations and future peace and stability in Asia. One direction is already visible. Japan feels it must act more independently of the United States and has sought an opportunity to become an equal partner with the super-powers in the effort to maintain world peace. Japan sees the future world as one of multi-powers, and feels it can best serve its own further development through creative diplomacy, not through military preparedness. To this end, Japan was quick to conclude a diplomatic normalization treaty with the People's Republic of China, responding positively to the Sino-American thaw. Japan has also improved her relations with the USSR.

RECOMMENDED READINGS

Akita, George, *Foundations of Constitutional Government in Modern Japan, 1868-1900*. Cambridge, Mass.: Harvard University Press, 1967.

Austin, Lewis, *Saints and Samurai: The Political Culture of the American and Japanese Elites*. New Haven, Conn.: Yale University Press, 1975.

Baerwald, Hans H. *Japan's Parliament: An Introduction*. New York: Cambridge University Press, 1974.

Beardsley, Richard, et al., *Village Japan*. Chicago: University of Chicago Press, 1969.

Beasley, W. G., *The Modern History of Japan* (2nd. ed.). New York: Praeger, 1973.

Beckmann, George M., *The Making of the Meiji Constitution*. Lawrence, Kansas: University of Kansas Press, 1957.

Benedict, Ruth., *The Chrysanthemum and the Sword*. Boston: Houghton Mifflin, 1946.

Brown, D. M., *Nationalism in Japan*. Berkeley, Calif.: University of California Press, 1955.

Brzezinski, Zbigniew, *The Fragile Blossom: Crisis and Change in Japan*. New York: Harper & Row, 1972.

Craig, Albert M. and Donald H. Shively, *Personality in Japanese History*. Berkeley, Calif.: University of California Press, 1970.

Curtis, Gerald L., *Election Campaigning, Japanese Style*. New York: Columbia University Press, 1971.

Dore, R. P., *City Life in Japan*. Berkeley, Calif.: University of California Press, 1958.

——————, *Land Reform in Japan*. London: Oxford University Press, 1959.

Duus, Peter, *Party Rivalry and Political Change in Taisho Japan*. Cambridge, Mass.: Harvard University Press, 1968.

Fukui, H., *Party in Power: The Japanese Liberal Democrats and Policy Making*. Berkeley, Calif.: University of California Press, 1970.

Harootunian, H. D., *Toward Restoration*. Berkeley, Calif.: University of California Press, 1970.

Hellman, Donald C., *Japan and East Asia*. New York: Praeger, 1972.

Ike, Nobutaka, *Japanese Politics: Patron-Client Democracy*. New York: Knopf, 1972.

Johnson, Chalmers, *Conspiracy at Matsukawa*. Berkeley, Calif.: University of California Press, 1972.

Kahn, Herman, *The Emerging Japanese Superstate: Challenge and Response*. Englewood Cliffs, N.J.: Prentice-Hall, 1970.

Kawai, K., *Japan's American Interlude*. Chicago: University of Chicago Press, 1960.

Krauss, Ellis S., *Japanese Radicals Revisited: Student Protest in Postwar Japan*. Berkeley, Calif.: University of California Press, 1974.

Kubota, Akira, *Higher Civil Servants in Postwar Japan*. Princeton, N.J.: Princeton University Press, 1969.

Langdon, Frank, *Politics in Japan*. Boston: Little, Brown, 1967.

Lockwood, W. W., *The State and Economic Enterprise in Japan*. Princeton, N.J.: Princeton University Press, 1965.

Maruyama, Masao, *Thought and Behavior in Modern Japanese Politics*. London: Oxford University Press, 1963.

Mason, R. H. P., *Japan's First General Election, 1890*. New York: Cambridge University Press, 1969.

Morley, James W., ed., *Dilemmas of Growth in Prewar Japan*. Princeton, N.J.: Princeton University Press, 1972.

Morris, Iran, *Nationalism and the Right Wing in Japan*. London: Oxford University Press, 1960.

Nakane, Chie, *Japanese Society*. Berkeley, Calif.: University of California Press, 1972.

Ogata, Sadako N., *Defiance in Manchuria: The Making of Japanese Foreign Policy, 1931-1932*. Berkeley, Calif.: University of California Press, 1964.

Packard, G. R., *Protest in Tokyo: The Security Treaty Crisis of 1960*. Princeton, N.J.: Princeton University Press, 1966.

Reischauer, Edwin O., *The United States and Japan* (3rd ed.) Cambridge, Mass.: Harvard University Press, 1965.

Richardson, Bradley M., *The Political Culture of Japan*. Berkeley, Calif.: University of California Press, 1974.

Sansom, George B., *The Western World and Japan*. New York: Knopf, 1950.

Scalapino, Robert A., *Democracy and the Party Movement in Prewar Japan*. Berkeley, Calif.: University of California Press, 1962.

_____, *The Japanese Communist Movement, 1920-1966*. Berkeley, Calif.: University of California Press, 1967.

_____, and J. Masumi., *Parties and Politics in Contemporary Japan*. Berkeley, Calif.: University of California Press, 1962.

Shillony, Ben-Ami, *Revolt in Japan: The Young Officers and the February 26, 1936 Incident*. Princeton, N.J.: Princeton University Press, 1973.

Shively, D. H., ed., *Tradition and Modernization in Japanese Culture*. Princeton, N.J.: Princeton University Press, 1971.

Silberman, Bernard S., *Ministers of Modernization: Elite Mobility in the Meiji Restoration, 1868-1873*. Tuscon, Ariz.: University of Arizona Press, 1964.

───────── and H. D. Harootunian, eds., *Japan in Crisis: Essays on Taisho Democracy*. Princeton, N.J.: Princeton University Press, 1974.

Smethurst, Richard J., *A Social Basis for Prewar Japanese Militarism: The Army and the Rural Community*. Berkeley, Calif.: University of California Press, 1974.

Steiner, Kurt, *Local Government in Japan*. Stanford, Calif.: Stanford University Press, 1965.

Thayer, Nathaniel B., *How the Conservatives Rule Japan*. Princeton, N.J.: Princeton University Press, 1969.

Tsunoda, Ryusaku, et al., *Sources of Japanese Tradition*, 2 vols. New York: Columbia University Press, 1958.

Vogel, Ezra, *Japan's New Middle Class*. Berkeley, Calif.: University of California Press, 1967.

───────── , *Modern Japanese Organization and Decision-Making*. Berkeley, Calif.: University of California Press, 1975.

Ward, Robert E., ed., *Political Development in Modern Japan*. Princeton, N.J.: Princeton University Press, 1968.

White, James R., *Sokagakkai and Mass Society*. Stanford, Calif.: Stanford University Press, 1970.

Yanaga, C., *Big Business in Japanese Politics*. New Haven, Conn.: Yale University Press, 1968.

───────── , *Japan since Perry*. New York: McGraw-Hill, 1949.

Chapter Three

China:
Giant Unbound

China unbound is a giant among the nations of the world. Territorially, China is among the largest political units. Its population of some eight hundred million amounts to roughly one-fourth of the world's population. Rich in cultural tradition, the Chinese people are extremely proud of their past greatness. The contemporary political expressions of the Chinese people are rooted in their history and their land and in their search for renewed national glory. The primary purposes of this chapter are to explain the measure of success and the meaning of the Chinese Communist revolution in historical context and to discuss the nature and struggle for development of the subsequent Chinese Communist regime.

THE LAND AND THE PEOPLE

With a continental expanse of 3,691,502 square miles, China stretches from Manchuria in the northeast to Tibet in the southwest and from the coast of the South China Sea northwestward to Chinese Turkestan in central Asia. This immense land is rich in topographical and climatic variation. In eastern Manchuria and northeastern Korea, thick forests provide natural boundaries. The vast arid expanse of the Gobi is in the north, and in the west is the Takla Makan Desert. The high plateau land of Tibet is to the south of these formidable desert areas. China is also separated from India and Burma by the Himalaya mountains and gorges, which until the days of the Burma Road, built during World War II, proved effective barriers to communication. In the south lies Thailand and the Indochinese peninsula, separated from China by infertile and rugged plateau land. Only the region of the Red River delta (in northern Viet-

CHINA

- ·····—— International Boundaries
- —— —— Indefinite Boundaries
- ············· Boundaries Defined by Communist China

Scale of Miles

0   100   200   300   400   500

Source: Ward and Macridis, 1963.

nam) is open to easy access from China, and the Chinese colonized this area from 111 B.C. to A.D. 939. Despite a long coastline, China was not inviting to early seafarers. Real and imagined hazards of the long sea voyage discouraged many. In the north the Chinese coastline lacks good ports, and the offshore water there is too shallow. The southeastern seacoast is more conducive to ocean traffic, but in early days this area, populated by minority races, was not under effective Chinese control.

Surrounded by impregnable natural fortresses, China had only a
limited contact with the outside world until the era of modern travel.
China maintained a tributary relationship with lesser neighbors. Through
intermittent contact with India, Buddhism was introduced, and it became
a popular religion in China. China was linked to the Persian world by the
famous "silk route" running from oasis to oasis around the edges of the
Takla Makan and the Yellow River basin. It was by this route that Marco

TABLE 3-1.
Chronological Chart

Principal Dynasties		Western Developments
c. 2000 B.C.	Hsia	
		Crete
c. 1500	Shang	
1027	Chou	
	Feudal states	
	Confucius	
	Taoist school	
	Legalist school	
	Warring states	
		Greece Reached its Greatest Height
221	Ch'in	
202	Centralized rule	
	End of feudalism	
	Han	
	Establishment of Confucianism	
		Rome at Greatest Period
A.D. 222	Six Dynasty Period	
		Fall of Rome
589	Sui	
618	T'ang	
	Bureaucracy	
	Examination system	
		Charlemagne
907	Sung	
		Crusades
1127	Southern Sung	
	Neo-Confucianism	
1260	Yuan	
	Conquests of Genghis Khan and Kubla Khan	
		Renaissance
1368	Ming	
		Reformation Thirty Years War
1644	Ch'ing (Manchu)	
1912	Republic	
1949	PRC	

Polo, the legendary Venetian world traveller, reached the imperial court in Peking during the height of the Mongol, or the Yuan Dynasty (A.D. 1260-1368) in China.

The earliest written records of the Chinese people date from 1200 B.C., and the first verifiable dynasty is the Shang Dynasty (1523-1027 B.C.). After the Shang, various dynasties followed in a cyclical rise and fall, woven together by their common heritage and a genius for maintaining their life-style, in spite of the relentless struggle with the forces of nature. China's imperial identity achieved a longevity far surpassing all the other great empires of the world, and a sense of history is deeply ingrained in the Chinese people.

In the Chinese dynastic cycle, the Shang dynasty was followed by the Chou dynasty (1027-250 B.C.). Chou was the great feudal period in Chinese history, and the demise of this dynasty moved the country into a long period of warfare among the feudal lords. Chou was the classic period, an intellectual golden age, highlighted by the coming of Confucius and other great thinkers. It was the period of intellectual ferment in which various aspects of the relationship between people and government were debated.

Out of the late Chou period of warring states, the Ch'in dynasty emerged to unify the country and set up a new, more centralized pattern of government. The lasting foundation of Chinese imperial government, however, was set up by the Han dynasty, which merged the Confucian moral precepts of government with the centralized political structure of the Ch'in dynasty.

CULTURAL INHERITANCE

To their own way of thinking, the Chinese are the most civilized people, and westerners, in comparison, are barbarians. The genius of their civilization is exemplified by the early invention of paper, printing, the compass, gunpowder, and by an infinite variety of artistic works.

Chinese thought has been historically concerned with how humans could live without discord, and they felt they had developed the perfect social organizations, economic institutions, and system of government. According to Confucian thinking, the basis of harmonious living is for each to follow "the way" or *tao*. Tao is the way of nature, and one's social roles, duties, and obligations are to be prescribed in accordance with it. It is a vision of cooperative living in which people strive to perfect social relationships devoid of antagonism and suffering.

The concept of tao predated the time of Confucius, but it was he who systematized it and gave it philosophical depth. Confucius was emulated, and his teachings were widely propagated by his followers. After the

Han dynasty, Confucianism became the state creed of Imperial China, and was viewed as the ethical and moral foundation for the behavior of the Chinese.

Confucius was born some twenty-five hundred years ago in the state of Lu of the Chou dynasty. At the time, the Chou dynasty was decaying and central control over the feudal states was breaking down. There was very little law and order, and the powerful engaged in exploitation of the weak. The common people were abused, and their interests disregarded. Wars between the feudal states and public and private armies raged unchecked. The young Confucius resolved to change this state of affairs by teaching harmonious and cooperative living.

To Confucius, the human was a social being, and the primary and perfect social unit was the family. He taught that it is natural for people to cooperate, and such cooperation is best realized when each maintains a proper place in society and performs his or her duties. Each person is to be judged on the basis of talent and performance. A ruler is measured by his ability to secure the welfare and happiness of the people.

The five basic Confucian social relationships are: (1) a wife is subordinate to her husband; (2) children are subordinate to their parents; (3) a younger brother is subordinate to his older brother; (4) a friend regards a friend as an equal; and (5) a subject is subordinate to the ruler. In other words, these relationships prescribe that males dominate females, age dominates youth, and government dominates the people. These superior-inferior relationships are morally justified by the goodness of people and their sense of love and obligation. Confucianism, variously altered in the course of history, has served as the governing creed of China for 2000 years.

In the Confucian state system, the monarch was at the apex of the government, and his legitimacy was sanctioned by "the mandate of heaven." He was the mediator between heaven and earth. He was the law of the land, and all the lands belonged to him. The people were his subjects. He governed the people through Confucian scholar-officials, who were recruited through examinations. After many years of study of Confucian classics, these scholar-officials were chosen to represent both in body and soul the best virtues of men and Confucianism. Not all Confucian scholars were government officials, but what official positions they held, extending through some eighteen or more traditional Chinese provinces and down to the district level, were appointive. Once appointed, an official was his own master and enjoyed much discretion in the performance of duties and responsibilities, although his performance as an official was subject to surveillance by the central government.

The sustained, unifying qualities of Chinese government over so many centuries and through a succession of dynasties lay in the socializing influence of the family and in the monopoly of political power by the self-perpetuating gentry. Merchants and artisans were despised. The sedentary Chinese masses were family-centered and lived simply, avoiding conflicts as much as possible. They were primarily poor, hard-working peasants who produced only enough food to feed their families. Confucianism offered a moral justification to these traditional Chinese practices. The Chinese family was not only the primary social unit, but also the primary socializing agent in Confucianism. Submission to authority was taught in the family. On a grander scale, the state was the family, with the monarch as the great patriarch.

The gentry was the most powerful class. They monopolized Confucian learning and therefore controlled the government. They set the patterns of life and thought of the people, and they were supported by the poor. Scholar-officials were recruited from the upper class through the examination system. They constituted the core government personnel, performing political, social, and economic activities. The demise of dynastic China in 1911, as will be explained later, was essentially the demise of China's gentry, and the Confucian philosophical foundation that had supported it. This demise was accelerated by forces external to China.

THE RISE OF MODERN CHINA

Western Impact

The first Europeans to arrive in China during the Ming dynasty (A.D. 1368-1644) were the Portuguese. They appeared in 1514. Gradually, their Dutch, French, British, and Russian rivals arrived. Trade was their primary objective, but missionaries came also.

At first, the Europeans' arrival was intermittent; their numbers few. They were not envied or emulated by the self-sufficient Chinese. They were taken lightly and mostly ignored. As long as the Chinese authorities did not regard them as disruptive, they were safe in China. The Chinese government was effective enough to exclude missionaries and traders from China at will, and these westerners were permitted to stay in China only at the dictate of Chinese indulgence. Increasingly, the conservative Chinese became annoyed by the presence of the foreigners.

The greatest rupture in China's contact with the West was the so-called Opium War (1839-1842) between Britain and China, and the Treaty of Nanking, which followed the war. It was not a war of conquest, and European expansion to China never resulted in the actual colonization of China by a European power. But this war proved more devastating than any war China had fought before. It eventually undermined the values and political order of the Chinese people.

The Opium War was a crude display of western military prowess in

Asia. The culprit was Britain, the most industrialized nation of the world at the time. The British were repeatedly irritated by the Chinese pretensions of superiority. China, with her huge population, was a potentially lucrative market; but British merchants encountered a Chinese unwillingness to trade and the obstacle of cumbersome official red tape. Canton was the only port open for trade. What immediately caused the war, however, was the quarrel over opium traffic. Opium traffic was made illegal in China, but proved highly profitable for British smugglers. Chinese efforts to squelch the smuggling encountered British military reprisals, and China was soundly defeated.

A series of humiliating treaties following the Opium War embittered the Chinese. The treaties imposed on China as a consequence of the war reflected western disdain for China. They extracted indemnities and forced China to accept territorial, political, and economic concessions. All the treaty powers acquired "most favored nation" status and were accordingly treated equally in their exercise of special rights and privileges. Every right and privilege initially extended to any one treaty power was to be automatically extended to the rest. The treaty powers enjoyed extraterritoriality in China. This system made a farce of Chinese sovereignty: it permitted foreigners and their activities in China to be governed by foreign, not Chinese, law.

The most far-reaching and contemptuous insult to China's sovereignty was perhaps the advance of Japan in the Sino-Japanese war (1894-1895) fought for dominance over the Korean peninsula. Chinese forces on land and sea proved no match for the Japanese who were experiencing their first test of international strength as a modern state. In the Treaty of Shimonoseki in 1895, the victorious Japanese were able to extract an atrocious price from China, which included the territorial acquisition of the Liaotung peninsula in southern Manchuria, Taiwan, and the Pescadores. Although the Liaotung peninsula was later returned to China by the intervention of Russia, France, and Germany, this defeat cost China the last vestige of status as a viable state in the eyes of foreign powers. China was thereafter mercilessly subjected to the scramble for concessions, and the empire was divided into foreign spheres of influence.

Rebellions, Reforms, and Revolutions

These foreign assaults against China's sovereignty exposed the inability of the dynastic system to cope with modern problems. The Manchu dynasty (1644-1911) had slowly decayed. Nothing was done to abate the periodic famines resulting from drought, flood, and war. An unprecedented population increase beginning in the mid-eighteenth century worsened the situation. The Manchu dynasty was at its weakest point at the time when the government was forced to contest the West. The western impact combined with Manchu deterioration, and a growing sense of nationalism among the Han Chinese against the Manchu domination accelerated the fall of the dynasty. The corrosion of the traditional Confucian value system also brought about permanent change to the Chinese way of life.

The Chinese reaction to increasing foreign pressure progressed through several stages, eventually culminating in the establishment of a Communist regime on Mainland China. Reform efforts emanated from various sectors of the society, and there were many disturbances and unsuccessful rebellions. The Taiping Rebellion, with the professed aim of establishing a new dynasty, a heavenly kingdom (*T'ien-kuo*) in China, lasted from 1851 to 1864 and threatened Manchu governmental authority over a large part of the country.

The traditional, conservative interpretation of "disturbance within and attack from outside" (*nei luan wei luan*) dealt in the main with China's own weakness in military preparedness, the moral corruption of officials, and the lack of able government personnel. The Confucian government of China was government by individuals and not by institutions and law; political adjustment was made by changing the personnel. Within this conceptual framework then, reforms, not a political revolution, were sought until these efforts proved too meek to successfully meet the challenge of the West. Nor could these reforms strengthen governmental authority over growing popular disenchantment with the Manchus.

Any drastic action to change the traditional dynastic constitution of the Chinese government, however, was anathema to the privileged class of Chinese society. The imperial court, the gentry, and scholar-officials reacted violently to constitutional reform efforts by such westernized intellectuals as K'ang Yu-wei, T'an Szu-t'ung, and Liang Ch'i-ch'ao. These leaders argued for a parliamentary, representative system of government and popular participation in the governing process, as in the West. China must learn from the West, they argued, in clear contradiction to the traditional Sinocentric view of the world. Such western tutelage was the surest way to defend the country against western invasion and hence the most direct route to the liberation of the country from the unequal treaties. Only in this way could the imperial glory of China be reclaimed. These arguments, which culminated in the so-called Hundred Days Reform (June-September, 1898), were supported by the young and well-meaning Kuang-hsu Emperor (1875-1908) in a revolutionary departure from previous monarchial policies.

The political revolution in China, although long in the offing, was periodically interspersed with staunch conservative reactions. The Empress Dowager T'zu-hsi successfully led the conservative reaction against the

Hundred Days Reform and scuttled the reform programs. When she supported the Boxer Rebellion (1900) against foreigners and Christians, an international relief mission to protect the westerners was dispatched to China. Peking came under the occupation of this mission, and the Empress Dowager and her court were driven into exile. China was no longer its own master. Only political inertia maintained the nominal sovereignty of the Manchu dynasty.

The final exodus of this last Chinese dynasty resulted from a simple act of mutiny, which began in a government garrison at Wuchang in south China in October, 1911. It spread beyond government control, and the revolutionary followers of Sun Yat-sen proclaimed a republic with their leader as temporary president. Sun was a medical doctor by training and his revolutionary activities against the Manchus had considerable following in China and abroad. The Manchu government in Peking meantime appointed Yuan Shih-kai as premier and commander of government troops to suppress the revolutionary forces. Instead, Yuan agreed with Sun to force the abdication of the last Manchu emperor. Yuan's price was the presidency of the republic.

A republic for all of China was officially born in February, 1912, and Sun resigned his provisional presidency in favor of Yuan. A new constitution was adopted establishing a parliament and a cabinet. The president was held responsible to the people and their chosen representatives. Political parties were assembled, and the first such party, the Nationalist Party (*Kuomintang*), was organized by Sun's followers in August, 1912, in preparation for a parliamentary election. Yuan, who was later to abolish all political parties and the parliament itself, created his own "Republican" political party. In the election held between the end of 1912 and beginning of 1913, the Nationalist Party won 269 seats in the House and 123 in the Senate as opposed to 120 and 53 seats, respectively, for the Republican Party.

The Nationalists saw the results of this first election as the dawning of representative government with themselves in power, but Yuan had no such illusions. A traditional monarchist at heart, he refused to share decision-making with the Parliament. The Nationalists in the Parliament obstinately contested Yuan's arbitrary exercise of power, revolting against him in 1913. But the revolt lasted only two months and Sun was forced to flee to Japan. The contest for power, however, continued and the outcome was a setback to China's newly won republicanism. Yuan was declared Emperor in 1915 by a national congress, which he convened to give the aura of legitimacy to his imperial ambition. But various opposition forces proved too strong for Yuan, and republicanism became the ideological rallying point against him. A broken man, Yuan died on June 6, 1916. Before his death, he was forced to declare the end of his short-lived dynasty, Hung Hsien (Great Constitution).

The Dilemmas of the Nationalists

Yuan's remedies for China's ills were anachronistic, but his death left a power vacuum. The next ten years were a period of warlords and internecine warfare, of political intrigues and assassinations, and of total ineffectiveness on the part of the central government. Even Sun Yat-sen and his Nationalist Party withdrew what support they gave to the central government in Peking and set up their own rival government in Canton. The Chinese Communist Party was organized in 1921.

Sun was an intellectual and a revolutionary, but Chiang Kai-shek, who eventually succeeded him, was a militarist and a pragmatic organizer. Where Sun might compromise, Chiang was forceful and adamant in his use of the military to unify the country. Sun was willing to court Russian assistance and cooperated with the Communists in promoting his three principles of the people (*San Min Chu I*): nationalism, democracy, and the people's livelihood. Chiang remained anti-communist. The availability of arms, funds, and a staff of military and political advisors which the Soviet government offered did not change his general position.

Sun Yat-sen died in 1925, and soon a division emerged within the Nationalist Party. The Kuomintang had permitted the Communists to join the party in 1923 under the first united front formula that the Soviet Union insisted upon. To the Soviet Union, the Chinese Communists were weak and unprepared for communist revolution in China. Therefore, the Chinese Communists were to work with the Nationalists toward the goal of bourgeois revolution and national unification. Chiang, however, became increasingly apprehensive over Communist influence in the Kuomintang and openly challenged them. Chiang was supported by the nation's banking interests and big business. On April 12, 1927, his forces marched into Shanghai in an extended military campaign against the warlords. It was at that time that Chiang ordered the round-up of Communist-led labor union members, in the so-called "White Terror." Given this success, Chiang's suppression of the Communists spread to other cities.

By spring of 1928, Chiang was the unchallenged leader of the Nationalist government. His military expedition against the warlords in the north was momentarily successful, and in June, 1928, Chiang proclaimed the completion of the military unification of the country. The warlords were never completely defeated, however, and some of them, especially in southwest and northwest China, remained in effective control of their territories. It was an uneasy alliance that made the warlords subservient to Chiang, and only nominal unification was possible in 1928. The Communists were then still at large and were able to set up various soviets (councils in areas under their control).

The military conquest of the warlords and the subsequent alliance were only the beginning of China's nation-building tasks. The peace that prevailed in China in the decade between 1928 and 1937 was deceptive. Peasants in the villages of China were not greatly affected by the changing political fortunes. Chiang's preoccupation with political stability left little time for the socio-economic revolution, so drastically needed in China. His military machine and police instruments, his penchant for conservatism, and his distaste for politics contributed to his eventual alienation of the masses and intellectuals.

The decade following Chiang's rise to power was one in which reformist zeal blossomed, but Chiang ruled so conservatively that many modernization programs were thwarted. China remained poor and disorganized. The size of the country and the growing population presented overwhelming dilemmas. The Japanese imperial ambition in China also tarnished Chiang's legitimacy and undermined his nationalist image.

Japan Humbles China

China's humiliation at Japanese hands began with the first Sino-Japanese war of 1894-95. Moreover, Korea had become a Japanese colony in 1910. And when World War I broke out, Japan declared war on Germany and seized the German leased territory of Kiachow Bay and the railway on the Shangtung peninsula. When China called upon Japan to withdraw, Japan presented China with the so-called "Twenty-One Demands," which not only justified Japanese claims over the occupied areas but also over other mining and railway rights. China was also warned not to lease any more territory to any power other than Japan and to employ Japanese financial and military experts in the Chinese government. These demands aimed at making China a satellite of Japan. Given its weakness, the Chinese government was forced to sign the agreement, but it refused to permit Japanese experts into their administration.

The articulate Chinese population was indignant at the news of their government's submission to Japan. The meekness of the government in Peking at the time was a source of great concern. Anti-Japanese as well as anti-government protests and demonstrations spread to every large city in China. Then, in April, 1919, the European powers at the Paris Peace Conference legitimated the Japanese seizure of German interests in China, and Chinese students and faculty members at Peking University launched the May Fourth Movement of 1919. They reacted strongly against Japanese territorial ambitions in China. The movement was the first mass outburst against Japan to be supported by Chinese students and intellectuals. It was also a protest against China's national humiliation at the hands of the leading western powers and the warlords who were selling the country out to foreign interests. Merchants, clerks, and factory workers followed the students and the intellectuals. Hundreds of underground papers appeared calling for a new China.

For Japan, a weak China was a guarantee of peace in East Asia. A strong nationalist government in China would have impeded Japan's imperialistic ambitions. Japan opposed a strong Chiang government and gradually undertook to control China, first by the seizure of Manchuria and Jehol in 1931 and then by extending its areas of operation into Inner Mongolia and northern China. Japan opened the second Sino-Japanese war in 1937.

Chiang's strategy against this blatantly imperialist Japanese scheme followed the lines in the ancient Chinese saying: "like the bamboo, to bend with the wind." He showed a patient disdain for an eventual showdown, a posture dictated by Chiang's awareness of the weakness of his Nationalist government. He also wanted to avoid a military struggle with Japan while he was still in the midst of an extermination campaign against the Communists in his own country.

The Rise of the Communist Party

When it was organized in 1921, the Chinese Communist Party (CCP) had some 50 members. It was a party of concerned and socially alienated Chinese intellectuals, strongly influenced by the West, the Comintern, (Communist International headquartered in Moscow), and the Russian Communist party. At the outset, the Chinese Communists sought a double-barrelled revolution for China: an anti-imperialist revolution in collaboration with the middle class nationalists and a revolution of the masses for social reconstruction.

Until Mao assumed the leadership of the party around 1935, however, the Chinese Communists were by no means united as to which revolutionary course to pursue and how to achieve it. Mao's leadership climaxed their search for a successful formula for revolution. Before then, the Chinese Communist Party had been small and powerless, relying on instructions from the Comintern. The Chinese Communists had been urged to collaborate with the Nationalists, subscribe to the program of "revolution from above," and support the political unification programs of Chiang Kai-shek. Such a united front was short-lived, however; and the split came in 1927, as stated earlier, when the Chiang forces struck against the Communist-led labor unions in Shanghai and rounded up many Communist leaders.

From the time of this rupture of the first Nationalist-Communist united front to the formation of the second united front in 1936, the Chinese Communists were subjected to successive Nationalist assaults. The Nationalists were bent on the extermination of the Communists. Only the most dramatic human determination and endurance saved the Communists from total annihilation. The huge expanse of China also helped the Communist cause by interfering with the Nationalist deployment of forces.

The Long March, the main column of some thirty-thousand party functionaries and their families—between one hundred-twenty- and one hundred-thirty thousand people in all—broke the Nationalist encirclement of the Communist concentration in Kiangsi province in the south. The Communists overcame several encounters with Nationalist forces and travelled for about a year to Shensi province in the northeast, far away from Nationalist control, where they secured a territorial base of operation. Many died on the way; many were lost; and many dropped out. According to one classic account of this march, the survivors dwindled to a third of their initial strength. Those who completed the march of some 6,000 miles endured eighteen mountain ranges, including five snowcapped the year-round, crossed twenty-four rivers, passed through twelve provinces, occupied sixty-two cities, and broke through the enveloping forces of ten local warlords. It was during this march that Mao consolidated his leadership. The close comradeship between the leaders of Mao's Communist party was formed during this period.

Once in Shensi province (Yenan, the capital city), the Communists effectively ruled their so-called "border area" thwarting landlords, "local bullies," and "bad gentry." The Communists were able to experiment with governing a large territory with meager resources. Support of the masses and the dedicated party workers were crucial to the survival of the Communist government against the superior forces of the Nationalist government.

Mobile guerrilla warfare proved the most successful way to fight until a strategic capability for direct confrontation was attained. Furthermore, as Chiang Kai-shek chose to fight the Communists rather than the Japanese, the Communists who fought the Japanese could exploit the nationalistic sentiment of the Chinese people for their own advantage. Communist leaders were aware of a growing dissatisfaction among Chinese intellectuals and others with Chiang's meekness in the face of repeated Japanese acts of aggression. Student strikes and demonstrations were evidence of the growing unrest.

Mao and his colleagues decided on an anti-Japanese people's united front of all the Chinese people including the Nationalists on August 1, 1935, and succeeded in forcing it on Chiang. Chang Hsueh-liang and Yang Hu-ch'eng, two warlords whom Chiang had placed in charge of the extermination of the Communists in northern Shengsi, were staunchly anti-Japanese and persuaded by Mao to agree to a united front. They kidnapped Chiang while he was on an inspection tour in Sian, and forced him to agree with the Communist formula for a united front in order to regain his freedom.

Chiang's Communist extermination campaigns were thus halted, and the Communists obtained a respite in the long civil war with Kuomintang forces. During the second Sino-Japanese war (1937-45), the Communists were supplied with Nationalist arms; they used their mobile guerrilla tactics effectively against the Japanese, and broadened their base of operation and nationalistic mass following.

When the Japanese surrendered in August, 1945, the Communists were in control of some one hundred million people spread over nineteen liberated areas. Their regular army consisted of about one million men, and their so-called "people's militia" had about two million men.

The Communists had several advantages over the Nationalists during the war. The Nationalists were identified with ineffective wartime government by peasants and intellectuals alike, and they were unable to dispel this negative image. The needs of the people were neglected by the government. Inflation was out of control. Official corruption and Japanese atrocities went unchecked.

The Communists, under the leadership of Mao, presented an attractive alternative to the Nationalist government of Chiang. Mao's Communists were on the rise. They felt they had a definite mission. In his wartime tract issued in 1940, Mao called for a new democracy in China that would be a government of "all revolutionary classes" and "all progressive political parties."

Economically, this new democracy was to be a mixed system. Only big banks, big industry, and big business were to be nationalized. The property of the large landowners was to be confiscated and distributed among the peasants, but all other forms of private property were to be protected. The intelligentsia, members of various minor parties, and the masses were called upon to unite behind the Communist Party and Mao's leadership. Mao and his followers set out to challenge the legitimacy of the Nationalist government. However, the final contest was on the battlefield, where the Communists were victorious.

At the end of the World War II, both Nationalist and Communist forces rushed into the power vacuum created by the areas that had been under Japanese occupation. Both repeatedly pronounced advocacy of peaceful solutions to their differences, but in actuality they seemed to be interested in establishing strategic positions and preparing for eventual armed clash.

Aided by the United States, Chiang's forces were able to dominate areas of Japanese surrender in south and central China, repulsing Communist challenges. In north China, however, Chiang's forces were unable to dislodge the Communists from their occupied areas. The Nationalists could not force their way into Manchuria, one of the most prized territorial possessions in China. Manchuria borders Siberia and the Korean peninsula, and China's great industrial centers were located there. In Manchuria, the Communists were aided by the Soviet Red Army, which had already disarmed the Japanese Kwangtung Army and transferred its weapons to the Communists. (The Soviet Union had agreed in the Sino-Soviet Treaty of Friendship and Alliance of August 14, 1945, to deal only with the Nationalist government and return Manchuria to their control after the defeat of Japanese forces.)

In late 1945, General George Marshall was sent to China by President Harry Truman to help bring about a coalition government. Once such a government was established, the United States promised aid for Chinese national reconstruction. A truce between the Nationalists and the Communists was signed on January 10, 1946, but it lasted only a very short time. Chiang embarked on a renewed drive to drive out the Communists.

Chiang's Nationalist government, however, was badly in need of reform and was financially bankrupt. Furthermore, his forces lacked the revolutionary morale that the Communists enjoyed. By late 1948, Chiang had lost his best troops in north China, mostly by defection. In the south and other parts of China, Communist guerrillas were successful in demoralizing the Nationalists by blockading the cities, cutting off supplies, and defeating the government forces.

In the spring of 1949, the Communist forces captured Peking and crossed the Yangtze River from the north almost unopposed. Rapidly moving south, they captured Nanking on April 23. By the end of that year, their conquest of the Chinese mainland was virtually complete. Chiang and his government retreated from city to city and finally evacuated to Taiwan with some five-hundred thousand members of the armed forces. Once in power, the Communists set out to consolidate their gains, reconstruct society, hoping to build a new nation out of the old.

GOVERNMENT INSTITUTIONS AND FUNCTIONS

The People's Republic of China (PRC) was officially proclaimed on October 1, 1949. Peking became the capital of the new regime. The Chinese Communist Party, headed by Mao, was unchallenged and assumed supreme dictatorial power.

The long revolutionary struggle had given the Chinese Communists experience in war and also in government. The territories under their control had to be governed by acting in the interests of the people and by constantly appealing for their support in the revolutionary cause. A revolutionary government must legitimize itself through force and/or persuasion. Under Communist control, the local populace was encouraged to go about its normal business. Local talent, including Nationalist personnel, were sought out and protected.

The first formal constitution of the PRC was adopted in September, 1954, underlining the basic framework of government. Earlier, the Chinese People's Political Consultative Conference (CPPCC) had convened in Peking on September 21, 1949, to consider Mao's guidelines for the "People's Democratic Dictatorship." The new state was to be an alliance of four classes: workers, peasants, petty bourgeoisie, and national bourgeoisie, who would exercise dictatorship over the "reactionaries," and who would govern democratically for the interest of all. This basic formula for the government was dictated by the need to ensure Communist hegemony in the new regime and at the same time to present a broad united front.

The Conference approved the three basic documents: the Organic Law of the Central People's Government, the Organic Law of the CPPCC, and the Common Program of the CPPCC. It also created six Great Administrative Areas, grouping the various provinces into the areas of north, northeast, northwest, southwest, east, and central south. These areas as units of government were abolished following the institution of a new constitution in 1954. They were becoming too powerful, and the central government in Peking feared any power independent of central control.

The constitution of 1954 was adopted by the newly established National People's Congress of some 1,200 delegates elected indirectly by the voters. This constitution established an interlocking hierarchy of the party, state, and army. But the supremacy of the party in governmental decision-making and supervision of the governmental bureaucracy was maintained as an integral part of the Chinese Communist system.

In the preamble and chapter one of the constitution, the concept of the People's Democratic Dictatorship and the "united front" is restated. The constitution described China as a unitary state, not a federal state as is the Soviet Union. No right of secession for any group was to be allowed. Rapid social change for China—from an agrarian to an industrial mode of life—was promised. Chapter two of the constitution dealt with the organization of the government (see Figure 3-1). The rights and duties of citizens are discussed in chapter three. Chinese citizens were all those who were permanent residents of China, regardless of nationality, and all people of the Chinese race living abroad, unless their status was changed by treaty or by naturalization.

Climaxing the political readjustment following the Great Proletarian Cultural Revolution (1966-1969), the constitution was revised, and this revised constitution was approved by the National People's Congress held in January, 1975. The amendments to the original constitution of 1954 were designed to help strengthen the party's centralized leadership over the government structure. The new constitution abolished the positions of Chairman and Vice-chairman of the Republic, and the functions of the

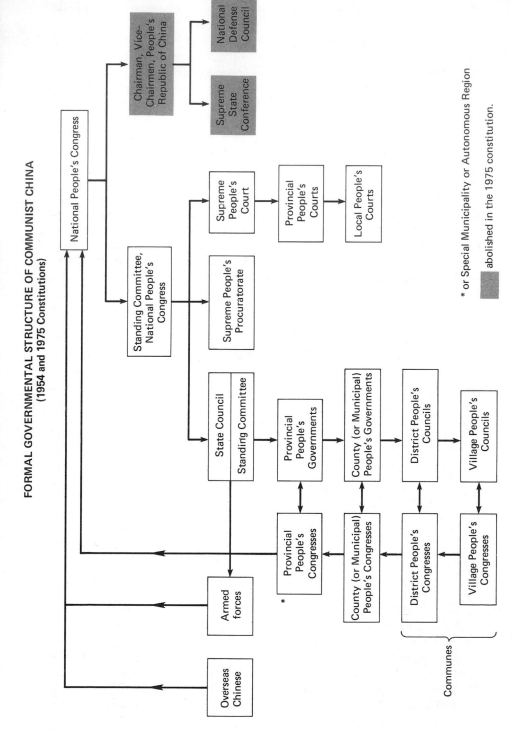

FORMAL GOVERNMENTAL STRUCTURE OF COMMUNIST CHINA
(1954 and 1975 Constitutions)

National People's Congress

Chairman, Vice-Chairmen, People's Republic of China

National Defense Council

Supreme State Conference

Standing Committee, National People's Congress

Supreme People's Court

Provincial People's Courts

Local People's Courts

Supreme People's Procuratorate

State Council Standing Committee

Provincial People's Governments

County (or Municipal) People's Governments

District People's Councils

Village People's Councils

Provincial People's Congresses *

County (or Municipal) People's Congresses

District People's Congresses

Village People's Congresses

Armed forces

Overseas Chinese

Communes

* or Special Municipality or Autonomous Region

abolished in the 1975 constitution.

74

head of state were assigned to the Chairman of the Standing Committee of the Congress. It also abolished the obsolete Supreme State Conference and National Defense Council.

Some key articles in chapter one of the revised constitution, which deal with the general principles governing the People's Republic of China, are:

Article 1:   The People's Republic of China is a socialist state of the dictatorship of the proletariat, led by the working class, and based on the alliance of workers and peasants.

Article 2:   The Communist Party of China is the core of leadership of the whole Chinese people. The working class exercises leadership over the state through its vanguard, the Communist Party of China. . . . Marxism-Leninism-Mao Tsetung thought is the theoretical basis guiding the thinking of our nation.

Article 3:   All power in the People's Republic of China belongs to the people. The organs through which the people exercise power are the people's congresses at all levels, with deputies of workers, peasants and soldiers as their main body. The people's congresses at all levels and all other organs of state practice democratic centralism.

In chapter three, which dealt with the rights and duties of citizenship, the people were given the right to strike and wage demonstrations following the example of the Cultural Revolution. They can speak out and hold debates. They can demonstrate publicly with written posters. They are, however, prohibited from unrestrained written and artistic creative works and change of residence without permission. The omission of these rights from the new constitution reflect the goals of the Cultural Revolution. The Peking regime clearly states that it will shape a new culture and remold intellectuals. It also attempts to eliminate differences between urban and rural life and between mental and manual labor.

Significant are the subtle politics of this new constitution. The new constitution is designed to institutionalize the practices of the Cultural Revolution and broaden the composition of the people's congresses at all levels to include not only workers and peasants, but also soldiers. Furthermore, the revolutionary committees, which were set up during the Cultural Revolution, are now regarded as permanent organs of the local people's congresses. Above all, the new constitution restates with unusual clarity the political supremacy of the party as "the core leadership of the Chinese people" and not only returns the relation of the party with other state organs to the pre-Cultural Revolution state but also elevates the role of the party to a new height. The document is a concise statement of the basic state structure, and much detail is left out for operational flexibility and continued experimentation.

The Central Government

The underlying principle of the government of the People's Republic of China is called democratic centralism and the National People's Congress is the highest organ of state power. It can amend the constitution, elect and remove the highest officials of the government, and sanction treaties and other important matters. It is elected for a term of five years (four years, previously) to meet at least once a year.

The National People's Congress is a colorful assemblage of delegates of diverse races and backgrounds, coming from various points in the huge territory of China. It meets for several days, as stipulated in the constitution; but its some 3,000 members (2,864 members for the 1975 congress) constitute a body too unwieldy for serious legislative deliberation. The Congress therefore elects a standing committee as its permanently acting body to exercise its power, especially when it is not in session. The standing committee of the National People's Congress has some sixty members. They are usually appointed by a higher organ of the party and the Congress approves the appointments rather than truly electing them. The Committee meets regularly, but it may be unrealistic again to assume that this body exercises any real constitutional powers of the Congress. The Committee has consistently consented and approved policies presented to it by the party decision-makers, thus further legitimizing their policies.

The Congress earlier had the power to appoint the chairman of the Chinese People's Republic, constitutionally the highest ranking office in the country, and two vice-chairmen. These offices were ceremonial, but the office of the chairman had gravitated toward some of the more powerful members of the party hierarchy. Mao was the first chairman. He was succeeded by Liu Shao-ch'i in 1959, who was at one time regarded as Mao's successor. In the aftermath of the Cultural Revolution, Liu was disgraced. In 1967 he was removed from power. The prime minister of the State Council and members of the Supreme People's Procuratorate and the Supreme People's Court are appointed by the National People's Congress on the recommendations of the chief party decision-makers.

The most important center for executive decision-making in the government is the State Council, chosen by the prime minister on the proposal of the party Central Committee. The State Council consists of some thirty or more ministers of administrative departments and heads of state commissions. It also includes various vice-premiers and a secretary-general who together with the prime minister constitute a standing committee of the State Council. The standing committee meets often and seems to play the powerful role of relating party decisions to the administrative branches of government and of directing and overseeing administrative decision-making. The executive powers of the State Council include: (1) formulating and issuing administrative directives and coordinating the work of ministries and commissions to be sure these directives are carried out; (2) administering the national economic plans and provisions of the state budget; (3) managing external affairs; and (4) guiding the development of defense forces.

Provincial and Local Governments

State administrative units directly below the central government include three special municipal governments (located in Peking, Shanghai, and Tientsin), 21 provincial governments, and 5 autonomous regions (Inner Mongolia, Sinkiang Uighur, Tibet, Ningsia Hui and Kwangsi Sh'uang). The provincial and regional governments are then subdivided into either counties (*hsien*) or municipalities (*shih*); each county is further divided into rural or urban communes and districts. These local units of government are the creations of the central government, and they owe their existence to it. They exist in an hierarchical order as administrative units to facilitate political communication between different levels of government.

Within this system the organizational principle of democratic centralism, while ensuring firm control at the top, calls for the people to have some voice in the selection of members of their congresses at the lowest level. As with the selection of members of the National People's Congress, these local delegates select delegates to a higher people's congress and so on up the hierarchical system. All Chinese citizens, eighteen years of age or older, have the right to vote and to be candidates for office, with the exception of landlords, "counter-revolutionaries," and those judged to be mentally unbalanced.

When government officials in the PRC refer to *hsit'ung*, they mean *systems*. These systems are functional organizations established nationwide for special purposes. They have their own personnel, and they are distinct from the principal channels of authority and communication, such as the regular party and government organs, at each geographical and administrative level. The relationship between these functional system organizations and the regular geographical and administrative structures is by no means clear in the PRC. The functional systems serve to accommodate new policies initiated by top central leadership and to establish a direct and speedy line of authority and communication between the central decision-making level of government and the operational level.

The Commune System

Since the winter of 1955, the central government in Peking has taken steps to reduce organizational complexity in its relationship with the various local administrative units. The number of counties was reduced from 19,000 in 1953 to 9,000 in 1957. The number of rural districts was reduced from 220,000 to 99,000 in the same period by combining two to three original districts into a larger one. Thus enlarged, the new district was to have "six benefits and one convenience": benefits of cooperation, production, transportation, communication, forestation, culture, and education; and convenience for the advancement of socialism. A large district was to have larger material resources and be better equipped for large-scale economic construction and mass mobilization. At the same time, local authorities were given more decision-making authority within the context of local conditions. In 1958 the commune system was instituted to collectivize every aspect of life under a single unit. The commune would oversee administration, production, and the development of agriculture, industry, trade, health, cultural, social, and political work, as well as military training.

As a major aspect of the Great Leap Forward for the industrialization and development of China, the commune movement quickly gained momentum. By the end of September, 1958, there were 23,384 communes in the rural districts, representing 90.4 percent of the total number of peasant households. The peasants were forced to forsake all of their material possessions to the communal organization. Their public kitchens, dormitories, and nurseries were designed to do away with traditional parochial orientation, familism, and inefficient production methods. The peasantry was to become an integral part of the total mobilization for social construction. They were to develop a new technical and scientific orientation. They were to be self-supporting and self-producing. Their sources of energy were to be more effectively channeled into useful agricultural and industrial tasks, under the management of party cadres.

In its original form, the commune lasted only a few months. Soon, the Communist leadership was faced with the adverse effects of the commune system: (1) there was inadequate food, clothing, and shelter, as well as unfulfilled production quotas; (2) local cadres proved over-zealous in their behavior; and (3) high accident rates affected production, and rising dissatisfaction caused the work pace to slow down. Chinese Communist decision-makers were forced to realize that the commune program was too radical a change from the past. There were weaknesses in the chain of command between the different levels of officialdom. Overconfident party cadres were generating false information that indicated successes more hoped for, than accomplished. Officially, the failure of the commune movement was blamed on the landlords and the weather.

Soon, the commune system was overhauled. Agricultural mechanization, rural electrification, and more extensive research and use of technicians for agricultural production were encouraged. Incentive pay and specific contracts were re-introduced to entice the peasants to increase their productivity. The peasants were allowed personal plots for cultivation. Organizationally, the size of the commune was made more manageable, and between 1961-1964 the large communes were broken into smaller units. The size of the farm was reduced by making the production team rather than the production brigade the basic accounting unit. (See Table 3-2.) The principle of the unity of the state and the commune has, however, been maintained as in the beginning of the commune movement, and the commune still remains an administrative, as well as a production unit.

Development Priorities

Development of the economy was given primary importance by the Communist leadership following 1949, but policies often fluctuated according to differing political positions in the party. Mao's initial plan was for a three-year period of recovery beginning in 1950, followed by three consecutive five-year plans aimed at establishing a balanced industrial system in China. In order to accomplish balanced growth, some accommodation between the industrial and agricultural sectors of the economy was desired.

The first five-year plan (1953-1957) was based extensively on the Soviet model, which emphasized development of heavy industry. Funding for this development came from the Soviet Union and from investments resulting from the collectivization of agriculture. Discussions, however, continued in the party leadership over the correct developmental policy. One position advocated strengthening light industry and labor-intensive agriculture in order to provide revenue for industrial expansion. The other position sought to concentrate on the development of heavy industry and mechanized agricultural production. During the Great Leap and commune programs, Mao momentarily terminated this debate and ordered complete collectivization. The resulting structure for China's development made compliance with the Soviet model difficult. Soviet credit also ended in 1957, and Soviet technicians were withdrawn by 1960.

The economic policy, termed "walking on two legs," was a practice of using the traditional labor capital to increase rural productivity, while urban resources and modern technology would promote industrialization. This developmental program, as discussed earlier, was a primary step in the initiation of the Great Leap Forward, which actually eclipsed the second five-year plan. The Great Leap was designed to show China's ability to modernize rapidly through the mass mobilization of labor in

TABLE 3-2.
Party and Government: Basic Leadership Hierarchy for Rural Policy-Making and Administration

| | Party Apparatus | | Governmental Apparatus | |
Level	Policy Making	Policy Supervision	Policy Implementation	General Administrations
National	Standing Committee of Politburo Politburo	Secretariat Rural Work Department	Agriculture and Forestry Office Ministries and Commissions	State Council
Provincial	Standing Committee of Provincial Party Committee	Secretariat Rural Work Department	Agriculture and Forestry Department	People's Council
County (Hsien) of Municipality (Shih)	Standing Committee of *hsien* Party Committee	Secretariat Rural Work Department	Agriculture and Forestry Department	People's Council
Commune	Commune Committee	Functional Departments (Some Merged)	Functional Departments	Commune Administrative Committee
Production Brigade	General Branch Committee			Brigade Administrative Committee
Production Team	Branch Committee			Team Administrative Committee
Work Group	Party Group		Section and Work Group Chiefs	

Source: Adapted from John W. Lewis, *Leadership in Communist China* (Ithaca, New York: Cornell University Press, 1963), p. 213. Copyright © 1963 by Cornell University. Used by permission of Cornell University Press.

order to maximize industrial and agricultural output. And the People's Communes were created as a means of distributing both economic and political power at the rural community level.

The errors of the Great Leap, however, had created some opposition. Peasant incentives were created in the form of private plots and free markets, and grain was imported to alleviate the pressure on commune production. The party leadership also called for improved economic planning and coordination, increased quality in output, and more production of consumer products. Communes were reconstructed accordingly.

In September, 1962, the Tenth Plenum of the Eighth Party Congress initiated a new policy, which again affected the economic development policy. Mao attacked the party's Post-Great Leap economic policy as "revisionist" and initiated the Socialist Education Campaign. This campaign was aimed at rural cadres and was intended to revive the rural party structure. Slogans attacked the "three great differences," or disparities, between town and country, agriculture and industry, and mental and manual labor.

The programs of the Socialist Education Campaign directly preceded the Great Proletarian Cultural Revolution. Mao contended that the commune was a practical means of transforming a collectivized society into a purely communistic society thus placing China ahead of the Soviet Union. It also promoted manual labor for all people, equality of income, economic construction by the military, and further use of the mass mobilization movement.

In the area of developmental policy, Mao and the party created a program that was not entirely based on a foreign model. Instead they took into consideration the various needs and nuances of the Chinese system. Mao consistently supported the development of agricultural productivity in order to invest in heavy industrial growth. The Maoist developmental strategy was aimed at rapid economic growth, while avoiding antagonisms between rural and urban areas.

THE PARTY AND IDEOLOGY

Party Structures and Functions

Ideally, under the Chinese Communist political system, the governmental structures including the armed forces are to be mere instruments through which the party exercises its control over the people and guides the execution of its policies and programs. The Chinese Communist regime allows other "democratic" parties and mass organizations to exist, but their political roles are minimal.

The CCP is organized in pyramid-fashion, roughly resembling the territorial tiers of the state administrative organizations. At the base of the pyramid are the primary party branches. They are set up where the personal presence of the party is needed. Primary party branches are present in factories, mines, enterprises, streets, government offices, schools, military units, and production teams. The party members in these administrative and production units occupy key positions providing necessary linkage with the party. They oversee the execution of party policies and programs at the worker's level. The primary party branches are then joined in the district commune, county, or city organizations, which in turn become the basis of the provincial, regional, or special municipal organizations. At the apex of this pyramidal party organization are the national organs. (See Table 3-2.)

The national party organs include the National Party Congress whose members are elected indirectly for a term of five years. The National Party Congress elects members of its Central Committee also for five years. As in the other electoral processes in Communist China, the National Party Congress approves a slate of members of the Central Committee presented to it by the inner core of the party surrounding the party chairman. Thus chosen, the members of the Central Committee include all the leading members of the party.

According to the party constitution (which periodically has been rewritten, the latest in 1973), the Central Committee creates and supervises the operational agencies of the party and performs the functions of the Party Congress when the Congress is not in session. The operational agencies of the party created by the Central Committee include the Politburo and its Standing Committee (since 1956), and "other necessary organs" such as the Central Secretariat, the Central Control Commission and the Military Affairs Committee. The members of these organs are to be elected by the members of the Central Committee.

The Central Committee itself has some two-hundred regular and alternate members and is too large for policy deliberation. Besides, it meets infrequently for short plenary sessions. Between plenums (fully assembled sessions) of the Central Committee, however, the Politburo and its Standing Committee are authorized by the party constitution to exercise the powers and functions of the Central Committee.

The Politburo is the most powerful organ in the Chinese Communist hierarchy, though during the Cultural Revolution it suffered a diminution of power. Its membership is small. It meets frequently in full session or in its Standing Committee session. For all practical purposes, it is the supreme decision-maker in Communist China. Since his rise to power, Mao has held the prerogative of appointing his close followers to the Politburo. The composition of the Politburo has not remained static, however, and

THE NATIONAL ORGANS OF THE CHINESE COMMUNIST PARTY

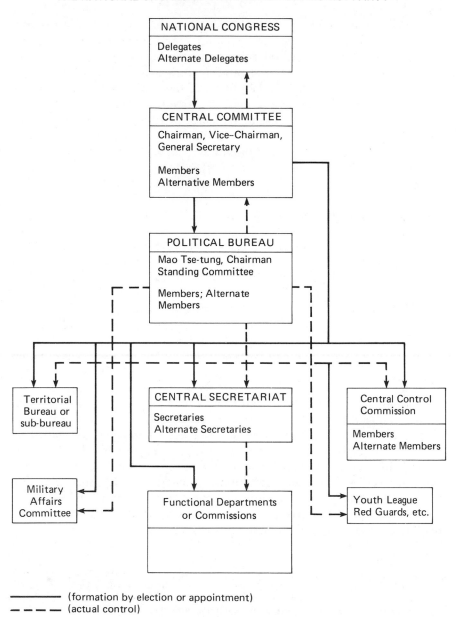

————— (formation by election or appointment)
– – – – (actual control)

FIGURE 3-2·

changes have reflected differing party leadership style and policy orientations.

The central party organization also includes various administrative and functional departments. The Central Party Secretariat in Peking is perhaps the most bureaucratic among the central party organs, and because of this it was attacked most severely during the Cultural Revolution. The Secretariat attends to the daily work of the Central Committee under the direction of the Politburo and its Standing Committee. Its work involves collating the reports and memoranda from the other sectors of party and other sources that must be directed to party leadership. The Secretariat also serves as the communication channel for party policies and decisions to all levels of the party organization. At the lower levels, individual branches of the Secretariat communicate party decisions.

Ideology of the Chinese Communist Party

Mao's philosophy derives many aspects from the Communist view of the world held by Marx and Lenin. But Mao has interwoven these ideas to serve the unique Chinese situation. Among his *Selected Works* are several treatises that show the development of his thought.[1] These treatises, largely dictated by practical necessity, are guides for action. Mao was an innovative, hard-fighting Chinese nationalist who spoke out against national humiliation. As a revolutionary he opposed the country's archaic traditions. He envisioned the Chinese people united by a self-perpetuating revolutionary cause. Emphasis is on struggle, not on harmony. His concept of "people", furthermore, includes all the Chinese people supporting his Communist regime and those who could eventually be made to support it through education and thought reform. In his "On Contradictions," Mao distinguishes between "antagonistic" and "non-antagonistic" contradictions. Antagonistic contradictions are found between exploiter and exploited, between imperialists and colonized people, and such contradictions require revolutionary resolution. Non-antagonistic contradictions, however, exist among the people in policy disputes, and they are amenable to peaceful adjustment. Mao stresses permanent struggle and policy readjustment as necessary elements in communism.

---

[1]For instance, "Report on an Investigation of the Peasant Movement in Hunan," 1927; "The Struggle in the Chingkang Mountains," 1928; "On Practice," supposedly written in 1937 but published in 1950; "On Contradictions," written in 1937 but published in 1952; "The Chinese Revolution and the Chinese Communist Party," 1939; "On New Democracy," 1940; "Let Us Reform Our Style of Work," 1942; "Against Party Eight-Legged Essay," 1942; "On Coalition Government," 1945; "The Present Situation and Our Tasks," 1947; "On People's Democratic Dictatorship," 1949; and "On the Correct Handling of Contradictions Among the People," 1957.

Theoretically, Mao subscribes to the philosophy by Marxism and Leninism. He believes in the scientific interpretation of history based on economic determinism and the inevitability of class struggle. He has taken an uncompromising anti-imperialist, anti-colonial, and anti-capitalist stance. He also prescribes a totalitarian dictatorship for China by the Chinese Communist Party as a necessary transition to the attainment of true communism. Under this system Mao emphasizes revolution to bring about change in backward institutions. In such revolutions, the peasants play a central role. As a son of a peasant family in Hunan province, Mao had firsthand experience with the peasant problems in China. Throughout his revolutionary career, he has been able to provide guidelines for organizing and directing the peasant revolt.

In the behavioral perspective, what is important is not the controversies surrounding Mao's theoretical position, but his unique Chinese adaptation of Marxism and Leninism. What is important is the fact that the Chinese people have been mobilized in the thoughts of Mao and have used them as guides for their actions.

Communism as an ideology and as a movement has had many different appeals throughout the world. In its development the CCP has embraced many divergent interests, and as the party grows in membership (now over twenty-eight million members) and status, it attracts members with different interests and motivations from those of the original, revolutionary ideologists. The elitist nature of the CCP has been, furthermore, a constant strain to Mao's formula for continuous revolution in China.

The path to party membership is not an easy one despite the seemingly simple requirements. Complete devotion to the cause is one requirement. The Young Communist League and increasingly the PLA (People's Liberation Army) and Red Guard units are proper channels for membership. Also activities in mass campaigns are oftentimes rewarded with membership. According to the CCP constitution (1973) a member must be eighteen years old, be working, accept the CCP program, and must obtain two recommendations from party members. Their recommendations must then be approved by the general membership of the party branch and by the next higher party committee.

Once in the party, the member must actively participate in party programs, while exhibiting absolute discipline, obedience, dedication, and submission to party indoctrination. In this fashion, the party insures that only those who prove themselves dedicated Communists will enter the party, thus maintaining the relatively high degree of ideological purity. As a party member, a person must undergo the *three-fold inner-party* education. This includes the study of Marxism-Leninism and the thoughts of Mao, as well as the study of current events, party and state tasks, and moral cultivation.

A more spectacular means of insuring ideological purity among party members, and sometimes the masses as well, is periodic *chen-feng yun-tung*, or rectification campaigns. As will be discussed shortly, the Great Proletarian Cultural Revolution, which started in 1966, aside from being a spectacular power struggle, has also served as a rectification campaign against the inherent bureaucratic tendencies of party and government officials and those taking a capitalist or revisionist road within the party.

Rectification campaigns have been waged often. These campaigns often coincide with a national crisis or a failure in the execution of government policy. The campaigns act as a safety valve to vent party frustration and to provide scapegoats. Those persons accused of causing a policy failure must publicly admit their errors and present an extensive self-critical review of their attitudes. The campaigns serve to eradicate factionalism within the party and generate support for the government from the general population.

The Cultural Revolution

The most celebrated of these campaigns was the *Great Proletarian Cultural Revolution*. The campaign had its roots in the failure of the 1958-1959 Great Leap Forward and commune movement, which raised serious doubts concerning the infallibility of Mao's prescriptions for rapid industrialization and communal structure within the country.

Mao was openly challenged by Politburo member, and Minister of Defense, P'eng Teh-huai, on the Great Leap Movement at the Lushan meeting of the Central Committee in July-August, 1959. Mao's power and influence in the party and government were on the wane in the early 1960s. Immediately preceding the Cultural Revolution, four main groups could be discerned, each with differing orientations and policy perspectives. The legitimacy of the PRC was not the concern of these groups. They differed regarding the best way to modernize the country. The most influential group was still the Maoist faction, which advocated an extremist-revolutionary mass-society for China. This group included Mao, Chiang Ch'ing (Mao's wife), Ch'en Po-ta and K'ang Sheng. The second group was led by Liu Shao-ch'i and Teng Hsiao-p'ing, and its power was found in the party bureaucracy, which was growing increasingly pragmatic and problem-solving in orientation. Government officials and administrators comprised the third group led by Chou En-lai. Finally, the fourth group was the military headed by Lin Piao. Of the non-Mao groups, the most critical challenge to Mao's leadership came from the Liu-Teng group, which differed with Mao particularly over: (1) the speed of collectivization; (2) the extent of mass mobilization in 1957-1958; and (3) the degree of independence from the Soviet Union.

By 1965 Liu's power had so increased that it threatened Mao's preeminent position. According to Mao, these revisionists were using old ideas, old culture, old customs, and old habits to weaken the proletarian dictatorship and the spirit of the people's revolutionary war. They sought, Mao argued, to establish the seeds of a bourgeoisie revolution. Mao had been fearful of the Chinese bureaucratic obsessions, fearful that all revolutionary fervor and initiative would be lost in a sea of paper shuffling. To Mao, the practice of his revolutionary ideals was vital to the long process of building the Chinese nation.

In his famous interview with Edgar Snow in January, 1965, Mao revealed his concern for the future of the revolution after his death. Would China's younger generation carry out his brand of permanent revolution? Mao even found himself in the minority within the leading circle of the party. In September, 1965, a secret meeting of the Central Committee of the party took place to examine the Vietnam crisis, and Mao was faced with a majority favoring the moderate revisionist policy stand of Liu Shao-ch'i. Mao's decision to fight for his indelible revolutionary imprint in the party was then made. He had cultivated the help of Defense Minister Lin Piao and his People's Liberation Army (PLA), which embodied Mao's revolutionary virtues. A mass campaign to follow the example of the People's Liberation Army had already been launched in February, 1964. As subsequent reports indicate, in the September 1965 meeting of the Central Committee of the party, Mao unsuccessfully argued for a cultural revolution. Nevertheless, on November 10, supported by the PLA, Mao and Lin issued statements in Shanghai condemning the playwright and historian Wu Han as a revisionist and a neo-capitalist. Some other minor authors were also criticized. The Proletarian Cultural Revolution officially began in May, 1966, when the *Red Guards*, composed mainly of young students, were organized as Mao's formative support group, and Liu Shao-chi's long time friend, P'eng Chen, Mayor of Peking and a leading member of the party, was openly denounced.

The intent of the Cultural Revolution, as stated by Chou En-lai in a speech delivered at Tirana, Albania, on June 27, 1966, was to meet a growing danger of revisionism in the revolutionary Communist state. By revisionism, Chou meant the restoration of capitalism. Chou explained:

> Owing to the corroding effect of the influence of the bourgeoisie and the spontaneous forces of the petty bourgeoisie, and owing to the presence and influence of the forces of habit from the old society, some persons within the party and government organs and cultural and educational institutions may degenerate and become new bourgeois elements. At the same time, imperi-

alism, modern revisionism and the reactionaries of all countries try every means to carry out encirclement and penetration against us, as well as subversive activities. All this creates in our country the danger of the emergence of revisionism and the restoration of capitalism.[2]

The Red Guards were organized in early May. They staged their first major rally in Peking on August 18. The Red Guards were given official state support and were provided with use of state railways and telegraphic networks. State facilities were also made available for their newspapers and wall posters. They were given permission to stage demonstrations against individuals in authority. The People's Liberation Army rendered its support for the Cultural Revolution by helping to create cadres in the ranks of the Red Guards.

An immediate result of the Cultural Revolution was great confusion in the line of political authority throughout the Chinese Communist system. The activities of the Red Guards were by no means centrally coordinated. Fights were reported between the Red Guards and Liu's adherents and between different groups of Red Guards. Work stoppages became widespread. Finally, the PLA was called in to return order.

The PLA was ordered first to support the left and second to prevent chaos. However, for a number of military commanders maintaining order and stability was more important than supporting the revolutionary left. Clashes between the Red Guards and some PLA units were reported. The Wuhan Incident in July, 1967 had far-reaching implications in this connection. A two-man, pro-Mao investigation team from Peking went to Wuhan to confront an anti-Red Guard military commander. The commander had them seized and beaten. This incident caused a resurgence of Red Guard activity aimed at removing all non-Maoists from positions of power within the PLA. Some army high commanders reacted by attacking the militant leftists. A quick compromise was worked out. The director of the PLA General Staff's Political Department, Hsiao Hua, was purged. At the same time some leaders of the Cultural Revolution Group were purged, including one member of the two-man Wuhan investigating team who had returned to Peking as a hero. The PLA was authorized to use force in defending itself against Red Guard violence.

Though the Red Guards were temporarily suppressed, the militants continued to attack the more moderate party members. Renewed Red Guard violence created a chaotic and confused atmosphere during the summer. Finally Mao was convinced that the Red Guard movement had gone too far. At this point the final step in the escalating military intervention was mandated by Mao. A Worker Provost Corps, also called "Worker-Peasant Mao Tse-tung Thought Propanganda Teams," and PLA

[2]Text released by *New China News Agency*, June 27, 1967.

units were ordered to disband Red Guard units using whatever force was necessary and to move the leadership of the Cultural Revolution to the working class. Revolutionary committees of "three-in-one combination" (revolutionary masses, revolutionary cadres, and armymen) were organized to replace the discredited party organizations.

Manuevers directly concerned with Mao's original goals for the Cultural Revolution ended with the Ninth Party Congress in April, 1969. At that time Lin Piao became the officially designated heir-apparent, giving the military increased control in party matters. A further political readjustment in the wake of the Cultural Revolution continued through the Tenth Party Congress in August, 1973. By then Lin Piao had died in a plane crash, according to an official explanation, while escaping from China after an unsuccessful attempt to assassinate Mao and stage a coup. Chou became more and more influential in decision-making, as did some old party and military leaders who were exonerated during the Cultural Revolution, such as Teng Shiao-ping.

In the Cultural Revolution, Mao was apparently the winner; Liu the loser. Mao's victory, however, left unanswered the basic policy disagreement that caused the Mao-Liu schism and produced the Cultural Revolution. Underlying the Mao-Liu schism is a longstanding controversy over the issue of "red and expert." "Red" means being ideologically correct; "expert" refers to professional and technical expertise. Mao has always insisted on the permanence of revolution and the importance of ideology, even if the revolutionary situation in which the Communists assumed political power in 1949 no longer exists. A revolutionary Communist party in power is no longer the same party it was out of power. As a party in power, the Chinese Communist Party undoubtedly requires more organizational and technical expertise. It must function as a problem-solving agency for the modernization of the country. Mao has demonstrated that he is prepared to forego some modernization if the country's ideological emphasis is threatened. Thus Mao had to pay dearly for his success in the Cultural Revolution, and so did China.

The Cultural Revolution shattered the old party organization, and in the ensuing power vacuum the PLA played a pivotal role in the CCP's reorganization. Thus there emerged a new power configuration in the party and the party-soldiers became, for the moment, the dominant group in the CCP. The party's Military Affairs Committee, with Mao as chairman, has emerged as one of the most powerful decision-making bodies in the country. The Ninth Party Congress of 1969 was attended by 1,512 delegates, and of this number the party-soldiers constituted the highest percentage. In the new Central Committee of the party, party-soldiers constituted close to one-half the entire membership. In the Politburo, 11 of the 21 regular members elected by the Central Committee were party-soldiers.

Developments Following the Cultural Revolution

The Cultural Revolution was more than a political event. One of Mao's primary concerns since his formative years as a revolutionary leader has been how to effect social change. His plan for China was one of continuous political and social revolution. In this way he hoped to avoid the seemingly inevitable bureaucratic stage in Chinese socio-political life. Mao's attempts to prevent stagnation of his social program are founded in his belief that harmony, unity, and social change depend upon controlled and disciplined political conflict and criticism. Therefore, the inability of the Red Guards to promote political struggle in a controlled fashion and the unwillingness of the cadres to accept criticism signify a failure of Mao's Cultural Revolution. Furthermore, the undisciplined excesses of the Red Guards were the foremost cause of the political intervention of the military.

With the conclusion of the Ninth Party Congress, a new political balance was established within the party. The government had become decentralized with a high degree of local autonomy and military control. Lin Piao was officially Mao's heir, and Chou En-lai was seemingly content with foreign affairs. The Congress had approved various programs that tended to reinforce the mass mobilization approach of Mao and were consistent with the political tendencies of Lin. These programs included measures aimed at restoring the conditions prevailing before the Cultural Revolution, such as large scale relocation of urban populations (especially Red Guards) to the countryside, and a limited return to the principles of the Great Leap.

During this period the political strategies of Lin and Chou began to diverge. Lin, perhaps supported by leading military leaders, in attempting to remain orthodox, continued to support the strategy of anti-American "imperialism" and anti-Soviet "revisionism." The difficulty with this policy, however, was that it placed American "imperialism" and Soviet "revisionism" on equal levels. Chou, on the other hand, began developing the policy of normalizing relations with the United States as a means of balance against perceived threats from the Soviet Union.

Following the Ninth Party Congress, major emphasis was placed on stabilizing the political situation, supported, in the main, by the army and the Maoists in Peking. In this process of rebuilding, Chou's capabilities were obviously more in demand than the programs of Lin Piao. This was also evidenced in an interview Mao granted to Edgar Snow in December of 1970. During the interview Mao expressed complete confidence in Chou to make major operational decisions in domestic and foreign policy, often without consulting him. As Chou's plans were initiated, certainly with Lin's opposition, relations with the United States improved, starting with "ping pong" diplomacy and climaxing in President Richard Nixon's visit to Peking in 1972.

The truth surrounding the death of Lin Piao and some military leaders in a plane crash is nearly impossible to determine, but the fact remains that Lin lost in a power struggle and was replaced by the more moderate elements of the party. Chou attempted to return to the situation that existed before the Cultural Revolution, including the removal of the military from political concerns. His aims were to rebuild the party apparatus with more freedom of action in the State Council, to initiate a period of economic growth characterized by material incentives and external economic ties, and to modernize the military with limited nuclear capabilities.

The Tenth Party Congress in August, 1973, indicated a consolidation of Chou's programs and position. The new Politburo consisted of both new and old party and military leaders, but with a generally moderate orientation. The power of the radical faction identified with Chiang Ch'ing was reduced in the Politburo. Also for the first time workers and farmers were elected to the highest party organs. The rise of Wang Hung-wen, a thirty-six year old, former Shanghai cotton mill worker, to the Politburo was phenomenal. The naming of five vice-chairmen on the Standing Committee of the Politburo for the first time suggested the recognition of a need for collective leadership in the event of Mao's disability. The communique released following the Congress emphasized this point by claiming that the "composition of the Tenth Central Committee fully demonstrates that our party is flourishing and has no lack of successors, and that it is firmly united on the basis of Marxism-Leninism-Mao Tse-tung thought." The new party constitution adopted at the Congress carries over the line adopted at the previous Congress with some minor changes. The main enemy is still revisionism, against which there must be continued vigilance, and cultural revolutions will be necessary from time to time to continue social transformation. The party is reestablished as the core, leading organs of the Chinese political system and all the other organizations, including the military, are mandated to accept the centralized leadership of the party.

POLITICAL DYNAMICS AND ACTIVISTS

Polity and Society

In the natural harmony of the Confucian view of human relationships, rulers were regarded as wise. The masses were to be taught and to follow their rulers. Authoritarian rule in traditional China was not, however, in any way like a modern dictatorship. Confucian government ruled through the force of moral principles. To the mass of people, the government meant trouble and was best avoided. The government that governed least was best. Away from the government, the people led their own lives in small, intimate family groups.

By 1949 China was much changed from what it had been traditionally. International and civil wars waged for so long had left the country in turmoil. The wars had forced people from their familiar surroundings. Poverty and destruction in the rural areas drove many people from their families into urban centers. Many young men had joined or were forcefully inducted into the armed forces.

Still the family was the most stabilizing influence in China in 1949. Because of political chaos, there was no governmental authority. With the Communist victory, however, the traditional family system and kinship-oriented social structure were no longer regarded as useful. Emphasis was laid on the building of a modern, industrial society along socialist patterns.

It was quite evident to any would-be reformers that the target of their efforts would have to be not only the traditional monarchial form of government, but also the family unit. Earlier in 1898, K'ang Yu-wei, a famous Chinese scholar-official and reformer, pointed out that the abolition of the traditional family was a condition for proper modern performance. Sun Yat-sen sensed the same incompatibility when he urged the expansion of familism into nationalism. For the Chinese Communist leadership to make the revolution a lasting success, there had to be not only a successful political and military victory, but also change in the people's thinking. This could only be accomplished by radically changing the family institution, which had for centuries ruled Chinese life and behavior. Long before the institution of the commune system, Mao sought to change loyalty from the small, tightly-knit, family groups to the party and government. To accomplish this it was necessary to strike hard against the base of the family, the marriage institution. In 1950, soon after the Communists attained power in mainland China, they introduced a new marriage law. Marriage was no longer merely an affair of the parents and the family. Women had equal rights. A minimum age for marriage was set at twenty for men and eighteen for women and no marriage was without consent of the marrying couple.

In a broader social sense, the CCP destroyed the landlord class in Chinese society and did not permit other group interests to develop. It destroyed the traditional social structure in the village and replaced it with a more egalitarian pattern of social mobility based on educational attainment and loyalty to the party. In place of the old diffused power structure of the village, it placed a centralized system of its own. The party established itself as the single center of power in the village through the cadres who worked and resided within it. These cadres, or leadership units, have been vital in bringing the village closer to a national political order.

Political Activists

Mao, as a Communist revolutionary, represented a new breed of Chinese leadership. In contrast to earlier imperial conservative leaders and reformers, Mao has no scholar-gentry background. In contrast to Chiang and his Nationalist leaders, Mao is anti-urban and anti-intellectual. Mao and his longtime, close followers share a predominantly rural, peasant background.

Mao's early life is typical of many of the leaders of the successful Chinese Communist movement. He was a son of a middle-class peasant family in a predominantly agrarian sector of Chinese society. A rebellious youth, he was intellectually curious and achievement-oriented. His career outlook was frustrating. He found his country immersed in political chaos and intellectual ferment. Finally he found inspiration in Marxism and the Communist party movement. The story can be repeated for most Communist leaders.

Mao demands total dedication from his close followers. He believes in the correctness of his road to reconstructing Chinese society as a modern, viable entity. He craves mass support. Mao envisions the masses vitally integrated with the development process. This involves use of cadres to initiate and promote a unified leadership between the party hierarchy and the people, a procedure the Chinese Communists call the "mass line" method. All cadres are not necessarily party members. The non-party cadres are nonetheless government officials. Party cadres include all party functionaries who come in daily contact with the people. The term *cadre*, though it has a variety of meanings, usually implies leadership and authority.

Among different types of cadres, there are *state cadres (kuo chia kan pu)* and *local cadres (ti fang kan pu)*. The state cadres are usually non-military officials in the bureaucratic hierarchies of government, and they receive their salary from the central government. The local cadres, on the other hand, are officials at the communal level and below, who receive their income from local institutions. Besides this state and local distinction, there are many informal groupings of cadres on the basis of seniority, experience in the revolutionary war, and so on. Thus, there are *old cadres* and *new cadres, long march cadres, Yenan cadres, anti-Japanese war cadres,* and *liberation war cadres*.

Since the practical application of party policies falls on their shoulders, the party cadres must be carefully trained. They must carry out a continuous study program, and they are periodically subjected to rectification campaigns. To become a member of the elite Communist party, one usually has to prove excellence in a chosen field of study or work. The new generation Chinese Communist Party members are no longer mere revolutionaries. The party membership has increased dramatically since 1950, and new recruits (particularly before the Cultural Revolution) have come more and more from the well-established and/or the upwardly mobile middle strata within Chinese Communist society. Many are graduates from institutions of higher learning. Once they are in the party, mandatory study of the political and theoretical aspects of Chinese Communism is enforced. They are further subjected to constant in-service education, which, according to an official document, includes research of the area of assigned duties. The recruit is expected to know his or her field in order to understand how party policies, regulations, and useful past work history can be made applicable. The party members must also acquire a specialized knowledge for the discharge of their responsibilities.

Some cadres are sent to school for further study; more often, however, cadres are organized into small study groups. The groups are small to encourage open confessions and mutual help. Intimate and active interactions among group members are encouraged. The principle of the unity of theory and practice is applied in various ways. One is the *2-5 system*. This means two days in the office for study and administration, and five days for actual participation at the production level.

The much publicized story about Wang Kuo-fan exemplifies leadership at the local and rural level. In 1934, at the age of 16, Wang ran away from his home in Hsip'u in the province of Hopei, a poverty-stricken village. He joined the Communists. His membership in the Communist Party began six years later. After the Communist victory in 1949, Wang refused an offer of a leading post in a *hsien* (county) and volunteered to return to his home village as a rank-and-file party member to help transform his homestead. Wang returned home and provided leadership for the land reform in his village, confiscating and redistributing landlord holdings. He organized mutual aid teams in the village and assisted the implementation of the party's decisions of December 15, 1951, on mutual aid and cooperation in agricultural production. In this instance he organized twenty-three households into a small agricultural producers' cooperative.

In the beginning this cooperative had an extremely poor financial base. Its hundred members comprised the poorest peasants in the village and owned only 230 *mou* (about 37.7 acres) of land. They had no carts, no draft animals, and no farm tools. Wang's creative leadership and his diligent and frugal operation transformed the cooperative into a self-sufficient and prosperous unit. Eventually it became a model cooperative.

Wang's Chienming Agricultural, Forestry, and Livestock Breeding Cooperative became widely known throughout the district and the country. Wang was elected to the National People's Congress, and articles he had written describing his experience appeared in *People's Daily* and *Red Flag*.[3] As a model cooperative, Wang's "paupers' cooperative" has become a point of attraction for the party's guided educational tours in the area.

Wang is a model cadre. Born in the era of revolutionary war, he joined the party as an ideologically dedicated revolutionary. Once the party came into power, he was willing to work where he could apply his talents for the good of the people. He was innovative when needed, but as a dedicated party cadre he was always able to interpret the leadership line of the party.

The Armed Forces

Officially, the new structure of power in the People's Republic of China is shared by workers, peasants, and soldiers. The People's Liberation Army is a main pillar of the Chinese Communist system. The Cultural Revolution has drawn the PLA into the vortex of Chinese politics. In the struggle for power at the height of the Cultural Revolution during 1967-1968, the PLA supplanted even party and government institutions throughout China's provinces and enforced direct military rule.

The PLA has been a potent political force throughout the Chinese Communist history. In one of his often quoted passages, Mao pointed out, "Every Communist must grasp the truth, political power grows out of the barrel of a gun." Indeed, the victory of the Chinese Communist revolution, as pointed out earlier, was in the end a military victory. In their long march to victory, the Communists fought against the Nationalist forces, expanded their areas of control, conquered the whole land, and established their legitimacy as the sole ruler of the country.

In the course of the revolution, the distinction between civil and military domains was blurred. Mao's leadership has been as much of the party, as of the military. As a matter of fact, together with Chuh Teh, Lin Piao, and P'eng Teh-huai, he was responsible for the organization of the so-called Red First Front Army in the Kiangsi Soviet area in south China. Mao, as Chairman of the Chinese Communist Party, has also been the Chairman of the Military Affairs Committee, the most powerful policy-making organ affecting the military.

Following the successful civil war, the PLA served a number of functions, insuring domestic control and public order, acting as an instrument of economic development through involvement in socialist

[3]*Hung-ch'i (Red Flag)*, September 1, 1959, no. 17, pp. 26-30.

construction, mobilizing popular support for party programs, and becoming a model for society.

The PLA contributed to the economy by growing much of its own food, by constructing roads, bridges, and other public works, by operating factories, and by aiding peasants in agricultural operations. Members of the PLA political apparatus were able to promote support of the party's programs through indoctrination and military training of the nation's youth.

The PLA is a huge national organization of some three million, organized into thirteen military regions. Its operation has consumed about 10 percent of the annual government expenditures since 1960. In the twenty year period from 1950 to 1970, the PLA's ex-servicemen numbered some fifteen million. After leaving the service, many were sent to their home villages as workers and supervisors.

Mostly infantry, the PLA's network embraces the entire country. The PLA general headquarters, constitutionally under the Ministry of Defense, consists of three departments: General Logistics department, General Staff department and General Political department, plus the service arm headquarters. The General Staff department, headed by the Chief of Staff, has operational military responsibilities.

Real direction and policy for the PLA come from the Military Affairs Committee of the party, which has been under the control of Mao, its chairman. Its membership has included many leading party and military leaders. In the Chinese Communist system, the military has been responsible not only for national security and internal peace-keeping, but also closely integrated with the political process for national development.

Many Chinese military professionals have been concerned with the political use of the military for socialist construction purposes. The prime concern of military professionals has been the fighting capabilities of their forces, rather than their political usefulness. Mao's emphasis, on the other hand, is that the PLA remain "red." This means that military modernization should not have priority over ideological and political considerations. The controversy over priorities has long been, and remains, a problem within the Chinese leadership.

From 1954 to 1957, with P'eng Teh-huai as the Minister of Defense, the Chinese military began to lean toward professionalism: military ranks were introduced, nuclear weaponry was under development, and modernized equipment was sought. By 1957, however, Mao and the party began to reassert the "redness over expertness." The Great Leap Forward mobilized the military. Along with intensive indoctrination sessions, the PLA provided massive labor inputs. In 1959 P'eng Teh-huai was purged and replaced by Lin Piao. The recall of Soviet aid, which forced China to become militarily self-reliant, also helped the party leadership in advocat-

ing the importance of political education. Lin Piao intensified indoctrination and political control, and by 1965 all ranks and varying uniforms
were abolished. The PLA became the model for the entire society, but as
a revolutionary rather than a professional body.

During the Cultural Revolution, the PLA actively participated in
politics, restoring order and managing the local governments. Revolutionary committees were formed, chaired in most cases by the military
commander.

China's new politics of the post-Cultural Revolution, however, are to
restore politics to the party and to reduce the political role of the military.
By 1970 the armed forces, under Chou En-lai's influence, were reverting
to military roles. Chou's death in 1976, however, has raised questions
about the future role of the Chinese military. Military professionalism has
been encouraged and there is a continuing need to modernize the conventional army and develop China's limited nuclear capability given the
Chinese leaders' perception of the Soviet threat. But the military's political voice has not been silenced.

CHINA IN WORLD AFFAIRS

History and culture have influenced China's foreign policy goals. For
instance, as Mao, the peasant revolutionary, has insisted on China's independence from its Confucian tradition, he has advocated disengagement
from its equally restrictive relationship with the Soviet Union. Just as Mao
recognizes the handicap of a passive and dependent peasantry existing
within China's political structure, he also realizes the consequences of the
identical characteristics being adopted by the PRC in its economic, political, and military relations with the USSR. Mao struggled to end the
politics of dependency, which characterized China's earlier domestic
scene, and he is engaged in the same kind of struggle on a broader scale,
in the realm of international politics—especially with regard to Soviet
Russia. Mao and the Chinese Communist Party have tried continuously to
destroy the superior/subordinate dichotomy that has existed in Chinese
society since Confucius. In like manner, the Chinese Communists refuse
to accept a subordinate position to the Soviet Union in the international
communist movement. Instead, China demands equality and the authority
to develop a unique path toward achieving the ultimate Communist state.
China's foreign policy goals have also included countering American influence in Asia.

During the first ten years after the establishment of the Peking
government, the PRC viewed the United States as the primary enemy.
The Soviet Union was China's foremost ally and source of economic and

military aid. To the third world nations, the PRC was a symbol of anti-imperialism, a nation willing to promote their wars of national liberation.

Sino-Soviet tensions, however, caused major changes in China's foreign policies. Stalin died in 1953. Mao considered himself second only to Stalin in the international communist movement. Although Stalin's successors demanded universal affiliation with their model of development, Mao denied the position of Moscow as the undisputed leader and arbiter of doctrine within the communist bloc of nations.

Mao had cause to concern himself with Soviet "revisionism" following the death of Stalin. Despite the Treaty of Alliance of 1950, and the PRC's entry into the Korean War to aid North Korea, the Soviet Union refused to come to China's aid when Mao wanted to liberate Taiwan in 1954. Soviet leadership refused to support him because of the American threat of nuclear retaliation. Worse still, Khrushchev's attack on Stalin in 1956 was also considered an attack on Mao and his leadership in China, as well as anyone who defied Moscow's new leadership.

The end of this period was marked by the leftward shift of Peking's outlook. Internationally, the PRC showed renewed interest in the forceful liberation of Taiwan in 1959 by intensifying propaganda against imperialism and "modern revisionism." With their more militant outlook, the Chinese regarded India, formerly a friendly neighbor, as a "reactionary power" competing for leadership in Asia. Old border disputes were reopened. The flight of the Tibetan Dalai Lama to India in March, 1959, did not help the situation. The first series of border clashes between India and China took place around the same time. At home, the country was swept by the fanfare of the Great Leap Forward.

In the early 1960s, the PRC found itself laden with problems. At home was the need to recover from the failure of the Great Leap programs. Abroad China was faced with hostile superpowers.

In the face of growing U.S. involvement in the Vietnamese War, the PRC opted for a cautious policy, limiting involvement in supplying arms and logistical support to Hanoi. However, China took a radical position against Khrushchev's growing détente policy. Chinese Communist leaders considered Khrushchev's policies too lenient toward "imperialism," and likely to compromise the principle of anti-imperialist revolutionary movements for the promotion of Soviet national interests. Khrushchev's show of force further aggravated the situation. In the summer of 1960 he cut off economic aid to China. Albania was faced with a similar situation in the spring of 1961. Furthermore, Khrushchev was courting India for further influence in Asia, and he wanted to hinder Chinese development of nuclear strike capabilities.

As the decade of the 1960s advanced, Sino-Soviet differences became more numerous and accentuated. They became more than ideolocial. One issue concerned conflicting national interests, including the highly sensitive question of border disputes. Brezhnev and Kosygin, as the successors to Khrushchev, failed to reverse the trend. In November, 1964, and again in February, 1965, their overtures for compromise were rejected by Mao. Mao's campaign against Soviet revisionism could not be easily compromised.

With the inception of the Cultural Revolution, Red Guards waged violent demonstrations against foreign embassies in Peking, and Red Guard demonstrations were reported along the Sino-Soviet borders. The Chinese Foreign Ministry was pressured by the Red Guards for a more militant foreign policy. Perhaps partly in response to these pressures, all Chinese ambassadors, except Huang Hua in Cairo, were recalled for political indoctrination at the height of the Cultural Revolution.

Moscow's reactions to the Cultural Revolution were negative. To Moscow, the Cultural Revolution and its anti-party manifestations were clearly a challenge to the Leninist principle of communist party control. The situation presented possibilities for Soviet intervention. In this connection, the application of the so-called Brezhnev doctrine to Czechoslovakia and the Soviet invasion there in August, 1968, had a shocking effect on the distraught Sino-Soviet relationship. Chou's answer was to seek a limited counterweight against possible Soviet pressures. Instead, Lin's solution, amplified by the militancy of the Cultural Revolution, was to provoke the famous clash with the USSR on the Ussuri River on March 2, 1969, only to be met by overwhelming Russian retaliation. Eventually, Lin's demise meant the rise of Chou's star and emphasis on diplomatic solutions for the achievement of foreign policy goals.

Following the Cultural Revolution, normalized foreign policy was reestablished. Most ambassadors were returned. The number of countries with diplomatic relations with the PRC increased. The PRC continued to insist on termination of relations with Taiwan as a prerequisite for formal relations, but generally allowed more flexible conditions. On October 25, 1971, the PRC gained the Chinese seat in the United Nations, and the Taiwan government was expelled.

Relations with the United States have also improved significantly, and even though great differences continue to exist, the Sino-American relations are somewhat less tense than those between the PRC and the Soviet Union. The PRC has much to gain from this arrangement: a balance to the Soviet threat, concessions in the Vietnam situation, concessions on the Taiwan question, improvement in foreign trade, and possibly the creation of certain amounts of dissension between the United States and

Japan. Finally, the Peking visit by President Richard Nixon, in 1972, improved mutual understanding between the two countries. Japan then quickly moved on her own to conclude normalization of relations with the PRC. At present, the PRC sees the Soviet Union as the number one enemy. China seeks to protect its national interests against the Soviet Union by improving relations with other countries in the world.

THE QUESTION OF TAIWAN

The question of Taiwan has created a number of problems for the PRC. There is disagreement as to whether Taiwan is part of China or whether it is culturally and socially distinct. Both governments (the PRC and the Republic of China) are in agreement that Taiwan is a part of China, but the leaders of the indigenous population claim otherwise. Unification is desired by the PRC, but this seems highly unlikely until the political influences of current leadership in the Chinese mainland and Taiwan have diminished.

In the past twenty years the Nationalist government on Taiwan has made solid economic progress. Several preconditions for this progress existed before the arrival of the mainland Chinese: the Japanese, who controlled Taiwan from 1895 to the end of World War II, left a considerable infrastructure and economic system; the location is beneficial to trade and shipping; the island is easy to govern and defend (with U.S. assistance); and the population is largely literate and educated.

The future prospects for the Taiwan government are uncertain, however. Lessening of trade with the United States, Japan, and European nations, due to pressure from the PRC, may force the Nationalists to turn to India and the Soviet Union to protect their sovereignty from the PRC. The most unlikely prospect in any case would be a coup by the native Taiwanese to overthrow the Nationalists.

American policy toward Taiwan did not develop until the Korean War, when Taiwan was included in the protective shield area set up by the United States. Strategic locations on Taiwan were used for air bases during the Vietnam War. Although the United States has continued to support the Nationalist government economically and politically, there has never been a definitive statement on the legal status of Taiwan. Following President Nixon's visit to China, a joint communique was issued that declared the question of Taiwan a domestic problem for the PRC.

The PRC has continuously sought to force the cessation of American support of the Nationalist government. The PRC seriously intends to liberate Taiwan or resolve the problem in some other way. Many methods have been attempted in the past, including propaganda measures during the Korean War, encouraging relatives of mainland Chinese to support unification, publicly urging the Nationalist government to join the PRC as an autonomous region, rejecting the two-China policy created by the United States, and carrying on low-level political talks.

PROBLEMS AND PROSPECTS

After establishing a new regime in 1949, the revolutionary Chinese Communists rapidly consolidated their political power and embarked upon ambitious programs of social change and economic development. Under Mao's leadership, until recently at least, they have maintained a unity almost unique in the history of revolutionary regimes. They have built the largest mass party in history and have kept it under tight discipline. They have unified mainland China, nurtured a new ruling elite at every level of society, indoctrinated the population in a new official ideology, and restricted all class relationships. The total population was mobilized for the Great Leap Forward, and frantic efforts are being made to expand output in industry and agriculture. These changes have made an indelible imprint on Chinese society.

Contributing to this success of the Peking regime and the maintenance of political stability have been Mao's charisma and his dedicated following, which made it possible to establish a strong, authoritarian government. This was accomplished in the political vacuum that existed following the long revolutionary war, but it was also made possible by the people, willing to experiment to improve their livelihood.

The failure of the Great Leap movement of 1959 and the subsequent communization program, however, emphasizes many internal contradictions within the Chinese Communist system. Mao's idealized concept of the ideal Chinese citizen requires him or her to sustain the revolutionary struggle. The ideal revolutionary is wholly obedient to party discipline, loyal and dedicated to the regime's goals, self-sacrificing and unconcerned about personal welfare, and always willing to place the good of the revolution above narrower interests. The irony of the situation, however, is that the process of modernization requires and helps create class differentiation and specialists, who tend to value professional competence over ideological commitment, and who are likely to push for at least some policies that the present leaders in China call "revisionist." In short, the consequences of modernization are likely to erode the basis for a continuing revolutionary dogmatism and ardor and tend to reinforce the long bureaucratic tradition of the Chinese people.

The "red and expert" controversy touches on the very essence of Mao's leadership. As long as Mao is alive, his charisma should give him the winning hand. However, Mao and his revolutionary colleagues are old and their days are numbered. Looming large on the horizon is an inevitable power struggle for the leadership of the country.

The Peking regime is confronted with many problems, and very often its assets have become its liabilities. The country is rich in natural resources and in the energy of its people. This has given China an impressive international power potential. But the task of mobilizing and modernizing so huge a population spread over so broad a territory is stupendous. The problem of communication is critical. The party's control is less tenacious in the provinces where peasant uprisings still occur. The revolutionary zeal of party cadres has enabled them to generate support for the regime, but it has also often caused them to misrepresent or distort the extent of that support. A serious communication gap exists between decision-makers and the masses.

The PRC's foreign policy will also parallel domestic policy in the future, in the sense that ideological concerns will be sacrificed in order to manipulate the balance of world power. Future relations with the Soviet Union may range from war to reconciliation. However, some political accommodation within the communist consortium is most likely. The tension between the United States and China has disappeared, and the Taiwan question remains the only significant problem before complete normalization of relations can occur. Economic competition and traditional dislike may create problems in Chinese-Japanese relations that could affect Asian stability. As a member of the United Nations, the PRC may take an effective role in promoting the interests of the Third World, while protecting its own national interests.

The Peking regime still has the problem of restoring what it claims to be lost Chinese territories in the areas bordering the USSR and India. The regime also has problems with minorities living in the border areas who have never been under the effective control of the central government of China. Peking's long range plans are to reclaim regions, most of them wastelands, in Manchuria, Inner Mongolia, Sinkiang and Tibet. The regime also intends to send settlers and workers into these areas to make better use of the land and to exploit the available natural resources.

Although many problems remain, the first goal of the Chinese Communists, to strengthen state power, has been met. They achieved this objective in the period from 1949 to 1953 with the liquidation of the landlords and other "class enemies." The second goal, the simultaneous development of the socialist revolution and socialist construction, was advanced in the three five-year plans (1953-1957, 1961-1965, and 1966-1970). Meanwhile, the regime also carried out rural collectivization, socialization of industry and commerce, the reform of intellectuals, the purge of "rightist elements," the Great Leap Forward to industrialization, the communization program, and the Cultural Revolution. This is an impressive record, but China is still a developing country with many problems and conflicts to resolve.

RECOMMENDED READINGS

Barnett, A. Doak, *Cadres, Bureaucracy and Political Power in Communist China.* New York: Columbia University Press, 1967.

———— , *China after Mao.* Princeton, N.J.: Princeton University Press, 1967.

———— , ed., *Chinese Communist Politics in Action.* Seattle, Wash.: University of Washington Press, 1969.

Belden, Jack, *China Shakes the World.* New York: Monthly Review Press, 1970.

Chang, Parris H., *Power and Policy in China.* University Park, Pa.: Pennsylvania State University Press, 1975.

Ch'en, Jerome, *Mao and the Chinese Revolution.* New York: Oxford University Press, 1967.

Cohen, Arthur C., *The Communism of Mao Tse-tung.* Chicago: The University of Chicago Press, 1964.

DeBary, William Theodore, et al., eds., *Sources of Chinese Tradition.* 2 vols. New York: Columbia University Press, 1964

Fairbank, John K., *The United States and China (3rd. ed.).* Cambridge, Mass.: Harvard University Press, 1971.

———— , ed., *Chinese Thought and Institutions.* Chicago: University of Chicago Press, 1957.

———— , et al., *East Asia: Modern Transformation.* Boston: Houghton Mifflin Co., 1965.

Fan, K. II., and K. P. Fan., *From the Other Side of the River.* New York: Anchor Books, 1975.

Fitzgerald, C. P., *The Birth of Communist China.* Baltimore: Penguin, 1964.

Gittings, John., *The Role of the Chinese Army.* New York: Oxford University Press, 1967.

Griffith, William E., *Sino-Soviet Relations, 1964-1965.* Cambridge, Mass.: M.I.T. Press, 1967.

Hinton, Harold C., *An Introduction to Chinese Politics.* New York: Praeger, 1973.

Hinton, William., *Fashen: A Documentary of Revolution in a Chinese Village.* New York: Random House, 1968.

Houn, Franklin W., *To Change a Nation: Propaganda and Indoctrination in Communist China.* Glencoe, Ill.: Free Press, 1961.

Hsii, Immanuel C. Y., *The Rise of Modern China.* New York: Oxford University Press, 1970.

Hsu, Leonard Shihlien, *The Political Philosophy of Confucianism.* New York: Harper & Row, 1932.

Johnson, Chalmers., *Peasant Nationalism and Communist Power: The*

Emergence of Revolutionary China, 1937-1945. Stanford, Calif.: Stanford University Press, 1966.

Lewis, John W., *Leadership in Communist China.* Ithaca, N.Y.: Cornell University Press, 1963.

——————— , ed., *Party Leadership and Revolutionary Power in China.* Cambridge, Mass.: Harvard University Press, 1970.

Lifton, Robert J., *Thought Reform and the Psychology of Totalism.* New York: Norton, 1961.

Lindbeck, John M., ed., *China: Management of a Revolutionary Society.* Seattle, Wash.: University of Washington Press, 1971.

Mao Tse-tung, *Selected Works of Mao Tse-tung.* 4 vols. Peking: Foreign Languages Press, 1961.

Mendal, Douglas, *The Politics of Formosan Nationalism.* Berkeley, Calif.: University of California Press, 1970.

North, Robert C., *The Foreign Relations of China (2nd ed.).* Encino, Calif.: Dickenson Publishing Co., 1974.

Prybyla, Jan S., *The Political Economy of Communist China.* Scranton, Pa.: International Textbook Co., 1970.

Pye, Lucian W., *The Spirit of Chinese Politics.* Cambridge, Mass.: M.I.T. Press, 1968.

Rice, Edward W., *Mao's Way.* Berkeley, Calif.: University of California Press, 1972.

Robinson, Thomas W., ed., *The Cultural Revolution in China.* Berkeley, Calif.: University of California Press, 1971.

Scalapino, Robert A., ed., *Elites in the People's Republic of China.* Seattle, Wash.: University of Washington Press, 1972.

Schram, Stuart R., *Mao Tse-tung.* Baltimore: Penguin, 1968.

——————— , *The Political Thought of Mao Tse-tung (rev. ed.).* New York: Praeger, 1969.

Schurmann, Franz, *Ideology and Organization in Communist China (2nd ed.).* Berkeley, Calif.: University of California Press, 1968.

Schurmann, Franz and Orville Schell, eds., *The China Reader: Communist China.* New York: Random House, 1967.

Schwartz, Benjamin I., *Chinese Communism and The Rise of Mao.* New York: Harper Torchbook, 1962.

Snow, Edgar, *Red China Today.* New York: Vintage Books, 1971.

——————— , *Red Star over China.* New York: Grove Press, 1961.

Solomon, Richard H., *Mao's Revolution and the Chinese Political Culture.* Berkeley, Calif.: University of California Press, 1971.

Townsend, James R., *Political Participation in Communist China.* Berkeley, Calif.: University of California Press, 1969.

——————— , *Politics in China.* Boston: Little, Brown, 1974.

Van Ness, Peter, *Revolution and Chinese Foreign Policy.* Berkeley, Calif.: University of California Press, 1971.

Vogel, Ezra P., *Canton under Communism: Programs and Politics in a Provincial Capital, 1949-1968.* Cambridge, Mass.: Harvard University Press, 1969.

Whitson, William W., ed., *The Military and Political Power in China in the 1970s.*
New York: Praeger, 1972.
—————— , and Chen-Hsia Huang, *The Chinese High Command: A History of Communist Military Politics, 1927-1971.* New York: Praeger, 1972.
Whyte, Martin King, *Small Groups and Political Rituals in China.* Berkeley, Calif.: University of California Press, 1974.
Wright, Mary C., *The Last Stand of Chinese Conservatism.* Stanford: Stanford University Press, 1957.
Zagoria, Donald S., *The Sino-Soviet Conflict, 1956-1961.* New York: Atheneum, 1964.

Heron Castle, Himeji, Japan

Geisha girl serving sake

A Japanese street scene

Modern Tokyo

Chinese children at play

A busy port scene

A Chinese commune

Chinese traditional architecture

Celebrating the Chinese Communist Revolution

A market place in rural India

Rural scene near New Delhi

2000 year old Sri Chamun-
duswari Temple on top of
Chamundi Hill, Mysore City

Street scene, Calcutta

River life in Bangladesh

A Pakistani Patriarch

Moghul architecture in Pakistan

A modern building in Pakistan

Chapter Four

India:
Democracy In Crisis

India's geographical setting is described as South Asia, or simply the subcontinent. These terms are derived from the region's peninsular appearance as it juts out from mainland Asia into the Indian Ocean. India, Pakistan, and Bangladesh are the larger countries in this vast Asian extremity. Together they total approximately 1,580,000 square miles—an area equivalent to four-fifths of Europe (less the USSR), and more than half that of the United States. India alone occupies approximately three-quarters of this territory. The dimensions of South Asia are matched by its topography, climate, and demographic diversity.

This region is separated from the Asian continent by the world's highest mountain barrier, the Himalayas. This mountain chain stretches for 1,500 miles across the northern perimeter of India and Pakistan and links with subsidiary ranges to the west and east. The latter ranges curve southward completing the natural boundary that envelops the entire region. Other prominent mountain ranges, such as the Vindyas, Satpuras, Western and Eastern Ghats, and the Deccan Plateau, although significant in both geographic and historic terms, when compared with the Himalayas give an impression of flatness.

The subcontinent also contains some of the world's more celebrated rivers. The Ganges, Brahmaputra, and Indus are most notable. All have their source in the Himalayas and carry life-giving waters and silt into India, Pakistan, and Bangladesh. They have made the Indo-Gangetic plain the most fertile region of its size in the world.

Although 60 percent of South Asia lies in the temperate zone, and all of it is above the equator, its climate is tropical. This phenomenon is due to the Himalayan range, which screens the cold northern winds while containing the monsoon that sweeps in from the tropical seas. The hot, sultry weather experienced in central, southern, and eastern South Asia contrasts with the decidedly hot, dry weather of the northwest.

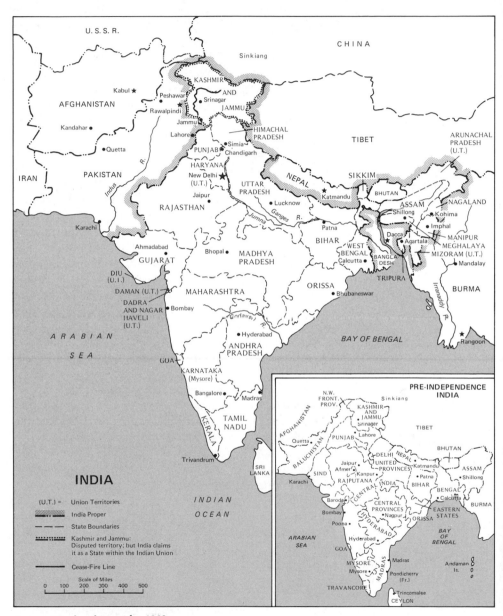

Source: Ward and Macridis, 1963.

Rainfall is usually the result of the monsoons, which strike inland from the Arabian Sea on the west and the Bay of Bengal in the east. In the former, there being no mountain barrier to release the force of the monsoon from the Gulf of Cambay to Karachi in Pakistan, rainfall is negligible. Hence, the territories of Sind, Baluchistan, Rajasthan, the Punjabs (in India and Pakistan), and the North West Frontier Province are arid and barren. The Indus and other major western rivers, however, are linked through an intricate network of irrigation systems, which has made the Punjabs and parts of Sind very fertile. More fortunate areas deriving benefits from the western monsoon (found almost exclusively in India) receive upwards of one hundred inches of rainfall. The eastern monsoon is renowned for its assaults on the Ganges delta and the hills of Assam. The rainfall there varies, but it is reputed to be the heaviest in the world. Both the Brahmaputra and the Ganges valleys receive ample rainfall, which may explain the heavy concentration of people found there.

India, with a population nearing 600 million, and Pakistan, before the emergence of Bangladesh with almost 130 million, represented the second and fifth largest countries in the world. Bangladesh's seventy-five million people now makes it the eighth largest country; Pakistan today is a nation of about sixty-five million. These figures also describe ethnic and cultural diversity of enormous magnitude. Extreme heterogeneity continues to characterize both India and Pakistan. By contrast, Bangladesh is more homogeneous. Major differences exist between the Dravidian peoples of South India [in Tamil Nadu, Kerala and Karnataka (Mysore)] and the Ido-Aryans of the North. Numerous languages separate these peoples from one another, as do religious preferences and rituals. The Hindu-Muslim controversy, which caused the division of South Asia into two sovereign states, addresses itself to the question of religious incompatibility. The independence of Bangladesh in December, 1971, is yet another example of the failure to assimilate cultural diversity. Problems of national identity can be traced to the tenacity with which people cling to regional and provincial life-styles. Moreover, the continuing reorganization of the Indian and Pakistan states and provinces is a response to linguistic and psycho-cultural differences. Atomization rather than homogenization is an important concept in the study of the politics of South Asia.

India has been the origin of many of the world's great civilizations. Hinduism, which is indigenous to South Asia, interacted with Buddhism, which also had its beginning there. Islam and Christianity came later from distant lands and shores. Of the two, the former is more conspicuous. Global civilizations aside, India contains religious communities that are less known in the outer world, such as the Jains, Sikhs and Parsis. Furthermore, the force of change has not left India untouched. Among younger Indians there is a shift away from cultures with religious foundations toward secular orders. Deviance from conventional norms may represent new civilizations in the making, and one cannot ignore communism or Indian Marxism. Like Islam and Christianity, communism and socialism have alien roots, but penetration has not occurred via physical invasion as much as through ideological importation. Moreover, the power of ideas has proven far more significant than the tenacity of foreign invaders, who have been swallowed by the vast reaches of the subcontinent.

HINDUISM AND GOVERNMENT

In Hindu tradition public office was given religious sanction. The first duty of the monarch was the protection of his kingdom, its subjects, and their property. According to the *Arthasastras* of Kautilya, the oldest surviving Hindu texts concerned with statecraft, rulers were free to use whatever means they deemed necessary to satisfy their obligations. The king is a paternalistic ruler among his subjects. Monarchy is perceived therefore as benevolent and fair, harsh only to those who would undermine the tranquility of the realm. The omnipotent and omnipresent king in Hinduism has been compared with the fountainhead of power in ancient China. Both would appear to suggest that the good fortune of the populace is mysteriously joined with the wisdom, drive, courage, and virtue of the maximum ruler.

A further point is the consequences to be suffered should the monarch fail to meet his responsibilities. What is the alternative to submitting to a despotic or incompetent king? Hinduism suggests the alternative is a state of anarchy, which is judged to be more disastrous than blind obedience. However, this is not to imply that a king cannot be forcibly deposed. The *Mahabharata*, another ancient Hindu text, in fact insists that a king who violates popular trust is no longer considered divine and "the people should take up arms and kill the king who plunders their wealth and fails to protect them . . . They should combine to slay him like a mad dog."[1] Yet there is virtually no evidence of such occurrences in early Indian history, unless palace revolutions are to be given prominence.

Finally, we come to an explanation for the apparent distance separating the governors from the ruled in pre-Muslim Indian civilization. It will also have relevance for an understanding of modern India and its people. Despite the symbiotic relationship between king and subjects, there is no awareness of the existence of statehood. Neither the king nor the folk are conscious of belonging to a political entity demanding their supreme allegiance. In India we are not always dealing with a corporate

---

Mahabharata, XIII, 61, 31-3, quoted in A. L. Basham, "Some Fundamental Political Ideas of Ancient India," in C. H. Philips, ed. *Politics and Society in India* (London: Allen and Unwin Ltd., 1962), p. 21.

arrangement, a fixed territory, an identity whose constancy transcends changes in the presiding elite. Rather, in India one is supposedly concerned with society and the individual who dwells within it. The Hindu stresses salvation, *Moksha*, the Buddhist, *Nirvana*, as the ultimate goal. To break the cycle of life to prevent rebirth to attain oneness with God is demanded of all Hindus. The doctrines of *Dharma*, or moral duty and *Karma*, the law of moral consequences, discourage mundane approaches to reality so intimately connected with secular, western life. In the pursuit of the ultimate, the individual Hindu learns to look upon the world as *Maya*, illusion. In India, this personalized mysticism tends to diminish corporate political feelings.

HISTORICAL BACKGROUND

Hindu civilization traces its origin from the Aryan invasions of approximately 1500-1000 B.C. Filtering into the northern and western regions of South Asia over many centuries, the Aryans eventually imposed their will on the indigenous population and drove them into the interior and southern regions. For two millennia the Aryans engaged in creating and destroying kingdoms, the more celebrated identified with Maurya, Gupta, and Harsha in the north, and Chola and Pallava in the south. Although Hindu kingdoms continued to dot the subcontinent's landscape, in the tenth century A.D., the Muslim invasions eclipsed Hindu importance for many centuries thereafter.

What stands out in the Hindu period, however, is not the political successes but the sophisticated social organization. India's cultural pluralism necessitated a unifying structure, and curiously, this was found in a complex socio-mystical order rather than in a centralized political edifice. The Hindu caste system highlighted interpersonal relations, which in turn emphasized a network of hierarchical roles, status, and occupations functioning within the overall society. The nature of the system was reinforced by its predictable behavior patterns, and this aided in its legitimization.

The caste system is the most celebrated institution of Hindu India. For most westerners it is synonymous with the subcontinent. Long associated with the Aryans, its principal purpose was social control. The caste system's four principal, stratified classifications (Brahmin, Kshatriya, Vaisya, and Sudra) unfortunately oversimplify a complex web of interpersonal and group relationships. Caste is linked with *jati*, a kinship group that is tied together by lineage and marriage and is more or less localized. The existence of literally thousands of jatis means the multiplication of castes by a similar number. Caste groups at the village level are the stuff that politics are made of to this day.

Although outcastes, or untouchables, are historically outside this network, since independence they have developed an equivalent and no less complicated jati order. The continuing importance of the Aryan-created and racially distinguished *varna* order of stratification has not been compromised. Caste arrangements remain fundamentally important, but the contemporary political process is producing change and more fluid relationships are possible. While not yet potent, transformations are taking place. Lower caste orders find increasing opportunities for upward mobility given their capacity to organize across jati lines through political alliances and emerging economic prowess.

Countries are politically modern not because of economic prowess or technological innovations, but because they can cope with the necessities of change and adapt accordingly. Change creates its own pace. Indian tradition and modernity comprise a unity, and instead of the latter displacing the former, one reinforces the other. Moreover, the oldest traditions are retained within new patterns of caste alliances, hence establishing the rhythm of ongoing change. The caste system, which westerners consider a vestige of India's primitive past, is responsible for the society's continuity and stability. In its changing state, caste assists India's peasant society to function in a representative democracy. It also fosters the growth of equality by making Indians see their common outlook and interests.

In order to understand India, it is necessary to use a different language from the one westerners normally employ. Indians tend to speak in several idioms, and not all are intelligible to the uninitiated. They are: the *modern*, the *traditional*, and the *saintly*.[2] Each has its own connotations. The modern language is the one the westerner finds most familiar. It is the language of the constitution and the courts, the parliamentary give-and-take, the sophisticated bureaucracy, and the upper levels of political party organization and behavior. This modern language speaks of policies, participation, recruitment, and interests. But it would be a travesty to insist that this is the full picture. Indian politics are considerably more. Modern developments are mere experiments, which depend for their success upon the more essential idioms, the *traditional* and the *saintly*.

The *traditional* idiom is usually ascribed to rural India. It is not so much interested in national India as it is in local India, and it certainly does not yield easily to sophisticated analyses. The traditional idiom is only marginally concerned with the nation-state. Its interest is the immediate society. At its core is caste, which cannot be absorbed by, but has nonetheless adapted itself to, the modern idiom. Caste must be seen as something intrinsically different from a group, for example, Roman Catholics in American politics, forming a unit within the modern system. In

[2]See W. H. Morris-Jones, "India's Political Idioms", *ibid*, pp. 133-54..

India, caste moves into politics as a way of life, not as a politically inspired group.

From a western vantage point, caste is in opposition to the nation-state and its development. The conventional reaction is to see it as an impediment to progress. But viewed from another perspective, caste is not necessarily a detriment to the new India. Within the context of its surroundings, caste produces social unity. Castes within an exclusive community are not only spiritually inter-linked, but functionally dependent. In some cases, caste stratification is sustained, in others it is possible to restructure status. Hindu social organization is not stagnant. Social groups have changed their positions in the social hierarchy. Nevertheless, stability is sustained as rising social groups tend to legitimize a change in their social position through the development of new classifications.

Changes in caste and caste status create change in the modern political system. In some ways that modern system may become traditionalized. As rural castes gain political leverage, old-line elites are displaced. A case in point is Mrs. Indira Gandhi's success in the 1971-1972 campaign, which is attributed to her cultivation of local leaders who control specific caste behavior. Traditionalization rather than modernization might prove a more accessible road to democratic development in India.

The third political idiom, *saintly* politics, introduces the metaphysical aspects of Indian life. It is commonplace to speak of Mahatma Gandhi as the personification of saintly demeanor. Lest it be misinterpreted, however, Indian saints are not superhuman. Rather it is their simple human qualities, their selfless devotion to cause, and spiritual courage in the face of physical frailties that identifies them with the Indian ethos. Gandhi's political style was very much a product of the Indian scene. Gandhi updated and organized the saintly style into a potent, modern force. He has no parallel in the modern western world. The saint in politics involves nothing less than the leader's total sacrifice. It is a personal, not societal phenomenon. The standards of the "saint-in-politics" are contrasted with the public's perception of the rank-and-file politician who may be obeyed but seldom respected. Although Mrs. Gandhi does not fit the saintly image per se, charisma surrounds her. Now that charisma has been reinforced with considerable authoritative power.

THE VILLAGE AND THE CITY

The human diversity that is India is mirrored in its villages and cities. Villages and cities share little in common, but in India, even villages in proximity to one another differ, and this fact is recognized by rural folk. The location of a particular village is significant. Location will determine language, custom, and dress. The groups that inhabit the village are also important. Sometimes Hindus, tribal peoples, Muslims, and Christians will all dwell in the same village. Often, however, there will be only one or two such groups.

Caste exists in all villages and especially where Hindus predominate. In one way or another, caste, whether religious, economic, social, or political, touches everyone. The number of castes found in a particular village is significant. Each caste has its own culture, and the structure of the village is made more complex as the number of castes increases.

In size, villages may range from a few hundred to several thousand persons. But the size of the village does not necessarily determine its consciousness of, or involvement in, national schemes. In this respect, communication and transportation are of particular importance. Access to a principal town or city is a prelude to enlightenment. The flow of ideas, similar to the flow of goods, is dependent on the existing structure. It may be worth noting that despite improvements in road transportation, most Indian villages are still remote from the nation's modern lifestream. Villages are sometimes difficult to reach, and there seems to be even less interest among their inhabitants to venture beyond them. Those visiting a village for the first time will be treated with suspicion. By the same token, leaving the familiar surroundings of the village invites loss of one's identity.

India is a land of numerous languages, let alone contrasting traditions and values. One need not proceed very far before being swallowed up by the unknown. Thus the unity of the village is far more meaningful to villagers than the unity of nation. Even more important is the unity of caste. Marriage and dining with members of other castes is forbidden. In their intimate lives Indians live in highly atomized circumstances. But village cohesion is found in economic enterprises and the relationships erected around them.

The dominant caste in a village is not necessarily the higher caste in the Hindu order. It is customary to think of the *Brahmins* (priests) at the top, the *Kshatriyas* (warriors) next, followed by the *Vaisyas* (merchants), and finally the *Sudras* (menials). The outcastes or untouchables are outside this network of relationships. But even they perform functions that are useful to the community. The dominant caste is usually the group having political and economic power. The dominant caste keeps the village peace and resolves disputes. Traditional values and practices are preserved in the intimacy of village life, which serve to strengthen the dominant caste. But with the intrusion of modernity, for example, the introduction of the secret ballot in village elections, dominant castes have had their grip on power loosened. As traditional loyalties and discipline are undermined, lower caste autonomy and unity tend to grow.

As the village power structure undergoes change, differentiation, or *fission*, occurs. This is followed by the development of caste federations and large associations with shared interests, symbols and norms, or *fusion*. A third stage is associated with *decompression* or the expansion of a peculiar caste's surroundings.[3] Given the goals of social mobility, self-reliance, and political power, caste associations and federations will play an increasing role in the decompression of village life. That is, they will reach out toward state and national legislative constituencies. In their own regions they will begin to influence community development blocs and *panchayat samitis* (a middle tier of local government in rural areas). It is also possible for caste associations to touch the bureaucrats, especially in the state secretariats. Moreover, through its own practices and policies, the central government has promoted this peculiar growth in caste conscious-ness. Decompression may not yet register significant impact on traditional India, but it does point to a future course of Indian development.

Change in village life is different from change in the cities, but in both settings ascriptive boundaries are being stretched. Twice-born *varnas* or castes (Brahmins, Kshatriyas, Vaisyas) are working with Sudras. West-ernization is influencing economic values, and secular movements are eroding sacred foundations. But these changes are still nominal in the villages.

Compared with the village, the Indian city is unstable and politically explosive. It is radical and periodically violent in support of progressive socialist dogma. The Congress party has persistently preached socialism in the cities, while practicing conservatism in the rural sector. Moreover, the country's leadership is almost exclusively drawn from urban centers where mobility is enhanced, and tradition is weaker. Although there were signs of elite displacement in the 1967 and 1971-1972 elections, India does not yet seem headed for rural renaissance.

HINDUISM AS A POLITICAL FORCE

Hindu India, prior to the Muslim invasions, must be viewed against a backdrop of political inactivity and socio-mystical dominance. Primary loyalties focused on kinship, caste, and village, and ties were usually based on blood relationships. Hence, perceptions of larger and broader political affiliations were limited.

In their prescribed intimate relationships, duties are seldom envis-aged as rights. With experience confined to a relatively small group and

---

[3]See Lloyd and Susanne Rudolph, *The Modernity of Tradition* (Chicago: The Univer-sity of Chicago Press, 1967). Copyright © 1967 by the University of Chicago Press.

with peculiar emphasis on metaphysical obligations, attitudes and behavior are predictable. Moreover, where individual dynamism is unanticipated, passivity tends to establish the parameters for social mobilization and growth, and change is left to that minority which is less inhibited by caste and resignation. Thus, although India's Aryan history features dynasties, their expansion, and eventual displacement, more important lessons are found in the crystallization of the Hindu psycho-social system. Despite episodic changes in elites, traditional patterns and conventions persist.

Hinduism is more than just the dominant civilization of India. Although it does not rule in an easily definable way, it permeates most segments of Indian society. Generally understood as an Aryan creation, Hinduism bears traces of numerous civilizations that settled in or passed through the Asian subcontinent. Hinduism has a sponge-like aspect, absorbing everything, yet unchanging in its basic form. Hinduism has affected the life-styles of diverse peoples, but differences between regions do exist. For example, the political climate of the Dravidian south was different from that of the Aryan north. Buddhist and Jain doctrines (espoused in the south), which embrace the concept of kingly authority, differ markedly from orthodox Hinduism. To some extent, political perception, as well as the philosophical orientation of Indians in the south, diverge from that held in the north. It may be appropriate to cite the more popular, and hence more liberal, stance of the Dravidian population. The Dravidians are more flexible and allow greater social mobility than in the north. Monarchy, however, has been the perennial form of government in India. Irrespective of regional variations, Hinduism conditioned the population to view government as an essential requirement: fear of anarchy produces a necessity for government. The ancient Hindu *Laws of Manu* (ancient texts that prescribe proper Hindu behavior) emphatically point out that the weak are easy prey for the strong in the absence of governmental order. Legend has it that the first king was appointed by the High God at man's request. Other stories indicate he was a divine being, sent down to earth by popular demand in order to restore and sustain law and social order.

The Hindu view of authority is cosmological in nature. In contrast, Buddhist kingship is pragmatic. Monarchy, identified as a human institution, was based on something approaching a social contract. The Jains stand somewhere between Hinduism and Buddhism, suggesting that life's complications produce leaders with wisdom greater than that of ordinary people. Such beings appear as a result of natural causation; thus they are revered by the population and have no reason to employ coercion in fulfilling their responsibilities. For Buddhists and Jains, it is the ultimate corruption of the human race, not their leaders, that compelled the use of force. In summary, the Hindu king was a charismatic personality of divine character. For the Buddhists and Jains the king was a necessary evil to avoid anarchy, but was always a human being. What tended to discourage Buddhist and Jain interpretations of kingship, however, was the wider appeal of Hinduism, generated by its conquering armies and formidable organization. Therefore, when Buddhist and Jain kings began to lay claim to divinity, it was the beginning of the end of their influence, vis-a-vis the Aryans. In India the doctrine of royal divinity came to occupy an unchallengeable position.

THE MUSLIM INVASIONS AND CONQUEST

The Muslim invasions of India commenced in the eighth century with the Arab infiltration of Sind. They were followed by more concerted Afghan and Turkish-Mongolian conquests culminating in the establishment of the Sultanate of Delhi in 1206. This success was eclipsed by the grandeur and power of the Muslim Moghul Empire founded in 1526. The Muslims attempted to integrate the vast subcontinent, and their ingenuity in coping with the atomized Hindu society cannot pass unnoticed.

Overall, Muslim rule was a combination of military and administrative aspects, rather than political. As the Moghuls pressed their invasion into the southern extremity of South Asia they met strong resistance. Various Hindu groups opposed their incursions, the Rajputs and Marathas being the most notable. Persistent conflict as well as cleavages, intrigues, and moral decay eventually weakened the empire to a point where it could not ward off the threat posed by the Europeans, particularly the British. Relative equilibrium was achieved between 1555 and 1707, but the Moghuls were ill-equipped to cope with new technologies of the eighteenth and nineteenth centuries. Nonetheless, the Moghuls represent the first serious effort to transform Indian society into a polity.

The rigidity of Muslim dogma collided with the more supple traditions of Hinduism. The militaristic invaders generally subdued the fragmented population, but there was relatively little cultural fusion. The building of a unified community was attempted by Emperor Akbar after 1555. His efforts failed, and the two civilizations tended to draw apart. With the passing of the last great Moghul Emperor Aurangzeb in 1707, bitterness between Hindus and Muslims had increased to such a degree that reconciliation was impossible. The appearance of the Christian Europeans at this time did nothing to reduce these tensions and may well have contributed to them. The oft-repeated phrase "divide and rule" explains Britain's emergence as the dominant power in India: there is no denying the opportunity that India's culturally disparate and inherently antagonistic "society" afforded the British.

Although the Hindus and Muslims were unable to coalesce, nevertheless they did influence each other. The followers of Islam adjusted to Hindu patterns of caste and occupation. The adaptation proved so useful that the establishment of the state of Pakistan did not obviate its functionality. For example, Muslim landlords are identified in higher castes than those who cultivate their land. A form of caste system is to be found among the Muslims of Pakistan, but it does not follow Hindu lines. On the other hand, Hindus learned lessons of Moghul administration, practiced Muslim art forms, and assisted in the development of sophisticated urban centers. The British took advantage of both the distance separating the two communities as well as the situations where they had converged. The Moghul administrative system, for example, gave the subcontinent a veneer of unity. They reformed the system, tightened and codified its rules and procedures, and separated the military from civil administration. Thus the foundation for British imperial rule was quickly established.

The intermingling of some Hindus, Muslims, and Christian Europeans, however, hardly affected the general population. The Indian masses went about their activities with no awareness of change in village customs or perceptions. Only in the cities, in the nineteenth century, was there any sign of a new consciousness.

THE GROWTH OF BRITISH POWER

British intervention provided the Hindu population an opportunity to undermine Muslim authority. The Moghuls could not prevent the growth of British power, and their hold on the general population weakened. Forces were set in motion, causing the Muslims to retreat to their exclusive traditions, while the Hindus appeared to welcome European techniques. The displacement of Moghul authorities stimulated a revival of Sanskrit culture. Both at the intellectual and governmental levels, Hindu-British interchanges stood in vivid contrast to the brooding isolation of the Muslims.

The British are credited with the establishment of a much needed equilibrium in India. Before their arrival the subcontinent was in a constant state of turmoil. Muslim-Hindu struggles multiplied during the reign of Aurangzeb and intensified after his death. Challenges to Moghul rule grew, the Maratha wars being perhaps the most outstanding instance. Bereft of leadership, the Moghuls could not sustain their preeminence. At that point, the British assumed their role in Indian history.

The British followed the Portuguese, Dutch, and French as they made their way to the subcontinent between the fifteenth and seventeenth centuries. The first order of business was trade. The establishment of the British East India Company in 1600, heralded a beginning that would not run its course for approximately 350 years. After defeating their chief European rival, the French, British ascendancy in India was virtually guaranteed. The Moghuls were no match for European technology, and just as they withdrew in face of the British advance, so too, rival Hindu rulers capitulated. The British were adept at alliance strategies, and although heavily outnumbered, they exploited indigenous antagonisms. Treaties with a multitude of princes sanctioned new relationships; British power imposed itself over an older framework resembling feudal arrangements, and an alien but structurally familiar bureaucracy engendered coherence. Subsequent legal innovations brought peace to the nation, and the British found themselves not entirely unwelcome.

The year 1857 was a turning point in Indian history. In the aftermath of a mutiny by indigenous troops of the British Indian army, the East India Company, under whose aegis the subcontinent had been subdued, ceased to function. After 1858, British rule was administered directly from Great Britain by the Queen-in-Parliament. The change was necessary because of the xenophobic forces created by the European presence. While traditionally privileged elements remained active, new elites slowly eroded the traditional monopoly of influence. Reforms introduced by the British did not drastically affect individual life-styles, but they did rearrange patterns of rule and power relationships in important commercial centers. The British colonial apparatus provided economic mobility, thus encouraging competition between rival groups.

British Indian government was bureaucratic, not political, in its early and middle stages. Nevertheless, the movement to accelerate urbanization produced a middle class of professional lawyers, teachers, journalists, and medical doctors. This group combined with new commercial and entrepreneurial elites to establish India's first cadre of politicians. Impressed with western concepts of freedom, liberalism, democracy, and socialism, they challenged the paternalistic colonial establishment, and the British found themselves in the embarrassing position of having indirectly spawned these attacks on their authority.

In the rural sector Indians admit that the *panchayat*, or village council, was revived by the British. The panchayat was the dominant political institution of ancient, rural India. Agrarianism was characterized by fragmentation, diffused power, and village self-sufficiency. As a basic form of government, the panchayat protected the village from external threats and resolved local problems. Endowed with taxing power, the panchayat provided public services and maintained village infrastructure. Cultural and intellectual activities also fell under its jurisdiction, and the village was able to perpetuate a self-contained, introverted life-style.

The panchayat was undermined by the Muslim invasions. Conquerors, unfamiliar with its operations and indifferent to its functions, were bent on developing larger communities. With the growth of towns and cities as centers for trade and government, the village panchayat became unnecessary. During the Moghul period, the village was incorporated in a new administrative structure, and outsiders dominated decision-making activities. The ancient Indian tradition was too weak to resist the impact of feudal control. Thus when the British arrived in India, panchayats were already useless administrations. The revival of village government is credited to Lord Ripon, a nineteenth century viceroy. Ripon's objective was to link India's villages with the general administrative system at a level familiar to the peasantry. However, his program met stiff resistance and was never truly tested. The rural scene was related to the distant district headquarters, but the villagers were left to the mercy of local *zamindars* (landlords) and corrupt bureaucrats. The question of revitalizing the village panchayat was raised again in the years before independence. But the institution's energy was gone, and village apathy was nourished by landlord and bureaucratic paternalism. Mahatma Gandhi insisted on separating the panchayat from the formal bureaucracy in order to revive the villagers' self-respect. He labored to interest the villagers in the education of their children, the improvement of their health and sanitation, and the settlement of their local disputes. His efforts were not without success, but rural government was a weaker feature of India's inheritance on the eve of independence.

REFORM AND REBELLION

Not all British reforms were beneficial. Some merely reinforced European controls. Others provided advantages only for certain groups, enabling them to acquire land, develop professions, expand their commercial activities, or join the colonial government. Still other controls undermined ritual leadership, and in a number of instances, sought to eliminate social customs abrasive to western sensibilities, for example, *Suttee*, or the burning of the wife on her husband's funeral pyre, and female infanticide. The reforms, however, stimulated a new consciousness among those living in close proximity to their foreign overlords. Organizations like the Brahmo Samaj, Arya Samaj, the Indian Association and the Indian National Congress were part of a new quest for identity. In the peculiar setting of the nineteenth century, it was inevitable that the quest should become a political movement.

Leaders like Ram Mohan Roy, Surendranath Banerjea, G. K. Gokhale, Dayananda Saraswati, Swami Vivekananda, Dadabhai Naoroji,

B. G. Tilak, Lajput Rai and Bipin Chandra Pal combined socio-religious and political objectives, which encouraged the demand for self-government In this array were liberals and conservatives, constitutionalists and revolutionaries, traditionalists and modernists. Hence some sought shared power and transitional change, while others insisted on total and complete *Swaraj* (self-rule). Gokhale symbolized the constitutionalists, while his counterpart and contemporary, Tilak, spoke for the revolutionaries.

Only in 1909, did the Indian Councils Act permit a few Indians to sit on the viceroy's councils. This small beginning whetted the appetite for greater representation and a "home rule" movement got underway shortly before the outbreak of World War I. Also in this period the Indian National Congress (established in 1885) was reorganized into a formidable political organization. During World War I the Congress party joined with the Muslim League (organized in 1906). They presented the British with a joint demand for self-government when the hostilities had ended. The British acknowledged the contribution made by the Indian forces in Europe and the Middle East. However, they were slow to respond to Indian demands. Finally, the Government of India Act (1919) introduced a form of parliamentary government. Although more in keeping with the concept of "guided democracy," it was clearly one step removed from total bureaucratic rule.

The 1919 Act brought a system of rule known as *dyarchy*, which meant certain specified powers were reserved for the viceroy and governors. Other powers came within the purview of ministers responsible to the provincial legislative council. A majority of these council members were to be elected under the Act. Thus some local government was granted the provinces, but national policies emanated from the viceroy's council, which remained a British club. The British "grant" was received with something less than satisfaction, and the Congress refused to cooperate. The intelligentsia felt justified in spreading their dissatisfaction to the illiterate masses. The Swadeshi movement demanded a boycott of foreign goods, but focused on the revitalization of village handicrafts or cottage industries. Street demonstrations supported the boycott, and the authorities felt constrained to use repressive measures.

The national elite, which was to bring India its independence, was formed under these circumstances. The Swadeshi movement brought together diverse interests. In the ranks of the militants were liberal-minded persons grown disenchanted with British promises. The British were accused of moral pretension and heavy-handed action, and their publicized humanitarian objectives could not be reconciled with their police-state tactics. The Swadeshi movement hoped to salvage the indigenous textile industry dislocated by English imports, but the real concern was the pursuit of self-government. Tutored by their conquerors, the Indians let it be known they were prepared to take charge of their own destiny.

GANDHI AND INDIAN NATIONALISM

The Congress party's sensitivity to societal grievances, their ability to organize demonstrations, and to enter into negotiations with the colonial authority attracted India's political reformers to its fold. The Congress had become the vehicle for Indian national aspirations. After World War I, those wishing to press the idea of Indian freedom were compelled to work within the framework determined by the Congress. Tilak dominated the party, having succeeded Gokhale who died in 1915. Tilak insisted on rejecting the Government of India Act of 1919. He cited the Rowlatt Acts, which would transform India into a police state, and he decried the Amritsar massacre of peaceful protestors. Britain, he complained, would maintain its empire at any cost. To a certain extent the Congress was radicalized, and a nationalist xenophobia, or hatred of foreigners, grew.

Xenophobic nationalism was not sufficient, however. British power remained intact, and although embarrassed by their more truculent subjects, effective administration was sustained. Moreover, vested interests neutralized the militants. Failing in their tactics, the Congress split between those insisting on terror as a means to an end, and those who retained faith in rational-legal processes. This was the prevailing situation when Mohandas Karamchand Gandhi captured the hearts and imaginations of the Indian population. The Congress was an established political organization. Its multi-dimensional character represented the aspirations of a cross-section of the populace, but it was in desperate need of a leader who could chart and direct a course of action acceptable to the numerous interest groups.

Gandhi's approach emphasized the role of the masses. While in South Africa he developed the technique of *satyagraha*, truth-force or passive resistance, and it was this tactic he urged the Congress to employ. The British were ill-equipped to cope with widespread civil disobedience. Satyagraha caused Congress leaders to restructure their organization, and the party's influence was spread into remote rural areas.

Gandhi's purpose was twofold. To rid India of the British was the first order of business. But Gandhi also wanted to ease the plight of the impoverished masses. Gandhi's perception of India was not one of throbbing cities and nascent industries. His concerns were for the peasantry and their simple villages. For Gandhi, India's quest for freedom would be meaningless if priorities were not given the peasant masses.

Mahatma Gandhi's writings and speeches provide insight to the Indian mind and experience. Early in the independence movement, India's spiritual leader wrote:

> My resistance to Western civilization is really a resistance to its indiscriminate and thoughtless imitation based on the assumption that Asiatics are fit only to copy everything that comes from the West. I do believe that if India has patience enough to go through the fire of suffering and to resist any unlawful encroachment upon its own civilization, which imperfect though it undoubtedly is, has hitherto stood the ravages of time, she can make a lasting contribution to the peace and solid progress of the world.[4]

Gandhi's concern extended beyond the immediate quest for independence. The mere withdrawal of British power, he cautioned, would not guarantee India's freedom. Gandhi contended that only when each peasant assumed the responsibility of self-government would the country be saved. Material and spiritual poverty were one and the same for Gandhi, and the impoverishment of the masses was the real dilemma:

> I would say if the village perishes India will perish too. India will be no more India ...The revival of the village is possible only when it is no more exploited. Industrialization on a mass scale will necessarily lead to passive or active exploitation of the villagers as the problems of competition and marketing come in. Therefore we have to concentrate on the village being self-contained, manufacturing mainly for use.[5]

Gandhi did not discount the importance of machines and new technology. What he vehemently opposed was the "craze" for machinery.

> The craze is for what they call labor-saving machinery. Men go on "saving labor" till thousands are without work and thrown on the open streets to die of starvation. I want to save time and labor not for a fraction but for all, I want the concentration of wealth not in the hands of a few but in the hands of all ...The supreme consideration is man. The machine should not tend to make atrophied the limbs of man.[6]

Gandhi deplored chauvinism. Economic development was significant when it benefited ordinary people; he received little solace from the thought that the state's power was measured in cold statistics. The slow, tedious road to human development may not be dramatic, but for Gandhi it was the only true path to progress:

[4]Mahatma Gandhi, *Young India*, August 11, 1927. Also quoted in Louis Fischer, ed., *The Essential Gandhi, An Anthology* (New York: Random House, 1962), p. 290, copyright © 1962 by Random House, Inc.

[5]Mahatma Gandhi, *Harijan*, August 29, 1936. Also quoted in Fischer, *Ibid.*, p. 291.

[6]Mahatma Gandhi, *Young India*, November 13, 1924. Also quoted in Fischer, pp. 291-92.

The machine produces too much too fast, and brings with it a sort of economic system which I cannot grasp. I do not want to accept something when I see its evil effects, which outweigh whatever good it brings with it. I want the dumb millions of our land to be healthy and happy, and I want them to grow spiritually. As yet, for this purpose we do not need the machine. There are many, too many idle hands. But as we grow in understanding, if we feel the need for machines we certainly will have them.[7]

Gandhi's strength was his unusual capacity for personal sacrifice. Having established an example that others might emulate, he pressured Congress leadership to follow his lead. The mass base that Gandhi fashioned gave the Congress a sense of unity and purpose. Gandhi was no orthodox politician. His nonviolent demonstrations and insistance on noncooperation frustrated the British. While galvanizing his countrymen into political activity, Gandhi simultaneously pricked the conscience of his alien rulers. He forced the Europeans to weigh their paternalistic stringencies alongside their declarations of justice and equity. *Realpolitik*, or power politics, was not beyond British capabilities, but Gandhi's tactics showed the hypocrisy in their democratic claims.

Gandhi's mass protest movements began in earnest in 1921 and continued through the early 1930s. Even when in prison, his refusal to accept proffered amenities and his long, debilitating fasts symbolized Indian will and determination. Gandhi's saintly performance was instantly transformed into legend, and the Indian population responded by endowing him with unprecedented adoration. Gandhi returned this veneration with more than philosophy. His practical interests lay in reviving village India, in reclaiming its legacy of social harmony and economic self-sufficiency. He rejuvenated handicraft industries. His spinning of *khadi* (hand-spun cloth) was no idle activity. By his example he hoped to instill a new confidence and self-respect in the peasantry. He was never dissuaded from the belief that India's future depended upon the viability of the rural sector. Progress for him would not be found in the complete expansion of modern industry in urban centers, but in a renaissance of village tradition, albeit with an infusion of contemporary ideas. Human development, rather than economic development, was his main objective. This is illustrated by his criticism of the caste system and his efforts at removing the stigma of untouchability, as well as his call for Hindu-Muslim amity.

India's nationalism was transformed into a positive program. Gandhi brought disparate and competing factions together: the Congress hierarchy came into proximity with the masses; the masses rallied behind the cause of Indian independence; village India was given special emphasis; and the

---

[7]Mathatma Gandhi, *Community Service News*, September-October, 1946. Also quoted in Fischer, pp. 292-93.

British were forced to question their legitimacy. Gandhi more than symbolized India. In a larger context, he dramatized the age that was still to
come.

THE TRANSFER OF POWER

For all of Gandhi's mysticism, he stands among India's more practical
personalities. The Congress party was a fragmented group when he took
up the work of shaping it into a coherent, disciplined organization. It was
his ideas to establish the small, elite Congress Working Committee and to
build it into the most authoritative arm of the party. Overarching the
much larger All-India Congress Committee (AICC), the Working Committee had the capacity as well as the power to make the hard decisions
without deferring to the AICC. Although Gandhi never became an official
member of the Congress Working Committee, he was its chief decision-
maker. Gandhi's dictatorial powers angered many within the Congress, but
his general popularity thwarted challenges even from well-known personalities, such as Subhas Chandra Bose, the charismatic Congress leader
from the populous Bengal province.
     Gandhi's charisma legitimated the operations of the Congress Work-
ing Committee, and it became an inner government. Moreover, it had the
capacity to negotiate with the British viceroy. No other political body was
so identified with the Indian nation. Under Gandhi's guidance District
Congress Committees (DCC) were created throughout the country. This
was in keeping with the Mahatma's ideas involving popular mobilization.
It reinforced the Congress' efforts against the British and also reminded
the party leadership of their continuing responsibility to the peasantry.
     Although the Congress exerted considerable pressure on the British,
it was not averse to suggestions that constitutional devices be used to
resolve societal conflict. Gandhi relaxed his passive resistance campaign
long enough to participate in the Second Round Table Conferences, which
opened in London in November, 1930. However, his disenchantment with
the British increased when he returned to India to find many of the
Congress leaders in prison. The Round Table Conferences resulted in the
Government of India Act of 1935. But few Indians believed the British
would seriously contemplate giving India its freedom.
     What disturbed Congress leadership most was apparent British ex-
ploitation of the Hindu-Muslim conflict. The British hoped to maintain an
empire by provoking clashes between the two principal religious communities, and the maintenance of the social fabric was supposedly dependent
on the British using coercive methods. Thus, despite the elimination of
dyarchy with the 1935 Government of India Act, and the concessions

permitting a measure of self-government, the Congress continued its attack on British rule. The Congress insisted the new 1935 constitution institutionalized communalism. Communalism described the division of India into two religious camps, the Hindu and Muslim, and thus undermined efforts at promoting a unified nation. Although the 1935 Constitution allocated more autonomy for the provinces, it also threatened the quest for national unity. Nevertheless, the Congress agreed to operate the 1935 Act and campaigned strenuously in the 1937 elections. They defeated their Muslim League opposition by an overwhelming margin and took control of eight of the country's most prominent provinces.

After the outbreak of World War II in 1939, India was declared a belligerent by the British government. This so infuriated the Congress leaders that they ordered Congress governments in the provinces to resign. The British reacted by assuming wartime powers, and they suspended the 1935 constitution. Gandhi responded by launching his famous "Quit India" campaign and insisted upon immediate independence. Pressed by the Japanese in Burma and fearing internal turbulence, the British arrested Gandhi and his close associates. Gandhi began one of his celebrated fasts and tension gripped the country. Riots spread throughout India while thousands of the faithful offered themselves up for arrest.

In 1942 the British sent Sir Stafford Cripps to India to meet with Gandhi. He promised virtual independence, but only upon termination of the war. The Japanese were approaching the eastern frontier, and Congress leaders thought it only a matter of time before the British war effort would collapse. Gandhi rejected the Cripps proposal as the tide of war began to turn in favor of the allies, and the Churchill government gave only passing notice to Indian demands between 1943 and 1945. With the end of hostilities, however, Churchill fell from power and Clement Atlee and his Labor party took up the reins of British government. Unlike the conservatives, the Labor party's position was clearly in favor of India's independence at the war's end.

The war was over, and Great Britain was exhausted and bankrupt. In addition, the United States was applying pressure to dissolve the empire, and Gandhi was again free to press his tactics. The demand that India be granted self-determination could not be diverted. For Prime Minister Atlee it was not so much a question of when, but how. The one drawback to a quick transfer of authority was the communal problem. The Muslim League, unlike the Congress, had more or less supported the British during the war. When the Congress provincial governments resigned in 1939, the Muslim League, which had been soundly beaten in the 1937 elections, was given new opportunity. The Muslim leader, Mohammad Ali Jinnah, characterized the Congress decision to leave the government as "a day of deliverance." In 1940, the Muslim League hastily convened in

Lahore and passed a resolution calling for the establishment of separate Islamic states in those areas where the Muslims predominated. The British did little to silence this demand. In fact they sought Muslim League support, and Jinnah anticipated his community would be rewarded once the hostilities ended.

Before World War II the Muslims fared poorly under British rule. It was the Muslim Moghuls from whom the British wrenched power, and it was again the Muslims that bore responsibility for the 1857 mutiny. Muslim reluctance to adapt English ways and customs and their avoidance of English educational opportunities put the Hindus in an advantageous position. As a result, the Muslims fell behind in economic and social affairs and eventually in administrative and political activities, as well. The growing power of the Hindus so distressed the Muslims that they were forced to redress the balance through belated acceptance of westernization. By this time, however, Hindu militancy was on the upswing, and the Muslims sensed a grievous threat to their culture. The partition of Bengal in 1905 was a case in point. The creation of a Muslim-dominant province in East Bengal was unacceptable to the Hindus. After several years of Hindu agitation, the British, despite their pledge to the contrary, rescinded the order and absorbed the province into a larger Hindu-dominant Bengal. The Muslims were convinced that their culture was in danger. Thus World War II was a catalyst for change. Jinnah and his Muslim League insisted that *two nations* inhabited the subcontinent, that they differed from one another in all respects, and therefore should *each* have the right of self-determination. It should be noted that Jinnah also had been a member of the Congress and had worked arduously for Hindu-Muslim unity in years past. But Jinnah disapproved of Gandhi's tactics, which he felt were too dogmatic and primitive. Moreover, he was repelled by the totally Hindu character of Congress entreaties. As an ardent constitutionalist, he deplored the extralegal devices employed to oust the British. Jinnah feared such devices could be used against the Muslims who, as a minority community, were dependent on constitutionalism for their protection and survival. Jinnah broke with the Congress and later with the Muslim League, as well. In the late 1920s, unhappy with both the Congress and his co-religionists, he sought refuge in London where he remained until the mid-1930s. It was only then that his supporters urged him to return to India to reorganize the Muslim League and help fight the 1937 elections. Although unsuccessful in the latter effort, World War II presented Jinnah with still another chance to lead the Muslims to independence. By the end of the war the British were prepared to entertain not only Indian independence but also the partition of the subcontinent between its two major communities.

Britain made one last attempt to retain the political unity of India in

1946. The Atlee government dispatched a Cabinet Mission to India with the purpose of finding a formula that would keep India intact. The failure of Viceroy Lord Wavell to reconcile Congress-Muslim League antagonisms, however, made division inevitable. Unable to bring the opposing sides together, the Cabinet Mission suggested its own plan on a take-it or leave-it basis. Instead of calling for partition, it emphasized federation. The object was the creation of an Indian Union: defense, foreign affairs, and communications were placed under federal government control, but in all other matters the federated units would enjoy full autonomy. According to the proposal, India would be divided into three zones, the two smaller being Muslim-dominant and the larger Hindu-dominant. In addition, a constituent assembly would be organized to draft a constitution and an interim government established to handle the affairs of state until the constitution was accepted. The commission let it be known that only one of the parties (the Congress or the Muslim League) need accept the plan in order to form the interim government.

The British had reason to believe the Congress would accept the arrangement. But to their chagrin, it was the Muslim League that responded in the affirmative. The Congress rejected the plan insisting it would lead to the permanent division of the subcontinent, and national unity would be made impossible. The Muslim League accepted the Cabinet Mission plan, expecting the British to call upon them to organize the interim government. The British, however, reneged on their pledge. Although Prime Minister Atlee would not give the Muslims control of the interim government, he did announce that the British would leave India no later than June, 1948. Lord Louis Mountbatten, a British hero of World War II, was rushed to New Delhi with orders to effect, with dispatch, the withdrawal of British forces and to settle the Hindu-Muslim controversy in the most expeditious manner.

By this time much of northern India was in flames. Muslim-Hindu bitterness had degenerated into acts of violence. Hundreds of thousands were slain in the ensuing months. Millions became refugees. It was the subcontinent's darkest hour. Mountbatten wanted to extricate Great Britain from an untenable situation. All alternatives to partition were put aside. Boundaries were hastily drawn and legitimated in the Radcliffe Award plan. The Muslims would be granted their separate state of Pakistan. Geographically, it would be something of a novelty with its two parts separated by approximately 1,000 miles of Indian territory, these being the areas where the Muslims were in a majority. The Indian Independence Bill was presented to the House of Commons on July 4, 1947, and approved within days. On August 14, 1947, Pakistan became an independent state. India was declared free and sovereign on the following day.

India remained a dominion within the British Commonwealth until the promulgation of its 1950 Constitution. When it was declared a republic, the nomenclature of the Commonwealth organization itself had to be changed. The Commonwealth of Nations replaced the old imperial organization, and the way was clear for the inclusion of other member-states, as one by one, Britain freed its colonies. But India's decision to retain the services of Lord Mountbatten came as something of a surprise. The last viceroy was now designated India's first Governor-General, and as ceremonial head-of-state, he, not Gandhi, presided over the initial transition. Hence the British departed India with remarkable goodwill.

GOVERNMENTAL STRUCTURE

By transferring power to the Congress party, the British ensured continuity of their political style. The new rulers of India resembled their immediate predecessors; they took pride in their British training and experience, and they harbored deep affection for the parliamentary system. This should not be interpreted as criticism. A European-type political system was judged an absolute necessity. Viable alternatives to this political design, if they existed, were considered inappropriate or regressive. Struggle as they must to maintain their nationhood, new countries, such as India, are hardly in a position to experiment with other systems. Urgent problems demanded attention, and government had to be purposive. Imitation was unavoidable under the circumstances.

Another explanation for the adoption of the parliamentary system was to prevent traditional rulers from demanding a return to the situation prevailing earlier. Convinced that their mode of operation was preferable, the politician-parliamentarians wanted to prevent the nobility from reasserting privilege and the bureaucrats from monopolizing decision-making functions. Hence they stressed their own legitimacy, denying it to these once-formidable vested interests.

The pre-independence experience established the pattern for the governmental system that was to guide India's decision-making process. And it might be added that it was the less than absolute nature of British rule that provided the Indians with the resiliency to ward off continuing crises. British imperialism in India was neither dictatorial nor democratic. As a *tutelary*, or guardian, system it left much to be desired, but nonetheless it did inculcate libertarian ideas. These ideas blended with indigenous tradition to create a unique contemporary experiment. While many countries have already discarded systems inherited from their predecessors, India continues to build upon its multiple legacy. Similar to the British

Salient Features of the Indian Constitution

1. The constitution of India is a written document. It is not based on accepted conventions like the British constitution.
2. The Indian constitution is considered the most detailed document of its kind in the world.
3. The Indian constitution is flexible in that it can be easily amended. The Indian parliament has the full authority to alter or modify many of the provisions of the constitution by a simple majority.
4. The Indian constitution provides for a unitary form of government, while the system of government is federal. The manner in which the Federation can be transformed into a unitary state is unique.
5. The Indian constitution establishes a parliamentary form of government and the parliament is described as a sovereign body.
6. Formally India has a presidential form of government, but the Indian president is supposed to be nominal head, and real power is wielded by the prime minister.
7. Every Indian citizen, male or female, is entitled to vote and there are no educational, property, income or any other restrictions.
8. The Indian constitution establishes a secular state. The government does not profess any religion.
9. Although Hindu is the official language and English has associate status, the constitution recognizes many more Indian languages and promotes them in culturally linguistic states.
10. India is divided into linguistic states.
11. The Indian constitution aims at the elimination of caste and class by giving all citizens equal status under the law.
12. Under the Indian constitution, in times of emergency, the "nominal" president can assume full powers.
13. Fundamental rights of all citizens are guaranteed in the constitution but may be suspended by a declared state of emergency.

before them, Indian leadership is not reluctant to use power, and Indira Gandhi's assumption of dictatorial authority, in the summer of 1975, is dramatic testimony to this fact. Nevertheless, India has been a poor nesting bed for tyrants, and the purpose of Indian government seems to be expressed in the concept of *managed anarchy* rather than sophisticated political competition.

The 1950 Constitution was anticipated by the Motilal Nehru Committee in 1928. It draws heavily on the Government of India Act of 1935: India is a federation guided by a parliamentary system. Although some believe parliamentarianism is too advanced for the country's illiterate, impoverished masses, there is no reason to believe a more traditional structure would be more functional. Moreover, there is no consensus for the establishment of an indigenous system. Little in the non-European Indian heritage addresses itself to the systematic unification of the Indian polity. India's survival and development, therefore, is heavily dependent on the degree of acceptance enjoyed by the parliamentary system. Similar to the English language, which bridges the communication gap, the parliamentary system makes coalitions of disparate political forces possible. Indians, as any other proud people, do not want to be reminded of their earlier condition of servitude. The representative system has been sufficiently "Indianized" to be considered a homegrown product. If it were not, it is doubtful it would have endured the years following Jawaharlal Nehru's passing in 1964. This also helps to explain Mrs. Gandhi's reluctance to terminate the parliamentary experiment despite her dictatorial handling of the parliamentary opposition.

India's constitutional system has the supreme task of maintaining national unity. Aided by an abundance of gifted leaders in the years immediately following independence, the institutions identified in the Constitution soon gained broad acceptance. The Indian system— federal and parliamentary—has cabinet-type executives in the individual states, as well as at the center. The prime minister is the national political leader, and chief ministers fill parallel roles in the states. The Constitution, however, sanctions the office of president and endows it with immense emergency powers. Moreover, the president appoints a counterpart, or governor, in the individual states. The federated units are thus linked with the central government and the governors are free from limitations that might otherwise be imposed by the respective state legislatures. India's presidents have always acted in concert with, and on the advice of, the prime minister. Hence the states' governors always have been asked by the president to suspend constitutional processes in their respective states on the advice of the prime minister. (See Figure 4-1 for a breakdown of India's government.)

The central government dominates in times of unusual stress. Despite periodic indications of a shift in political power toward the states, the central government remains preeminent. The relative ease with which the constitution can be amended, and the general reluctance on the part of national leadership to assume a rigid posture vis-a-vis the states, however, has contributed to the maintenance of the Indian union. Nevertheless, it is the strength of the prime minister, the Congress party, and the professionalism of the bureaucratic establishment that reinforces the national fabric. National unity is uppermost in the thinking of Indian leadership, and efforts have been made to redress state grievances without weakening that leadership.

ORGANIZATION OF GOVERNMENT OF INDIA

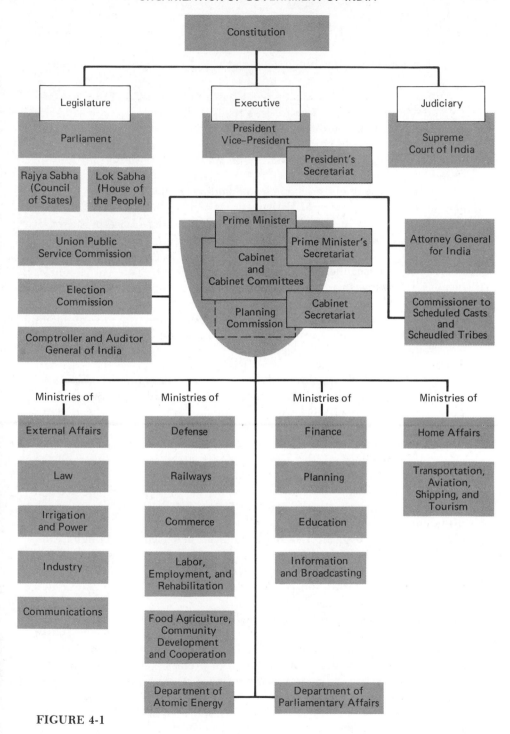

FIGURE 4-1

The President

Since the promulgation of the Constitution in 1950, India has had five presidents: Rajendra Prasad, Sarvapalli Radhakrishnan, Zakir Hussain, V.V. Giri, and Fakhruddin Ali Ahmed. The latter took office in 1974, and his election tended to emphasize Prime Minister Gandhi's successful neutralization of her opposition. Fakhruddin Ali Ahmed is the second Muslim to hold that high office.

The president of India is elected indirectly by the state legislators and members of the central Parliament. His or her term is for five years, and the president may stand for re-election. India's vice-president is elected for a similar term, but this election is confined to a joint sitting of the central Parliament. The prime minister is elected by the dominant party or coalition in the central Parliament. The Parliament is bicameral (having two legislative chambers), the upper house or Rajya Sabha (Assembly of States), is presided over by the vice-president who is ex officio chairman. Should the president die in office, the vice-president succeeds to the position until such time as a new president is elected. The Constitution calls for such elections within six months of the president's death.

Similar to the president, India's upper house is supposed to be more ceremonial than influential. But should the Lok Sabha, or lower house, prove unstable and Cabinet government falter, the president and Rajya Sabha can take command. The prime minister is responsible to the Parliament, but the president has the power to appoint him.

Other members of the Council of Ministers are appointed by the president on the advice of the prime minister. Should the prime minister fail to acquire a majority in the Lok Sabha, an ambitious president could use his special powers. In the event of instability, the knowledge that the prime minister holds office at the pleasure of the president, and that the president can dissolve the Lok Sabha and call new elections, is significant. Of course, much depends on the personality of the president should circumstances require the use of emergency powers. A point worthy of note is that the Constitution is vague on how far the president can go in a crisis situation.

The president as commander-in-chief of the armed forces is endowed with exceptional powers. In critical situations, the presidency may yet prove the most important institution for sustaining national equilibrium. Although the Constitution was supposed to protect the nation against the use of arbitrary power, in grave circumstances the strength of the democratic system dissipates rapidly. The select, but increasingly frequent use of President's Rule in individual Indian states from 1967 can now be viewed as a precursor of more unfortunate events in 1975. Turbulence in the states and the inability of their coalition governments to perform efficiently tended to concentrate greater powers in the central government. Emergency became a common condition, and in this situation the Indian executive branch insisted on maximum powers, unencumbered by legal practices.

The Parliament

The Indian parliamentary system remains intact, but its independence has been seriously battered, and its future utility is in doubt. The 525 members in the Lok Sabha are elected through direct adult franchise with each state divided into constituencies of near equal population. As with the president, members of the Lok Sabha are elected for five year terms. But as has been mentioned, the Assembly can be dissolved by the president, or in rare circumstances, extended for an additional year. The speaker, elected from among the membership in the Lok Sabha, presides over the House and possesses wide-ranging powers in organizing the affairs of the body. The Lok Sabha usually exerts influence over the executive branch (the Cabinet) and passage of a "no confidence" motion can prompt the creation of a new government. After Nehru's death in 1964, the Lok Sabha practiced considerable independence. But opposition to Congress rule has been historically weak. Failure of an opposition party to control fifty seats in the Lower House would leave India without an official opposition.

The Rajya Sabha, or Council of States, is comprised of 250 members. Twelve are nominated by the president with the remainder coming from the various states: their numbers are fixed by population with special allowances given the smaller ones. Members of the Rajya Sabha are elected by the state assemblies and serve for six years. Unlike the Lok Sabha, it cannot be dissolved. Compared with the prerogatives of the Lok Sabha, however, its powers are of minor consequence. It cannot, for example, impede the operation of Cabinet government. Revenue and spending bills can only be introduced in the Lower House (Lok Sabha), and even if the Rajya Sabha rejects legislation passed by the Lok Sabha, the latter body need only repass the measure and further it to the president for signature for it to become law. The Rajya Sabha theoretically protects the constitutional prerogatives of the states. It also enjoys equal power with the Lower House in amending the Constitution. As already noted, the Indian Constitution is easy to alter. Simple majorities in both Houses of Parliament, followed by ratification by a majority of Indian states and the president's automatic assent, is all that is required. From 1950 to 1975, the Constitution was amended thirty-nine times.

India had little experience in parliamentary democracy when independence was achieved in 1947. Admittedly a borrowed institution, the parliamentary system seeks to provide stability to a society that seems perennially on the edge of chaos. In a country as vast and diverse as India, representative bodies can be considered necessary. They provide a forum for competing ideas where discontent is tempered and energies are channeled away from bigotry and fanaticism. But the parliamentary system is extremely fragile, and its future in India is not assured.

The Prime Minister

India has had three prime ministers since achieving independence in 1947. Jawaharlal Nehru (1947-1964). Lal Bahadur Shastri (1964-1966), and Indira Gandhi from January, 1966, to the present. The stability of the prime minister's office has sustained the political edifice. Although controversies have swirled around the prime ministers, especially Mrs. Gandhi, there have been few serious challenges to their authority. The prime minister is the fulcrum upon which virtually all political decisions rest in India. Indeed, it is the prime minister who employs powers constitutionally invested in the president. A brief explanation is therefore in order.

Indian constitutionalists and politicians saw the need to protect the new nation from the power of the country's traditional rulers. There was no mistaking the institutional majesty and privilege of India's many royal potentates. Their almost absolute power dramatized the meaning of personal rule in the subcontinent. India's numerous princes, however, lost their private kingdoms after independence, and the integration of their territories into the Indian Union was completed with great speed. Their power was effectively neutralized. The British viceroy's office presented a different kind of problem. Although the office was abolished after independence in 1947, its powers came to rest in the presidency, or the governor-general, prior to the promulgation of the Constitution. However, by making Lord Mountbatten their first governor-general, the Indian leaders emphasized the purely ceremonial character of the office. Opposite Prime Minister Nehru, the governor-general thus presented no problems, and a new tradition appeared to have been established.

Moreover, Mahatma Gandhi wanted no part of political office, and Nehru insisted on becoming prime minster. These personal decisions reinforced the parliamentary experiment and deflated the traditional executive. One need only contrast this Indian experience with that of the Pakistanis. It was suggested that Mountbatten should also act as Pakistan's governor-general. But this idea was rejected. Instead, the leader of the Pakistan movement, Mohammad Ali Jinnah, became Pakistan's first governor-general. The possibly unintentional result was the lowering in stature of the Pakistani prime minister and the consequent undermining of the Parliament. The powers of Pakistan's Parliament were blatantly usurped by a later governor-general in 1953 and 1954. Martial law in 1958 brought an end to Pakistan's first experiment in representative government. Pakistan had strengthened the autocratic vice-regal tradition, while India's leaders consciously endeavored to confine it to history. Nevertheless, vice-regalism is deeply rooted in subcontinental government, and it is constantly reappearing, albeit in different forms. Hence even India's longer experience with parliamentarianism cannot insulate the country from this dominant trait in its political character. There is considerable evidence that power continues to mass at the center and in a particular individual or institution.

Nehru's personality, along with his seventeen years of unbroken service, added luster to the parliamentary experiment, but it also kept alive the phenomenon of vice-regalism. India was fortunate in having a phalanx of respected and able colleagues at Nehru's side. Their existence also acted as a check on the uses of arbitrary power. The swiftness with which the Indian Union or Federation was consolidated and the Constitution completed tells us much about their dedicated but collective leadership. Nehru seemed to personify India: but his colleagues were not inconsequential.

Hence Nehru's passing was less traumatic than anticipated. The political apparatus had gained legitimacy, and many staked their future on its stability. For a time after 1964, political power was more diffused. Nehru had dominated Cabinet committee deliberations. Moreover, he created and led the Emergency Committee, a super decision-making body within the Cabinet. His successor, Lal Bahadur Shastri, shared governmental responsibilities with his associates in the party hierarchy. Also, the individual states played more significant roles under Shastri, and the new prime minister could not ignore their separate demands as he strove to achieve a unity of purpose. The Shastri transition demanded a type of collective leadership with key Congress officials, the Syndicate, assisting in the making of important decisions. The Syndicate, or Grand Council, comprised Congress personalities with political power in the states as well as at the center. This "inner government" was responsible for Shastri's elevation to prime minister, and they worked in reasonable harmony. This behind-the-scene political maneuvering, however, did not weaken the legitimacy or threaten the mystique of the prime minister's office.

Shastri's sudden death and the selection of Nehru's daughter, Indira Gandhi, as his successor shattered the decorum and ultimately the character of shared responsibility in the Syndicate. Mrs. Gandhi had been the overwhelming choice of the Syndicate. She was considered the least controversial of the possible candidates. Her appointment, somewhat unorthodox in that she was a member of the Upper and not the Lower House at the time, was made in order to maintain party unity. Some of the older, durable politicians wanted the office, but a protracted struggle threatened the party's somewhat precarious hold on the country. Mrs. Gandhi's elevation to prime minister, it was believed, would restore waning confidence in the Congress party. The fact that she was also Nehru's daughter was judged an asset in uncertain times.

Mrs. Gandhi was not in power very long when general elections were held. The new prime minister had little time to restore public faith in the Congress party, and when the ballots were counted the organization went down to a humiliating defeat. Mrs. Gandhi's personal success, however, attested to the aura surrounding the prime minister's office. It was also a tribute to her acumen, as well as her family legacy. Above all, the election results portended a shift of power from the Congress Syndicate to the prime minister's office. From hindsight it is now obvious that the 1967 elections, which shattered the influence of the old guard in the Congress party, heralded a period of power concentration and indeed, of vice-regalism, in India. Events from that election to 1975 tended to transfer more and more power to Prime Minister Indira Gandhi, who proved to be a very astute manipulator of political forces.

Indian Federalism

India's federal structure is more pronounced today than at any other time in its young history. Whereas the Constitution's Union (Federal) list of powers provides the central government with exclusive authority in matters of defense, currency, taxation and foreign affairs, and the central government has the power to impose its will on individual states, there is no avoiding the swelling of state influence. Parliament has the power to create new states, to alter the boundaries of existing ones or even abolish states altogether. It can also make laws that are reserved by the Constitution for the states under the state list of powers. But all these powers, along with those enabling the center to take over the management of a particular state, must be treated with circumspection.

If the Constitution emphasizes the center's dominance, political pressures highlight the prerogatives of the states. Central government leaders cannot afford to ignore state grievances. Their future, as well as that of the nation, rests on the capacity of institutional devices to reduce tension and promote cooperation. Implementation of central government policies is dependent on the relatively smooth operation of state government. The center-state group forms a link in the bargaining process between central and state leaders. A major amount of brokering is involved in which cooperation, persuasion, and compromise are the accepted norms. Leadership in each state is especially mindful of the demands of their constituents. Closer to the firing line, success is measured by their ability to reduce local pressures and satisfy provincial aspirations. Hence local leaders, irrespective of party affiliation, seek to realize the individual needs of their constituents. Competition for scarce resources drives them to protect limited reserves. Moreover, given the existence of non-Congress governments in some of the states, new accommodations are imperative. Although it can be argued that Congress preeminence is constantly being challenged, it is also true that Indian federalism is quite vigorous. What has managed to save Congress government is something peculiar to the Indian experience: conflicts are often so regionalized that they seldom influence other states.

As presently constituted, the Indian states represent several stages of transition. The first involved integration into the Union of more than 500 princely kingdoms. The second occurred with the States Reorganization Act of 1956, which redrew the older colonial map of India. This geographic reorganization emphasized the development of states using specific linguistic criteria. The third stage witnessed the further extension of the language-area principle and Bombay State was partitioned in 1960, Nagaland was made a state in 1963, and the Punjab was divided into separate Sikh and Hindu states in 1966. Himachal Pradesh was declared a state in 1971. Three more states in the eastern tribal belt were created in 1972. Moreover, in April, 1975, the Sikkimese ousted their monarch and voted overwhelmingly for Indian statehood. Thus, the present Indian federation comprises twenty-two states, with possibly more changes being a reasonable expectation:

States and Territories of the Indian Union, 1976

	States	Principal Language
1.	Andhra Pradesh	Telegu
2.	Assam	Assamese, Bengali
3.	Bihar	Hindi
4.	Gujarat	Gujarati
5.	Haryana	Hindi
6.	Jammu and Kashmir	Kashmiri, Dogri, Urdu
7.	Kerala	Malayalam
8.	Madya Pradesh	Hindi
9.	Tamil Nadu (Madras)	Tamil
10.	Maharashtra	Marathi
11.	Karnataka (Mysore)	Kannada
12.	Nagaland	Naga, English
13.	Orissa	Oriya
14.	Punjab	Punjabi
15.	Rajasthan	Rajasthani, Hindi

States and Territories of the Indian Union, 1976 *(Continued)*

States	Principal Language
16. Uttar Pradesh	Hindi
17. West Bengal	Bengali
18. Himachal Pradesh	Hindi, Pahari
19. Meghalaya	Hindi, Assemese, Khasi, Garo
20. Tripura	Tripuri, Bengali
21. Manipur	Manipuri
22. Sikkim	Sikkimese, Hindi, Nepali

Union Territories

Delhi	Lakshadweep Islands
Andaman and Nicobar Islands	Gao, Daman
Dadra and Nagar Haveli	Diu
Pondicherry	Chandigarh
Arunachal Pradesh (NEFA)	Mizoram

State governments resemble the Union prototype. Each state has a governor appointed by the president, who in turn appoints the chief minister, the rough equivalent of the Union prime minister, within the state. The chief minister commands a majority in the state legislature. Governors play significant roles. They can dissolve state governments and often monopolize authoritative decision-making on behalf of the center. President's Rule permits the governors to bypass the state apparatus and assume virtual dictatorial powers. After the 1967 elections, coalition governments were formed in a number of states, but their inability to function led to repeated breakdowns causing severe dislocation. Given these power vacuums, the governors step in with emergency powers. Since Mrs. Gandhi became Prime Minister in January, 1966, the central government has taken over states on approximately thirty occasions. By contrast, in the sixteen years after the Constitution took effect (1950-1966), emergency powers were used only ten times. In 1973 alone, Congress-run governments collapsed in Uttar Pradesh, Bihar, Gujarat, and Orissa due to the loss of local support. Critics of Mrs. Gandhi's government attributed these seizures to a mounting strain on the political system and the inability of effective government, short of the use of emergency powers.

State parliaments vary. Some are unicameral, others bicameral. Where the latter prevails, the power of the upper chamber is so circumscribed as to leave it powerless. With few exceptions, such as in Tamil Nadu, the legislatures are dominated by traditional landed interests, and the spreading of participatory politics is minimal. Government in the states remains more administrative than political.

Bureaucracy

India's states and territories are divided into 342 districts, each containing more than one and one-half million people. District administration is a throwback to Moghul times, but the British have contributed to most aspects of its present form. The elite class of civil administrators, known as the Indian Civil Service (ICS), controlled district life. The chief officer in the district, the Deputy Commissioner, combined the powers of law enforcement, judge, and tax collector. For a considerable period of time only British citizens were allowed to fill these roles. But in the decades immediately leading to independence, indigenous personnel were recruited, trained, and given a place within the system. This group, along with those Englishmen who remained at their stations after 1947, formed the core for the new ICS, later to be designated the Indian Administrative Service (IAS). With the 1950 Constitution, members of the IAS found their powers reduced, especially their judicial prerogatives. Nevertheless, their preeminent position in the districts remains intact.

The Deputy Commissioner, or Collector, is not only charged with traditional responsibilities, but also has been given the burden of overseeing rural development and social welfare programs. In order to place the administrator within the political framework, however, the IAS has been "provincialized" and decentralized. Officers are assigned to individual states and are guided by standards that bring them under local or regional political control. Still, it must be reiterated that both the Deputy Commissioners' legacy and the continuing need for their expertise reinforces their paternalistic authority and status among the villagers.

Assisting the Deputy Commissioner are numerous subordinate officers who, in theory, permit government to reach into remote villages. Districts are divided into sub-units called *Talukas* or *Tehsils*, each one containing several hundred villages. The chief officer at this level is usually referred to as the *Talukdar*. The primary function of the chief officer is the collection of land revenue. The actual work of keeping village landholding records and taxing the peasantry falls upon the village *Patwari*. This lower functionary's reputation for misbehavior and corruption is legendary in the subcontinent.

The most celebrated structure of rural self-government is called *Panchayati Raj*. Panchayati Raj is derived from the traditional village council of five elders (*Panch* meaning "five") who governed the local community in times past. The modern Panchayat system has several tiers: the *village panchayat* at the bottom, the *panchayat samiti* above if (comprising all the elected chairmen of the village panchayats and co-opted experts and administrators), and the *zila parishad* at the top, which links with district administration. Although initially linked with the traditional bureaucracy, the Mehta Report of 1959, recommended more self-reliance and greater political freedom for this structure. Although community development is reported to have suffered as a result, the awakening of political consciousness in the rural regions cannot be minimized. Political linkages between Panchayati Raj and the state legislatures may even give the villagers a voice in the central Parliament. Until that moment arrives, however, one can expect the Indian bureaucracy, despite its somewhat ambiguous powers, to dominate the rural scene. Panchayati Raj has been plunged into party politics and the villagers have been diverted from their progressive tasks of improving rural agriculture, health, sanitation and education. Thus economic development suffers as village factions compete frantically for political influence.

India's urban communities house approximately 18 percent of the country's population. Calcutta, Bombay, Delhi, and Madras represent the larger cities. The governing bodies in the cities are the municipal corporations, which are popularly elected bodies. But as with other levels of government, the executive is appointed. In these instances the chief executive is an administrative officer called a Commissioner and is appointed by the state government. Unlike the villages where civil strife is usually contained, the cities are arenas of unrest. Strikes, demonstrations, and riots are linked with middle-class restlessness. In these activities, the urban intelligentsia plays a prominent role. The extra-constitutional nature of street politics is frowned upon, but it also provides a forum for groups that are not able to register an effective voice in Parliament. Because political party activity is associated with agitation and public protests, and not orderly debate, the bureaucrats remain important fixtures.

The Judiciary

India's judicial system is highly unified and national in structure and purpose. This conflicts with the principle of federalism, but it remains one of the principal means for sustaining the nation's cohesiveness. At the top of the judicial hierarchy is the Supreme Court. It possesses both original and exclusive jurisdiction and until August, 1975, could hear any case that even remotely involved the Constitution. The Supreme Court has been the guardian of the Constitution, but it has also been careful to avoid political collisions. The clash between Prime Minister Gandhi and her detractors, in and outside the Congress party, however, has disturbed the Court's non-political role. The future of the Court is intertwined with the events challenging the Indian political system. It remains to be seen what role the Supreme Court will play in the country's political life. The Supreme Court has had the power to render an act of Parliament unconstitutional, but this power has been undermined by the crisis that erupted in 1975. Moreover, the Supreme Court's powers are questionable, given the "emergency" articles that have been written into the Constitution, and the way in which those emergency powers have been used.

The Supreme Court usually consists of a Chief Justice and thirteen Associate Justices. Justices are appointed by the president from those judges filling positions on the High Courts, the tier just below that of the Supreme Court. Appointments to the High Courts are also made by the president, in consultation with the Justices of the Supreme Court and other members of the legal fraternity. Judges have tenure until the mandatory retirement age of sixty-five. The Constitution also specifies that judges can be removed for proved misbehavior or incapacity. The size of the High Courts varies with the individual states but ranges somewhere between three and thirty-three members.

The High Courts do not have their powers spelled out by the Constitution, but some of their acknowledged responsibilities include: appellate powers, original jurisdiction in revenue cases, and protection of the rights granted the citizenry by the Constitution. The remainder of the judicial structure involves district and lesser courts.

During the British period, the judiciary was linked with the bureaucracy and hence was a career service. The State Judicial Service (SJS), similar to the IAS, recruits its personnel on the basis of competitive examinations, but also insists on several years of legal experience. The lower courts are staffed exclusively by members from the SJS. Lateral appointments do occur at the appellate level. Britain's chief legacy in India was respect for the rule of law and the legal institutions erected to uphold that principle. By and large, India has perpetuated this legal design.

POLITICAL DYNAMICS

India's leaders are hard put to satisfy the demands of their many publics. Population growth and desperately limited resources, combined with complex psycho-social conventions and diversity, make the quest for a western system unrealistic. One should not be misled by the knowledge that India's parliamentary system, its political parties, its entrepreneurial and scientific elites have western roots. The federal parliamentary system aims at promoting national unity among a people who are still unable to transcend the immediacy of their circumstances and the influence of ancient traditions. Since independence, maximum attention has been given to the creation of a community of common interests. This is the foundation for the ideological emphasis on secularism and socialism, two ideological pillars of modern India. It also contributes to an explanation of personality politics and the disarray of political parties.

Politics dominate the urban scene, just as bureaucracy does in the rural sector. Ideology and its concomitant, national unity, therefore, focus on the groups vying for power in the more sophisticated city atmosphere. Hence it is not unusual that opposition parties concentrate their activities in the cities, while endeavoring to extend their tentacles into the countryside.

Nehru's personality, the incomparable organization of the Congress Party, the fidelity of the civil and military services, an ambiguous but popular program of reform, and a supporting cast of entrepreneurs, landlords, and intellectuals prevented any genuine challenge to Congress authority before 1964. Given the Congress' monopoly of power, the opposition accused the regime of maladministration and corruption. But their capacity to publicize governmental scandals in no way satisfied their yearning for political influence. Events were often turbulent, but when calm settled on the country the Congress was still supreme. The demonstrations that rocked Madras, the Punjab, Bombay, and Calcutta were troublesome but not a great threat—as long as Nehru guided India. His passing, however, left many questions unanswered.

Lal Bahadur Shastri was selected by the Congress Syndicate to succeed Nehru. A compromise selection, he was the least ambitious of the contenders. India's leaders showed they were reluctant to come to grips with the consequences of Nehru's death. The party had broken into several factions, drastically affecting the Congress' monopoly. The brief Indo-Pakistan War in the autumn of 1965, gave the party a temporary respite. It aided the Shastri image, but public confidence improved only slightly. Shastri's sudden death at Tashkent in January, 1966, plunged the party into deeper trouble. Again the Congress elite was forced to choose a leader. Once more they stifled the more ambitious seekers. This time Indira Gandhi became their compromise selection.

Through Indira Gandhi, the Congress party hoped to exploit the Nehru legacy. Mrs. Gandhi was expected to act within the boundaries established by the collective leadership, as was Shastri before her. She was to take her cues from the elder statesmen within the party syndicate. However, the Congress had already lost much of its popular appeal. Its image tarnished by years of alleged ineptitude, it bore responsibility for the severe economic dislocation, expanding restlessness, and a lack of international influence. The Congress was criticized for holding power too long, for failing to deliver on a multitude of promises and for acting indifferently to the suffering of the Indian people.

This dissatisfaction was amply registered in the 1967 election. The Congress kept control of the Central government, but the party was defeated in seven of the Indian states. Twenty years of one-party rule had ended. Moreover, some of the Congress' leading personalities went down to defeat. These included the Congress president and the political bosses in the critical areas of Bengal and Bombay. The syndicate was badly shaken. Mrs. Gandhi survived the test, however, and insisted on plotting her own course and making her own decisions.

Congress prevailed over the opposition by being all things to all Indians. It was quick to adopt rival programs, to yield on issues of minor consequence, and to hold out opportunities for individual members of opposing parties who wished to transfer their loyalties. The Congress could posture as a socialist organization, while facilitating the expansion of private entrepreneurial and industrial empires. It could emphasize the doctrine of secularism and Muslim-Hindu amity by electing Muslims like Zakir Husain and Fakhruddin Ali Ahmed to the presidency. It was also ready to champion Hindu traditions and culture. While denouncing and outlawing the caste system, the party made use of it by exploiting local rivalries. The fragility of Congress rule lay in the time-consuming, day-to-day manipulation of the political process. "How long could the Congress continue its precarious high-wire act?" was a question raised with increasing frequency after the death of Jawaharlal Nehru. Its revered leader gone, popular grievances coalesced and the discontent was dramatically portrayed in the 1967 election results. Mrs. Gandhi could not fail to ignore the lesson that the elections had to teach.

Prime Minister Gandhi and the Transformation of the Congress Party

The days of Congress hegemony had come to an end. India's electorate had come of age. Ways had to be found to moderate popular dissatisfaction. Indira Gandhi's election amid the broad collapse of so many party luminaries was significant. The Prime Minister sensed she had been given a mandate to carry through revolutionary reforms. Not only did the Congress need restructuring, new leadership, and an updated, more consistent philosophy, there was also the unpleasant task of tackling deep-seated inequities. Popular demands focused upon a more satisfactory distribution of wealth and a more responsive governmental apparatus.

After independence in 1947, the Congress transformed itself from a national movement into a national political party. After 1967 the Congress required yet another metamorphosis. The party no longer epitomized Indian aspirations. A new generation clamored for an end to special privilege. Prime Minister Gandhi could not avoid this challenge and quickly executed policies that brought her into conflict with her erstwhile supporters in the party hierarchy. She ignored the views of the inner council in the Working Committee and publicized her intention to part company with the decision-making syndicate. By 1969, the rift between the Prime Minister and the party leaders was unbridgeable.

The death of President Zakir Husain and the search for his successor crystallized these differences. The Prime Minister wished to divest the syndicate of influence in making public policy. Mrs. Gandhi believed only a socialist emphasis would make her administration credible, and she abused those who disagreed with her. Her initial program involved nationalization of the major commercial banks, aggressive land reforms, restrictions on industrial holdings, general limitations on income and private property, and the abolition of pensions allotted to former princes. As a result of this program, Congress leadership was hopelessly split. For ideological, as well as pragmatic reasons, there could be no meeting of the minds.

The foundation of Congress power had been undermined by the Prime Minister's actions. When Mrs. Gandhi revealed the candidate of her preference to fill the vacant presidential office, Congress balked and nominated the Speaker in the Lok Sabha, Sanjeeva Reddy. Instead of yielding to the overwhelming vote of the syndicate, Mrs. Gandhi continued to support her candidate. Her nomination of V. V. Giri, then acting president of India, was an unprecedented and defiant maneuver. There was no longer any doubt that she wanted to liquidate the syndicate.

Sensing an opportunity to weaken the Congress, a number of opposition parties supported Mrs. Gandhi against her own party members in the Parliament. Thus the Samukta Socialist Party (SSP), the Dravidia Munnetra Khazhagam (DMK), the Muslim League, the various Communist party factions, and the United Front governments in Kerala and West Bengal declared their support for Giri and Mrs. Gandhi. The parties of the right (Swatantra and Jan Sangh) put up their own candidates, while the Praja Socialists did not compete. Convinced that she had sufficient votes, Mrs. Gandhi purged her Cabinet and removed her arch rival, Morarji Desai. Desai was Deputy Prime Minister, as well as Finance Minister—the most important Congress politician excepting Mrs. Gandhi. With Desai out of the way, Mrs. Gandhi ordered the nationalization of fourteen major banks, which together held approximately 70 percent of the country's total bank assets. Privileged families, such as the Dalmias, Tatas, Jains, and Birlas, were directly affected by the action, and the political advantages and risks had to be carefully weighed. Mrs. Gandhi claimed her actions were for the common people of India. The act forced Congress members in the Parliament to make their positions known, and the vote for the new President proved a decisive struggle between the syndicate and the Prime Minister.

The election was complicated by the number of candidates, but V. V. Giri emerged the victor. Mrs. Gandhi's success was due to her support from the opposition. Congress defections also aided the Prime Minister's choice. Mrs. Gandhi won a victory, but given the mood of the Congress elite, the war was far from over. After removing all Cabinet officials who voted against her candidate, she turned on the presiding Congress President, Nijalingappa. Mrs. Gandhi argued she controlled a majority in the

All-India Congress Committee (AICC) and could command the loyalty of most of the states' Chief Ministers. She moved against Nijalingappa and insisted he resign. Nijalingappa, however, retaliated by ordering the Prime Minister's supporters on the Working Committee to vacate their seats. Mrs. Gandhi countered this action by calling her own meeting of the AICC. Her move was tantamount to the establishment of a separate Congress organization. Assisted by Y. B. Chavan, then the powerful Home Minister, Mrs. Gandhi's AICC met in Delhi in November, 1969, and elected their own party president.

Nijalingappa and Kamaraj, the previous Congress president, along with Morarji Desai, accused Mrs. Gandhi of unconstitutional activities. On November 12, 1969, the Congress Working Committee expelled her from the organization. The Working Committee called upon the Congress Parliamentary party to elect a new leader, who they hoped would be the new prime minister. But this order was rejected, and Mrs. Gandhi received a much needed vote of confidence. Under Desai's leadership the syndicate called another meeting. This time 111 Congress members in the Parliament attended. The conference elected Desai as its chairman and announced it would form an opposition party in the Parliament. The new organization took the name of the Congress Parliament party and has since been called the Congress (Opposition) Party. Moreover, given its size, it received recognition as an official opposition party. It was also the first time in the history of the country that an official opposition in the Parliament had been recognized. Dr. Ram Subhag Singh became the first leader of the opposition.

Indira Gandhi's support in the Lok Sabha was reduced to slightly more than 200 Congressites, not nearly enough to claim a majority. Thus it was only the votes of the DMK, the Communist Party of India, and a number of independents that gave her a precarious hold on the government. On December 27, 1970, finding this an untenable situation, she called for a showdown. The Prime Minister requested President Giri to dissolve the Parliament, permissible under the Constitution, and call a new election. General elections were not scheduled until 1972, but Mrs. Gandhi believed the only remedy for parliamentary inertia and growing public discontent and terrorism was the realignment of political forces. If successful, her program could be revitalized and the country hopefully stabilized. Parliament was dissolved and new elections were scheduled for March, 1971.

The 1971 Election and its Aftermath

India held an important election in the winter of 1971. Prime Minister Gandhi led her new Congress party in a compaign aimed at restoring one-party government to India. Mrs. Gandhi traveled throughout the country carrying her message to the largest number of persons ever to hear, firsthand, the election addresses of an incumbent prime minister. Nevertheless, the election issues were not readily received by the listening masses. Her speeches were national, rather than local in content, and too philosophical to be of interest to India's predominantly rural population. Moreover, ballots would be cast not for a specific platform, but for or against the daughter of Jawaharlal Nehru. The Prime Minister, therefore, could only hope to project her personality and overcome voter apathy by her presence. She knew a large voter response (estimated to total about 275 million) would give her party the advantage.

The decision to hold mid-term elections was directed against the parties that gave Mrs. Gandhi a majority in the Parliament, as well as at her Congress opposition. The Prime Minister did not make many friends in the Communist Party or the Dravida Munnetra Khazhagam (DMK), but she apparently felt their support was more expedient than genuine. It was an all, or nothing, effort. The Prime Minister wanted no interference with her policies, and the time was right for a test of her popularity.

This was the first parliamentary election held separately from that of the states. Only in three states, West Bengal, Orissa, and Tamil Nadu would there be simultaneous elections. The prevailing situations in those states could do no harm to the Prime Minister. Mrs. Gandhi did not expect to win in Tamil Nadu. The coalition government, organized by the Swatantra in Orissa, had collapsed, and new alliances were being forged. Similarly, in West Bengal, the Naxalite terrorists had so shaken the state government that even the Marxist Communist Party could not sustain a United Front Government. Under these circumstances, Mrs. Gandhi expected to pick up some seats in West Bengal and Orissa.

Eight important parties and some forty lesser, or regional, parties contested the 1971 parliamentary election. The large number of political parties may explain why the Congress party, even when led by Jawaharlal Nehru, never received a majority of the votes cast. Up to 1971 the largest success came in 1957 when the Congress received approximately 46 percent of the vote. A lowpoint was reached in the 1967 elections when it totalled something less than 40 percent. Congress dominance, therefore, must be viewed against a background of multi-party politics in which divisions are so numerous that Congress wins almost by default.

When the March, 1971 results were tallied, Mrs. Gandhi's tactics proved successful. She had won a stunning victory. Mrs. Gandhi's Congress party gained a two-thirds majority in the Lok Sabha, winning 350 of 515 seats, but with less than 50 percent of the total vote. By contrast, the opposition Congress won only 16 seats. The Jan Sangh and Swatantra also lost ground to the new Congress party. Collectively, the Communist parties gained a few seats, but separately, the pro-Moscow CPI lost ground, and the pro-Peking CPI (Marxist) improved its position slightly.

Mrs. Gandhi's closest supporters in the ruling Congress party were re-elected. Jagjivan Ram, Fakhruddin Ali Ahmed, Y. B. Chavan, and Swaran Singh were made Ministers of Defense, Food and Agriculture, Finance, and External Affairs, respectively. Morarji Desai, leader of the opposition Congress, V. K. Krishna Menon, Nehru's former Defense Minister running as an independent, and A. K. Gopalan, leader of the CPI (Marxist) also were successful. Among the defeated were members of the old Congress syndicate. They were: S. K. Patil, Ram Subhag Singh, Asoka Mehta, and N. Sanjeeva Reddy. Moreover, the leader of the Swatantra, M. R. Masani, was humiliated at the polls.

The DMK swept Tamil Nadu. The CPI (Marxist) won a large number of seats in the West Bengal Legislature, but the ruling Congress made a striking comeback and only seven seats separated it from the CPI. In Orissa, Mrs. Gandhi's Congress also moved into a strong position. Mrs. Gandhi was overjoyed with the results and was convinced that a great revolution had taken place in the country.

A year later, Mrs. Gandhi celebrated still another electoral success. The remaining state elections were held on schedule and the Prime Minister's party walked away with fourteen of the sixteen state elections In all, the Congress party won 70 percent of the State Assembly seats, defeating their foes on both the right and left. The new Congress party regained its pre-1967 stature and now added to its control West Bengal, Bihar, Andhra Pradesh, Maharashtra, Karnataka, Gujarat, Himachal Pradesh, Haryana, Punjab, Madya Pradesh, Rajasthan, Assam, Kashmir, and Tripura.

EAST PAKISTAN AND THE RISE OF BANGLADESH

One week after Mrs. Gandhi's victory at the polls in 1971, civil war erupted in East Pakistan. Just when the government was about to tackle its socio-economic problems, long lines of impoverished Bengali refugees moved across the Indian frontier. When Bengali resistance crumbled under heavy Pakistan army pressure, the trickle of refugees became a raging torrent. Reports circulated that the Hindu minority in East Pakistan had been charged by Pakistani authorities with primary responsibility in the secessionist movement. According to Pakistani officialdom, the Hindus aimed to destroy the state of Pakistan. Moreover, the Indian government's support of an independent Bengal in East Pakistan reinforced this conclusion.

Tales of genocide and the destruction of Hindu property were carried by the refugees as they moved into makeshift sanctuaries in Indian West Bengal and Assam. The plight of the homeless, wretched masses aroused the world, but India had to house, feed, and immunize them against disease. Although exact figures were impossible to verify, by November, 1971, the estimated count topped nine million. The Pakistan government insisted the refugees should return to their homes and that others should cease leaving. However, there was no evidence that the killing, torturing, burning, and looting had been terminated in East Pakistan. Prime Minister Gandhi declared the refugees would be returned, but it became clear this could be accomplished only after Indian arms defeated the Pakistan army. In the absence of such a military venture, the refugees, particulary the three-quarters that were said to be members of the Hindu community, were in India to stay.

Mrs. Gandhi noted that no country had ever been faced with so large a problem in so short a time. It had come when the country was poised for rapid economic advance. Now India would have to allocate its scarce resources to meet the demands of a desperate people. Moreover, a large portion of the refugees were in West Bengal, India's most turbulent state at the time. The situation threatened the state with even more violence. There were incidents of the local inhabitants turning on the refugees. Incidents involving Indian Muslims and Hindu militants were also on the increase, and the country faced the possibility of intensified Hindu-Muslim disunity. The coalition government of West Bengal collapsed on June 27, 1971. It had been in power a few, short weeks when Chief Minister Ajoy Mukherjee announced law and order could no longer be maintained. Pakistan's future was in doubt, but India's survival as a democratic and unified polity suddenly assumed new urgency.

In view of this, Indian leadership prepared a strategy to sever East Pakistan from Pakistan and hence help establish an independent Bangladesh state. With the Pakistan army and their collaborators inflicting losses against the Bengalis in East Pakistan, leaders of the Awami League in the Pakistani province, took refuge in Calcutta and set up a provisional government of Bangladesh. With Indian assistance the Mukti Bahini, or Bangladesh liberation army, was trained and equipped. It infiltrated the embattled province to harrass, disrupt, and weaken the Pakistan army. In the meantime, India mobilized a sizeable military force, which dug in along the 1,500 mile frontier of East Pakistan. With the Indian army in a position to shell East Pakistan at will, the Pakistan army was compelled to position contingents on its borders. A limited Pakistani military capability was thus stretched beyond its meager resources. As the Pakistanis were increasingly deployed on the frontier, the rest of East Pakistan was exposed to the raids of the Mukti Bahini. As pressure increased on the Pakistan garrison, the Pakistan government tried to divert Indian attention by launching air raids into India's western region. They also attacked in

Kashmir. This Pakistan action was all India needed to justify its major offensive against East Pakistan.

On December 4, 1971, the Indian army crossed into East Pakistan with the expressed purpose of overrunning the province and destroying the Pakistan army. The Indian Parliament, which had been calling for action from the time the refugees started arriving in India, was ecstatic on learning the news. Mrs. Gandhi had returned empty-handed from a trip to the United States and other western capitals, and this aroused India's politicians to new heights of indignation. Given the pact signed between India and the Soviet Union in the summer of 1971, and the apparent indifference of the western powers, the politicians were overjoyed that Prime Minister Gandhi ordered the Indian forces to cross the Pakistan frontier. In the United Nations, the Security Council proved unable to stem the invasion as the Soviet Union sided with India. The support provided by the USSR was contrasted with that of the United States and China, both of which assisted Pakistan, labelling India the aggressor.

Despite the pleadings of the United Nations and the United States for a ceasefire, Indian arms overwhelmed the Pakistani defenders. Surrounded on three sides, blockaded on the fourth, the Pakistan army could not be re-supplied, and once its air force had been defeated over East Pakistan, the main Indian offensive commenced. Ultimately, the Pakistani forces were compelled to surrender or face total liquidation. Despite declarations suggesting a fight to the bitter end, the war in the east drew to a close only thirteen days after the initial Indian assault. Before the formal surrender, however, India had already recognized the new state of Bangladesh, and East Pakistan ceased to exist.

On December 16, the Indian government announced it would unilaterally cease all hostilities, and it called upon the Pakistan government to accept a ceasefire and negotiate a permanent settlement. Although the Pakistanis hesitated to accept the Indian demands, on December 17, 1971, President Yahya Khan announced his government would comply. The second Indo-Pakistan War in six years was over.

In military terms, India won a striking victory. However, the emergence of Bangladesh was a mixed blessing for the Indian government. Although approximately ten million refugees returned to their homes in Bangladesh, the new state looked to its liberators to help rebuild their country.

DEMOCRACY AT THE CROSSROADS

Electoral successes and battlefield triumphs can prove to be ephemeral. Political leaders have been known to attain crowning achievements only to find their enormous popularity short-lived. Winston Churchill has been

identified as one of the truly distinguished leaders of the twentieth century, yet on the eve of his greatest victory, the defeat of Nazi Germany in
World War II, the English voted him out of office. Richard Nixon and
Lyndon Johnson conducted extremely well-supported campaigns for the
American presidency, but both men eventually left office under shattering
public criticism. History is full of such events, and therefore it is not
surprising to find comparative developments in India. What is of particular interest in this area is not that Mrs. Gandhi found it impossible to
sustain her popularity of 1971-1972, but the way in which she endeavored
to protect her government given the attacks made upon it.

It is obvious that Mrs. Gandhi gained considerable political leverage
as a result of India's victory in the Indo-Pakistan War of 1971 and the
subsequent emergence of the independent state of Bangladesh. The
sweeping successes at the polls in the Indian states' elections in 1972,
capped her triumph over old Congress party members who refused to
follow her lead in 1969. By and large, the elections also demonstrated the
continuing weaknesses of the opposition parties that for so many years had
sought to displace Congress party rule. Unable to break the grip that Mrs.
Gandhi and her Congress party held over the nation, the opposition
repaired to their local domains to reorganize their battered legions and
form new strategies. It was a foregone conclusion that those who had
devoted their lives to politics were not about to surrender their avocation.
Moreover, these professional politicians had spent virtually all their lives
in the opposition ranks, both before and after India's independence, and
were not about to retire. In addition, they understood that India's problems of too many people and too few resources, especially food, would
continue to defy remedy, and that under such circumstances, no government could long escape condemnation. Despite her foreign policies and
military achievements, domestic issues eroded the popular support that
Mrs. Gandhi's administration formerly enjoyed.

The Indian economy has challenged the most able economic strate-
gists. Still, Mrs. Gandhi sought to identify her domestic program as
Gharibi Hatao, or the "abolition of poverty." Politicians must speak the
idiom of the masses, and there can be no mistaking the broad impact of
such a message on the Indian population, most of whom subsist on a
minimum diet and whose purchasing power is almost nil. Moreover, in a
moment of great national exuberance, such as that experienced with the
defeat of Pakistan, both leaders and followers tend to believe that the
impossible is possible. However, positive results are what count. India was
hardly prepared to live up to the Prime Minister's exaggerated rhetoric for
several reasons.

First, traditional status, epitomized by the caste system, militated
against significant changes in superior-inferior relationships. The economic

structure, which had been built on a philosophical foundation that stressed the co-mingling of public and private sectors, could not be destroyed without first developing a viable alternative. Even in those areas where the government had displaced private financiers and entrepreneurs, the end product did not improve the lot of the masses. Corruption was also an obstacle to coherent government programs. Officials were no less greedy than their counterparts in the private sector. Added to this were forces of nature that either left crops stunted through prolonged drought, or washed them into the sea during times of flooding. Also beyond anyone's control in India was the global economy on which India is so dependent. In 1973, that economy went into a sharp decline as oil was first embargoed by the Arab states and then raised to inordinate price levels by the Organization of Petroleum Exporting Countries (OPEC). India had to pay out of scarce reserves for the precious fuel it could not supply for itself. Already wracked by inflationary spirals, the country underwent further dislocation. Prices for essential commodities rose beyond the meager ability of the Indian working man and woman; the government plunged the nation into deeper indebtedness, as a result of its dealings with the more economically advantaged nations. Coupled with a rapidly increasing population that now approaches six hundred million, despite strenuous attempts by the government to introduce birth control, economic progress quickly was overtaken.

When India detonated its first atomic device in May, 1974, national pride was stimulated for the moment. But then questions surrounding the nation's priorities arose. Should a country with so many people living in abject poverty use its limited resources for such ventures? The Indian government's reply to its domestic and foreign critics was affirmative. As a great nation and the largest power on the Indian Ocean, India had no alternative. Moreover, Mrs. Gandhi and her Ministers argued that the country's ultimate development depended on its technological and scientific advances, and nuclear energy was basic in the construction of a modern state. Indeed, the Indira Gandhi government took great pains to explain the peaceful purpose of Indian nuclear experimentation. But the clear fact remained that India was struggling for an inner equilibrium that showed itself to be elusive under conditions of intensified and expanded poverty.

Thus despite the inclusion of the Planning Commission in the Cabinet in 1971, and the renewed stress on socialism in government and society, progress was minimal. Political expediency compelled the ruling Congress party to avoid bold displays of radicalism. Nationalization schemes were implemented but, by and large, the private sector retained an important position. The government also refrained from taxing agricultural property, the key tax base in any redistribution of wealth program.

One problem in this area lay in the Constitution, which reserves to the Indian states the power to tax the agricultural sector. State governments are reluctant to impose heavy taxes because the large landowners are politically influential. Mrs. Gandhi could press for an amendment to the Constitution in order to transfer agricultural taxing power to the Center. However, many of the landlords have been her supporters, and she is reluctant to act against them. Times are changing, however, and the political climate has been dramatically altered (as will be recounted below). The new land reforms being pressed by the government might yet produce the innovations that heretofore have been so stubbornly resisted.

Even in good periods, approximately two hundred million people in India earned only 18 cents a day, while 80 percent of the country's children suffered from malnutrition. The Indian government reported that 1972-1973 was an especially difficult year. In 1970-1971, India, produced a record 108.4 million tons of food grains and still had to import many millions of tons to feed its population. In 1972-1973, food production was cut by a severe drought that left the country with a yield of less than one hundred million tons. Famine conditions spread from Rajasthan in the west, to Bihar and Orissa in the east. Food riots became commonplace, and the Gandhi government was made the target of repeated abuse. The government was accused of authoritarian rule, hypocrisy, massive bribery, and administrative failure by the revitalized opposition. The electorate, it was suggested, has not failed the democratic system. Rather it was the avarice and unscrupulousness of its leaders in collaboration with a selfish and unprincipled educated elite. The politicians attacked at a time when Mrs. Gandhi sought desperately to put together a coalition of political and apolitical elements, which she hoped would address itself to India's more dire questions.

The political opposition's attack on the Gandhi administration was echoed and reinforced by the media, led by India's free and erudite press. In 1973 and 1974, their criticism focused on food shortages and the government's unsuccessful attempt to control the sale of wheat. In the wheat situation, the government's policies blundered by having the reverse effect: instead of guaranteeing wheat at reasonable prices, there was considerable hoarding, which resulted in the development of an intolerable black market. Ultimately, costs of food grain and other essentials rose by 15 percent in 1972-1973, and from 15 to 20 percent in 1973-1974. It did not take an economic statistician to confirm that the country was threatened with social unrest, as well as economic chaos.

As a consequence of these developments, Mrs. Gandhi's regime began to lose political popularity and control. The opposition sensed an opportunity to seize power and began to organize under a series of banners. Finally, a number of important opposition parties began to draw together despite their disparate philosophies and different long range objectives. In the short run, they agreed that Mrs. Gandhi had to be discredited and her party defeated at the polls. It was toward this end that the five leading opposition parties merged. The Congress (Opposition) that represented the old line Congressites who split with Mrs. Gandhi in 1969, the ultra-militant Hindu Jan Sangh party, the Socialist Party, the Sikh Akali Dal, and the conservative Bharatiya Lok Dal comprised a United Front. The Front was led by two men: Prakash Narayan, a disciple of Mahatma Gandhi and a socialist leader of heretofore apolitical humanistic causes; and Morarji Desai, a prominent Congress party leader and former Deputy Prime Minister under Mrs. Gandhi. They assembled massive rallies and wherever a by-election (an election to fill a vacancy) for the Indian Parliament or a special election of a state legislature was held, they proved to be vigorous compaigners. The success of the opposition can be measured by their achievements at the polls, especially in Bihar and Gujarat in 1974-1975. But the opposition was not satisfied with these token gains. What they wanted was a new test of strength in a general election, which Mrs. Gandhi was not required to grant until the winter of 1976. In the absence of a fullblown election campaign, the oppositon settled to the task of consolidating their gains, while increasing pressure on Mrs. Gandhi and her government.

Opposition speeches began to attract the multitudes. Speaker after speaker hurled invectives at the Gandhi administration and at the Prime Minister, personally. These open-air sessions often led to rowdiness. Under the cloak of growing disorder, other elements sought to raise havoc in the country, some for private gain and others for political ends. In the latter category, the extremist political order known as the Naxalites again began committing acts of sabotage and murder. The Naxalite movement had been inactive since early 1972, after its leader Charu Mazumdar died, and many of his associates were killed in open clashes with the Indian army and police. But in June, 1975, the Naxalites were reportedly on the move in West Bengal, Andhra Pradesh, and Orissa. Tension between landlords and peasants in those states was increasing, and the Naxalites sought to assist the latter. Because of the Maoist affinities of the Naxalites, even the pro-Moscow Communist Party of India (CPI) described the movement as a militant form of agrarian struggle. Prime Minister Gandhi was alarmed by the resurgence of the Naxalites and other terrorist groups. She alerted all the state governments to practice increased vigilance wherever extremism was in evidence, especially after the assassination of her Railways Minister, L. N. Mishra, in January, 1975, and a subsequent attack upon the Chief Justice of the Indian Supreme Court. Law enforcement was ordered to improve their machinery and tactics. At the same time, land reforms, which all the states had adopted, fixing minimum holdings be-

tween seven and forty acres, were to be duly adhered to. Mrs. Gandhi was
aware that many state governments were ignoring their responsibilities in
this area, increasing the likelihood of clashes between the landed and
landless elements and providing the extremists with opportunities for
exploitation. The last thing, Mrs. Gandhi wanted was public sympathy for
groups such as the Naxalites, who were already being hailed as champions
of the poor by some of the press.

Also at this time, the High Court at Allahabad, in Uttar Pradesh,
handed down its verdict in a case that had been initiated in 1971, and
directed at the Prime Minister. Mrs. Gandhi had been charged with
violating India's electoral laws in her campaign for re-election in 1971.
Her opponent, Raj Narain, a socialist, had been defeated by a 2-1 margin
in that election, but had immediately processed a case accusing the Prime
Minister of a series of illegal acts. After years of trial and deliberations the
Court handed down its verdict and found Mrs. Gandhi guilty on two of
the fourteen charges filed against her. The judge in the case ordered her
disqualified from holding any political office for a period of six years, but
said she could remain Prime Minister while appealing her conviction to
the country's Supreme Court. In point of fact, Mrs. Gandhi had been
found guilty on the minor charges of having permitted a government
employee to act as her campaign manager and of using local police and
officials to help prepare a political rally. She was acquitted on the more
serious charges of bribing voters, spending more money than the allowed
maximum, using government airplanes for political purposes, or employing
religious symbols as political party symbols. The verdict, however, sent
shock waves throughout the country. The opposition believed that Mrs.
Gandhi could now be forced to resign, and that new elections would be
ordered. The government, on the other hand, was near panic, and sought
to organize popular support for the Prime Minister.

Emboldened by a new sense of power, the political opposition assembled. Their speeches consisted of one theme: the Prime Minister must
resign, along with her entire Cabinet, and new elections must be called by
India's president. Jaya Prakash Narayan was in the forefront of this campaign. He called for civil disobedience, *satyagraha* in Mahatma Gandhi's
days, and he urged his listeners to maintain pressure on the administration. Narayan believed the Gandhi government was transforming India
into a dictatorship and he pledged himself to prevent it. J. P., as Narayan
is best known, insisted that the Gandhi government was no longer legal,
hence its orders were unjust and should be ignored by all government
workers, including the military and police. Moreover, he allegedly said, no
one need pay taxes until a new government was organized. The fact that
the Supreme Court had not yet acted on the appeal and that the Lower
Court had permitted the Prime Minister to continue in office in the
interim went unnoticed by the vociferous opposition.

With the possibility of large scale civil disobedience in the offing, the government moved to defend itself with stron, decisive action. On June Moghuls was institutionalized with the consolidation of British rule. emergency under Article 352 of the Constitution. Mrs. Gandhi maintained it was a necessary action in order to thwart a conspiracy aimed at destroying her government, thus circumventing the Constitution. In an address to the nation, she reiterated that she governed through consent of the majority and that she was duty-bound to preserve the democratic system from its identifiable, as well as hidden, enemies. The Prime Minister gave special attention to J. P.'s appeal to the armed forces and police to disobey the orders of the Gandhi government. If the forces of opposition were to be given license to continue with their plan, chaos could be visited upon the country and its democratic heritage completely overwhelmed. In the days and weeks that followed the declaration of the state of emergency, all dissident and suspected dissident leaders were seized by the Indian police and imprisoned under Security Acts. This meant that no formal charges were brought to bear against them. Censorship descended on Indian society, and Indian newswriters and editors were also taken into custody. Foreign correspondents were ordered to sign a pledge not to publish anything that was not approved by the authorities. Many declined and chose to leave the country. Others were forced to leave on short notice. A number of foreign publications were banned in the country, and ultimately only those newspapers and periodicals favorable to the government were permitted to continue publication.

Twenty-six political organizations were declared illegal, although the government was constrained to note that none of them were represented in the Parliament. The principal groups affected by this action were:

1. the Rashtriya Swayamsevak Sangh (RSS), a reactionary organization that seeks to convert India into a Hindu state (it was a member of the RSS group that assassinated Mahatma Gandhi in 1948);
2. the Jamiat-ul-Islam, a pan-Islamic group accused of being pro-Pakistan and thus the Muslim counterpart of the RSS;
3. the Ananda Marga, a secretive sect that emphasizes mystical rituals and renounces the present political system; and
4. the Naxalites whose exploits have been described above.

Efforts were made to round up the leaders and active members of all banned organizations.

In a short time the net was broadened to entrap the leaders of the major opposition parties as well. Although their parties were still left to function in the Parliament, the arrest of their leaders brought their activities to a standstill. J. P. Narayan, Morarji Desai, Asoka Mehta, Piloo Mody, Ram Dhan, Chandra Sekhar, K. R. Malkani, and Samar Ghua—a veritable who's who of the Indian opposition—were arrested without prior warning and jailed without charges or trial. It is alleged that approximately 55,000 political dissidents had been detained by mid-August, 1975. With the principals isolated from their followers, and especially from the general public, Mrs. Gandhi asked the Parliament to confirm the sweeping emergency powers granted to her under the Constitution. What remained of the opposition boycotted the proceedings of the Parliament, and the emergency measures were approved without a dissenting voice.

Under the state of emergency all fundamental rights, for instance, free speech and free assembly, were suspended. As has been observed, efforts were made to prevent the free flow of information. The severe restraints imposed on the nation transformed India into a closed society. The situation was unprecedented. Prime Minister Gandhi has justified her actions, saying they were in the national interest. Explaining the silencing of the press, she has been reported as saying:

> It is not a good thing to have censorship, but we must realize that liberty, or any kind of right which democracy gives can never be a privilege without its corresponding responsibility and obligation.[8]

The calm that settled over the country was judged to be beneficial and worth the exercise in police power. Mrs. Gandhi revealed that she did not act in haste or in panic, that all her actions were seriously weighed before decisions were arrived at. The Prime Minister used every opportunity to assure her listeners that democracy, rather than being undermined by her use of extraordinary powers, is really being protected. The functioning of Parliament, where she held an overwhelming majority and from which the opposition had retreated, apparently is all the evidence she requires to justify her posture. Striking a chord heard in many other third world countries in recent years, the Prime Minister contends political liberty and political rights exist only so long as political order remains: a state of anarchy can only lead to quick erosion of every freedom and political right of the individual. With comments such as these from India's key authority, one is reminded of the origins of Indian monarchy previously discussed. The Prime Minister has moved with the spirit of the times, but this spirit also seems to be very much in harmony with ancient Kautilyan prescription. If the time comes to choose between authoritarian government or anarchy, natural laws demand the selection of the former. This is reminiscent of yet another political tradition, which has long been central to this vast society. Vice-regalism which was identifiable under the Moghuls was institutionalized with the consolidation of British rule. Therefore, vice-regalism was close to the surface of Indian politics for the first twenty-five years of the country's history. It appears to have burst

---

[8]Indira Gandhi, quoted in *The New York Times*, September 8, 1975, 19:1.

through the veneer of constitutionalism that had been so carefully laid by India's founding fathers. Indira Gandhi's critics allude to her as the new "Empress of India." This point is debatable, but it would not be irreverent to suggest that the vice-regal tradition, the ultimate source of all power, resides in the prime minister. Thus it was Indira Gandhi who could order the postponement of the general elections that were scheduled for 1976. She also demanded and obtained an amendment to the Constitution that nullified the actions taken against her by the Allahabad High Court. The thirty-ninth amendment to the Indian Constitution also prevented the Supreme Court from interfering with the Prime Minister's election policies, as well as her office administration.

But if Mrs. Gandhi is able to avoid judicial scrutiny, she is still accountable to the people, who in the ancient admonitions, can take matters into their own hands if the reigning monarch no longer serves the interest of society. In order to establish a new equilibrium and thereby protect her administration, Mrs. Gandhi has followed the course developed by all previous Congress governments. As an umbrella organization capable of bringing together diverse views, the Congress has always been successful in adopting programs that opposition politicians have originated. Whether it be a socialist program or a capitalist one, the Congress has had no difficulty in absorbing the essence of them both and presenting them to the Indian public as its own national prescription for the country's improvement. In this way the Congress meant different things to different constituencies, and the larger segment of the Indian voters continued to support the Congress party. This flexibility has sustained the Congress through repeated organizational crises. Certain aspects of the Congress are reminiscent of Hinduism itself, with its incredible ability to absorb alien beliefs and practices without undergoing significant intrinsic change. Mrs. Gandhi and her advisors on the inner Political Committee, formed in 1973-1974, understood that J. P. Narayan had hit a responsive chord, and that they could not ignore the demands for an improved life-style. Hence from the moment that the state of emergency was declared, strenuous efforts were made to incorporate Narayan's program into official government policy.

Mrs. Gandhi is now leading the struggle to redistribute land to the landless. Price stabilization is another absolute requirement, and no time was wasted in notifying the commercial sector that they should be content with reduced profit margins. Generally, the Prime Minister insists on the practice of austerity at all levels of Indian society and in all sectors, both private and governmental. The regime has amply demonstrated its determination to use strong measures, and the threat of imprisonment and loss of property and position threatens those who feel the conditions prevailing in the country make it easy for them to aggrandize themselves. Mrs.

Gandhi has described the state of emergency as a new lease on life for the Indian nation. She believes the opportunities for improving the lot of the common people have improved as a result of this new concentration of power. The government's inability to act, or its reluctance, is traced to a perception of democracy that stressed license and personal greed, not obligations, responsibilities, and civic consciousness. She has repeated the concept that all Indians must develop and practice *discipline* in their private, as well as public lives. Discipline and *unity* are the key ideas in this new campaign.

Both national concern and self-serving interests are reflected in the actions and statements of the Prime Minister. Mrs. Gandhi has been described by her compatriots as indispensable and the very personification of "Mother India," the inference being that without Mrs. Gandhi, India's future would be bleak. Obviously, this position is far-fetched. It is for this reason that her arrogation of unlimited powers (although within the construction of the Constitution) disturbs and frightens the middle-class intelligentsia. It is, after all, this element of society that is directly affected by the Prime Minister's maneuvers. It is they who encouraged, supported, and took pride in the constitutional/parliamentary system. The masses of Indians, some 80 percent of the population who reside in hundreds of thousands of primitive villages, are barely touched by the state of emergency. Indeed, in the first flush of excitement, the rural and urban poor, were the first to reap benefits as fearful merchants and traders reduced their prices. It is therefore no simple matter to understand what is happening in India. While there is no question that the democratic experiment is facing its most severe test, there is also sufficient evidence to show that internal and external forces were (and still are) at work to destroy that very experiment. There is also no doubt that not only Mrs. Gandhi, but her aides as well, wish to remain in power. Some of the latter certainly aspire to succeed her when she eventually steps down: they seek to be in an advantageous position when that time comes. On the other hand, it is not clear if there is another coherent political organization capable of assuming the responsibilities associated with Indian government. The Congress party has been the undeniable preference of the Indian voters since independence in 1947. No other party has achieved even relative *national* status in the almost three decades that have passed. And as a one-party dominant state, India has managed to evoke a dynamic equilibrium in which national unity has been sustained without necessarily achieving national integration. If the Congress party disintegrates, the anarchy that Mrs. Gandhi foresees may not be idle comment.

On November 7, 1975, the Indian Supreme Court ruled unanimously that Prime Minister Indira Gandhi was legally elected to Parliament, hence reversing the earlier decision of the Allahabad High Court. India's senior jurists produced separate opinions in which they upheld the retroactive amendments to the country's election laws. The justices argued that Mrs. Gandhi did not violate election practices, nor had she exceeded the prescribed ceiling in election expenses. The Prime Minister was especially pleased with this judgment, and she took the opportunity to again condemn the opposition for "raising false slogans" and "posing as champions of democracy." In spite of this victory, the Prime Minister gave no indication of lifting the state of emergency and intimated that that act had no connection with her court battle. In essence, the Supreme Court had rendered its decision on the basis of the changed law, not on the principles of jurisprudence and their interpretations. The court had in fact refused to contest the authority of the legislature in passing the retroactive law exonerating Mrs. Gandhi from any wrong-doing. By so doing the Indian Supreme Court had yielded to the supremacy of the Parliament and had therefore avoided a struggle over the Court's judicial review prerogatives.

Speaking to the nation on November 11, the Prime Minister described her victory as a national, not an individual, triumph. Her principal theme was that any attempt to bring the Prime Minister into disrepute would do serious harm to the nation. Alluding to the coup, which swept Bangladesh's celebrated leader, Mujibur Rahman, from office, the Prime Minister said, "You have seen how governments have been overthrown in our neighborhood."[9] Mujib's unexpected demise was a shocking example of what can happen to a country when a government does not practice vigilance.

On November 17, 1975, the Indian government reiterated its determination to control any dissident voices in the nation. The state of emergency was extended providing for the re-arrest of a person on the same charge at the end of a period of detention or even after being released by the courts or government. Until this latest amendment to the state of emergency powers, Indian legal experts had said that once someone was released under the Internal Security Act, it was not possible to detain that person again on the same charges. It is noteworthy that Jaya Prakash Narayan had been released by the government on November 12, and on that occasion had announced his intention to continue his fight with Mrs. Gandhi and her Congress government.

In February, 1976, the central government took over the administration of the state of Tamil Nadu which had long been governed by the provincial DMK party. The government charged that the DMK was planning the secession of Tamil Nadu. Although the DMK leaders denied the accusation many were arrested along with hundreds of party workers

[9]Quoted in *The New York Times*, November 10, 1975, 8:1.

and state government officials. The seizure of Tamil Nadu left only the Indian state of Gujarat without a Congress dominated government. But rumors were circulated that the instability in the Gujarat government was forcing the central administration to take over its affairs too. More significant was the report that the Gujarat government had resisted the emergency decrees of the Gandhi administration. Thus it came as no surprise when on March 12, 1976 President's Rule was imposed on Gujarat as well. This act completed the centralization of the Indian political system and ten years of political activity which aimed at the devolution of authority to the states appeared to have been reversed.

On top of these developments was the systematic dismantling of judicial safeguards. Although repeated often that everything the Gandhi government had done was within the defined limits of the constitution, it was obvious that the traditional protections provided by the constitution were no longer operative. This observation was made abundantly clear when on April 28, 1976 the Supreme Court of India reduced some of its own powers by ruling that the Prime Minister had the right to imprison political opponents without court hearings. In a 4 to 1 judgment the Supreme Court held that the traditional right of *habeas corpus*, guaranteeing the accused a court hearing and protecting him from arbitrary arrest, had been suspended for the duration of the emergency. And under the constitution the State of Emergency can last as long as the government determines it necessary.

Another significant effect of the State of Emergency has been the revitalization of the civil and police bureaucracies. The constitution had been designed to remove the bureaucrats from their pre-independence power positions. In these circumstances, however, the bureaucracy was moved back and into the decision-making arena where it had to work on a more intimate basis with Congress party officials. It was thus possible to hypothesize either the politicizing of the bureaucrats or the bureaucratizing of the Congress politicians. Neither arrangement, however, seemed to suggest the development of Indian democracy.

Finally, the impression was growing that Prime Minister Gandhi was permitting her colleagues to fabricate something resembling a "cult of the personality." Not only did the Congress President D. K. Borooah declare that all Indians must dedicate themselves to the policies of their "beloved leader," but the Congress Party's youth wing came under the control of Mrs. Gandhi's son, Sanjay. The youth wing was supposed to counter opposition student movements and clashes with demonstrators were unavoidable. Moreover, Sanjay became a key member of Prime Minister Gandhi's inner circle of advisors and the feeling was widespread that Mrs. Gandhi was grooming him to succeed her within the current decade. It did not require much arithmetic to note that the Nehru family had governed India since the country's independence, with the exception of the nineteen month administration of Lal Bahadur Shastri.

The Prime Minister wields virtual dictatorial power in which the press has been silenced, smuggling reduced, production increased, tax evaders forced to pay significant penalties, and inflation generally controlled. Indeed, even the proverbial trains were running on time. It was doubtful, having tasted the power of success through strong government, that Mrs. Gandhi would desire to return to the more familiar aspects of Indian politics. A member of Parliament commented on the new conditions prevailing in the country in the following manner:

> She finds it convenient to have an emergency. It's a great convenience, for instance, not to have the newspapers saying bad things about you, not to have the opposition around making a lot of noise, with strikes and fasts and things like that. As I told her she'll get used to the convenience, and it will then be very, very hard to go back to the way it was.[10]

RECOMMENDED READING

Aggarwala, R. C., *Constitutional History of India and National Movement*. Delhi: S. Chand and Co., 1964.

Andrews, C. F., and Girija Mookerjee, *The Rise and Growth of the Congress in India*. London: Allen and Unwin, 1938.

Austin, Granville, *The Indian Constitution*. New York: Oxford University Press, 1966.

Bailey, Sydney D., *Parliamentary Government in Southern Asia*. New York: Institute of Pacific Relations, 1952.

Barnds, William J., *India, Pakistan, and the Great Powers*. New York: Praeger, 1972.

Basu, Durga Das, *Introduction to the Constitution of India*. Calcutta: S. C. Sarkar and Sons Ltd., 1966.

Bhambhri, C. P., *Bureaucracy and Politics in India*. Delhi: Vikas, 1971.

Bhatia, Krishnan, *The Ordeal of Nationhood*. New York: Atheneum, 1971.

——————— , *Indira: A Biography of Prime Minister Gandhi*. New York: Praeger, 1974.

Bombwall, K. R., and L. P. Choudhry, *Aspects of Democratic Government and Politics in India*, Delhi: Atma Ram and Sons, 1968.

Braibanti, Ralph, ed., *Asian Bureaucratic Systems Emergent from the Imperial Tradition*, Durham, N.C.: Duke University Press, 1966.

Brecher, Michael, *Nehru's Mantle: The Politics of Succession in India*. New York: Praeger, 1966.

——————— , *Political Leadership in India*. New York: Praeger, 1969.

[10]Quoted in *The New York Times*, November 10, 1975, 2:4.

Brown, J. M., *Gandhi's Rise to Power: Indian Politics 1915-1922*. Cambridge: Cambridge University Press, 1972.

Chatterjee, Basant, *The Congress Splits*. Delhi: S. Chand and Co., 1971.

Chatterji, Saral K., *Political Prospects in India*. Madras: Diocesan Press, 1971.

de Mesquita, Bruce Bueno, *Strategy, Risk and Personality in Coalition Politics: The Case of India*. New York: Cambridge University Press, 1976.

Fisher, Louis, ed., *The Essential Gandhi: His Life, Work and Ideas*. New York: Vintage, 1962.

Franda, Marcus, *West Bengal and the Federalizing Process*. Princeton, N.J.: Princeton University Press, 1968.

Ghose, Sankar, *The Western Impact on Indian Politics (1885-1919)*. Bombay: Allied Publishers, 1967.

Gledhill, Alan, *The Republic of India*. Westport, Connecticut: Greenwood Press, 1951.

Goel, Madan Lal, *Political Participation in a Developing Nation: India*. New York: Asia Publishing House, 1976.

Gupta, N. L., ed., *Nehru On Communalism*. New Delhi: New Age Printing Press, 1965.

Hanson, A. H., and Janet Douglas, *India's Democracy*. New York: Norton, 1972.

Hardgrave, Robert, L. Jr., *India: Government and Politics in a Developing Nation* (2nd ed.). New York: Harcourt Brace Jovanovich, 1975.

Hardy, P., *The Muslims of India*. Cambridge: Cambridge University Press, 1972.

Hodson, H. V., *The Great Divide*. London: Hutchinson, 1969.

Iengar, H. V. R., *Administration in India: A Historical Review*. Bombay: Bharatiya Vidya Bharan, 1967.

Joshi, G. N., *The Constitution of India*. Bombay: MacMillan, 1966.

Karunakaran, K. P., *Modern Indian Political Tradition*. New Delhi: Allied Publishers, 1962.

Kochanek, Stanley A., *The Congress Party of India, The Dynamics of One-Party Democracy*. Princeton, N.J.: Princeton University Press, 1968.

Kothari, Rajni, *Politics in India*. Boston: Little, Brown, 1970.

Maheshwari, B., *Studies in Panchayati Raj*. Delhi: Metropolitan Book Company, 1963.

Menon, V. P., *The Story of the Integration of the Indian States*. Bombay: Orient Longmans, 1956.

————— , *The Transfer of Power*. Princeton, N.J.: Princeton University Press, 1957.

Misra, R. N., *The President of the Indian Republic*. Bombay: Vora and Co., Publishers Limited, 1965.

Morris-Jones, W. H., *Parliament in India*. London: Longmans, Green, 1957.

Narain, Iqbal, ed., *State Politics in India*. Meerut: Meenakshi Prakashan, 1965.

Nehru, Jawaharlal, *Independence and After*. New York: The John Day Company, 1950.

Norman, Dorothy, *Nehru: The First Sixty Years*. New York: The John Day Company, 1965.

Palmer, Norman D., *The Indian Political System*. Boston: Houghton Mifflin, 1961.

_____ , *Elections and Political Development: The South Asian Experience*. Durham, N.C.: Duke University Press, 1975.

Panikkar, K. M., *The State and the Citizen*. Bombay: Asia Publishing House, 1960.

Park, Richard L., and Irene Tinker, *Leadership and Political Institutions in India*. Princeton, N.J.: Princeton University Press, 1959.

Phillips, C. H., ed., *Politics and Society in India*. New York: Praeger, 1962.

Pylee, M. V., *Constitutional Government in India*. Bombay: Asia Publishing House, 1965.

Rahman, M. M., *The Politics of Non-alignment*. New Delhi: Associated Publishing House, 1969.

Ramana Rao, M. V., *A Short History of the Indian National Congress*. Delhi: S. Chand and Co., 1959.

Rudolph, Lloyd and Susanne, *The Modernity of Tradition*. Chicago: Chicago University Press, 1967.

Sen Gupta, Bhabani, *Communism in Indian Politics*. New York: Columbia University Press, 1972.

Shah, A. B., *Planning for Democracy and Other Essays*. Bombay: Manaktalas, 1962.

Singh, Balgit, *Indian Foreign Policy: An Analysis*. New York: Asia Publishing House, 1976.

Smith, Donald E., *India as a Secular State*. Princeton, N.J.: Princeton University Press, 1963.

_____ , *South Asian Politics and Religion*. Princeton, N.J.: Princeton University Press, 1966.

Srinivas, M. N., *Caste in Modern India and Other Essays*. Bombay: Asia Publishing House, 1962.

_____ , *India's Villages*. Bombay: Asia Publishing House, 1963.

Veit, Lawrence A., *India's Second Revolution: The Dimensions of Development*. New York: McGraw-Hill (for the Council on Foreign Relations), 1976.

Weiner, Myron, *Party Building in a New Nation: The Indian National Congress*. Chicago: Chicago University Press, 1967.

_____ , *Party Politics in India*. Princeton, N.J.: Princeton University Press, 1957.

_____ , *State Politics in India*. Princeton, N.J.: Princeton University Press, 1968.

Chapter Five

Pakistan and Bangladesh: Quest for Identity

Political developments in Pakistan and Bangladesh necessitate adapting a different approach from that followed in discussing Japan, China, and India. In Pakistan and Bangladesh, socio-political unrest, inchoate government structures, and regional conflict inhibit the emergence of coherent politico-administrative systems. Therefore, this chapter is more concerned with political forces and personalities, than with political structures and functions. Pakistan has only recently re-established a formal political system. Bangladesh has yet to do so. Martial law was in effect in Pakistan from March, 1969 to March, 1972. It had also been imposed from October, 1958 to March, 1962. Bangladesh felt the pressure of martial law in 1975, and the consequences of the 1971 civil war are evident in this nation's near anarchy. Pakistan has already experienced two parliamentary constitutions (1956 and 1973) and a presidential constitution (1962). Bangladesh's 1972 constitution has been discarded. Given so much political uncertainty, it is not surprising that both countries are heavily influenced by members of their higher bureaucracy or army. The elevation of Zulfikar Ali Bhutto to the leading position in Pakistan, to be discussed below, suggests new directions for Pakistan. The death of his counterpart, Sheikh Mujibur Rahman, in Bangladesh at the hands of young army officers, however, portends further turmoil for that poor nation.

PAKISTAN

Pakistan was born in confusion, precipitated in part by the feverish British retreat from South Asia. A product of Indian Muslim history, Pakistan's emergence as an independent state was paradoxically predictable and yet surprising. It was predictable because the Muslims of India tended to view

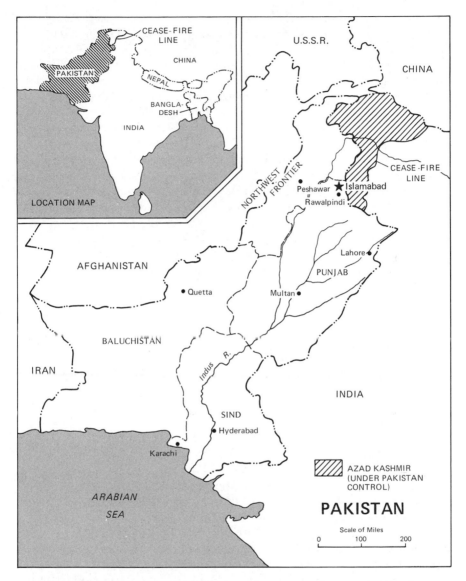

Source: Lawrence Ziring, *The Ayub Khan Era: Politics in Pakistan, 1958-1969* (Syracuse: Syracuse U. Press), 1971, p. xii. (Adapted and modified).

themselves in authoritative roles vis-à-vis their Hindu neighbors. With British departure and the imminence of Hindu political dominance, only a separate state would placate Muslim fears and satisfy Muslim aspirations. The Muslims of India insisted they represented a distinct nation, due the right of self-determination. The partition of British India was the only way to realize this claim. But Pakistan's independence was also surprising. The haste in which the British proceeded to carve up their colony provided little time to think through the questions of a new political design. Fearful Muslims registered a demand for a separate homeland; the Hindus made little effort to ameliorate the minority community's hysteria; and the British were eager to disassociate themselves from the subcontinent's civil conflict. A combination of forces, none of which the principals seemed interested in controlling, set the course of future developments.

As Pakistan was formed, its boundaries consisted of two geographic parts, one separated from the other by more than a thousand miles. These areas were determined by the presence of Muslim majorities in these two separate locations. Moreover, because Pakistan's leaders were schooled in a version of British parliamentary government, and the British advocated a system of representative government in Pakistan, no serious consideration was given to alternative plans. Realistically, how could culture, geography, and imperial legacies be adapted to the sophisticated system of the parliamentary model? How, for example, were the Bengalis in the east wing of the country to relate to the Punjabis, Baluchis, Sindhis, and Pathans in the western sector? The theme of Islamic unity ruled out prior discussion of this salient issue. Pakistan's leaders had brought forth a state, but subsequent developments would show that building a nation was a far more formidable challenge.

ISLAM IN INDIAN HISTORY

The *two-nation theory* was postulated by leaders of the Muslim League. It was directed at the British and held that the sizeable minority of Muslims living within the Indian subcontinent were *de facto* a nation and hence entitled to self-determination and *de jure* recognition. As adherents of Islam and descendents of a conquering people, they found it difficult to entertain the thought of Hindu rule. Contrasted with Hinduism, Islam is relatively simple, but also inflexible. Compared with Hinduism's ability to absorb diverse aspects, Islam is rigidly doctrinaire and resists innovation. Whereas Hinduism epitomizes pantheism, Islam stresses monotheistic beliefs. Both represent socio-religious organization, however, and are often described as encompassing total ways of life. This being the case, it is not unusual that friction should exist between them. It is a curious myopia that would perceive Hindus and Muslims as forming a single community simply because they have long been cohabitants of the subcontinent. In point of fact the two communities maintained distance from one another. This was true in the manner of worship, dress, dietary habits, and worldly outlook. Hindu mysticism insists that change is the only constant factor in life. By accentuating the metaphysical, Hindu outlook clashes with orthodox Islam. At this juncture, it is necessary to add a brief word concerning Islam.

Islam swirled up and out of the sands of Arabia in the seventh century. The Prophet Mohammad, armed with God's revelations, galvanized a heretofore fragmented Arab nation into a world force. After his death in A.D. 632, Mohammad's disciples collected these revelations and recorded them in the *Quran*, the holy scripture of the Muslim people. *Islam* means "surrender," and a Muslim is one who surrenders himself to God by obeying the teachings set down in the Quran. The activities permitted Muslims are assembled in the *Hadiths* or traditions of the Prophet. Together the Quran and the Hadiths comprise the Muslim *Shari'a*, or Divine Law, that all Muslims are duty-bound to observe. Later it was necessary to add flexibility to Muslim observances, and *Ijma* (consensus of the learned) and *Qiyas* (reasoning by analogy) provided a wider spectrum of behavior. No priesthood existed and those learned in the Quran and Hadiths became the interpreters of the religion. These were the *Ulema* to whom the people displayed their respect. The main tenets of Islam have been described as the five pillars, the obligations incumbent on all Muslims. They are:

1. A profession of the faith that "There is no God but God and Mohammad is His Prophet";
2. prayer five times each day;
3. fasting during the month of Ramazan;
4. alms to the poor; and
5. for those who are able, a pilgrimage to the Holy City of Mecca during one's lifetime.

A sixth pillar has often been described by observers as *Jihad*, or Holy War, but this is usually discounted by students of Islam. There is no doubting the importance of Jihad for Muslims, however.

Upon the death of the Prophet, the question of who should lead the Muslim community arose. Mohammad had not named a successor. The problem was resolved momentarily by the election of his intimate disciples. There were to be four immediate successors, or Caliphs, with Ali, the Prophet's son-in-law being the last of this line. Hence it was during Ali's tenure that controversy developed. One school insisted that on his death Ali's sons should succeed to the Caliphate. Another school argued for election. In the conflict that ensued Ali's sons were murdered. The perpetrators of the act proceeded to ignore the elective principle and established a dynasty instead. It was under this dynasty, the Umayyad, that the Caliphate came to represent and to protect the *Sunni* (orthodox), the largest sect within Islam. Those who emphasized the martyrdom of Ali's sons became followers of a somewhat mystical line of *Imams*. Their sect is identified by the term *Shiah*. The Sunnis and Shiahs represent the two principal divisions within the Islamic world today, although others also exist. South Asian Muslims represent both Sunni and Shiah Islam.

Muslim invaders pressed into the subcontinent from Arabia in A.D. 712, conquering the area known as Sind in present-day Pakistan. This move into India was not different from other Arab invasions, which swept across the Fertile Crescent into Persia and Central Asia, or up through Egypt, across North Africa and into Europe. When the Arabs lost their momentum and internal quarreling began, their empire split and eventually withered. Islam had been implanted, however, and other peoples carried the faith into new territories. Hence more lasting Muslim impacts in India were to be registered by non-Arabs. In South Asia the authority of the Arab Caliphate remained in force in Sind only, until the ninth century, but the area's inhabitants had been converted to Islam, and their descendents remain Muslims to this day.

EARLY ISLAM IN INDIA

It was Mahmud of Ghazni, an Afghan of Turkish lineage from Central Asia, who between A.D. 999 and 1025, set the character for later Muslim conquests of the subcontinent. Mahmud seized the Punjab, and from there he set out to destroy the symbols of Hinduism. Mahmud justified his indiscriminate destruction of Hindu life and property on the theory that Hinduism was contrary to God's will. But his empire did not survive his passing. Eventually another Turkish dynasty, that of Ghur, seized his lands and extended them to Delhi where a substantial Muslim kingdom was organized in 1192. Until 1526 the Sultanate of Delhi, or the Kingdom of Pathan Kings, ruled almost the whole of northern India.

Efforts to infiltrate the southern reaches of the subcontinent were not as successful, however, and the Delhi sultans consolidated their control only over the upper regions of the south. The Turkish-Afghan Muslim rulers of India were rigid in their Islamic observances, and initially the Hindu population was placed under severe pressure. Muslims recognize only those religions similar to their own. They must be revealed religions and possess holy scriptures (such as Jews, Christians, and Zoroastrians). Lacking these aspects, the Hindus were treated as heathen. In time, however, the Muslim conquerors came to require the services of the Hindu population. Hindus were thus given the status of *dhimmis* and were permitted to practice their religion, provided they paid a head-tax known as the *jizya*.

Lest it be concluded that Islam was spread by the sword alone in India, mention should be made of the Muslim missionaries, saints, mystics, and scholars who played a significant role in converting the outcastes, backward castes, and pagan tribals. By song, ritual, and simple persuasion they drew people into the fold even before the approach of Muslim armies. The results of their special endeavors are to be witnessed in Bengal, where people living in total subordination to the caste system greeted the new faith with enthusiasm. The promise of equality and God's grace was most welcome.

Although northern India became a Muslim bastion, it is important to understand that the Muslims were never more than a fraction of the total population. Nonetheless, their rule was rarely, and then only locally, challenged by the Hindu majority. The comparative unity of the Muslims was more than a match for the fragmented Hindu civilization. Of no small importance was the impact of Hinduism on Islam, however. It would be a serious error to suggest that there was no interaction between the Muslim and Hindu communities as the Muslims advanced. The conquerors settled and married Hindu women, whose rituals and customs they could not completely ignore. Only recent converts themselves, the new Muslims venerated those responsible for their conversion. They subsequently worshipped relics and made sacred their leaders' gravesites. The impact of Hinduism is evident in these observances. Aspects of the caste system were also assimilated, as well as certain marriage practices and other Hindu ceremonial appurtenances. Observing these influences, Mohammad Iqbal, the illustrious Indian Muslim poet of the twentieth century, exclaimed;

> We have out-hindued the Hindu himself; we are suffering from a double caste system—the religious caste system, sectarianism and the social caste system, which we have either learnt or inherited from the Hindus.[1]

The blending of aspects of Hinduism and Islam, however, did not engender unity or a common brotherhood. Indian architecture, which appears to symbolize the union of the two peoples, also obscures the gulf that separates them. The Turkish armies, which sustained the Delhi Sultanate and later the Great Moghul Dynasty (1526-1858), borrowed from other cultures, as well. For example, in the more sophisticated Moghul period, Persian civilization formed the foundation of the state. Moreover, the Persian language, alone, and then a mixture of Persian, Arabic, and Turkish combined with Hindi to form the new language of Urdu in the Moghul court.

[1]Quoted in Richard Symonds, *The Making of Pakistan* (London: Faber and Faber, 1950), p. 21.

THE MOGHULS AND BRITISH POWER

The Moghuls of India represent the golden age of Islam in India. Contemporary Muslims remember the grandeur and progress achieved in its time, and there is an irrepressible yearning to repeat this performance. The Moghuls were a warrior people of Turkish-Mongol origin. While it is true that they pressed their empire into southern India, it is equally important to recognize the benefits of their attempt to organize a single polity. The building of new cities, the creation of a unified administrative system, and the encouragement given to people of arts and letters, cannot be minimized. Under Akbar (1556-1605) strong efforts were made to bridge Hindu-Muslim differences. The Jizya was withdrawn, and cow slaughter was banned. Hindus were recruited in the civil administration and army, and scholars worked on ways to form a common faith. Those who succeeded Akbar were less interested in the latter activity, however, and this dream of an integrated India died with him.

When Aurangzeb (1658-1707) assumed the Moghul throne he proceeded to accelerate the trend away from community-building and sought to reinvigorate Islamic tradition. Aurangzeb's perception of the Moghul kingdom left no place for anything but Islamic practices. Once more the Moghuls made war on their Hindu adversaries. Thus, Hindus were purged from the government and persecuted en masse. The Jizya was reimposed, Hindu temples were demolished, and the subcontinent again became a great battleground.

Aurangzeb's failure to conquer his Hindu Maratha enemies, however, strained the capacity of the Moghul treasury. The collapse of the empire's economy set the scene for the intervention of European powers and eventual British succession. Moreover, the internecine conflict within the royal family consumed the dynasty. After Aurangzeb, Moghul emperors were weak and ineffective. The empire had not yet succumbed, but leadership had gravitated to specific regions where local rulers sought to reinforce their personal authority.

The Muslim rulers of Hyderabad, Bengal, Mysore, Oudh, and Rohilkhand sought to consolidate their control as British, French, and Dutch settlements began to flourish on the coasts. Once the British had disposed of their European competitors, they moved against the individual Muslim states, and in 1803, occupied Delhi. With the Afghans taking advantage of the Moghul decline and extending their kingdom into Sind and the Punjab, the British joined in the scramble for territory. By 1843, Sind was also in British hands. The Punjab, which the Afghans took from the Moghuls, was then seized by the Sikhs. In turn, they were defeated by the British and the region was annexed in 1849. By mid-century the once magnificent empire of the Moghuls was gone. The Moghul emperor was secreted behind the walls of the Red Fort in Delhi, and only Oudh and

Hyderabad were significant regions of Muslim rule. The absorption by the British of the former in 1857 was partly responsible for the famous mutiny of that same year. Hyderabad was of less strategic value, and the good relations cemented between the British and ruling Nizam allowed it to continue until independent India absorbed it in 1948.

The banishment of the last Moghul emperor after the 1857 mutiny, and the rise of the British Indian empire, as well as its passing, were related in Chapter Four. What concerns us now is the renaissance of Muslim power, the growth of Muslim nationalism, and the establishment of the state of Pakistan.

THE EMERGENCE OF PAKISTAN

Syed Ahmad Khan symbolizes the rejuvenation of the Muslim psyche. After the British victory, the Muslims isolated themselves, turning away from the opportunities that their English superiors offered in return for their loyalty. Syed Ahmad Khan was convinced that the Muslim community's survival was dependent on its adopting British education and European science. He urged a reconciliation with the British and in 1875, founded the Muslim Anglo-Oriental College, later to be called Aligarh University. Many of the individuals who would stand in the vanguard of the later Pakistan movement, as well as those Muslim leaders who remained in India after 1947, are identified with this university. Aligarh University combined an English educational curriculum with Islamic practical and religious training. The student was prepared both for service in the government and leadership in the Muslim community.

Syed Ahmad Khan was knighted by England in 1876, and his ability to ingratiate himself with his European overlords was of no small consequence for his followers. The principle of separate electorates was first suggested by Syed Ahmad Khan. It was accepted first in principle by the British and then given substance in later years. The modernization of the two-nation theory was also the handiwork of this man. A critic of the Congress party, he feared that Muslims would lose their cause by joining that party. He warned:

> The proposals of the Congress are exceedingly inexpedient for a country which is inhabited by two different nations... Now suppose that all the English ... were to leave India ... then who would be the rulers of India? Is it possible that under these circumstances two nations—the Mohammedan and Hindu—could sit on the same throne and remain equal in power? Most certainly not. It is necessary that one of them should conquer the other and thrust it down. To hope that both could remain equal is to desire the impossible and the inconceivable.[2]

[2]Symonds, *op. cit.*, p. 31.

Those who followed Syed Ahmad Khan after his death in 1898 built upon his work and ideas. Amir Ali, a westernized intellectual, lawyer, and government official, spoke to Indian Muslims in his famous book, *Spirit of Islam*. His principal purpose was to reconcile classical Islam with modern needs. Amir Ali contended that Islam was a positive force, adaptable to contemporary conditions and necessary for spiritual enlightenment and practical advancement. His theme emphasized that the Muslims of India had strayed from the teachings of the Prophet. Were they to recognize this, correct their course, and apply themselves to progressive tasks, their religious and temporal life would be renewed. In his short *History of the Saracens*, Amir Ali expands this theme by emphasizing the great contributions that the Islamic world has made to human civilization. The resurgence of Muslim pride became the battle cry of the Muslim intelligentsia, and the concept of a separate Muslim polity gained new meaning.

It was Mohammad Iqbal who crystallized Muslim thinking in regard to their political and cultural future in the Indian subcontinent. As poet-philosopher of the Indian Muslim renaissance, he chose to ignore the dynastic past and emphasized recapturing the spirit of community. His call was a plea for sacrifice and selflessness, compassion and development, cooperation and spiritual devotion. He was critical of those who would take advantage of an unknowing, submissive, impoverished people. His barbs were directed at temporal lords, as well as reputed religious leaders. His concern was for those whose innocence paved the way for unscrupulous demagogues. He was emphatic in his belief that European dominance of India was caused by selfish men, blinded by the pursuit of personal gain. Iqbal, though heavily influenced by western philosophies and practices, counseled his people to avoid emulation. Although he admired Europe's power, he condemned the means employed to acquire and sustain it. Iqbal's nationalist theme was implicit in much of his poetry and writings. Through him Muslim culture was deftly joined to a political consciousness, and the community had its rallying cry.

Iqbal was also concerned with practical politics. He avoided the Congress party for the same reasons offered by Syed Ahmad Khan. Iqbal pursued the idea of separate electorates for Muslims and advocated Muslim quotas in the administrative services. In 1930, he became the president of the Muslim League (which had been organized in 1906 to counter the influence of the Congress). In his Muslim League presidential address, he made the first clear demand for the establishment of a Muslim state either within or outside the British empire. Iqbal was to have a number of unsatisfactory experiences with the British. He cautioned his colleagues to build a mass, grassroots organization to achieve their objectives. It was Mohammad Ali Jinnah, however, who led the Indian Muslims to independence. Armed with Iqbal's philosophy, Amir Ali's scholarship, and Syed

Ahmad Khan's pragmatism, Jinnah is credited with the creation of the nation of Pakistan.

THE CRYSTALLIZATION OF INDIAN MUSLIM NATIONALISM

The first decades of the twentieth century shaped the course of Hindu-Muslim relations. Moreover, the major political parties appeared more to reflect than influence those relations. The British were inclined, though slowly, to transfer some responsibility for the conduct of Indian affairs to the indigenous population (the Indian Councils Act of 1892 and the Ripon Reforms of 1882 accomplished this). Furthermore, the formation of the Indian National Congress in 1885, and the Muslim League in 1906, provided political platforms from which the articulate members of the Indian population could pressure the British Raj for a share in the decision-making process. The Morley-Minto reforms (1909) for the first time provided indigenous representation on important government councils and gave substance to the Muslim insistence on separate electorates. But in 1912, the rescinding of the order to partition the province of Bengal intensified the conflict between Hindus and Muslims. The British had broken a sacred promise to the Muslims and had given in to militant Hindu and Congress demands. Muslim distrust of the British and Congress party resulted, and the Muslim League gained support due to this distrust.

True, not all Muslims heeded Syed Ahmad Khan's advice not to join the Congress, and efforts were made by these individuals to bridge Hindu-Muslim antagonism. Maulana Mohammad Ali (1878-1930) and Maulana Abul Kalam Azad (1888-1958) not only supported the Congress but held the highest positions in that organization. Devout Muslims, they did not envision a separate Muslim state within the Asian subcontinent. They endeavored to provide political representation of their brethren. It is important to note that Maulana Azad opted to remain in India after 1947. Given a high post in the new government, he undoubtedly felt duty-bound to assist those tens of millions of Muslims who were to remain within India. Included among those Muslims who sought to bring closer the major communities was Mohammad Ali Jinnah.

Mohammad Ali Jinnah was a successful Bombay lawyer, whose early political loyalties were divided between the Muslim League and the Congress party. In 1916, he was instrumental in bringing the two parties together through the Lucknow Pact. This agreement represents the only time that the separate organizations would share common views on a future Indian constitution. The Lucknow Pact specified that Muslims were to be permitted one-third of the elective seats in any future All-India parliament. Moreover, they were to command 50 percent of the seats in the Punjab legislature, 40 percent in Bengal, 30 percent in the United Provinces, 25 percent in Bihar, 15 percent in the Central Provinces and Madras, and 33.3 percent in Bombay. Thus both at the center and in the provinces the Muslims were to be granted separate electorates. Unfortunate for the fate of Indian unity, however, the Lucknow Pact was soon a dead letter, and Jinnah's reaction could be anticipated. He accused the Hindu leadership in the Congress party of reneging on the agreement, and the gap between Hindu-Muslim cooperation widened.

The Montagu-Chelmsford Reforms of 1917, aimed at self-governing institutions, and the Government of India Act of 1919, gave concrete form to the proposals for self-government, albeit in a strictly tutelary context. The principle of dyarchy (two rulers), which left the British Raj in substantial control of Indian society, infuriated the Indian politicians who had anticipated a more satisfactory transfer of authority in light of Indian support for the Allied war effort in World War I. The bitterness thus engendered resulted in widespread protests, strikes, and violence. The British responded with repressive legislation and measures. The massacre of non-violent demonstrators by troops under the command of the British General Dyer at Jalianwalabagh was the catalyst for still one more attempt at Hindu-Muslim reconciliation.

At this time Gandhi began to mobilize his followers for a concerted attack on the British establishment. However, Jinnah was offended by Gandhi's tactics, which placed emphasis on civil disobedience. Jinnah was not comfortable with street demonstrations and preferred a more moderate, constitutional approach. But the time was not propitious for disciplined maneuvers.

In the Muslim community there was concern for the Ottoman Sultan who was also Caliph of Islam. After World War I, the Sultan-Caliph was a virtual prisoner of the Christian Europeans. Muslims were roused to assist him. What in South Asia was to become known as the Khilafate Movement, therefore, involved saving the Ottoman Caliphate. Maulana Mohammad Ali and Mahatma Gandhi believed they had found an issue that would aid Hindu-Muslim amity. While Hindus were called upon to provide moral support and possibly help to finance the movement, the Muslims were to join in a general passive resistance campaign against the British in India.

But the plan proved a disaster. The Muslims of India, though religiously attached to the Caliphate, were in no position to prevent the Turks under Mustafa Kemal (Ataturk) from taking matters into their own hands. Long a symbol of backwardness, the nationalist Turks terminated the rule of the Sultan, eliminating the Ottoman Empire after more than 600 years of uninterrupted rule. With it went the Caliphate, as well. Ataturk's emphasis on the restoration of the Turkish nation was multi-dimensional, but there could be no mistaking the secular blueprint. Thus, the Indian Muslims were left with an empty movement and the Hindus with a meaningless cause.

Hindu-Muslim cooperation faded rapidly and the old animosities commenced. Communalism, the South Asian term for inter-community bloodletting, increased in the years that followed. Moderate Indian leaders were helpless to prevent the slaughter of the innocent. Jinnah's fear that the subcontinent's masses could be politically activated, but not controlled, was given wider credence.

Jinnah had ceased to play an active role in either the Muslim League or the Congress but appeared as the leader of an independent delegation at an All-Party Conference in the late 1920s. It was at this meeting that Jinnah again called for a recognition of Muslim demands, which were documented in his Fourteen Points. The Congress, however, insisted on the acceptance of the Moltilal Nehru Report (Moltilal was the father of Jawaharlal Nehru), which all but ignored Muslim claims, particularly for separate electorates. Jinnah's defiance of the Congress hierarchy reinvigorated what had become a somnolent Muslim League organization. With the British replacing the 1919 Act with the more liberal Government of India Act of 1935 (which brought an end to dyarchy), Jinnah was urged to return from his self-imposed exile in England in order to assist the rebuilding of the Muslim League.

JINNAH AND THE MUSLIM LEAGUE

Armed with a clear, unconditional mandate, Jinnah returned to reactivate the party for the 1937 elections (which were to implement the 1935 Act). But he failed to carry his party to victory at the polls. The Congress party took control of seven of eleven provinces (Bombay, Central Provinces, United Provinces, Madras, Orissa, Bihar, and the North West Frontier Province). The Muslim League had to be satisfied with coalition governments in Bengal and the Punjab that put their co-religionists, but not necessarily their party, in positions of authority. The Congress offered the Muslim League leadership some positions in the central government Cabinet on condition that it disband its parliamentary organization and order its members in the legislature to join the Congress party. It was obviously a condition the Muslim League could not accept without destroying itself. Indignation was immense: if proof was needed that the Muslim community was in jeopardy, this provided it. The Muslim League was organized around the theory that the Muslims were a separate nation. Acceptance of the Congress terms meant repudiation of the two-nation theory. Hence,

Islam was judged to be in mortal danger; and it made little difference that the Congress acted within legally acceptable parliamentary customs.

The Muslim League leaders had the issue they could fruitfully exploit. A number of important Muslim personalities were compelled to leave the Congress, and they gave their support to the Muslim party. All the old fears were resuscitated. Jinnah moved to make the Muslim League accessible to the masses by reducing membership fees. He and his lieutenants set out on speaking campaigns, which spread through the Muslim areas of the subcontinent. Their principal theme stressed how much more serious would be the Muslim plight under Hindu rule than under the British. The goal was to attract Muslims away from the Congress standard, and to correct the impression gained by the 1937 elections that the Congress could represent both Hindus and Muslims equally. This field work was not without its rewards. Between 1938 and 1942, the Muslim League eroded Congress power by taking forty-six of fifty-six secondary elections. In addition, the chief Ministers of Bengal and the Punjab identified with the Muslim League. Moreover, when the Congress ministries resigned in 1939, in protest of the British declaration citing India as a belligerent in World War II, Jinnah declared a "day of deliverance" for all Muslims. It is reported that the Muslim leaders were jubilant and used the opportunity to plot new strategy.

The key to Muslim demands was publicized in Lahore in March, 1940. A resolution was passed at the annual convention of the Muslim League calling for the establishment of independent states in those areas where the Muslims represented a majority of the population. Later to be known as the Pakistan Resolution, it drew its name from a suggestion made by a Muslim student studying in London in the early 1930s. The student, Rehmat Ali, supposedly took the first letter from the regions identified as the Punjab, Afghania (North West Frontier Province), and Kashmir, and then added Iran, Sind (including Kutch and Kathiawar), Turkistan, Afghanistan, and Baluchistan to get the acronym *Pakistan*. Rehmat Ali also noted that the word *Pakistan* could be translated in both Urdu and Persian as the "land of the pure," but he could not have known at the time that his handiwork would be adopted by the Muslim League, or that the name would be used to identify the new nation.

It is perhaps no less important to recognize that the Lahore, or Pakistan Resolution, spoke of independent "states." The implication clearly suggested that more than one Muslim state should be constituted within the subcontinent. The other "state" obviously was to be formed from the eastern region centering on Bengal. But as time would show, the Muslim League leaders had second thoughts on this interpretation of the Lahore Resolution.

When the final push toward independence was launched in

1946-1947, the goal was for the establishment of a single state, represented by a single party, and led by a single personality. Thus Pakistan, the Muslim League, and Mohammed Ali Jinnah became the symbols for Muslim independence in India.

THE INDEPENDENCE OF PAKISTAN

Under Jinnah's leadership, the British transferred their authority to the Muslim League, and on August 14, 1947, the Pakistani nation was declared free and sovereign, although remaining a dominion within the British Commonwealth. (This was fully discussed in Chapter Four, p. 136.) Jinnah was both leader of the Muslim League and governor-general of the state, but with a parliamentary system in operation, the everyday tasks of government fell to his closest aide who was now the prime minister, Liaquat Ali Khan. The burden of governing the new state weighed heavily on Liaquat, as Jinnah's health had deteriorated in the struggle for independence. Only a year after realizing the fruits of his labor, Jinnah succumbed to tuberculosis.

Liaquat was determined to make the parliamentary experiment work, but with Pakistan a reality and the Qaid-i-Azam (Great Leader) Mohammed Ali Jinnah dead, divisions were already in evidence, within and outside the Muslim League. The country was divided into five principal provinces, four in the west (Punjab, North West Frontier Province, Sind, and Baluchistan) and one in the east (East Bengal). The Punjab and Bengal had been partitioned by the Radcliffe Award, and in the case of Bengal, the more urban and industrialized section was given to India. The division of these, the two most important provinces of the Pakistani state, created problems of special complexity, but nowhere was this so evident as in the eastern wing.

THE BENGALI PROBLEM

The Bengalis shared a common bond through the Islamic religion, but in every other way differences abounded. In the first phase after independence, it was the cultural differences, particularly that of language, which brought the two wings of the country (separated by more than a thousand miles) into conflict. Muslim League leaders decided that the country required an indigenous *lingua franca*. The continued use of the English language seemed to militate against the creation of a sustained Pakistani-Muslim nationalism, and it was hoped Urdu could be substituted without great difficulty.

Urdu was declared to be a more genuine Islamic language, being written in the Persian-Arabic form. Bengali, on the other hand, was written in the *devanagri* character which is undeniably linked with Sanskrit, the classic language of the Hindus. Although some efforts were made to get the Bengali script altered, the problem of communication remained, and Urdu was judged to be the one truly viable alternative. The Bengalis, however, were incensed. They represented approximately three-fifths of Pakistan's total population and argued that Urdu was only spoken by some 8 percent of the population. If Urdu were to be imposed upon the people of the eastern province, it seemed evident that not two, but three, languages would have to be learned. The difficulty in learning both Urdu and English meant the Bengalis would be governed and controlled by "outsiders," namely refugees from India where Urdu was their mother tongue, and people from the Punjab who dominated the civil services and army. The emphasis on Urdu, therefore, heightened tension between the two parts of the country and from the start, the sensitive and volatile Bengalis asserted they were being turned into a colony. Subsequent developments raised Bengali to an equal position with Urdu. Both were declared to be national languages in 1954, with English remaining the official governmental language. But by this time there were even deeper rifts between east and west.

TERRITORIAL ISSUES AND MILITARY RESPONSE

If problems with Bengal were not enough to hinder Liaquat Ali Khan's administration, it also had to contend with the princely states, which the British gave the opportunity to remain independent if they so desired. These kingdoms had to be handled with finesse, as were the historically restless tribal Pathans of the North West Frontier. Their semi-independence, but loyalty to Pakistan, seemed a satisfactory arrangement. It was not until 1955, that Khairpur and Bhawalpur were amalgamated along with the four provinces of West Pakistan to form the administrative and political entity called the *One Unit* of West Pakistan.

India also was a constant dilemma. Within a year from the date of independence, the Congress government had absorbed more than 500 princely states into the Indian union. Muslim-ruled princely states of Janagadh on the coast of Kathiawar, and Hyderabad in the south of India, were taken over forcibly by the Indian army. Muslim complaints over these seizures reached as far as the United Nations—but to no avail. The most celebrated dispute, however, was over the state of Kashmir with its Hindu king and predominantly Muslim population. Even before independence was achieved a guerrilla-type struggle had broken out in the mountainous northern kingdom as the Muslims sought to remove the Hindu Maharaja. After independence, the conflict intensified and it did not abate before regular Pakistani and Indian armies were directly involved. The problem was complicated further with the abdication of the Maharaja in favor of the Indian government, and the subsequent handling of the controversy by the United Nations. Although the Security Council was able to secure a ceasefire in January, 1949, the dispute could not be resolved.

Since 1957, India has insisted on the inclusion of Kashmir in the Union, but the United Nations urging of a plebiscite still stands, and Pakistan remains unreconciled. The 1965 war between India and Pakistan, which could not be contained in Kashmir, spread to the Punjab and Sind frontiers, as well as to the borders of East Pakistan. It is symbolic of the frustrations experienced by Pakistan vis-à-vis its larger neighbor. Although the 1971 hostilities severed East Pakistan from the Pakistan state, the Kashmir dispute remains unresolved. Because each nation considers the other its principal adversary, and because the hostility between them is unrelenting, resources which might better be spent for social improvements are largely siphoned away by the military. In Pakistan's case, the country is dependent on outside sources of supply for military parapher-nalia. Its fear of India, which is only in part linked to the Kashmir dispute, caused Pakistan to establish high priorities for defense. Alliances, such as the Baghdad Pact (Central Treaty Organization) and the Southeast Asia Treaty Organization (SEATO), were entered into with United States encouragement in 1955 and 1954, respectively. It was through these alliances that the country hoped to acquire the arms it could not manufacture.

The alliance systems were an unmixed blessing in the mid-1950s; and they became a heavy burden in the 1970s. Since the 1965 war with India, United States military assistance to Pakistan was sharply curtailed. As a consequence, the country ceased to play a more than symbolic role in the alliance organizations, and in 1972 Pakistan withdrew from SEATO. Moreover, concern with Indian military power forced Pakistan to compensate for its weakness by seeking aid from Communist China. Chinese friendship after the 1965 war led to Pakistan's receiving development loans and Chinese military assistance. Peking also permitted Pakistan International Airways (PIA) to fly between the two countries. However, Chinese-Pakistani amity did not quite equal India's good relations with the Soviet Union. Both countries continued to jockey for a more favorable international posture when their longstanding dispute erupted in widescale conflict in December, 1971. The Soviet Union's support of India and the latter's eventual success in establishing an independent state of Bangladesh (formerly East Pakistan) is discussed later in this chapter.

THE PARLIAMENTARY EXPERIMENT
AND ITS TERMINATION 1947-1958

Pakistan's political system was parliamentary and federal in the first decade after independence. It had a national and several provincial legislatures, with powers divided between the center and the federal units. Initially, there were only two significant political parties, the Muslim League and the Congress party of Pakistan, the latter representing the approximately twelve million Hindus remaining in Pakistan (virtually all in East Bengal). By 1952, however, numerous other parties emerged, a number having split from the Muslim League.

The first challenge presented to the Muslim League originated in East Pakistan. It was the last of the five original provinces to conduct provincial elections, and in the campaign of 1954 the Muslim League was dealt a stunning defeat which not only liquidated its influence in that province, but also led to its defeat in West Pakistan.

The period from 1947 to 1958 can be separated into three parts: 1947-1953, 1953-1956, and 1956-1958. Each part tells a separate story: when combined, the reasons for the failure of parliamentary democracy in Pakistan become clear.

1947-1953. The first years after independence saw the fledgling state struggle to consolidate its place in the firmament of nations. It was thought the country would succumb to its many unique problems within six months from independence. However, given Jinnah's popular personality and considerable sacrifice, the nation not only survived, but during the Korean War was able to move its feeble economy into what was generally described as a "boom." Politically, the nation was engaged in preparing and drafting a constitution, a job India was to complete in 1950. But the Pakistanis ran into difficulty. The question of representation loomed large, and the Constituent Assembly was ill-prepared for the responsibility of drafting a constitution. Failure to accommodate diverse interests led to an impasse.

East Bengal had the larger population and therefore insisted on a larger number of seats. The politicians in the western provinces refused to accept proportional representation, however. The Punjabis, in particular, were reluctant to give their eastern cohorts a majority in the national legislature. Hence the debating dragged on interminably. Moreover, because the Muslim League was controlled from West Pakistan, the Bengalis found themselves supporting provincially-oriented parties. The Awami League, Krishak Sramik Party, and Ganatantri Dal were more notable in this latter category. They eventually took their places in the Constituent Assembly, and the resulting exchanges were highlighted by an undisguised acrimony. The Muslim League gained acceptance for its Objectives Resolution, declaring that the future constitution should be Islamic in principle, as well as spirit. But their Basic Principles Reports only emphasized the deep division in the assembly and constitution-making proved to be an impossible task. As the politicians became locked in strenuous debate, the responsibility for running the country fell more and more to the bureaucracy, the "steel frame" of the British colonial era.

The Civil Service's elite organs, the Civil Service of Pakistan (CSP), the Finance Services, and the Police Service of Pakistan (PSP) along with the army were becoming impatient. Historically, they had little respect for politicians, and with the death of Jinnah in 1948, and the assassination of Prime Minister Liaquat Ali Khan in 1951, they felt that no single political personality could stabilize the situation. Riots were commonplace. The streets had become the only forum for airing demands and popular discontent. Hence the civil and military services were called upon to restore order with increasing frequency. Moreover, the services blamed the politicians for the domestic strife.

The governor-general's office had been filled by a Bengali, Khwaja Nazimuddin, after Jinnah's demise. The same Nazimuddin assumed the role of prime minister upon the assassination of Liaquat Ali Khan, the governor-general's post then going to the civil servant and "financial wizard," Ghulam Mohammad. It is said Nazimuddin stepped down in order to become prime minister because the governor-general's post was only symbolic. Real authority was supposed to rest with the prime minister in a parliamentary system. Or at least this is what Liaquat tried to stress and what Nazimuddin believed. In reality Pakistan lacked an indigenous constitution, and the parliamentary system rested on the Indian Independence Act of 1947, passed by the British Parliament. Moreover, Ghulam Mohammad interpreted the Act differently from Nazimuddin and his supporters.

In 1952 the Urdu-Bengali language issue caused severe rioting in East Bengal, which only the army could quell. In Karachi, later that year, disturbances broke out involving the student population. Given the general disorder, the army was again called upon to intervene. In 1953, however, violence in the Punjab reached a peak of intensity not witnessed since the days leading up to and immediately following independence. Triggered by religious elements seeking to punish a Muslim sect known as the Ahmediyas, the incident grew into a major disturbance that could not be terminated until arson, burning, and murder had taken a terrible toll on life and property. Nazimuddin was a central figure in each tragic episode. As prime minister, he was expected to handle such events decisively. But this was neither Nazimuddin's style, nor his forte. Governor-General Ghulam Mohammad assumed it was his responsibility to fill the leadership vacuum. He ordered the dismissal of Nazimuddin and quickly designated his successor. With this act the bureaucracy moved into the mainstream of decision-making in the young nation, and the parliamentary experiment was already on the verge of collapse.

1953-1956. The ambassador to the United States, Mohammad Ali (Bogra), was selected by the Governor-General, not elected by the Muslim League party in the Constituent Assembly, to be the new prime minister. Nazimuddin had been ousted without the traditional parliamentary vote of confidence and his supporters insisted that the governor-general's action was illegal. Such comments meant little, however. Nazimuddin's Cabinet remained intact, except for the dismissal of two members who also happened to be the prime minister's advisers in the Muslim League. The bureaucrats had mangled the parliamentary process and their surreptitious handling of Nazimuddin did permanent harm to the Muslim League. Of no lesser importance was the behavior of the politicians who seemed more concerned with their individual welfare than with proper constitutional procedure. In view of what was to follow it is possible to argue that Nazimuddin had been conspired against by persons associated with the Punjab who, together with important members of the bureaucracy, elevated their narrow interests above that of the nation. Put another way, they equated their personal interests with national purpose. What the conspirators wanted was a constitution that protected their privileges and preeminence. In order to guarantee such a document they had concluded that the government must be seized *in toto*.

Within a year Ghulam Mohammed acted again. This time he ordered the dissolution of the Constituent Assembly. As the Assembly was still dominated by the Muslim League, its members, somewhat belatedly, took steps to limit the powers of the governor-general. After being made aware of this challenge to his authority, Ghulam Mohammad ordered the convention closed and insisted he had the right to lift its mandate. With army support the Governor-General's maneuver was successful. Ghulam Mohammad's justification for his action was the inability of the Constituent Assembly to draft a constitution. Moreover, the Muslim League had been trounced in the East Pakistan provincial election held earlier in the year, and the Muslim Leaguers sitting in the Constituent Assembly were no longer considered representative of East Pakistani interests. Thus the same Governor-General who prevented the newly elected United Front from governing East Pakistan (martial law was put into force in East Pakistan just weeks after the conclusion of the 1954 provincial election) received support for his action from Bengali political circles. In fact the Bengalis sensed the dissolution of the Constituent Assembly would aid their cause.

It was obvious that divisions in the ranks of the politicians played into the hands of the bureaucratic and military elites. Although Ghulam Mohammad would pass his mantle to Iskander Mirza in 1955 (illness being the principal cause), a pattern had been established. Mirza was an honorary Major General, a graduate of Sandhurst and an experienced administrator. Named Defense Secretary by Ghulam Mohammad, he eventually presided over the destiny of East Pakistan after the cancellation of the 1954 provincial elections. His dictatorial ways marked him as Ghulam Mohammad's successor. Similar to the former Governor-General, Iskander Mirza never participated in political party activities. He took no part in the Pakistan movement and looked contemptuously on all politicians. Mirza, however, had to accept the assembling of a Second Constituent Assembly. Although he would have preferred a system more in keeping with Pakistan's vice-regal or authoritarian tradition, he was compelled to approve a parliamentary constitution. This constitution was finally adopted and put into force on March 23, 1956. On that date Pakistan became a republic, and Mirza was the country's first president.

1956-1958. The destruction of the Muslim League in East Pakistan meant coalition politics were now unavoidable. Pakistan still had a multiparty system, but this was made far more chaotic by the elimination of the once dominant Muslim League. This too played into the hands of the bureaucrats and military. Political coalitions were not meant to succeed. Political opportunism was too much a part of the scenario and the issues between the parties, as between the regions, were becoming increasingly divisive. The emergence of the Republican Party in the west wing, which represented the powerful landlords and was supported by President Mirza, made it impossible for the Muslim League to play an effective role even in West Pakistan. In East Pakistan, the Awami League and Krishak Sramik Party could not sustain their United Front. A bitter feud raged between them. These East Pakistan parties consorted with either the Republicans or the Muslim League in West Pakistan, and the ever shifting configurations made a shambles of the orderly processes of government. When the National Awami Party was organized in 1957, more fuel was added to the flames as this leftist party played one coalition against the other. The result was a breakdown in party discipline, a succession of weak governments, and interminable bickering. During this period the country suffered severe economic dislocation, and even the bureaucracy could not perform its tasks without being burdened by political infighting.

When altercations broke out in the East Pakistan legislature and militant and/or separatist movements pressed their objectives in both regions of the country there seemed to be no alternative to a declaration of martial law and a general military takeover. It was under these circumstances that General Mohammad Ayub Khan, Commander-in-Chief of the

Pakistan army, asserted his authority. Under a proclamation of President Iskander Mirza issued on October 7, 1958, General Ayub Khan was made Chief Martial Law Administrator and the army was called upon to take control of the country. A constitution almost ten years in the making and in force for a short time was summarily abrogated. All the legislatures were closed and political parties banned. One parliamentary phase was over, and the presidential period was about to begin.

THE AYUB KHAN ERA

One man dominated the political scene in Pakistan from October, 1958, until March, 1969: Mohammad Ayub Khan. The first Pakistani Commander-in-Chief of the army was an important personality during the parliamentary period (1947-1958). Officially, his position was one of support of the parliamentary experiment. Nonetheless, he was often asked to put down domestic unrest, which the politicians had provoked but were unable to terminate. Given the army's role in maintaining domestic peace, Ayub eventually lost confidence in the politicians and soured on the parliamentary system. He did not object when Nazimuddin was illegally dismissed in 1953. Ayub assisted the governor-general in the dissolution of the First Constituent Assembly in 1954. He joined Ghulam Mohammad's "cabinet of talents" as Defense Minister and was soon writing memoranda calling for the improvement of the governmental process. Simultaneously, he did not ignore his work in building the Pakistani military establishment. Ayub's arrangements with the United States and the decision to join the Southeast Asia Treaty Organization (SEATO) in 1954, and later the Baghdad Pact in 1955 (to be renamed the Central Treaty Organization or CENTO), both occurred in the same period of time.

Ayub feared India and sought with the help of the United States to assemble an effective military organization of adequate size to defend Pakistan. Although the United States perceived international communism as the primary threat, the military assistance it gave to Pakistan could not be controlled. Although Pakistan considered India, not the Soviet Union or China, its principal foe, under Ayub Khan the country was still one of the largest recipients of United States military aid.

Ayub Khan's success in converting the Pakistan army into a modern force contrasts with his failure to reorganize the political system. Although Ayub Khan insisted he was democratically motivated, he became so contemptuous of politicians that his vision of a new political order ignored casting influential roles for them. Because he wielded significant powers as president and Chief Martial Law Administrator, Ayub was able to neutralize politicians challenging his authority.

Although the troops returned to the barracks soon after Ayub consolidated power, martial law remained in force for forty-four months, until
a new constitution was promulgated in March, 1962. During this period of
martial law, Ayub Khan ruled by personal fiat. Legislation came in the
form of executive ordinances, and the Pakistani bureaucracy was omnipresent. Although some bureaucrats were purged and others screened out,
demoted, or reprimanded for having been in league with the politicians,
the great majority escaped scrutiny. Ayub Khan depended on the career
bureaucrats and especially the elite service, known formally as the Civil
Service of Pakistan (CSP). The CSP were the legatees of the Indian Civil
Service (ICS), which had permitted Britain to rule their South Asian
subjects with minimum difficulty. Much of the arrogance and paternalism
of the ICS influenced the attitude of the CSP. In the absence of viable
political party activity, the CSP, along with the other services, performed
important political as well as administrative functions. Thus Ayub expected the services to execute his directives, and the bureaucrats in turn
accrued powers reminiscent of colonial authority.

Ayub Khan, as a career officer in the Pakistan army, was a product
of the civil-military bureaucracy. It was natural for him to trust his fellow
servicemen in the military and civilian branches. Unlike politicians, who
he perceived as excessively quarrelsome, he considered the administrators
as professionals dedicated to their special functions. Moreover, unlike the
politicians, the administrators were considered more patriotic, as well as
talented. The bureaucrats were better educated, modern, and more familiar with national problems. It is also true that members of the permanent
services, whether from the military or civil administration, could more
readily communicate with foreign governments and their advisors. Their
idiom very much resembled that used in the United States and Great
Britain, and this was of considerable importance in forming programs to
build the nation.

Ayub believed the politicians had wasted not only precious time but
also the country's meager resources. Foreign assistance could be maximized only when political constraints were lifted. Ayub ordered the Second Five Year Plan (1960-1965) executed with an emphasis on flexibility.
Furthermore, the administrators were given responsibility for encouraging
and directing the development of national infrastructure, industry, and the
raising of crop yields. Free enterprise was also given advantages it did not
enjoy in the parliamentary period.

Ayub had the more outspoken politicians disqualified from participating in any form of political activity. The Elective Bodies Disqualification Order (EBDO) isolated numerous dissidents. Although cries of dictatorship were often heard, they were not sufficient to gain widespread
support.

Basic Democracies

The generally passive reaction of the population to Ayub's strict control can be attributed to two major factors: (1) the maintenance of the rural power structure with traditional landlord-peasant relationships, and (2) the dominance of the bureaucracy. With a population 85 percent of whom live in villages and an illiteracy rate perhaps even higher; with per capita income among the lowest in the world; and with a peasantry exceptionally impoverished, malnourished, and subject to a variety of diseases, little political activity could be expected outside the urban centers.

The permanent services (the bureaucracy) policed the cities and towns, leaving Ayub free to launch a program envisaged to make the peasantry more productive, as well as to engender support for his regime among the masses. After approving land tenure reform in West Pakistan (East Pakistan experienced reform in 1950), Ayub announced his Basic Democracies scheme. Ayub said the Pakistani masses were ill-equipped for a sophisticated parliamentary system—clay in the hands of demagogic politicians. Basic Democracies (BD) was designed to promote a higher standard of living for the average villager. It was also slated to make the villager more conscious of local responsibilities. (See Figure 5-1.)

BDs put enormous stress on training and education through demonstration. A five-tiered arrangement in its original form, the very lowest tier of Union Councils (Union Committees in the cities) comprised persons directly elected by the populace. As initially conceived, a Union Council would have half of its membership appointed. This arrangement, however, was scrapped in 1962 in favor of all-elected Union Council bodies. The BD system not only represented a substitute for the parliamentary system, it also aimed at socializing the peasantry into a system controlled by the higher bureaucracy. The key to the BD system was the field administrator, and there was no mistaking the revitalization of a pre-independence colonial legacy in the form of district administration. The bureaucrats exerted influence on the Union Councils. Also their continued dominance of the tiers above, namely, the Tehsil/Thana (or sub-district), the District, and the Division, left their influence unimpaired. The fifth tier, or Provincial Council, was dissolved in 1962, with the coming into force of the Constitution.

The more educated city people looked upon the BD system with contempt. BDs were contrived to both deny them access to politics and to bring them more firmly under bureaucratic control. They believed the BD system did not promise rural development; rather, it was seen as a clever device to sustain a privileged semi-colonial system. Ayub disagreed with this appraisal, and he was even more determined to keep the city dissidents in check.

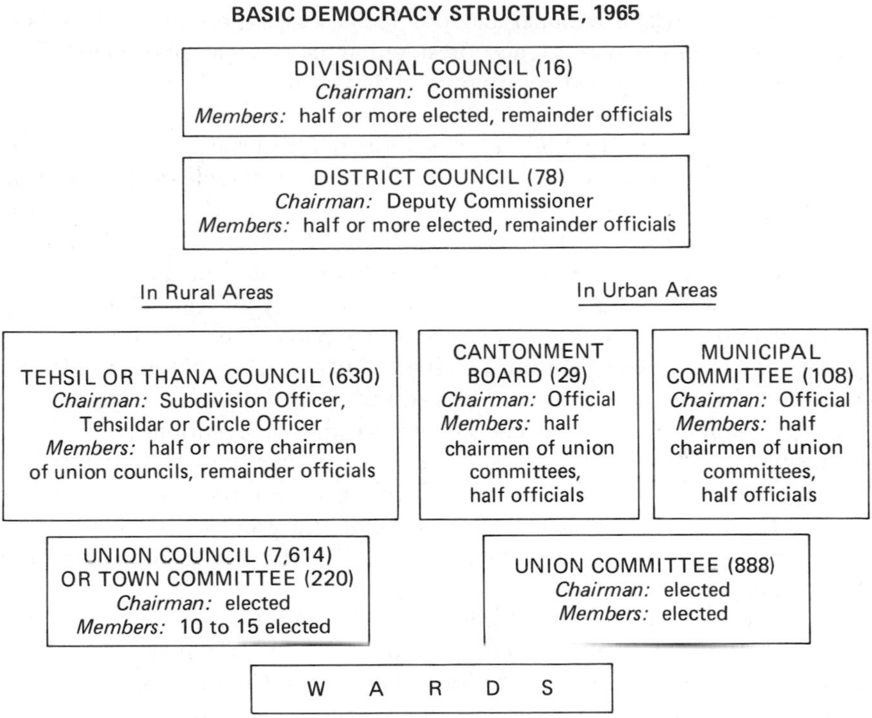

BASIC DEMOCRACY STRUCTURE, 1965

> **DIVISIONAL COUNCIL (16)**
> *Chairman:* Commissioner
> *Members:* half or more elected, remainder officials

> **DISTRICT COUNCIL (78)**
> *Chairman:* Deputy Commissioner
> *Members:* half or more elected, remainder officials

In Rural Areas   In Urban Areas

> **TEHSIL OR THANA COUNCIL (630)**
> *Chairman:* Subdivision Officer,
> Tehsildar or Circle Officer
> *Members:* half or more chairmen
> of union councils, remainder officials

> **CANTONMENT BOARD (29)**
> *Chairman:* Official
> *Members:* half
> chairmen of union
> committees,
> half officials

> **MUNICIPAL COMMITTEE (108)**
> *Chairman:* Official
> *Members:* half
> chairmen of union
> committees,
> half officials

> **UNION COUNCIL (7,614) OR TOWN COMMITTEE (220)**
> *Chairman:* elected
> *Members:* 10 to 15 elected

> **UNION COMMITTEE (888)**
> *Chairman:* elected
> *Members:* elected

> W   A   R   D   S

Note: The municipal corporations of Karachi and Lahore are also represented
        at the divisional level and are administratively subordinate to the
        West Pakistan Department of Basic Democracies and Local Government.
        These two corporations have component union committees.

FIGURE 5-1
Basic Democracy Structure for Pakistan, 1965
Source: Guthrie Birkhead, ed., *Administration Problems in Pakistan* (Syracuse: Syracuse University Press, 1966), p. 32.

Political Dynamics
in the Administrative State

Ayub's administration emphasized the sustaining of traditional coalitions in Pakistan. Ayub, like his predecessors looked to the army, the bureaucracy, the landed interests, and a small but growing entrepreneurial elite. Arrayed against him but remaining disorganized, were politicians, the professional intelligentsia (lawyers, journalists, literati, teachers), lower middle-class propertied and labor interests, members of the ulema (leaders in the religious community), and the nation's educated youth. When Ayub gave the country a new constitution in 1962, he explained that his aim was stability and national unity. The Constitution described a presidential-type system in which national and provincial legislatures would be subordinate to executive will. Hence presidential power was maximized. The legislatures were required to approve actions already taken by the executive.

Ayub had no intention of reinstating political parties. But with the reconstituting of the assemblies in 1962, pressure to release the political organizations was unrelenting. Ayub succumbed, and the ban on the parties was lifted, albeit with many of the pre-1958 luminaries silenced by the disqualification order (EBDO). Ayub later wanted his majority in the legislatures (the legislators were elected indirectly by the 80,000 Union Council Basic Democrats) to organize along party lines. Ayub named his party after the defunct Muslim League, which angered old guard Muslim Leaguers. In response, they too revived the Muslim League name. Hence, the government party became known as the Conventionists, and the opposition Muslim League took the name of Councillors. Although Ayub's Conventionist Muslim League never developed the sophistication expected of a dominant political party, the power of the groups supporting Ayub Khan made it unbeatable when compared with the demoralized and feuding opposition parties.

Moreover, the indirect elections, which Ayub established for electing the president and members of the national and provincial assemblies, tended to neutralize opposition efforts. The Union Councillors in the Basic Democracies system formed an electoral college, and the voting population had no say in the election of the president or parliamentarians. To summarize, the population elected only those who served on the Union Councils in the BD system. The 80,000 elected BDs (40,000 from each wing of the country) sat as an electoral college. This electoral college cast ballots for the president every five years and in subsequent elections for the members of the assemblies.

The opposition political parties, representing the more politically conscious urban population, opposed the BD system, the indirect election, and the devices used to arrive at decisions. Given an opportunity, they would have scrapped the BDs and returned the country to the parliamentary system and direct adult suffrage. Moreover, the nation had been promised, but had never experienced, national elections. The opposition also had difficulty in wooing the Basic Democrats, given their continuing demand that the Basic Democracies system be dissolved.

The Basic Democracies Election: 1964-1965

The 1964 election for the Basic Democracies was greeted with considerably more enthusiasm than had been the case in the initial campaign in 1959. In the five years that had passed the Basic Democrats acquired a degree of acceptance, if not legitimacy. A Rural Works Program had been introduced on a national basis in 1963, and the Basic Democrats were given some responsibility in the utilization of development funds at local levels. Moreover, the role the Basic Democrats played as an electoral college could not be ignored. Although the political parties could not directly identify with BD candidates, there was much jockeying for position after the winners were announced. The parties were more interested in influencing the decisions of the electoral college than in the election of the BDs. The second generation of Basic Democrats represented a different cross-section of the population than that of the earlier body. More landlords, retired civil and military officers, professional and commercial interests, as well as some politicians competed in the elections. Clearly the new Basic Democrats were better educated and more prosperous than their predecessors.

When the election was held for president in January, 1965, and the assemblies later that year, the changing character of the BDs was evident. Ayub won re-election, and his party dominated the national and provincial legislatures, but the opposition made a formidable showing. The opposition parties coalesced long enough to form the Combined Opposition Party (COP) and selected Fatima Jinnah, the sister of Mohammad Ali Jinnah, as their candidate. Miss Jinnah ran a strong campaign, and on the eve of the ballotting there was a possibility she might defeat President Ayub Khan. When the results were tabulated, however, Ayub emerged the victor. His success was not overwhelming. Miss Jinnah and the COP carried the principal cities in both East and West Pakistan, namely Karachi and Dacca. Ayub won by only a slight margin in the east wing. The scales apparently were tipped in the government's favor in the rural areas. Ayub carried rural East Pakistan and was an outstanding success in rural West Pakistan. The rural power structure, the bureaucratic system, and traditional voting patterns were clearly instrumental in his re-election. Although the opposition accused the bureaucrats of exerting undue pressure on helpless rural-based Basic Democrats, Ayub was unassailable.

Ayub Khan's Second Term

The spring of 1965 was the highwater mark for the Ayub administration. Ayub Khan had promised stability, and it had been achieved. He had pledged a new constitution, and it was put into force. He had sought to induct the rural community into nation-building activities, and Basic Democracies and the Rural Works Program were operative. He had encouraged industrial growth, and statistical progress was remarkable. The Second Five Year Plan (1960-1965) drew to a close at this time, and foreign advisors assisting the Planning Commission were ecstatic about its success. Pakistan was heralded as a model of how best to use foreign assistance. But nowhere in these successes was there credit for the politicians. The work had been carried on by civil servants and influential entrepreneurs. In the countryside, tubewell (power driven water pump) construction in West Pakistan signalled a new emphasis on high-yield farming techniques. Nor could anyone ignore the infusion of large sums of economic and technical assistance from the United States.

The United States funded the Rural Works Program. It was heavily involved in building hydroelectric and flood control installations, as well as combatting water-logging and salinity. It was difficult to find a project that did not bear a United States aid stamp. Education, medicine, journalism, agriculture, population control, not to mention military assistance programs were ubiquitous United States activities. United States presence was a burden as well as an asset for Ayub Khan, however.

As a member of both the SEATO and CENTO alliances, Pakistan not only acquired military hardware, it also hoped to draw the United States and other alliance partners into its problem with India. Pakistan believed that India posed a threat to its existence. Of immediate importance to Pakistanis, especially those in West Pakistan, was the question of Kashmir, and India's insistence that the mountain state was an integral part of the Indian union. There was no escaping the conclusion that Pakistan perceived India its chief enemy. It joined the western alliances not so much to defend itself against the spread of international communism (Pakistan recognized Communist China in 1950 and high level visits were exchanged as early as 1956-1957), but to develop a modern army for possible use against its South Asian neighbor. Pakistan had no quarrels with the Soviet Union, and early in the Ayub administration opened up economic and cultural avenues with that nation. It also demarcated the frontiers with China in 1963, and opened an international air link between major Chinese cities. But India was another matter.

Relations With India: Domestic Impact

Pakistan and India had waged war from the first year of Pakistan's independent existence. Kashmir was the primary battleground. When the United Nations arranged a ceasefire in January, 1949, there still was no resolution of their disputes. India earlier absorbed Hyderabad and Junagadh and removed their Muslim rulers. India argued that the regions in question were Hindu-dominant and that their populations wanted to join the Indian union. When Pakistan chose to use the Indian argument in Kashmir where a Hindu maharaja ruled over a Muslim population, India ignored the similarities and stressed the nation's secular ideology. But arguments aside, Pakistan simply did not have the capability to wrest Kashmir from Indian control. As Pakistani frustrations mounted, hatred for India intensified.

The Pakistanis believed India was bent on occupying the Pakistan state. Tensions periodically led to the assembling of troops, but there was no significant clash until the mid-1960s. Skirmishes on the frontiers became frequent as did claims and counterclaims regarding the treatment of minority groups in the respective countries. Both countries belonged to the Commonwealth of Nations and maintained diplomatic relations, but few peaceful exchanges between the two countries occurred. Suspicions were therefore heightened. In such an atmosphere the politicians could easily exploit the bitterness existing between the two peoples.

Pakistan's political opposition sensed new opportunities to press their attack when relations between India and China became strained. Neither the United Nations nor the United States or its alliance partners could put Pakistan one inch closer to success in Kashmir. When India faced Chinese penetration of territory over which it claimed sovereignty, Ayub Khan suggested joint defense of the subcontinent. The offer was rejected by Prime Minister Nehru, who believed acceptance of Pakistani assistance would necessitate a settlement with Pakistan. It would certainly mean the introduction of Pakistani troops in areas long held by India. Given the Indian position, it is curious Ayub Khan should restrain his armies when India found itself humbled by the Chinese Communists who pushed their way into India's northeast frontier, as well as the Ladakh area north of Kashmir in 1962. Ayub's inaction antagonized many in West Pakistan who accused him of being restrained by the United States. Kashmir was for the taking given India's predicament, but Ayub did not act.

Moreover, discontent became more pronounced when the United States aided the Indian army, which suffered a humiliating defeat at the hands of the Chinese. Pakistanis demonstrated considerable anger, and Ayub Khan obviously was embarrassed by the United States gesture of support to India. Ayub was forced to publicly declare that the arms the United States gave India would never be used against the Chinese but definitely would be turned on Pakistan. The clash with the United States came at a most unpropitious moment for the Ayub Khan administration. A few months earlier, the country had been given a new constitution, martial law was officially lifted, and political parties had been reinstated. The politicians wasted no time in condemning the President's action, and Ayub's system came under new criticism. The more sophisticated sections of the country supported the opposition.

Thus Ayub's reluctance to take advantage of India and the subsequent shipment of United States military paraphernalia to India complicated Ayub's tasks. Instead of receiving grudging acceptance for his new "democratic" order, the opposition politicians chose to exploit this opportunity to weaken Ayub's grip on the nation.

The 1965 election of the President has been cited, and the results show how Ayub failed, despite economic gains, to win the cities. Statistically, the economic development during the Ayub Khan era is significant. Industrial development cannot be obscured. West Pakistanis were being drawn from the countryside toward the cities where jobs were opening in the new factories. But the cities also housed an intelligentsia that could not be placated. It was they who sought to stir popular emotions against the Ayub Khan administration. In an attempt to neutralize this attack, members of Ayub's government spoke out against Indian cunning and United States duplicity. Leading the charge against the United States from within the government was the Foreign Minister, Zulfikar Ali Bhutto. He threatened to remove Pakistan from its western alliances (he later was to declare Pakistan would leave the United Nations if Pakistan's interests were not served in Kashmir) and announced that Pakistan would "free" the Kashmiris after the 1965 elections took place.

In the spring of 1965, Pakistani and Indian armies fought a short but violent battle in a region to the east of Karachi called the Rann of Kutch. A marshland, the territory is virtually uninhabited, and the border between the two countries is ill-defined. The Pakistanis got the better of their Indian counterparts, and although the dispute over who controlled the Rann of Kutch was passed to an arbitration panel in Geneva, the clash convinced the Pakistan government and army that it might launch a more elaborate assault in Kashmir.

The Indo-Pakistan War of 1965

In August, 1965, sporadic fighting broke out in Kashmir. The Pakistanis insisted the struggle was indigenous, claiming the Kashmiris wanted their freedom and had resorted to arms when negotiations proved fruitless. The Indians, however, gave another account. They contended Pakistan was directly involved in not only training and equipping the Kashmiri Liberation Front, but that regular members of the Pakistan army led the insurrection. When India brought heavy weapons into the struggle and deployed its aircraft, Pakistan quickly matched the effort. Logistically, the Pakistanis had the advantage, and the Indian forces were hard-pressed to maintain their positions. It was feared a Pakistani thrust could cut India's land supply route into Kashmir, hence more drastic action was required.

Indian actions in early September surprised the Pakistanis. India sought to draw Pakistani forces away from the Kashmir front by assaulting West Pakistan proper, putting maximum pressure on the Punjab in the areas around Sialkot and Lahore. The Indian air force flew raids into the Pakistani interior striking at Peshawar, Rawalpindi, and near Karachi. The Indians threatened East Pakistan. Limited air attacks frightened the people of East Pakistan, who realized they did not have the force to repel a concerted Indian drive. The Pakistan army's inability to assist East Pakistan in the ensuing circumstances left an indelible impression on the Bengali population.

The Indian strategy was successful. Although no decisive battles were fought, the war was over almost before it had started. Pakistan forces were withdrawn from Kashmir and put into a defense of West Pakistan. Moreover, Pakistani military stores were consumed at an accelerated rate on the plains around Sialkot and Lahore and could not be replaced. Although the Chinese Communists threatened India with an invasion a few days after the attack on West Pakistan, Pakistan was in no position to continue the fight. India's superior numbers and larger quantities of weapons would eventually give it the advantage. Although the determination in West Pakistan was to fight on, regardless of the odds, Ayub Khan could see no logic in such an exercise.

Pakistan had too much to lose. Even if China was taken seriously in its ultimatum to India, Ayub did not want Chinese presence in South Asia. Hence Ayub's decision was to accept the United Nations' resolution calling for a cease-fire. The decision was extremely unpopular in West Pakistan, especially among those considered pillars of Ayub's support, the army and the bureaucracy. The demonstrations that preceded and followed Ayub's decision involved the country's youth, and they became extremely violent.

The United Nations, however, was in no position to satisfy Pakistani aspirations. Despite the pleadings of Foreign Minister Bhutto, the world organization only insisted that the two countries agree to the *status quo ante*. The opposing armies faced one another and each occupied some minor territory on the Punjab frontier. The U.N. peace observation team worked to restore the pre-September border. The hatred exhibited by each side led to intermittent engagements. Some believed, especially in West Pakistan, that the hostilities would resume after the breakdown of U.N. deliberations.

The United States placed an embargo on arms to both India and Pakistan and the restriction fell particularly hard on the latter country. Even the effort to secure arms from Turkey and Iran, sister CENTO and Muslim states, could not satisfy Pakistani requirements. Moreover, United States pressure was brought to bear on those countries not to transfer arms to Pakistan. Under the circumstances it is not surprising that Pakistan looked to China for help. The Soviet Union had been a principal supplier of weapons to India, and they continued to do so despite the ceasefire. Furthermore, India had a sizeable industrial base for the manufacture of sophisticated weapons, aircraft, and trucks. Therefore, India did not face the dilemma that confronted Pakistan. China seemed to offer the only option, and while it might meet Pakistan's long range needs, there was no escaping the present emergency situation. The delivery of aged MIG aircraft, tanks, and assorted vehicles helped to cement relations between the two countries.

The United States, which had seen its image in Pakistan altered from that of supreme savior in the mid-1950s to despised exploiter in the mid-1960s, became a weighty burden for Ayub Khan. It was also at this point that members of the military wondered if Ayub Khan had outlived his utility. The answer to their musings was not long in coming. Ayub wanted to normalize relations with India and put the country back on the road of development. The elections of 1964-1965 followed by the war took their toll of Pakistani resources. In order to again stress development and return to the Third Five Year Plan (1965-1970) meant seeking United States support. But Pakistan was increasingly anti-American. The United States had reached a high point of involvement in Vietnam, and its interest in Pakistan slackened appreciably. The United States was in a poor position from which to mediate the dispute between India and Pakistan. Hence diplomatic initiative was left to the Soviet Union.

The Tashkent Affair

Ayub Khan at first rejected a Soviet offer to negotiate, but sensing no other viable alternative he agreed to travel to Tashkent in Soviet Central Asia. Prime Minister Shastri who succeeded to the helm of the Indian government on the death of Jawaharlal Nehru in 1964, and who piloted the country through the war with Pakistan, also accepted the invitation. In January, 1966, the two leaders, under Soviet guidance, met to discuss their differences. It was a *coup* for the Soviet Union and illustrated the success of Soviet diplomacy in South Asia. The fact that the United States enthusiastically greeted the Soviet initiative is informative. But if the United States and the Soviet Union wanted the restoration of peace in the subcontinent, their desires were quite different from those of the Pakistanis. The West Pakistanis did not want the talks to succeed. No one in Pakistan believed that Kashmir would be granted independence at Tashkent, and it was expected Ayub would come away from the conference with ample justification for renewing the hostilities. Pakistan had time to regroup its forces, arms had been acquired from China and Iran, new infantry units had been formed and quickly trained, and the belief persisted that in a new struggle, China could be depended upon to draw away significant segments of the Indian army.

As the negotiations dragged on without an agenda being agreed upon, the talks appeared bankrupt, and Ayub was expected to return immediately. But with dramatic suddenness word spread that Ayub Khan and Lal Bahadur Shastri had signed a document drafted by the Soviet

Union calling upon the two countries to withdraw their forces from the seized territory and restore normal relations. When this news reached West Pakistan it was greeted with stunned disbelief. Demonstrations protesting the Tashkent Declaration ensued. Ayub Khan now had to cope with the formal opposition and his disenchanted government, as well.

Zulfikar Ali Bhutto, who was present at Tashkent, symbolized the dissatisfaction within Ayub's Cabinet. Bhutto wanted to seek larger Chinese support and to sever Pakistan's links with SEATO and CENTO. For Bhutto, the United States was no longer a useful partner. Bhutto wanted Pakistan to woo China in order to balance the Soviet Union's support of India. Only then could Pakistan hope to gain advantage over its neighbor. But Bhutto's thinking also involved a program to transform Pakistan into a socialist state, albeit with Islamic overtones. When the Foreign Minister indicated a desire to resign from Ayub's Cabinet, the President at first refused to consider it but later acquiesced. Once out of government office, Bhutto began a verbal assault upon his once respected leader.

With Ayub on the defensive in West Pakistan, the East Pakistanis, under the leadership of Sheikh Mujibur Rahman of the Awami League, renewed the old issue of East Pakistan autonomy. At a meeting of opposition parties convened in Lahore in February, 1966, for the purpose of denouncing the Tashkent Declaration, Mujibur Rahman presented his Six Point Manifesto for East Pakistani autonomy. Mujib was less interested in Tashkent and the Kashmir issue than those who had organized the session. The latter did not greet Mujib's demands with acceptance. Thus what was to be a unity conference quickly fell apart, and Mujib's party, the only East Pakistani contingent at the session, walked out.

West Pakistani opposition did not give up the struggle against Ayub. They tried to exploit the Tashkent issue, and the government, under the Defense of Pakistan Rules that allowed for preventive detention, moved to imprison them. Given their divided circumstances, the Ayub administration had no difficulty in controlling the politicians, but the President's legitimacy had not been improved.

Ayub's Demise

With the West Pakistani opposition either in prison or disorganized, the government turned its attention to East Pakistan. Mujib was seized and imprisoned for advocating his Six Point Program. Some in the Ayub administration feared the program would precipitate a secessionist movement. Under the Six Points, only defense and foreign affairs remained central issues. In all other matters the Bengalis were to determine their own policies and future. Vested interests in West Pakistan sensed the liquidation of their assets, and pressure was brought against the government to take preventive action. Ultimately, Ayub Khan was compelled to declare that civil war could not be ruled out, but that he was determined to avoid such a calamity. In December, 1967, several months after Mujib's imprisonment, the government publicized what became known as the Agartala Conspiracy. An official spokesman announced a plot had been uncovered that aimed at the secession of East Pakistan with the connivance of the Indian government. Mujib was identified as the culprit in this intrigue.

Simultaneously, Ayub was struck down by viral pneumonia, and for several weeks his life hung in the balance. Although seriously weakened by the ailment (rumors circulated that he would soon resign), Ayub resumed his duties ten weeks later. During that summer the Agartala Conspiracy trial began. Manzur Qadir, often credited with writing the 1962 Ayub Constitution and one of Pakistan's leading lawyers, pleaded the case for the government. The government's case was less than convincing. And although the allegations were dramatic, the evidence was flimsy.

As the trial dragged on, the government staged an elaborate celebration to publicize the Decade of Development, 1958-1968. The government could certainly claim substantial material progress in the ten years since Ayub seized power, but Pakistani society had accrued few benefits. The government's expensive publicity campaign was not only in poor taste, it angered an already embittered population. Riots broke out throughout the length of West Pakistan. The disturbances were clearly a protest against the government's attempt to flatter itself.

Ayub Khan became the principal target of the demonstrators. Years of martial law, the atrophy of political institutions, a semi-muzzled press, educational grievances, a self-serving entrepreneurial elite, rising inflation and static wages, the misadventure in Kashmir, and continued dependence on the United States all found violent expression on the tenth anniversary of Ayub's rise to power. West Pakistani cities and towns erupted as first students, and then other segments of the population, took to the streets. Zulfikar Ali Bhutto became the leader of a new political organization called the Pakistan Peoples Party (PPP), which called for an end to the Ayub system. Other politicians followed, but it was Bhutto who stood out most prominently.

The government tried to quell the protestors, but wide-spread rioting was inevitable. Scores of deaths occurred, and the principal politicians were seized and imprisoned in an effort to end the turbulence. But mayhem continued. It now spread to East Pakistan where Sheikh Mujibur Rahman's Six Points became a feature issue. Given the difficulties of law enforcement, government functionaries began to question their role. Doubts concerning Ayub Khan's capacity to rule overtook the higher echelons, and these soon filtered down among line personnel. The death of youthful martyrs and the imprisonment of unrepentent political leaders shook the confidence of a growing number of civil and military officials. Demands publicizing the scrapping of the Basic Democracies, the re-establishment of a parliamentary system, and a more equitable distribution of wealth impressed senior and junior officers alike.

Actions in West Pakistan sought the termination of Ayub Khan's administration. Once the President was removed, events were expected to take a productive course. This naivete was not echoed in East Pakistan, however. There, Ayub Khan was merely a means to an end. What the Bengalis wanted was an end to West Pakistani dominance. Although the demonstrations in East and West Pakistan were linked, it was the East Pakistanis who sought a new political design for Pakistan. Moveover, the West Pakistani rejection of Mujib's Six Points suggested more was at stake than the status and reputation of Ayub Khan. But this was obscured by the immediacy of events.

Ayub's administration displayed a reluctance to act, and an inability to quell the demonstrations. The President was therefore forced to retreat. He offered to redress educational grievances. He lifted the Defense of Pakistan Rules and released politicians, such as Bhutto, from prison. He terminated the Agartala Conspiracy trial and exonerated Mujibur Rahman from wrongdoings. Finally, he invited political party leaders to meet in Rawalpindi to thrash out their differences. When the politicians balked at this invitation (Bhutto and Mujib insisting that Ayub maintained a capacity for intrigue), Ayub declared he would not stand for re-election and intended leaving office in January, 1970. After this announcement the opposition agreed to meet with Ayub, but Bhutto still refused to attend. During the meeting Ayub revealed he would permit the Constitution to be modified, and he said he would not stand in the way of the reinstatement of the parliamentary institution. At the same time Ayub was cognizant of Bhutto's and Mujib's radical demands and that this offer would not satisfy them. Ayub's gesture was too little and too late.

The intensification of the disturbances in East Pakistan revealed that no amount of political reform, short of the full implementation of Mujib's Six Points, would bring an end to the turbulence. Thus on March 25, 1969, Ayub Khan asked the army to restore tranquility to Pakistan. Ayub Khan announced he was resigning from the presidency and that the Commander-in-Chief of the army, General Agha Mohammad Yahya Khan, would replace him and reimpose martial law on the country. In his last official address to the nation, Ayub explained he had labored to satisfy the demands of the political community but had failed to achieve a consensus. For him, no alternative remained but to permit the army to restore order.

March 1969 was a repeat of October 1958. As in the latter case, the Constitution was abrogated, the legislatures closed, and all political parties banned. General Yahya Khan announced his first task was the establishment of "sanity" in the country. Achieving this goal he would give new thought to the goals of Pakistani society. For the time being, however, the full force of martial law would be employed, and the country would be given an opportunity to ponder its condition. With Ayub no longer a target for their discontent, and with the army determined to create a new equilibrium, the rioting subsided. All eyes and ears were now directed at Yahya Khan who indicated he would transfer authority to responsible civilian leaders at an appropriate moment.

Yahya Khan Takes Over

General Yahya Khan inherited the dilemmas of his predecessors. Although he pledged to restore democratic and civilian government, he was a prisoner of Pakistan's past. Twenty-two years of independence had failed to alter the pattern established by the British. Colonial administration, not political representation prevailed. Pakistan was an administrative state after Liaquat Ali Khan's assassination in 1951. Ghulam Mohammad's rule demonstrated this fact. Pakistan continued as a civil and military administrative state under Iskander Mirza between 1955 and 1958, despite the drafting and promulgation of a parliamentary constitution. After 1958, and throughout the Ayub decade, the decision-making apparatus was the virtual monopoly of the bureaucrats. The 1962 presidential constitution actually reinforced their status. In 1969, when Ayub could no longer officiate, Yahya Khan assumed the executive function.

Martial law had been imposed so often that it could be judged the normal functioning of the administrative state under crisis conditions. Constitutions were flagrantly disregarded and unceremoniously discarded. The legal instruments in force protected members of the permanent services and higher bureaucracy, not the politicians. The status and privilege of the former group were safeguarded by statute and custom developed in the pre-independence era, and this explains much about the condition of government and politics in Pakistan.

The vice-regal tradition is significant. It might be stretching the historical record to look for an explanation of the vice-regal tradition in Islamic culture, particularly in the institution of the Caliphate. But Pakistanis consider themselves members of an Islamic state, no matter how incipient, and the place of the *Great Leader* cannot be ignored. Of no less importance is the blending of the British experience in South Asia with that of Muslim tradition. The office and person of the viceroy, the maximum ruler, blend with Muslim tradition, particularly in its monarchial form as experienced under the Moghuls. Nor can the agencies of executive authority be discounted in this picture. The executive's administrative and

military arms are conditioned and trained to display allegiance to personalities, not constitutions. Constitutions imply limitations on the uses of
power, particularly arbitrary power. The vice-regal tradition and the administrative state obviates development of a popularly based political
system. Hence the declaration of Yahya Khan that he would restore
constitutionalism to Pakistan must be seen against a background of political impotence and administrative dominance. Pakistanis are disposed to
talk about democracy and its restoration. But realistically, there is little in
the historic record to suggest they can live with it. General Yahya Khan's
insistence that he wanted no part of politics and would return the government to the people at the earliest moment may be taken as sincere, but it
was also misleading.

Yahya, as Ayub had done earlier, publicized the purging of corrupt
officials. The Pay and Services Commission Report of 1962, which called
for an integrated civil service, had never been released. It was now given
to the newspapers. A new commission was assigned the task of scrutinizing
the activities of the privileged bureaucrats. The old provinces of Sind,
Baluchistan, Punjab, and the North West Frontier amalgamated into the
One Unit in 1955, were reconstituted under pressure from the local
politicians. The parliamentary system was accepted in principle, and a
new constitution was promised. Anti-monopoly ordinances were issued in
order to limit or control the holdings of the large entrepreneurial and
industrial families who dominated the country's economy. East Pakistan
was promised a significant portion of development revenues and a larger
voice in political decision-making. Pakistan's first general elections were
scheduled for 1970, and the entire adult population would have an opportunity to register their preference for candidates in national and provincial
assemblies.

THE SIX POINT PROGRAM
AND THE EAST PAKISTAN DILEMMA

The Bengalis did not trust Yahya Khan. Too many past pledges had been
broken for the East Pakistanis to be mollified by the new martial law
authorities. Sensing that it was their movement that forced Ayub Khan
from power, the Bengalis with their chief spokesman, the Awami League
member Sheikh Mujibur Rahman articulating their aspirations, pressed for
the acceptance of the Six Points Program. Those points were outlined as
follows:

  1. Pakistan should be a federation under the Pakistan or Lahore Resolution
      of 1940, which implied the existence of two similar entities. Any new
      constitution according to the Bengalis had to reflect this reality.

2. The federal government should deal solely with defense and foreign affairs.

3. There should be two separate but freely convertible currencies. East Pakistan would have a separate banking reserve as well as separate fiscal and monetary policies.

4. The federated units would have the sole power to tax. The central government should be granted funds to meet its expenditures.

5. Separate accounts from foreign exchange earnings would be maintained. The federating units would be free to establish trade links with foreign countries.

6. East Pakistan would have a separate militia.

These were the same Six Points that Ayub had rejected, and now Yahya Khan was forced to come to grips with them. Since Ayub's fall from power, Bengali ranks closed rapidly. The East Pakistanis called for not a federation, but the loosest form of confederation. Even the suggestion that foreign affairs remain in the central government was dubious given the demand that East Pakistan should enter into trade relations with foreign countries and maintain separate accounts. Where defense was concerned, it is difficult to imagine how the central government could provide for a common defense if it was absolutely dependent on the federated units for its operating currency.

Clearly the Six Points, as interpreted by the Yahya Khan government, was nothing less than a subtle form of secession. Still, the government did not confront Mujib, as had Ayub Khan, with an ultimatum. The government did not wish to add to Mujib's popularity, and they refused to silence him. Also, the government realized that the Bengali autonomy movement, though widespread, was also desperately in need of leadership. The decision in 1970, therefore, was to proceed with caution in East Pakistan.

Yahya Khan promised general elections and machinery was set up to make good the pledge. Reviewing previous political activities, Yahya and his advisors believed that there would be so many parties contesting the election that no single organization would emerge with dominant support. Moreover, when coalitions are necessary, it is mandatory for individual political parties to modify their programs. Coalitions are tenous alliances at best. Hence, there was a continuing dependence on the permanent services. And it was obvious that the Pakistan bureaucracy, although somewhat demoralized, would remain intact. The Third Five Year Plan (1965-1970) was something less than a total success, and the government was eager to push on with the fourth plan (1970-1975), which envisaged a 6.5 percent growth target. In this work the bureaucracy played a major role. Nonetheless, the government had the following to say about future development:

In reviewing the actual progress made and the causes of discontent, it is important to remember that economic development is a long and arduous process under *any system* and that we as a nation are too poor to satisfy people's aspirations in the immediate future. It will perhaps be necessary to satisfy the people not only through economic reward and a rapidly improving standard of living, *but also by non-material motivation and by participation in the political process.*[3] *(italics added)*

A broader sharing of political power was in the offering, but the bureaucracy still commanded the larger share.

As preparations got underway to hold elections and revitalize the nation's economic life, a disaster of unprecedented proportions struck East Pakistan. On November 12, 1970, a tidal wave more than thirty feet high and lashed by cyclonic winds of 120 miles per hour blasted five of East Pakistan's coastal districts. It was called the worst natural catastrophe in modern history. Estimates put the death toll above one million, and total property damage affected the region. There was an immediate need for all forms of assistance, and the Bengalis turned to their leaders in West Pakistan. But the Pakistan government was slow to react, or so it appeared. Yahya Khan did not visit East Pakistan or the devastated areas for some days after the calamity. By that time, international relief activities were underway, and reports filtering out of the country contrasted this help with the apparent indifference of Pakistani officialdom. The Bengalis were convinced that their countrymen in the western sector cared little for their well-being, and their bitterness waxed into outspoken hatred.

The Yahya Khan government faced yet another unexpected challenge. Large numbers of Pakistanis were in need of food, shelter, and medical aid. Resources were in short supply. Pakistan is among the poorest of countries, and the government was faced with the agonizing dilemma of reserving national treasure for development projects, or making funds and facilities available for relief purposes. It seems fair to suggest that the government took a middle ground position. A sum of money was earmarked for sustenance and rehabilitation, but an all-out effort was rejected. To the Bengalis the proffered assistance was meaningless. They believed it was aimed at relieving international pressure, not the destitute survivors. Sheikh Mujibur Rahman's Six Point Program was now an even more credible demand, and the Awami League emerged as the beneficiary of an otherwise indescribable human tragedy.

Yahya Khan originally slated October, 1970, for general elections, but the annual summer flooding had been so severe in East Pakistan that the date was changed to December. Now, in the aftermath of the Novem-

---

[3]Government of Pakistan, *Pakistan's Third Five Year Plan, 1965-1970*, Interim Report Series, Vol. XI, No. 5 (May, 1970), p. 3.

ber cyclone and tidal wave, it was suggested they should be postponed again. The Yahya Khan government desired such a postponement, as the time was hardly propitious for holding elections. The government wanted Mujib to dilute his Six Points. But under the circumstances, the Awami League's position could scarcely have been stronger, and to postpone the elections again would run the risk of precipitating a violent reaction, which the government wished to avoid. The decision was to proceed with the elections.

Yahya Khan gambled that the elections would take some heat out of the tense situation prevailing in East Pakistan. He insisted that the elections were essentially a means for assembling those persons who would be charged with the drafting of the new constitution. Yahya was also emphatic in declaring that such an assembly would have to follow the general guidelines laid down by the martial law authorities, and the delegates would have 120 days to complete their work. Given failure to write a constitution in this period, President Yahya Khan warned he would dissolve the body and call another election. Hence, Yahya felt the deliberations of the assembly could be controlled. Consensus would be achieved, or there would be no constitution. In any consensus the Six Point Program would have to be modified. Thus Yahya Khan's decision was to proceed with the election despite the trouble in East Pakistan.

The general election, the first in Pakistan's twenty-three year history, commenced on December 7, 1970. Approximately fifty-six million people cast ballots for the National Assembly in a peaceful and orderly atmosphere. The ritual was repeated again on December 17, for the legislative assemblies of East Pakistan, Sind, Baluchistan, the Punjab, and the North West Frontier Province.

POLITICAL PARTIES AND IDEOLOGY

The number of parties contesting the election demonstrated the divisions in Pakistani society. There were nine political parties of note and many lesser congeries. Listed below are the principal parties and their positions on the more prominent issues:

Party	Support	Program
1. Awami League (Sheikh Mujibur Rahman)	All sectors in East Pakistan	Bengali autonomy. Separate economy. Prefers withdrawal from CENTO and SEATO.

Party	Support	Program
2. Council Muslim League (Mumtaz Daultana)	Landlord and industrial class of Punjab. Some upper-class Sindhi support.	Strong center. Opposed dissolution of One Unit of West Pakistan. Capitalist-inclined. Somewhat pro-West.
3. Qaid-i-Azam Muslim League (Qayyum Khan)	Upper-classes of North West Frontier Province. Some support in Punjab and Sind.	Strong center. Capitalist. Pro-West. Lip service to Muslim solidarity.
4. National Awami Party (West Pakistan) (Wali Khan)	Tribal chiefs of NWFP and Baluchistan. Some lower middle-class following in Karachi.	Most ardent supporter of break-up of One Unit. Supports Awami League's Six Points. Pro-Moscow foreign policy.
5. Sind United Front (G. M. Syed)	Cross-section of Sind population. Emphasis on landlords and intelligentsia.	Sind for the Sindhis. Supports other provincial movements. No foreign policy.
6. Pakistan Democratic Party (Nurul Amin, Nasrullah Khan)	A congeries of dissatisfied personalities from East and West Pakistan. No particular support.	No program. Respects private enterprise.
7. Pakistan People's Party (Zulfikar Ali Bhutto)	Nationalist industrialists. Left-leaning youth in West Pakistan. Workers and peasants and some landlords in Sind and Punjab.	Hesitant support of breakup of One Unit. Ambiguous on matter of Six Points. Socialism but also supports private ownership of industry. Anti-West, decidedly anti-Indian.
8. National Awami Party (East Pakistan) (Maulana Bhashani challenged by Toha-Abdul Huq group)	East Pakistan peasantry. Some members of intelligentsia and labor.	End to One Unit. East Pakistan autonomy. Radical social change. Anti-West. Some-

Party	Support	Program
		times identified as substitute for Pakistan Communist Party banned in 1955.
9. Jamaat-i-Islami (Maulana Maudoodi)	Religious and lower middle-class elements in urban areas of West Pakistan. Some land-lord support in Punjab.	Supports One Unit in West Pakistan and opposes autonomy for East Pakistan. Basic-ally supports private property. Opposes Sino-Pakistan cooper-ation. Pro-West and wants close affiliation with Saudi Arabia. Chief supporters of Islamic state.

The most obvious characteristic of the political parties is their negative nature. Pakistan did not possess even one genuine national political party. Parochialism, the narrow manifestation of provincialism, stalked the country from its birth. It continued to do so at this crucial hour. Given divided movements in Pakistan, national unity has always been paramount, but singularly elusive. It was little wonder then that the permanent services repeatedly invaded the domain of the politicians. Although the bureaucracy and military were conspicuous by their absence in the struggle toward independence, once having achieved statehood it was left to them, the "steel frame," to sustain the fledgling nation.

Even the original Muslim League was more an extension of the personality of Qaid-i-Azam Mohammad Ali Jinnah than a popularly based organization. While Jinnah lived, separatists and individualists were held in check. When he died in 1948, Prime Minister Liaquat Ali Khan assumed his role. Although not as successful as Jinnah, he did manage to neutralize the opportunists. But Liaquat's assassination in 1951 removed the last person with any chance of taming parochial politicians. His successor, Nazimuddin, was a well-meaning individual, but he was ill-equipped to play the role that circumstance thrust upon him. Nazimuddin could not control the ambitious personalities and they simultaneously destroyed him and irreparably damaged the Muslim League.

If there was a national organization it would be found in the permanent services, particularly the higher bureaucracy and army. This is amply
demonstrated in the Ayub Khan decade. Ayub, reluctantly, sought to
build a national party in the Conventionist or Pakistan Muslim League.
However, the organization never had his full support, lacked capable
leaders, and was consistently undermined by bureaucratic actions. Moreover, Ayub Khan never developed a taste for politics, and used the party
not to mobilize mass support but to legitimize his programs. Thus his
party also failed.

National politics atrophied. However, politics as such could not be
eliminated from the Pakistan scene. Despite the dominance of the bureaucracy in the decision-making process, the very act of convening legislative
assemblies meant there would be political activity in one form or another.
Given the peculiar emotional issues rampant in Pakistani society, it was
not surprising that varieties of local nationalism should be spawned. The
results of the election were to be expected. Provincialism had carried the
field. Although two parties won the larger portion of the seats in the
National Assembly, the cleavages in the Pakistan design were dramatically
demonstrated.

Yahya Khan hoped the election results would force Mujibur Rahman
to yield on his Six Point Program. He also expected a number of parties to
emerge with significant leverage in both East and West Pakistan. But he
was disarmed by the tallies, and his opportunity to manipulate a favorable
coalition was lost. Sheikh Mujibur Rahman's Awami League swept East
Pakistan. His party was an overwhelming success in both the provincial
and national assemblies. The Awami League counted 288 of 300 seats in
the East Pakistan Legislature and 167 of 300 seats in the National Assembly. Nevertheless, the Awami League did not carry a single West Pakistan
constituency. Thus it was hardly a party of national unity. On the contrary, the vote was more a declaration of independence for East Pakistan.
The elections gave the Six Point Program the legitimacy of a legal document; it was now a veritable constitution. Moreover, with such a popular
mandate Mujibur Rahman, even if he wished to, could not compromise
with his West Pakistani counterparts.

Bhutto's Pakistan People's Party (PPP) won a large, but not nearly
so decisive a victory in the Punjab and Sind. The PPP did represent the
second largest party in the National Assembly, however. With 83 seats in
the latter body no other party came even close to making a challenge. The
convening of the National Assembly and the drafting of a new constitution
rested on the ability of Mujib and Bhutto to accommodate one another.
The two men never expressed friendship, and Bhutto, as a member of
Ayub Khan's Cabinet, sought to stifle the Awami Leaguer. But eventually
it was expected the two electoral champions would reach an agreement

TABLE 5-1.
Results of the Elections of December 7 and 17, 1970

	East Pakistan	Punjab	Sind	NWFP	Baluchistan	Total in all Prov.	Seats in National Assembly
Total General Seats	300[a]	180	60	40	20	600[d]	300[b]
Awami League	268 288[e]					268	151 167[e]
Pakistan People's Party		113	32[c]	3		148	81 83[e]
Independents	6	28	10	6	5	55	16[e]
PML (Qayyum)		6	5	10	3	24	9
NAP (Wali)	1			13	8	22	6
CML		15	4	1		20	7
Jamiat (Ahle Sunnat)		4	7			11	7

Jamiat (Hazarvi)	2	4	2	8	7
PML (Conventionist)	6	2		8	2
PDP	4			6	1
Jamaat-i-Islami	1	1		4	4
Nizami-i-Islam	1			1	
Jamiat (Ahle Hadith)	1			1	
NAP (Pakhtoonkhawa)			1	1	
Baluchistan United Front			1	1	
Sind MPPM Mahaz	1			1	

[a] Elections held for 279 seats only.
[b] Elections held for 291 seats only.
[c] Including four independents backed by the party.
[d] A number of provincial seats remained undetermined.
[e] Final results.

Embassy of Pakistan, *Pakistan Affairs*, Vol. XXIV, No. 1 (January 15, 1971), p. 1.

knowing that the army was observing their actions. But this apparently was not their intention. Nor did they consider the army a formidable obstacle to personal ambitions.

CIVIL WAR AND BANGLADESH

Mujibur Rahman could not slow the momentum of the autonomy movement. Although it would have been prudent to consolidate his gains, Bhutto's success in West Pakistan also drove his movement toward more extreme posturing. His success at the polls convinced him that West Pakistan's destiny had been deposited in his hands. He apparently assumed an obligation to represent West Pakistan interests (which were equated with all-Pakistan interests) in the struggle with Mujib and the Awami League. Bhutto vacillated on the Six Point Program during the campaign, and his position remained unclear on election day. He rejected the proposals at one time, accepted them on another. But the time for political hesitancy had passed. Bhutto declared the Six Point Program must be modified, or he would boycott the National Assembly, which was scheduled to convene on March 3, 1971.

Bhutto demanded compromise and adjustment from the Awami League or there could be no drafting of a constitution. The debate was reminiscent of older struggles, which delayed the writing of Pakistan's first constitution. That document took nine years to produce: in essence, because the West Pakistanis refused to grant the Bengalis representation commensurate with their numbers. Proportional representation would have given the Bengalis a dominant voice in the National Assembly, and this was unacceptable to West Pakistan's first-generation politicians. The second-generation politicians indicated they learned something from the mistakes of their predecessors. Moreover, the Legal Framework Order of 1970, prepared and issued by the Yahya Khan government, specified that the East Pakistanis would receive a true proportion of the seats in the National Assembly. Failure to honor the 1970 election results forecast impending tragedy.

With the final results for the 313 seat National Assembly revealing that Sheikh Mujibur Rahman commanded 167 and Bhutto 83 seats, the scene was set for an epochal clash. Bhutto informed his supporters of his decision not to attend the National Assembly meeting, as Mujib promised his compatriots that no one would be able to make the Awami League accept anything less than a constitution based on his program. Mujib never doubted his right to press for his demands. Under parliamentary procedure, his party held a majority and was entitled to form the government. And even with martial law still in force, the enthusiasm generated

TABLE 5-2.
Distribution of National Assembly
Seats under the Legal Framework
Order (1970)

	Distribution of Seats
East Pakistan	169
Punjab	85
Sind	28
Baluchistan	5
NWFP	19
Tribal	7
	313°

°   Thirteen seats were reserved for women.

by the election could not be ignored. Bhutto's adamance, while serious, was not considered decisive. Hence the Awami League proceeded with their draft version for a new Pakistan constitution. Bhutto, on the other hand, could not have taken his position without the support and/or encouragement of the Yahya Khan government. Yahya Khan failed to get Mujib to dilute the Six Point Program and the Awami League's electoral victory gave a new dimension to the autonomy quest. Moreover, faced with Mujib's overwhelming mandate from East Pakistan, Yahya could not declare the elections null and void without serious consequences.

Yahya Khan, like Ayub before him, sensed a threat to the Pakistan state. The elections confirmed the fundamental disunity inherent in the Pakistan design, and unfortunately the parliamentary system envisaged by the Legal Framework Order crystallized rather than dissolved differences. Bhutto's refusal to attend the convening of the National Assembly gave the Yahya Khan government ample reason to postpone the proceedings. Without Bhutto, it was argued, West Pakistan could not be represented. On March 1, 1971, Yahya Khan announced his decision to put off the convention. The reaction in East Pakistan was predictable. Mujibur Rahman condemned the action and brought pressure on the administration by calling a general strike. The population in the East wing responded enthusiastically, and the provincial capital ceased functioning. In Dacca and throughout the province, acts of violence involving looting and burning followed. There was a complete shutdown of transportation, business, industry, and air services in East Pakistan. At this point the Awami League could not retreat. The outstanding question remained Yahya Khan's response. Yahya called a meeting of all parliamentary leaders and asked that they assemble in Dacca. Bhutto and Mujibur Rahman, however, refused to attend. Yahya then announced that the National Assembly would convene on March 25. Another postponement, he implied, would be Mujib's responsibility alone.

With East Pakistan's provincial administration paralyzed, matters quickly drew to a climax. On March 6, 1971, the Awami League declared it was establishing a parallel administration. It derived legitimacy from the elections conducted under the auspices of the Yahya Khan government. Mujib called upon all those serving in the government of East Pakistan to honor the wishes of the Bengali people. The response from the Bengali members of the administration was positive, and Mujib became virtual ruler of East Pakistan.

Mujibur Rahman next outlined four conditions under which he would agree to attend the National Assembly convention on March 25. They were:

1. That martial law be terminated.
2. That the army return to its barracks.
3. That an inquiry be opened into the alleged killing of civilians by the army.
4. That power be transferred at once to the province's elected officials.

He reiterated that the general strike would continue until the central government yielded to his demands. The East Pakistanis were ordered not to pay taxes, and all Bengali administrators in civil and judicial capacities were expected to follow the dictates of the Awami League. Moreover, Pakistan flags were taken down and black flags of protest flown in their place.

The situation in East Pakistan had its initial impact on the West wing in the area of the economy. West Pakistani holdings in East Pakistan were extensive, and with the breakdown of banking transactions between the two segments of the country the national economy was seriously dislocated. Moreover, commercial establishments owned and/or operated by non-Bengalis were invaded, ransacked, and often burned. Non-Bengalis were massacred, and others fled. The more fortunate were flown to West Pakistan. By March 14, the courts ceased to function, telecommunication links with West Pakistan were severed, and foreign personnel began an exodus by sea and air.

On March 15, Yahya Khan flew to Dacca and met with Sheikh Mujibur Rahman. These talks failed. By this time it was doubtful that even Mujib, if he wished to do so, could restore order. Passions reached an extreme stage and the highly volatile Bengali students, intoxicated by their victories, insisted on the establishment of an independent Bengali state. President Yahya Khan hurriedly ordered the parliamentary leaders from

West Pakistan to Dacca where they met with him and Sheikh Mujibur Rahman. After first refusing to attend, Bhutto agreed to join in the deliberations.

When the Awami League leader demanded the establishment of two committees within the National Assembly, one for East and one for West Pakistan, Bhutto speaking for the latter refused to consider the arrangement. Mujib insisted on two constitutions and possibly a third. The East Pakistanis wanted a constitution independent of the one operating in West Pakistan. The idea of still another constitution was implied by the suggestion that a third confederated plan would bridge the two units. Neither Bhutto nor Yahya Khan appreciated this design, and the talks broke off.

March 23 was the thirty-first anniversary of the Lahore or Pakistan Resolution, which called for independent Muslim states in India. The day was renamed by Sheikh Mujibur Rahman as "Resistance Day," and at an enormous meeting in Dacca the flag of Bangladesh was flown officially for the first time. Pakistan flags that still flew over foreign consulates were seized by students, and the new Bengali standard raised in its place. Elsewhere, rioting, looting, burning, and murder continued with only the Awami League's own para-military organization in a position to restrain the demonstrators.

On March 25, as Yahya Khan and Bhutto were returning to Karachi, the army struck at key points in Dacca, the port of Chittagong and throughout the province. The target according to the government was the Awami League, and Sheikh Mujibur Rahman was arrested at his home and flown secretly to West Pakistan. The Awami League and its leader, said President Yahya Khan, had committed treason and would be punished. A ban was ordered on all political activity and the convening of the National Assembly was postponed indefinitely. Once more Yahya Khan stated he would return power to the people's elected representatives when the country was returned to normalcy.

It was less than twenty-four years since Pakistan gained its independence, but the country's survival in its 1947 form hung in the balance. The Pakistan army showed no mercy in putting down the Bangladesh movement. Fighting raged for several weeks with the army being reinforced and resupplied on a round-the-clock basis. Unable to fly over India, troops were put aboard ships for the long voyage around India. Aircraft used a similar route, refueling in Ceylon. With the disarming of Bengali military and police units, the indigenous population had few arms to use against the sophisticated firepower of the Pakistan army. Moreover, the Punjabi, Baluchi, and Pathan members of the Pakistan army were ready to take their revenge on the Bengali population.

When the Bengalis realized their fight was hopeless, that only the government of India had indicated support (the Chinese Communist government supported Yahya Khan), the conflict subsided. But the Pakistan army had not completed its work. The large Hindu minority, approximately ten million, was singled out as aiding and abetting the secessionist movement. The whole incident was an "Indian plot," declared Pakistani officialdom. This harkened back to the 1968 Agartala Conspiracy. Clearly, the Yahya Khan government needed to justify, essentially for its international image, the violence that it inflicted on East Pakistan. Hence India was the villain, with the most to gain. Bangladesh would be reunited with West Bengal and absorbed in the Indian Union.

Although published statistics are only estimates and it is more than likely that the actual count will never be known, the Pakistan army and its supporters are reputed to have killed in excess of one-half million Bengalis. The Bengalis, in turn, are said to have taken the lives of thousands of non-Bengalis, particularly migrants from Bihar in India. In this initial phase, military casualties were estimated at several thousand. In the latter stages, the Hindus of East Pakistan bore the brunt of the casualties. Refugee figures indicated that of the ten million who are estimated to have fled East Pakistan for refuge in India, about seven million were Hindus. The devastation done to the Hindu quarter in Dacca and other cities was mute evidence of the particular vengeance meted out to this community.

DISMEMBERMENT OF PAKISTAN
AND ITS AFTERMATH

Guerrilla activity increased as the bloodletting unleashed by the Yahya Khan government continued in East Pakistan. The India-based Mukti Bahini, or Bangladesh Liberation Army, filtered across the 1,500 mile border to sabotage communications, paralyze the province's economy, and assassinate government officials and collaborators. When India began its buildup of forces on the East Pakistan frontier, the Pakistan army was compelled to leave the security of their garrison cities, towns, and cantonments. Moreover, in the tense atmosphere, the two armies could not be kept from skirmishing, and such engagements led to a mutual exchange of artillery barrages that took a toll of the innocent on both sides of the border. With the Pakistan army thus forced to cope with a potential Indian advance, the hinterland of East Pakistan was more exposed to the raids of the Mukti Bahini. By the autumn of 1971, it was evident the Bengalis were not about to yield to the firepower of the Pakistani army. A long war of attrition was in the offing, and neither party in the conflict displayed any sign of accepting a compromise solution.

The trial of Sheikh Mujibur Rahman was reported underway in Pakistan, but everything relating to that procedure was kept in strictest secrecy. Without Sheikh Mujib, the provisional government of Bangladesh was bereft of spiritual leadership. Awami League leaders, such as Tajuddin Ahmed and Nurul Islam, were unable to securely grip the revolutionary movement. A prolonged guerrilla struggle held out the possibility of bringing extremists to power. The Yahya Kahn government ignored this possibility, however.

The Indian decision to invade East Pakistan and establish an independent state is hardly surprising. The Pakistan government not only made a series of gross miscalculations, it was unable to appraise the consequences or the magnitude of its mistakes. The Indian thrust into East Pakistan and the quick capitulation of the Pakistan army forced reality upon Pakistan's leaders. Yahya Khan apparently anticipated a Chinese maneuver that would have relieved his beleaguered and hopelessly surrounded forces in East Pakistan. For this reason he urged his commanding officer in the province to fight on, no matter the cost. Chinese assistance, however, never materialized, and Yahya Khan's hand was forced by members of his entourage within the army and air force. India's terms for a ceasefire were finally accepted.

Pakistan suffered a grievous blow. The knowledge that Pakistani leaders were primarily responsible for giving India the opportunity to not only humiliate the country's armed forces, but also facilitate the secession of East Pakistan, in no way eased the plight of the nation. The country of Pakistan, of Jinnah, and Liaquat Ali Khan could never be the same. Bangladesh was a fact, even if the world community was slow to recognize the new international actor. Pakistan had been reduced from a country of approximately 130 million to something closer to 65 million. The latter were demoralized and openly disenchanted with its leadership.

In mid-December, 1971, President Yahya Khan appointed Zulfikar Ali Bhutto as Deputy Prime Minister and sent him to the United Nations to lead the Pakistan delegation before the Security Council. On December 15, Bhutto castigated the Security Council for "legalizing aggression" and emotionally declared he saw no purpose to remain any longer. Leaving his seat he shouted, "We will fight. My country harkens for me." On December 17, however, Pakistan accepted India's terms for a ceasefire. Bhutto returned to Pakistan almost immediately, after meeting with President Richard Nixon hours earlier (the United States had given symbolic support to Pakistan in its short war with India). When he arrived in Pakistan, Bhutto was informed that Yahya Khan had vacated his office, and that he was to take his place. On December 20, 1971, with Yahya Khan sitting to his left, the papers of transfer were signed. Zulfikar Ali Bhutto, leader of the Pakistan People's Party (PPP), became Pakistan's first civilian president since Ayub Khan seized power in 1958. In some respects he can be considered Pakistan's first political head-of-state since the dismissal of Khwaja Nazimuddin in 1953.

Bhutto's PPP won a majority of West Pakistan seats in the December, 1970 elections. Although he was partly responsible for the decision to postpone and then to cancel the meeting of the Constituent Assembly in March, 1971, and thereby bore responsibility for the tragedy that subsequently followed, he was not a party to the atrocities committed in East Pakistan. Nor was he implicated in the military policy that resulted in Pakistan's ignominious defeat. As the most popular political figure in West Pakistan, and one who consistently worked to further the interests of the military establishment, he was the one person capable of bridging the population of West Pakistan with their conventional but seriously discredited governmental apparatus. The military required time to restore its shattered image. It was in no position to officiate over a crestfallen population, especially one demanding vengeance.

Bhutto had long coveted the highest political office in Pakistan. At one time Ayub Khan had given some thought to grooming the young man as his successor. That events conspired against the realization of that particular expectation can now be viewed with some irony. Bhutto inherited a truncated, demoralized, and seriously dislocated country. It is doubtful that his dreams of power had included the circumstances that now surrounded him. Drastic surgery was in order and the new President, with the new military leadership looking over his shoulder, immediately undertook his responsibilities.

With Yahya Khan's resignation a signal to action, Bhutto ordered the retirement of a score of top army and navy officials. Civilians were placed at the head of the Punjab, North West Frontier, Sind, and Baluchistan provincial governments. The press was freed and the first candid articles and editorials criticizing the previous government were published. Perhaps the most important single decision in Bhutto's first month as President of Pakistan was his insistence on the release of Sheikh Mujibur Rahman. Mujib met with Bhutto shortly after the latter was installed in the presidency. Their secret talks appeared to center on salvaging something of the original Pakistan design. A loose confederation was rumored to be Bhutto's hope for the country. The actual freeing of Mujibur Rahman on January 8, 1972, without preconditions, and the Sheikh's subsequent tumultuous return to Bangladesh, however, brought down the curtain on a drama that took almost twenty-five years to unfold.

THE BHUTTO ADMINISTRATION

The President's initial acts were designed to renew the population's spirit. In March, 1972, concrete steps were taken to reorder Pakistani society. Land reforms were instituted, which placed a ceiling of 150 irrigated acres and 300 unirrigated acres on individual holdings. This cut by two-thirds the acreage permitted under the Ayub Khan regime. Governmental officials who had been allowed to acquire lands were forced to give up everything in excess of 100 acres. Moreover, the government seized other forms of land holdings and either distributed these to poor farmers or reserved them for the use of the landless. By October 31, 1972, the government announced more than four million acres had been resumed.

In addition to cutting down individual agrarian holdings, the government took steps to make the cultivators more secure. They could no longer be arbitrarily ejected, and the landowners were made responsible for the payment of water rates and agricultural taxes. Cooperatives were reestablished to assist the poor farmer, and a new rural works program that envisaged agrarian-based industries, villages and cottage industries was pressed.

Other major reforms involved the educational system, protection of labor, and a broadscale health program. In addition, life insurance was made the responsibility of the government. Monies acquired from the sale of such insurance were to be utilized in the construction of housing for the poor. In this context, thirty-two industrial units representing 18 percent of all industrial assets were seized by the administration and placed in the public domain. Banking reforms sought to increase the accountability of financial institutions, as well as promote easier credit to farmers and small businesses.

The most important reforms of the Bhutto administration are in the area of political change. Martial law was lifted within months after Bhutto assumed the presidency and an interim constitution was enacted by the National Assembly. The National Assembly selected a constitutional committee, which was charged with the responsibility for drafting a new constitution with a target date of August 15, 1973. Although there was considerable tension between the various factions, particularly over Bhutto's desire to maintain the presidential form of government, the opposition was successful in having the parliamentary system reinstated.

On April 12, 1973, the new draft constitution was approved by the National Assembly. It came into force on August 14, 1973. The constitution established Pakistan as a federal republic with a parliamentary political system. The president is identified as the constitutional head of state, but the prime minister is the chief executive, and his advice must be followed by the president. This explains Bhutto's decision to resign from the presidency to become prime minister. Chaudhri Fazal Elahi was named President of Pakistan by the National Assembly on August 10, 1973. Whereas the prime minister is the leader of the majority in the legislature, the president is elected by the National Assembly, must be a Muslim, and is a purely apolitical figure. The legislature for the first time

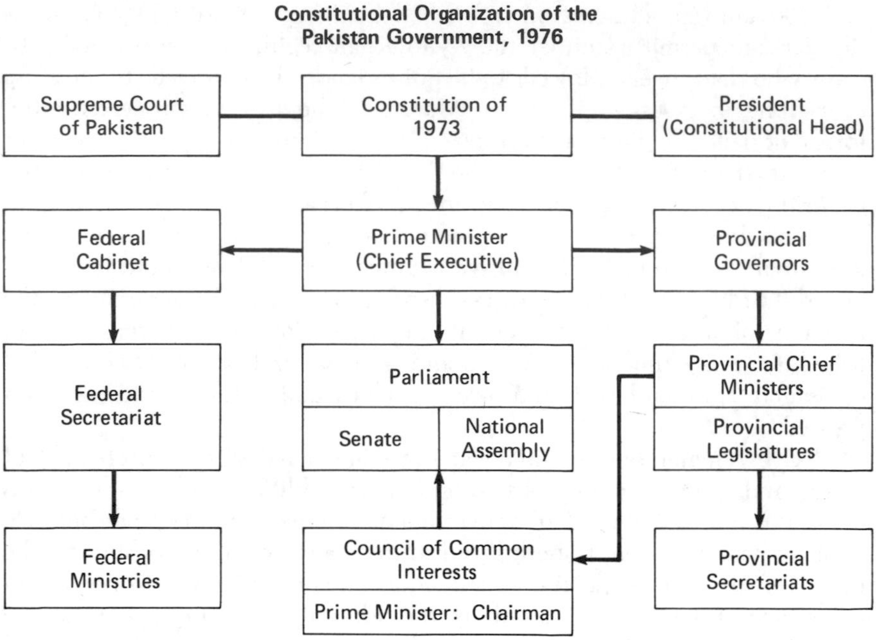

**Constitutional Organization of the
Pakistan Government, 1976**

Supreme Court of Pakistan	Constitution of 1973	President (Constitutional Head)

Federal Cabinet	Prime Minister (Chief Executive)	Provincial Governors

Federal Secretariat	Parliament Senate | National Assembly	Provincial Chief Ministers Provincial Legislatures

Federal Ministries	Council of Common Interests Prime Minister: Chairman	Provincial Secretariats

FIGURE 5-2
Constitutional organization of the Pakistan government, 1976

is bicameral with the National Assembly, or lower house, consisting of 200 members (ten additional seats have been reserved for women for a period of ten years), and a Senate consisting of 63 members (fourteen from each province, five from federally administered tribal areas, and two from the federal capital area). Members of the National Assembly are elected on the basis of a direct, free, and secret ballot. However, senators are elected indirectly by the members of the four provincial legislatures.

Attempts have been made to bolster the position of the prime minister by making a no-confidence motion which could be brought against him by members of the parliamentary opposition also contain the name of his possible successor. A majority is required to pass a no-confidence motion, but the prime minister is empowered to dissolve the National Assembly and order new elections by calling upon the president to so act.

There are two groups holding positions of power enumerated by the constitution—the federal list and the concurrent list. This arrangement stresses the division between the central government and the provinces and permits residual powers to rest with the province. Provincial governors are appointed by the president on the advice of the prime minister. However, the governors take their advice from the chief ministers within the provinces, as the latter are considered heads of the provincial parliaments. Chief ministers are elected by a majority in their respective provincial assemblies.

The federal character of the constitution can also be observed in the establishment of a Council of Common Interests, which consists of an equal number of representatives from the provinces and the federal government. The functions of the Council of Common Interests includes formulation and regulation of policies in relation to federal concerns in which the provinces have a vital interest. This would involve such utilities as the railway system and other federally-controlled institutions. The Constitution also establishes a National Economic Council to advise the government on developmental planning and a National Finance Commission, which recommends the allocation of revenue between the federation and the provinces.

The highest court in Pakistan is the Supreme Court and its justices are appointed by the president. It has both original and appellate jurisdiction. The most important court in each province is the High Court, and the president also appoints these justices.

Perhaps the most interesting feature of the new Constitution is the establishment of Islam as a state religion. This was not done in either the 1956 or the 1962 Constitutions, although the country was called an Islamic Republic. The Constitution now permits a Council of Islamic Ideology to advise the government on how to bring existing laws into conformity with Islamic guidelines.

Bhutto and the Problems
of the New Pakistan

When Zulfikar Ali Bhutto received the transfer of power from General Yahya Khan in December, 1971, Pakistan was a shambles. Pakistan's garrison had been forced to surrender to India and Mukti Bahini forces, and Bangladesh became an independent state. The Pakistan of Mohammed Ali Jinnah lost 60 percent of its population, and the loss of East Pakistan seemed to threaten economic dislocation and mass insecurity. Of psychological importance was the weakening of Pakistan's *two nation theory*—the belief that the Muslims of South Asia were a separate and distinct community, entitled to a separate political state founded upon Islamic principles. It has been said that Bhutto inherited a demoralized country without a future. Subsequent events have proved this to be an exaggeration. Those Pakistanis who *were* shocked by the defection of Bangladesh belong to a sophisticated, well-informed minority. The vast majority of West Pakistanis, those who inhabit the rural areas or urban slums, were not affected by the dismemberment of their country. Even those who were genuinely shocked by events have shrugged off their loss.

In considerable measure, this has been due to Bhutto's vigorous efforts to reconstruct Pakistan.

Bhutto is both Pakistan's Prime Minister and Chairman of the dominant Pakistan People's Party (PPP). Although he urges his people to build and respect institutions and place less emphasis on individual leadership, he has contributed little to this transformation. Dominance over decision-making, not delegation of responsibility, has been Bhutto's style. He not only stands at the apex of the government, he perceives himself as personifying the political system in Pakistan. Much of his background is responsible for Bhutto's pronounced self-confidence. For example, his experience as the scion of one of the well-known families of Sind's landed aristocracy; his education in some of the western world's more renowned institutions of higher learning; his status in President Ayub Khan's administration; his capacity to build a new political party where others failed; and ultimately, his selection by the Pakistan military establishment to head a new civilian government following the dismemberment of the country; all these factors reinforce his self-image.

Bhutto shows little confidence in the ability of the western-educated class to provide positive leadership. He tends to rely on an expanded police establishment, and he feels that his own performance must be resolute and unyielding. Therefore PPP disorganization is more or less inevitable. When first launched in 1967, the PPP's purpose was the dislodging of Ayub Khan. Toward that goal the party enlisted numerous dissidents from among Pakistani society. Radical students and feudal aristocrats, as well as factory workers, share-croppers, and members of the intelligentsia and professional classes found themselves in strange alliance. Ostensibly a leftist party, the PPP has had to explain its apparent willingness to admit so-called "reactionaries" to its ranks. Chairman Bhutto proceeded to note that "the capitalists and feudal lords who have joined my party have already taken an oath before me to abide by all conditions laid down in the PPP Manifesto."[4] Chairman Bhutto was satisfied that no contradictions existed in the acceptance of the propertied class as members of the PPP, which silenced any complaints from other party officers. Because a broad coalition was needed in the 1970 election campaign, there was little initial quarreling with this approach.

After Bhutto took power, a nationalization program was implemented, which whetted the appetite of the leftists in the PPP. Land reforms provoked some of the more radical members of the party to call upon the peasantry to seize the estates of landlords. Basic industries, insurance companies, and national banks were expropriated by the government. It seemed the country was moving toward a fully socialized econ-

[4]Zulfikar Ali Bhutto quoted in the daily newspaper *Dawn* (Karachi), January 26, 1975.

omy. But Bhutto began to veer away from this trend. He insisted the country should have a smooth transition to socialism and that the steps already taken needed consolidation before new programs were attempted. He was particularly interested in stabilizing the agrarian scene, and he protected those landlords who had been subjected to arbitrary seizure of their holdings. Instead of permitting the landless to take matters into their own hands, he ordered the parcelling of properties to those peasants who were likely to lend their support to the rural PPP. In this way, the number of those possessing land were multiplied while the landlords maintained their privileged status. This posture did not satisfy the more vocal radicals in the PPP coalition who interpreted the Chairman's policies as favoring the landlord.

The party's ideological cement had been poorly mixed. The doctrinaire leftists criticized Bhutto's cautious approach, as well as his recruitment of old line bureaucrats to key government positions. Above all, they were disturbed by Bhutto's determination to be acknowledged as the dominant ruler not only within the party, but throughout the country. The disarray in PPP ranks was caused in part by a reluctance to reconcile ideological pronouncements with practical performance. As a result, those assuming important positions in the PPP administration often had little interest in original party principles. Thus, except for Bhutto's looming presence, the PPP has become a congeries of small provincial factions, each with its own accepted leader. None of the latter maintain much political leverage in the absence of Bhutto's support. Although the PPP is the preeminent political organization in the country, it would be powerless without Bhutto to help rally its divergent interest groups. Chairman Bhutto expects loyalty and obedience from his lieutenants. If such is demonstrated, he is prepared to tolerate their mistakes, and he will often ease them through difficult situations. But if there is any kind of insubordination, that particular office-holder must be prepared to face the consequences. The strength of the PPP, therefore, lies in Bhutto's capacity to impose his will. Thus united, the PPP will give the political opposition a difficult time.

The political opposition had been meticulously disassembled by Bhutto's tactics. The United Democratic Front (UDF), which brought the conservative and radical opposition parties together, has never achieved distinction. The principal parties in the UDF were the National Awami Party (NAP) led by Wali Khan and the Jamaat-i-Islami whose spiritual leader has long been Maulana Maudoodi. The leader of the Tehrik-i-Istiqlal, Ashgar Khan, however, has consistently refused to join the UDF. Thus the Front has never been truly unified and does not pose a significant threat to the PPP.

The more successful members of the opposition have been the

Jamaat-i-Islami and the National Awami Party. Although poles apart in philosophy, they share a common desire to destroy Bhutto and his PPP. The Jamaat, however, has been more guarded in its activities and statements than has the NAP. As a consequence, the government has been more concerned with the latter organization. But before examining the PPP-NAP conflict, which caused the government to ban the NAP and arrest its leaders, it would be useful to briefly review the religious parties.

Pakistan's profession that it is an Islamic state has always given prominence to the ulema (Muslim scholars) and the political organizations with which they have been associated. To some extent the ulema are more politically influential in the current period than at any time in Pakistan's brief history. It is noteworthy that in 1970, the Jamiat-e-Ulema-e-Pakistan was organized as a political body under the leadership of Maulana Shah Ahmad Noorani. Representing the ulema of Pakistan, it is significant that this party won some seats in the national and provincial assemblies in the general elections of 1970.

Another ulema organization is the Jamiat-e-Ulema-e-Islam (JUI). The JUI is more politically experienced, stemming from the pre-independence Deoband School of Ulema. The Deoband School has always been extremely nationalistic and it has gained many adherents in Baluchistan and on the North West Frontier. It was also in these provinces that the JUI won their seats in the 1970 elections. Later, the JUI and the NAP combined forces to form coalition governments in both frontier provinces, but they were short-lived due to PPP intervention. Nevertheless, the JUI and the NAP maintain considerable appeal.

The Jamaat-i-Islami is a religious party, but it does not claim to represent either the ulema or the pirs (descendents of Islamic saints). The founder of the Jamaat, Maulana Abul Ala Maudoodi, is neither a member of the ulema, nor is he a pir. He created his organization in India before 1947, and moved to Pakistan when British India was partitioned. The Jamaat has been more concerned with political education than with winning seats in the assemblies. It has always worked with a small nucleus of disciplined followers drawn from the educated middle and professional classes, and it has been primarily active in the Punjab. Since 1971, however, it has expanded its program and has recruited members from the entire country. The Jamaat has concentrated its efforts in the universities. It is alleged that virtually all student unions in the country's universities and colleges are controlled by students who are members of the Jamiat-e-Tuleba-e-Islam, the Jamaat's student wing. The Jamaat's appeal among the students can be attributed to their disillusionment with the PPP. Pakistani youth is idealistic and the PPP, which had their support in the period immediately following Bhutto's assumption of power, could not retain their confidence. Generally, the student population has been angered by the PPP government's apparent divergence from its supposed socialist goals. They are searching for a movement and a leader that will adhere to their idealistic principles. Moreover, it has been said that the strict adherence to ideology, the consistency of the Jamaat argument, and the discipline demanded of its members have a peculiar attraction for young intellectuals seeking a new beginning for Pakistan. The PPP has responded to the students by criticizing their participation in politics.

Although the PPP is not overly concerned with religious parties, the National Awami Party has been a persistent dilemma. The NAP has long stood for secularism, but the resurgence of Islamic sentiment since Pakistan's 1971 military defeat convinced the party of the need to adopt religious issues. Thus it was the NAP on the North West Frontier that pressed the first resolution calling upon the government to declare the Qadianis (an unorthodox Muslim sect) a non-Muslim minority. In 1974, the PPP-dominated National Assembly approved legislation declaring the Qadianis to be non-Muslims, in order to avoid the possibility of communal violence being exploited by the NAP in the Punjab.

More significant, however, was the charge that the NAP had conspired with Afghanistan to further fragment the Pakistan state. The 1973 coup in Afghanistan that returned Sardar Mohammad Daud to power heralded the intensification of Pakistan-Afghanistan troubles. Daud quickly reasserted his support for Pushtunistan, the concept that the Pushtu-speaking people on the North West Frontier of Pakistan should constitute an independent state. The NAP and Afghanis were also accused of inciting the tribes of Pakistan's Baluchistan province, and Baluchi insurgents were allegedly trained and armed in Afghanistan. Although the NAP leaders rejected charges that they were in league with foreign forces to destroy the country, the Bhutto government was determined to take strong action. Thus after the assassination of a high-ranking member of the PPP in the NWFP, Bhutto ordered the arrest of all NAP leaders and banned the party. The Constitution was promptly amended to permit the government to extend the state of emergency without seeking the National Assembly's approval every six months, and even members of the national and provincial assemblies could be arrested and detained under the new law. Prime Minister Bhutto explained that the country was facing the "politics of violence," and he was duty-bound to liquidate all anti-national elements. It could be inferred from the Prime Minister's speeches, as well as the actions of his government, that Pakistanis had not yet learned the lessons of the Bangladesh tragedy.

Bureaucratic Reforms

In his initial address to the nation in December, 1971, Zulfikar Ali Bhutto announced that the country was in desperate need of a new, dynamic administrative system: one that could put the colonial legacy to rest. In April, 1972, he formed an Administrative Reforms Committee, which was charged with reviewing previous efforts at administrative reform. More important, the committee was required to recommend a program that could be implemented in the immediate future. As has already been noted, the elite or higher bureaucracy in Pakistan held enormous power and enjoyed exceptional privilege. Their contempt for the politicians and their paternal management of the public produced the abrasive reactions that characterized Pakistan government. Furthermore, inter-service rivalries isolated the dominant bureaucrats from the larger administrative system, and the higher bureaucracy had to contend with opposition from without, as well as within. Given this combination of factors, it was somewhat remarkable that the higher bureaucracy sustained its preeminence as long as it did. In the end it was obvious that the military held the key to administrative change. As long as the military controlled the policy-making process in Pakistan, the privileged bureaucracy was assured of its status. When that military support was removed, however, the bureaucratic establishment could not protect itself from a combined opposition of enraged politicians, service rivals, intellectuals, and citizenry. Thus the collapse of the Yahya Khan regime heralded the beginning of the end of a tradition that spanned several centuries of imperial rule and two republics. Pakistan's third republic could not leave the bureaucratic legacy untouched.

Prime Minister Zulfikar Ali Bhutto adhered to his party's manifesto when he declared an end to the administrative system originally fashioned by the British in India. On March 20, 1973, Bhutto soberly announced the termination of what he chose to call *Naukarshahi* (servant-kings). The use of the term was deliberate. Civil officials had become rulers, not servants of the people. Another term that he used on this occasion was *bara Sahib*, a description that in the colonial period was reserved for the white European overlord. The term remained after independence and from that time on was usually ascribed to leaders in a variety of sectors, but especially to high-placed administrators. Bhutto underlined this reality with his allusion to the bureaucrats who, he contended, had developed a bara Sahib attitude. The use of such terms and the context in which they were employed were clearly aimed at enlisting the support of a population grown weary of administrative inaction and indifference. Thus Bhutto's declaration was met with a positive response, which no doubt reinforced his popular standing. This was especially true among segments of the intelligentsia who sensed new opportunities when the Prime Minister noted "the country could no longer condone a system which elevated the generalist [administrator] above the scientist, technician, professional expert, artist or the teacher."[5]

[5]Quoted in *The Pakistan Times (Lahore)* August 21, 1973.

Pakistan's "Brahmins" and "Mandarins," as they were called by Bhutto, tumbled from their lofty perches at a time of political change. The Pakistan People's Party expected to profit from the action of the Prime Minister. Not only could the party anticipate increasing its legitimacy, but the posts vacated by members of the higher bureaucracy could now be filled by political officials. The PPP manifesto and Bhutto's subsequent speeches made it clear that only those dedicated to the PPP and hard work would be chosen to serve the new socialist regime.

The principal target of Bhutto's reforms was the celebrated Civil Service of Pakistan (CSP). The CSP was ordered disbanded, along with all the other services, in order to be integrated into the new All-Pakistan Unified Grades. The CSP's protected status was terminated, and new functional categories made workers dependent on meritorious performance. Competition appeared to be the key concept in the new arrangement. Although a number of distinguished officers were purged, hundreds of generalist administrators were retained. These bureaucrats could be expected to cooperate, but to what extent remains an unanswered question. Not all former members of the CSP can be expected to adapt to a diminution in their status. Thus eliminating organizations like the CSP is no panacea. The government is still dependent on many of the same individuals for the implementation of its reform program. The success of the reform program will illustrate that the charges levelled against the CSP were well-aimed. The failure of the reforms, however, might lead to a contrary conclusion. The CSP has argued that they were a necessary organization, and that the country could not progress without them. This was the explicit argument presented by those CSP officers who disagreed with the recommendations of the 1962 Administrative Reforms Commission. The CSP members of the Commission stressed that "the present system, which has stood the test of time, not only during the British regime but also during the tumultuous and important years since independence, should be permitted to continue."[6] However, no amount of counter-argument has been successful, and the CSP ceased to exist as a privileged institution.

The Bhutto administration is certainly not without faults. If the intention of the government is to politicize the bureaucracy, then it must also be prepared to entertain an opposition from within it. Bhutto needs the loyalty of the bureaucracy, and it remains to be seen if the dissolution of the CSP will weaken his position. Moreover, is it in the country's interest to make the bureaucracy an extension of the PPP?

The All-Pakistan Unified Grades is an attempt to simplify the bureaucratic system. There are currently twenty-two grades where once there

[6]Government of Pakistan, *Report of the Pay and Services Commission, 1959-1962* (Karachi: Government of Pakistan Press, 1962), p. 447.

were several hundred. All service cadres have been merged into a single structure, and equality of opportunity is supposedly assured. In theory, this would mean that a peon or watchman could rise in the system to attain the highest post available. On the surface this appears to be a noble gesture, but there are those who attribute much of the present-day labor unrest to such notions. The rigid superior-inferior relationships, fashioned over the centuries, are apparently coming undone, and management is hard-pressed to meet the demands of a more achievement-oriented lower-class. Another aspect of the new administrative system is the opening of the heretofore closed cadres, so that horizontal movement between them is possible. In this way technical personnel can take up positions that in the past were reserved for generalists. This also makes it possible for outstanding officers to earn out-of-turn promotions. Each post is graded through scientific job evaluation, and seniority has ceased to be a major consideration.

Provision has also been made for entry into government service through lateral appointment. Talented persons in the private sector are being recruited for key positions in defense procurement, finance, industrial management, and both domestic and international commerce. Such lateral appointees are given immediate status, while career officials who once coveted these posts, are forced to serve their alien superiors. The government seeks its recruits from the scientific, engineering, medical, teaching, and professional communities. In the latter, serious efforts have been made to draw economists and accountants into government service. The lateral appointment program apparently has been well-received, and some persons have made personal sacrifices by joining the government in which pay scales are much lower.

It has been suggested that the CSP could have preserved its autonomy had it been prepared to accept some fundamental changes in the administrative system. It is said that the action taken on August 20, 1973, could have been avoided had the CSP hierarchy agreed to minimum demands for change. However, it appears more than likely that the CSP was doomed, given PPP concern with building a new political order. Significantly, the PPP cannot tolerate a government within a government, which is what the CSP represented. Furthermore, the CSP represented vested interests, and given the PPP's emphasis on socialist reconstruction, the CSP was judged expendable. This does not ignore the Bhutto government's need for astute, efficient administrators. Nor does it invalidate the need for attitudinal change among future administrators if nation-building is to be pursued in earnest. But genuine nation-building may be as far from realization today, as it was under the older system. How will the Bhutto government conduct itself, given its decision to neutralize its opposition and avoid a true test of its popularity at the polls?

Pakistan will not experience another round of general elections until 1977. This means the present government will have governed Pakistan (1) as a result of the outcome of the now questionable 1970 election, and (2) by dint of its determination to prevent the political opposition from organizing an effective challenge to its highly centralized rule. Finally, the new Constitution, which Bhutto gave the country in 1973, clearly serves the interest of the party in power. Therefore it is not likely to promote a competitive political situation. Arbitrary actions, rather than limited political power, continue to characterize the Pakistan political system.

BANGLADESH

The Bangladesh government, in exile, moved from Calcutta to Dacca after the surrender of the Pakistan army on December 16, 1971. In January, 1972, Sheikh Mujibur Rahman returned to his native country and was met by a tumultuous and enthusiastic population. He was immediately sworn in as president of the new republic. Soon thereafter, Mujib resigned the presidency in order to become the country's prime minister. His confidant, Abu Sayeed Chowdhury, was declared the nation's president and was given ceremonial powers. A provisional constitution was put into force on January 11, 1972, and a Constituent Assembly (Ganoparishad), comprising members of the national and provincial assemblies in the defunct East Pakistan, was organized. The Constitution gave all powers to the prime minister, his Cabinet and the Constituent Assembly. Moreover, due to the Awami League success in the 1970 All-Pakistan elections, it became the overwhelming force in the Constituent Assembly. Thus Bangladesh began its first year of independence as a one-party state.

As a result of the Constituent Assembly's deliberations, an official Bangladesh Constitution was promulgated on December 16, 1972, just one year after the Pakistani army had laid down its arms. The Constitution's principal features included the following:

1. Bangladesh was a republic and a parliamentary democracy. Authority rested with the Parliament and was exercised by the Cabinet headed by a Prime Minister. The President acted on the advice of the Prime Minister.
2. The Parliament was unicameral and consisted of 300 members who were directly elected from single territorial constituencies for five year terms. Fifteen seats were reserved for women.
3. The country's principal ideology was declared to be socialism, which was considered to embody nationalism, secularism, and democracy.
4. The Judiciary was independent but did not have the power of judicial review.

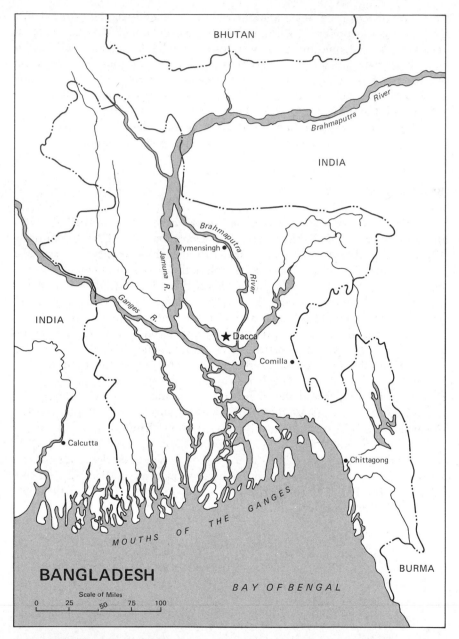

BANGLADESH

Source: Ziring, *The Ayub Khan Era*, p. xiii. (Adapted and modified).

5. The Constitution established the office of an ombudsman to investigate complaints against the administration. Its primary purpose was to expose corruption or general behavior deemed detrimental to the health of the nation.

Few countries have had to grapple with the dire questions facing the Bangladesh government in its first year of independence, and the picture did not improve in subsequent years. An historically impoverished society had been scourged by civil war. Food production, industrial output, transportation, and communication were disrupted to the extent that restoration could not be contemplated for years to come. Meanwhile, hundreds of thousands of people were already dead from starvation, and famine threatened millions more. Possibly 10 percent of the country's estimated seventy-five million were homeless or refugees within their own country. Disease was rampant and health facilities seldom reached the most needy. The state had virtually no treasury, nor the capacity to readily acquire one. Indeed, Bangladesh was referred to as that "international basket-case." The country was absolutely dependent on external assistance for its most basic requirements.

The Awami League politicians were generally unfamiliar with running a welfare government, let alone coping with the calamity that confronted them. They fell back upon the civil bureaucracy. Relief and rehabilitation were made the responsibilities of the administrators, while the politicians endeavored to erect and operate a political system that would guarantee their personal security. Political stability was the first priority, and ordinances were issued limiting the holding of arms. Private armies spawned during the civil war, along with criminal and terrorist elements, were challenged, and strenuous efforts made to subdue them. Reforms aimed at improving police and civil services in the municipalities, as well as at the village level, were forecast. Awami League leadership was particularly cognizant of the need to control the activists, if it was going to retain its preeeminent position. Hence rebuilding the army received considerable attention, but significant resources were also directed at the expansion of the police service and the Awami League's private armed militia.

MUJIBUR RAHMAN, POLITICS, AND TERRORISM

The Awami League had its origins in 1949, and the party was successful in forming the provincial government in East Pakistan from 1955 to 1958. Sheikh Mujibur Rahman gained prominence at this time. As General Secretary of the party in its early days, he was known for his fiery, outspoken speeches against the central government. On numerous occasions he was arrested, threatened with bodily harm, and charged with treasonous acts. But his emergence as a charismatic figure is not traced to those events. It was Mujib's attack on the Ayub Khan administration, his Six Point Program for East Pakistan autonomy, first publicized in 1966, and his incarceration and trial in the controversial Agartala Conspiracy (1968-1969), that set the stage for this metamorphosis. *Banglabandu* (friend of Bengal), as he was affectionately known, never yielded to the authority of the central government, and this earned him the respect of his East Pakistani brethren. Thus when Ayub Khan fell from power in March, 1969 and his successor Yahya Khan proceeded to call for general elections, it was Mujib who had the support of the Bengalis.

With the East Pakistan National Awami Party boycotting the election in December, 1970, the Awami League succeeded in taking 167 of the 169 seats allotted to East Pakistan. The party also won 288 of the 300 seats in the Provincial Assembly. The Awami League demonstrated it was the most developed political party in the province. Its youthful student branch, the East Pakistan Student League (EPSL) and the Jatiyo Sramik League (JSL), or National Worker's League, recruited and trained a dedicated, if not disciplined army of followers. This force was unequalled by any of the other provincially-based parties. The Awami League was a rallying ground for a variety of groups and associations, and herein lay one of its principal problems. How could the party, both ideologically and in a practical sense, begin to satisfy the diverse elements that gave it its strength? Factions were not unknown to the Awami League. Factional splits caused the loss of its momentum in the 1950s, and there was always the possibility of history repeating itself in the 1970s.

Mujibur Rahman banned all so-called right-wing parties in December, 1971, and as a consequence left-wing organizations proliferated. The Bangladesh National Awami Party (NAP) posed a potential but distant threat to Awami League dominance given its division into pro-Moscow and pro-Peking factions. The same could be said for the Communist Party, which had been outlawed by the Pakistan government in 1955, and now had been resurrected. Other parties of consequence were the Bangladesh Jatiya League (National League) and the National Socialist Party. An underground terrorist group, identified as the Naxalites, rounded out the picture. Nonetheless, these leftist parties posed little, if any, electoral threat to the Awami League. Moreover, Bangladesh was hardly prepared for competitive politics.

Anything resembling normal political activity was out of the question, and reports of assaults, murder, and political assassination mounted. In the summer of 1974, the government announced that approximately 3,000 politicians had been killed by terrorists and that the Awami League had suffered losses greater than the other parties combined. A resounding electoral victory of the Awami League in March, 1973, only seemed to increase the level of violence. In that election the Awami League won 291 of 300 seats in the Parliament. But neither this outstanding success nor the decision to bring the pro-Moscow branch of the NAP and Bangladesh Communist Party into the government brought peace to the country. Given the manner in which Bangladesh gained its freedom, there was obvious concern that the country could fall under the sway of local warlords. Regional guerrilla leaders showed considerable hesitation in responding to the government's demand that weapons be turned over to the army. In one celebrated instance, Mujibur Rahman ordered the armed forces to crush a Marxist-Leninst group located near the capital.

In December, 1974, seeing no other alternatives, Prime Minister Mujibur Rahman declared a state of emergency throughout the country and commenced a drive to root out the terrorism plaguing his regime. Reinforced army units were ordered to take up permanent stations in key areas. Every major city and many towns came under direct military surveillance. Bangladesh's President also empowered Mujib to take whatever measures he deemed necessary to restore the nation's economic system. Moreover, the government controlled newspaper urged Mujib to purge the opposition. This same note was struck by government spokesmen: "Political killings, acts of sabotage, hoarding, profiteering, smuggling and antipeople activities should not be tolerated."[7] Mujib's actions were apparently prompted by the assassination of still another Awami League member of the National Parliament (the sixth), but as a consequence the Bangladesh army was destined to play a larger role in the country's political life.

A SCENARIO OF DESPAIR

The "Golden Bengal" frequently alluded to by Mujibur Rahman was a fantasy. Bangladesh was confronted with economic problems that it could not resolve. Worldwide economic dislocation, exacerbated by the sudden price rise in petroleum meant that few countries would be able to lend significant assistance. The aid Bangladesh received did not improve the lot of the country's desperate and poor. Moreover, the inability to stabilize the political scene, due to the terrorism performed by factional groups, made serious efforts at innovation impossible. On the occasion of Bangladesh's National Day in December, 1974, Mujibur Rahman spoke disconsolately of the miseries of "Sonar Bangla" (Golden Bengal). He cited the ravages of starvation and the outrages committed by the ter-

[7]*The New York Times*, December 30, 1974.

rorists. Although he was quick to identify Pakistan as the source of these evils, he could not ignore the natural disasters, which periodically took their toll. Nor could he avoid the prevalence of governmental corruption, ineptness, and his government's overall accountability.

It is estimated that aid totalling more than two billion dollars had been given to Bangladesh between 1972 and 1974. Moreover, Bangladesh received an additional billion dollars worth of assistance in 1975, but there was noticeable reluctance of foreign donors to continue such support. Members of the Aid Consortium for Bangladesh had begun to question why the country should not be permitted to collapse in 1976, rather than at a later date. Indeed, that collapse was believed inevitable given the country's multiple problems. For example, in 1973 Bangladesh imported over one and one-half million tons of rice, and it is reported that one million tons were smuggled into India! In 1974-1975 the government asked for more than two million tons. But few countries could deliver such a quantity, and Bangladesh's insolvency ruled out its paying for such shipments. The Soviet Union, Bangladesh's key supplier, was unable to provide needed foodgrains, and the United States, Canada, and Australia had less to offer given a mounting worldwide demand. In fact, the United States had agreed to sell most of its grain reserves to the Soviet Union, which had suffered a disastrous harvest in 1975. Little relief was in sight.

Bangladesh's economy never recovered from the civil war. The principal industry and cash crop had been jute, but by 1974 output was still only 60 percent of what it had been in 1969-1970. Much of what was being produced found its way into smuggler dens, where it was promptly sold to purchasers across the border in India. Tea, the second largest commodity with which Bangladesh hoped to earn precious foreign exchange, suffered the same fate. In addition, shortages in cloth, fuel, and spare parts for machinery, along with a high rate of inflation, gross unemployment (between 35 and 45 percent in 1974), and a declining Gross National Product presented a picture of nation-wide economic bankruptcy.

Contributing to this dismal picture were those few who had enriched themselves at the expense of the many. Not everyone in Bangladesh was suffering. Those having intimate connections with the government hierarchy, including Mujibur Rahman's family, had prospered in the years following the country's independence. Mujib himself continued to live simply, but his immediate family and close relatives gave the impression of an ostentatious life-style. Such inequity had proved to be a principal issue in the campaign to overthrow Ayub Khan in 1969, and now it threw a shadow over Mujib's government. Mujib was extremely protective of his family, and as he grew more suspicious of those around him, he developed a heavy dependence upon his close relations. Ultimately they formed the inner circle in the Awami League government. As a consequence, intimate advisors and long-time associates were ignored.

Mujibur Rahman had also organized a personal militia called the Rakkhi Bahini. Rather than the army, it was this force which engaged in battles with so-called radical and anti-state elements. The Rakkhi Bahini was estimated to have approximately 20,000 men under arms, and they had a reputation for terrorizing the countryside, burning villages, and murdering opponents of the regime. The wanton destruction visited upon the country by the Rakkhi Bahini was linked with Mujib's desire to cling to power no matter the cost; however, it also was Mujib's response to terrorist elements.

The Rakkhi Bahini also harassed and abused the public. Eventually, they antagonized virtually all sectors of society including the army, which blamed Mujib for their excesses. Mujib's defense of the Rakkhi Bahini widened the gulf between himself and the armed forces.

Another disturbing feature was Mujib's personality cult. *Mujibism* was portrayed as an ideology comparable to Marxism or Leninism. A draft of Bangladesh's First Five Year Plan used the term "Mujibism" to signify the country's resolve to attain the goals established by its great leader. But the real meaning, if there was one, was never explained. Mujibism seemed to be created to suggest such slogans as "democracy," "secularism," and "socialism." Mujibism was supposed to be the sum total of these concepts in a Bengali context, elevating Mujib to the status of the embodiment of the Bangladesh nation. Certainly those within his inner circle promoted this notion, but as they came more and more to believe their own propaganda, events in Bangladesh were already moving out of their control.

Violence had become a way of life in Bangladesh. Moreover, a group of militant radicals argued in favor of stepping up their campaign of terror. These nihilists were convinced that the country could achieve its goals, but only after millions more had died. Mujib could not ignore the approaching anarchy into which Bangladesh was rushing.

MUJIB'S DEMISE

With the announcement of a state of emergency in December, 1974, Mujib assumed dictatorial powers. On January 3, 1975, the government issued a series of directives including the power of the government to impose press censorship, intercept mail, ban political parties, and deport foreigners. Fundamental rights were already in suspension, detention and arrest without trial being commonly practiced. The right of assembly was also withdrawn, and all criticism of the government was made subject to stern penalties. The directives, however, implied a form of martial law imposed by civilians rather than the military. But on January 25, Sheikh Mujibur Rahman took the next inevitable step. The Constitution was swept aside, and a presidential system was foisted upon the nation. The Parliament was dissolved by decree, and even the Awami League was neutralized. A new national party was forecast, but its name and role were to be disclosed at a later date. Mujib called the abandoned three-year-old constitution a legacy of colonial rule. He also insisted that an "international clique was making Bangladesh a playground" and promised swift punishment for those "in the pay of foreign powers."[8]

The precipitous decline in civil order provided the impulse for drastic action. But it also tended to obscure the fact that the Mujib government, at both the political and bureaucratic levels, had spawned many of the problems that threatened the nation's survival. Mujib's personal performance was no doubt a contributing factor, but when the new Cabinet was announced, neither a change in administration nor governing style was forecast. Many of the same people who had served in the previous government were given positions in the new one. Thus the initial excitement aroused by Mujibur Rahman's decision to experiment with a new political system was quickly dissipated. Mujib may have been concerned with the restoration of the nation's equilibrium, but he also wanted to neutralize or eliminate those elements within his own Awami League who he thought were conspiring against him. In the months following the imposition of dictatorship, Mujibur Rahman looked less to his Cabinet and withdrew into the security of a tight family circle. Little effort was given to the construction of a new political party. The government bureaucracy was uncertain of its role, and Mujib was not present to lead them. Meanwhile, Mujib's political opponents were again set upon by the Rakkhi Bahini.

On August 15, 1975, without prior warning, elements of the Bangladesh army attacked the home of Mujibur Rahman, killing him and his family, with the exception of two daughters who were abroad. Other groups assassinated Mujib's powerful relatives and close supporters. The headquarters of the Rakkhi Bahini were attacked and put out of action. The exact reasons for the military coup have not been clarified, but it is alleged that the young officers who engineered the enterprise were motivated by intense, personal dissatisfaction with Mujib's relatives and sons. One of Mujib's sons had recently returned from the British Military Academy at Sandhurst, and rumors had circulated that he would assume the number two position in the army, thus further personalizing the regime. Mujib had also recently appointed a number of district governors who were to take control of all police and local armed forces on Septem-

---

[8]Quoted in *Dawn* (Karachi), January 26, 1975.

ber 1. The conspirators apparently concluded that their plan to force Mujib to relinquish control of the government would be impossible under the new arrangement, hence their decision to take decisive measures.

Within hours of the coup, word had spread that the Father of Bangladesh was dead, and a new government was being organized under the leadership of Khondakar Mushtaque Ahmed, an experienced politician and long-time associate of the dead President. Martial law was imposed by the army, and the new President's importance was disregarded. Real power rested with the military, although the army rulers represented several different factions. Strangely enough, there were no demonstrations of grief on the part of the Bengali public, which over the years had come to think of Mujib as a savior. The plight of Bangladesh, the collapse of its economy, and the rampant terrorism, both official and clandestine, had taken a toll. Mujib's charisma had vanished, and although the new government buried him with state honors, few Bengalis grieved his loss.

President Khondakar Mushtaque Ahmed's first acts attempted to create a workable equilibrium. He endeavored to enlist heretofore outspoken dissidents by returning newspapers to their original owners. One paper had been the official organ of the Awami League, before Mujibur Rahman had ordered its seizure. Another represented the views of the National Socialist Party, a political organization that had publicly proclaimed its intention to overthrow Mujibur Rahman. The restoration of these newspapers revealed a plan to reorganize the Awami League and to recruit into the government those who had been ostracized by Mujib. The new President announced the release of 1,000 political prisoners, commuted all pending death sentences, and granted full amnesty to those whom the previous government had marked for punishment. He said his government would not permit full-fledged political activities for at least one year. Mushtaque Ahmed spoke of new elections, which were officially scheduled for February 28, 1977, but his government intended to rule by decree, and the civil-military establishment (the privileged bureaucratic and military elite) was called upon to create a stable political environment.

This expectation, however, was apparently dashed on November 6, 1975, when President Mushtaque Ahmed was overthrown in yet another military coup. He was replaced by the Chief Justice of the Bangladesh Supreme Court, Abu Sadat Mohammed Sayem. The new President claimed that Mushtaque Ahmed had resigned and had asked him to assume the office. All indications, however, pointed to a clash within the military itself. Bangladesh continues to suffer from the events which caused its emergence as an independent state, and the military has not been spared. Factions within the armed forces were the apparent reason for Mushtaque Ahmed's fall. In this instance, Major General Ziaur Rahman had been dismissed as the army chief and Major General Khalid

Musharaf had taken his place. This development followed the killing of four of Mujibur Rahman's closest associates while they were detained in a Dacca jail. Apparently, the younger officers who had overthrown Mujib were provoked by the lingering loyalty for the slain leader. Fearing their own demise, they executed Tajuddin Ahmed and Mansoor Ali, former Prime Ministers of Bangladesh; Syed Nasrul Islam, an ex-Vice-president; and A. H. M. Kamuruzzaman, one-time Minister of Commerce. All four men played instrumental roles in Bangladesh's struggle to achieve its independence from Pakistan.

The reported deaths of these celebrated leaders greatly disturbed older officers within the army, as well as rank and file troops who still thought affectionately of Mujibur Rahman. When General Ziaur Rahman moved to have the responsible officers arrested, they forced the President to replace the army chief with someone more sympathetic to their cause. This resulted in a total breakdown of government at the highest level. Clashes ensued between opposing elements until forces loyal to General Ziaur Rahman were successful in neutralizing their adversaries. Mushtaque Ahmed made it possible for seventeen of the young officers implicated in the killings to fly to Thailand for asylum. Major General Khaild Musharaf, however, was killed, and Mushtaque Ahmed was compelled to resign his office.

Three military leaders, General Ziaur Rahman, who regained his charge of the Bangladesh army, Commander Mosharraf Mossain, the navy head, and air Vice-marshal G. M. Tawab, comprised the military council advising the President. While the President insisted he was the Chief Martial Law Administrator, these military leaders were the real rulers of Bangladesh. To underline this fact they drastically limited the President of Bangladesh's power. The country's 315-member Parliament, as well as the Council of Ministers, had been abolished by the declaration of martial law. No political parties were permitted to operate, and strenuous efforts were made to save the country from complete anarchy. The calamitous events of the past year had revived many local armed bands throughout the country, and the breakdown of the central government's authority was a signal for them to resume their individual quests. Outside the capital city of Dacca, private armies engaged in sporadic violence and looting. Some of these assaults had political implications, but most were attributed to personal vendettas. In general, however, Bangladesh had shown that it was not ready to establish a coherent governmental framework, let alone operate a sophisticated political process. The future of this impoverished land seemed to foretell even more turmoil. Indeed, even its most concerned neighbor, India, was showing signs of alarm. On November 17, 1975, Prime Minister Indira Gandhi denied that India was contemplating intervening in Bangladesh's domestic affairs. Nevertheless, she has intimated that India is concerned with the continuing instability in the area of its eastern states. The Indian government also was outraged by the attempt on the life of the Indian High Commissioner and threatened the Bangladesh government with redress, if the terrorist campaign remained unchecked. Increasing strains in India-Bangladesh relations added to the uncertainties of a region already permeated by crisis.

INDIA, PAKISTAN AND BANGLADESH

The dramatic political changes in Bangladesh heavily influenced its relationships with India and Pakistan. Pakistan was the first country to recognize the new regime in Dacca, and by the end of 1975 both countries agreed to exchange ambassadors and commence negotiations on improving commercial and cultural ties. Bangladesh's association with India deteriorated, however, as skirmishes erupted on their mutual frontier. The new Bangladesh government indicated a desire to be less dependent on India; it also raised anew the problem of the Farakka Barrage in India which diverted needed water from the Ganges river and prevented its even flow into Bangladesh. This twenty year old issue had long been a source of friction between the two countries, and in April, 1975, Mujibur Rahman and Indira Gandhi had concluded an agreement on the sharing of the precious water. After Mujib's death the issue was revived and it became the centerpiece for a running controversy between the two countries. In March 1976, in order to show its good faith, India announced it would unilaterally reduce the quantity of water permitted it under the agreement and called upon Bangladesh to enter into new talks to resolve their differences.

While India was having difficulties with Bangladesh, both countries sought to normalize their relations with China. In the Spring of 1976 their respective governments announced that they would restore communications and post ambassadors in Peking. In April 1976 India also announced that Prime Minister Gandhi had reacted favorably to Zulfikar Ali Bhutto's request that their countries should resume full diplomatic relations, air and rail communications as well as overflights of their territory. On May 14, 1976 all of these arrangements were enshrined in a formal agreement. On the one hand, it appeared Bhutto had capitalized on India's concern with developments in Bangladesh. On the other, however, it could be said that Prime Minister Gandhi was conscious of the need to reduce tensions with India's principal enemies, Pakistan and China, especially as her government was making strenuous efforts to establish a new course for the country. Moreover, any improvement in the international climate was welcome to all of the governments of South Asia as each of them sought to stabilize their political systems and consolidate the power that they had seized under extraordinary circumstances.

RECOMMENDED READING

Abdulla, Ahmed, *The Historical Background of Pakistan and Its People.* Karachi: Tanzeen Publishers, 1973.

Ahmad, Kabir Uddin, *Breakup of Pakistan.* London: The Social Science Publishers, 1972.

Ahmad, Mushtaq, *Government and Politics in Pakistan.* Karachi: Space Publishers, 1970.

Ali, Tariq, *Pakistan: Military Rule or People's Power?* London: Jonathan Cape, 1970.

Amir Ali, *Short History of the Saracens.* London: MacMillan and Co., 1916.

Ayoob, Mohammed, *India, Pakistan and Bangladesh—Search for New Relationship.* New Delhi: Indian Council of World Affairs, 1975.

————— and K. Subrahmanyam, *The Liberation War.* New Delhi: S. Chand and Co., 1972.

Ayub Khan, Mohammad, *Friends Not Masters: A Political Autobiography.* New York: Oxford University Press, 1967.

Banarjee, D. N., *East Pakistan: A Case-Study in Muslim Politics.* Delhi: Vikas Publications, 1969.

Bhutto, Zulfikar Ali, *The Myth of Independence.* Lahore: Oxford University Press, 1969.

Birkhead, Guthrie S., ed., *Administrative Problems in Pakistan.* Syracuse, N.Y.: Syracuse University Press, 1966.

Braibanti, Ralph, *Research on the Bureaucracy of Pakistan.* Durham, N.C.: Duke University Press, 1966.

Brines, Russell, *The Indo-Pakistani Conflict.* London: Pall Mall Press, 1968.

Brohi, A. K., *Fundamental Law of Pakistan.* Karachi: Din Muhammadi Press, 1958.

Callard, Keith, *Pakistan: A Political Study.* London: Allen & Unwin, 1957.

Choudhury, G. W., *Constitutional Development in Pakistan* (2nd ed.). London: Longman, 1969.

—————, *Documents and Speeches on the Constitution of Pakistan.* Dacca: Green Book House, 1967.

—————, *The Last Days of United Pakistan.* Bloomington, Ind.: Indiana University Press, 1974.

—————, *India, Pakistan, Bangladesh and the Major Powers.* Riverside, N.J.: The Free Press, 1976.

Costa, Benedict, *Dismemberment of Pakistan.* Ludhiana: Kalyani Publishers, 1972.

Feldman, Herbert, *From Crisis to Crisis: Pakistan 1962-1969.* London: Oxford University Press, 1972.

—————, *Revolution in Pakistan.* London: Oxford University Press, 1967.

Hasan, K. Sarwar, *The Genesis of Pakistan.* Karachi: Pakistan Institute of International Affairs, 1950.

Ikram, S. M., *Modern Muslim India and the Birth of Pakistan (1858-1951)*. Lahore Shaikh Muhammad Ashraf, 1965.

Jackson, Robert, *South Asian Crisis: India, Pakistan and Bangla Desh*. New York: Praeger, 1975.

Jahan, Rounaq, *Pakistan: Failure in National Integration*. New York: Columbia University Press, 1972.

Jennings, Ivor, *Constitutional Problems in Pakistan*. Cambridge: Cambridge University Press, 1957.

Khan, Fazal M., *Pakistan's Crisis in Leadership*. Islamabad: National Book Foundation, 1973.

LaPorte, Robert Jr., *Power and Privilege: Influence and Decision-making in Pakistan*. Berkeley: University of California Press, 1976.

Loshak, David, *Pakistan Crisis*. New York: McGraw-Hill, 1971.

Mankekar, D. R., *Pakistan Cut To Size*. New Delhi: Indian Book Company, 1972.

Maududi, Sayyid Abul, *The Islamic Law and Constitution*. Lahore: Islamic Publications Ltd., 1960.

Qureshi, I. H., *The Muslim Community of the Indo-Pakistan Subcontinent*. 'S-Gravenhage: Mouton, 1962.

Rashiduzzaman, M., *Pakistan: A Study of Government and Politics*. Dacca: Ideal Library, 1967.

Rushbrook Williams, L. F., *The East Pakistan Tragedy*. New York: Drake, 1972.

——————— , L. F., *The State of Pakistan*. London: Faber & Faber, 1962.

Sayeed, Khalid B., *The Political System of Pakistan*. Boston: Houghton Mifflin, 1967.

Siddiqui, Kalim, *Conflict, Crisis and War in Pakistan*. New York: Praeger, 1972.

Singhal, Damodar P., *Pakistan*. Englewood Cliffs, N.J.: Prentice-Hall, 1972.

Stephens, Ian, *Pakistan*. New York: Praeger, 1967.

Wheeler, Richard, *The Politics of Pakistan: A Constitutional Quest*. Ithaca, N.Y.: Cornell University Press, 1970.

Wilcox, Wayne A., *The Emergence of Bangladesh*. Washington, D.C.: American Enterprise Institute, 1973.

——————— , *Pakistan: The Consolidation of a Nation*. New York: Columbia University Press, 1963.

Ziring, Lawrence, *The Ayub Khan Era: Politics in Pakistan 1958-1969*. Syracuse, N.Y.: Syracuse University Press, 1971.

——————— R. Braibanti and W. H. Wriggins, eds., *Pakistan: The Long View*. Durham, N.C.: Duke University Press, 1977.

Chapter Six

Indochina and Thailand: Change and Continuity

Between China and India are the states of Southeast Asia. This region, roughly the size of Europe, contains in excess of two hundred million people. The Chinese have historically referred to the area as *Nan Yang*, the southern seas; the Indians called it the "Golden Peninsula," or "Further India." It was during World War II that the term Southeast Asia came into general use. This area now includes Thailand, Indochina, the Malay peninsula, and the island states of Indonesia and the Philippines. The countries discussed in this chapter are Thailand, Vietnam (North and South), Cambodia (Khmer Republic) and Laos.

Southeast Asia is rich in historical experience. The indigenous populations of the region have intermingled and have also been subjected to Chinese and Indian influence. Political stability has always been elusive. Boundaries have been altered to suit the dominant political force. No single power, however, has ever succeeded in controlling the entire region. Moreover, the ethnic diversity of the region contributed to the overall picture of disunity. As the British, French, Dutch, Portuguese, and Spanish divided Southeast Asia among themselves, "divide and rule" was already a well-tested principle.

Southeast Asia falls within the tropical zone. It is a region of jungles, rice paddies, and rubber plantations. Mountains have long isolated small tribal elements, who tenaciously cling to primitive life-styles. The more congenial low-lying areas have witnessed the growth of complex societies with elaborate cultural systems. Southeast Asia is an anthropological and archaeological treasure-trove. The temples and palaces of ancient Angkor, Borobudur, Pagan, Amarapura, and Mandalay stand in vivid contrast with the westernized cities of Singapore, Manila, Djakarta, Bangkok, and Saigon. The vast differences between rural and urban worlds are also reflected in the life-styles of rich and poor. Southeast Asia is a portrait of beauty and squalor.

THE PHYSICAL SETTING

Thailand, Vietnam, Cambodia, and Laos comprise a significant section of mainland Southeast Asia. These countries are traversed by great river-valleys, which generally run from north to south. It is along these river-valleys that the principal civilizations of the region have developed. Thailand depends upon the Menam Chao Phraya river, while life in Cambodia and Laos has been nourished by the Mekong basin. North Vietnam's life-line has been identified with the Red River delta, whereas South Vietnam has drawn sustenance from the Mekong delta. The areas between the great valleys consist of high mountains and plateaus. These heavily forested elevations have made movement between the valleys difficult, and passage has been mostly confined to the river-valleys. The delta areas are extremely fertile and sustain a substantial segment of the population.

Rainfall is adequate in the region but subject to seasonal wet and dry periods. The annual monsoon rains extend over a period of several months. In some areas structures have been erected to conserve the run-off for the dry months. The control of water resources means that crops can be grown throughout the year. The region has been known for its high rice yields, and up through World War II enormous quantities were exported.

Western traders were lured to Southeast Asia by the rice trade, but once established they quickly introduced cash crops, such as rubber, copra, sugar, and coffee. Today, nearly 90 percent of the world's rubber, 75 percent of its copra, and most of its tin come from Southeast Asia. The discovery of off-shore petroleum along the coasts of Vietnam suggests an even more important commercial role for the region. But this economic activity cannot conceal the fact that the overwhelming majority of people in Indochina and Thailand are peasants, with strong and enduring ties to the land.

THE EARLY HISTORY

Both Java man and Peking man go back to the dawn of human evolution. There has been considerable speculation concerning their origin and possible relationship. Theories suggest that Java man is connected with the emergence of the Mongoloid racial strain, the major type found in Asia. If

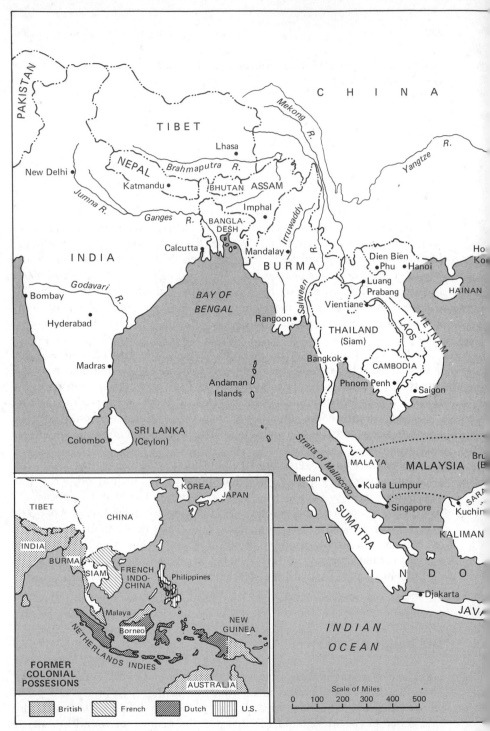

Source: Adapted from Ward and Macridis, eds, *Modern Political Systems: Asia* (Prentice-Hall, 1963).

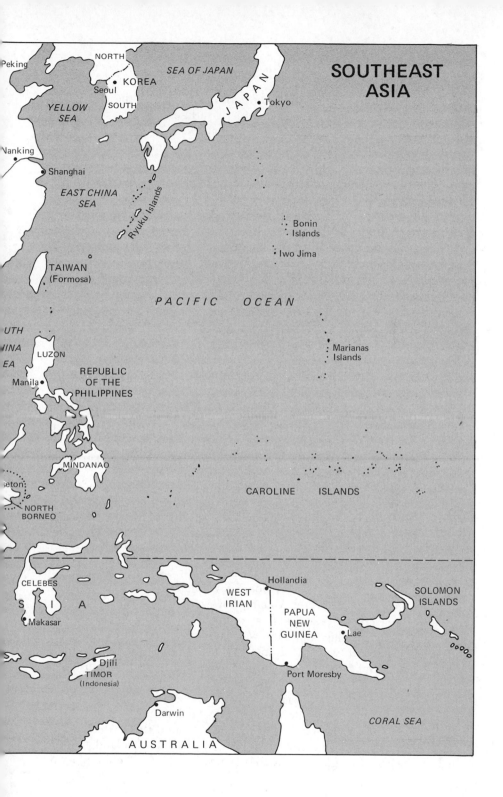

SOUTHEAST ASIA

Peking

NORTH

SEA OF JAPAN

● KOREA
Seoul ●

YELLOW
SEA

SOUTH

JAPAN

● Tokyo

Nanking

● Shanghai

EAST CHINA
SEA

Ryuku Islands

Bonin
Islands

Iwo Jima

TAIWAN
(Formosa)

PACIFIC   OCEAN

UTH
INA
EA

LUZON

Marianas
Islands

REPUBLIC
OF THE
PHILIPPINES

Manila ●

MINDANAO

CAROLINE   ISLANDS

eton

NORTH
BORNEO

CELEBES

Hollandia
●

WEST
IRIAN

SOLOMON
ISLANDS

S   I   A

PAPUA
NEW
GUINEA

● Lae

● Makasar

● Djili
TIMOR
(Indonesia)

S

Port Moresby
●

● Darwin

CORAL SEA

A U S T R A L I A

valid, these theories show possible northern movement by the Mongoloid peoples. Historical records present an entirely different picture. Migrations north to south, particularly from China, and west to east from India, inform us about the early composition of the people inhabiting Southeast Asia. In addition to the Mongoloids, a Negrito people are also known to have lived in the region. Descendants of this race are still to be found among the Semang of Malaya. Verified facts reveal that the Indonesian or Malayan branch of the Mongoloid type arrived in the region from southwestern China approximately four thousand years ago. The Vietnamese people are also believed to have come from western China. These people arrived in the Red River delta about two thousand years ago and settled the areas that were to be known as Tonkin and northern Annam. The Chams, of reputed Indonesian stock, developed a small state in the vicinity of Annam and Cambodia. They did not, however, interact on any significant scale with the Vietnamese to the north. The Khmers, also from China, established their hold in central Cambodia centuries later. It was not until after the thirteenth century that the Thais and Laos, also originating in southwest China, filtered into the area.

An ethnic map of Indochina today would show the Vietnamese people inhabiting the coastal region from the Red River in the north to the Mekong delta. The Khmers occupy Cambodia, and the Thais dominate the central Mekong valley. The Laos are a thinly spread people with some elements extending into present Thailand. Tribal groups can be found in the mountain recesses of all the states, but the war that raged through Indochina from 1945 to 1975 has forced a change in their situation. The Annamese make up approximately 75 percent of the total population of Indochina. The Khmers represent approximately 10 percent, and the remainder are mainly Chinese, Chams, and tribals. The Thais comprise 85 percent of the population of Thailand, with Chinese, Laos, and tribals making up the difference.

Folklore dates the history of Indochina as far back as 3000 B.C., but there is genuine belief that a kingdom of Vietnam did exist in 207 B.C. The earliest recorded history of Annam, however, is traced to 111 B.C. At this time, the Chinese established a kingdom stretching from southern China into Tonkin. This kingdom was later absorbed within the Han Empire of China. It was not until A.D. 939 that a native Annamese kingdom called Dai Viet was established following a revolt against their Chinese overlords. The Chinese again intervened in the fifteenth century. The effectiveness of this rule was short-lived, as a new Annamese kingdom emerged. This kingdom was later divided into Tonkin and Cochin China.

The kingdom of Cambodia had its origin around the second century A.D. It extended from the lower Mekong River into Thailand, and attained the height of its glory between A.D. 600 and 1200. The temples and buildings of Angkor, and the celebrated wealth of the Khmer civilization are associated with this period. Cambodia later collapsed under the blows of Thai tribes that had been pushed out of southwest China by the Mongolians under Genghis Khan and his successors.

As a result of these continued migrations, it was the Chinese and Indian cultures that dominated the region. What records exist of the region's early history are due to the efforts of Indian and Chinese chroniclers. The Chinese, however, were the better record-keepers, given the Indian poetic style of writing. The Indian influence was most strongly felt in southern Indochina and on the shores of the Gulf of Siam. They also migrated through the Straits of Malacca, stopping in Malaya before moving on to Java and beyond. The sophisticated and even temper of the Indians was emulated by the indigenous population of Southeast Asia. When the Portuguese arrived in the region in the beginning of the sixteenth century, Indian influence dominated everywhere except Tonkin, Annam, and Cochin China, present-day Vietnam. In Vietnam, the Chinese culture was unshakeable.

The development of seaborne commerce followed the rhythm of the monsoon winds in an age of sailing vessels. Indian, Chinese and even Arab traders were interested in Southeast Asian perfumed woods, resins, gold, precious stones, and spices. Goods for exchange included: silken yarns and fabrics, tea, and porcelain from China; high quality textiles from India; glass items, rugs, and tapestries from the Middle East; and objects of art from other parts of the world. The result of this trade made Southeast Asia a crossroads for commerce, and struggle for control of the trade routes became inevitable. Kingdoms and states rose and fell with the shifting centers of commercial activity. Chinese involvement in Indochina was stimulated by the development of a shortened trade route to India, which passed through Southeast Asia.

The first empires in Southeast Asia were trade empires, and the fact that these were "Indianized" empires attests to the importance of Indian trade. Numerous states developed along the Indian trade routes. Until commercial routes were developed through the Straits of Malacca, the traders crossed the Malayan isthmus and traveled along the coast of the Indochinese peninsula to the ports of southern China. The Indians spread Buddhism throughout Southeast Asia and into China. It was the Confucianist practices of the Chinese, however, that influenced the development of politico-administrative institutions in Southeast Asia. With the establishment of the Dai Viet kingdom in the Red River basin in the tenth century A.D., China was obliged to accommodate a Vietnamese establishment which resisted all attempts to subdue them. At the same time, in return for a vassal or subordinate relationship, China permitted the Dai Viet to maintain its autonomy. Nevertheless, China remained the dominant civilization and it, not India, had a profound impact on the culture of the North Vietnamese. Their governmental organization and society was influenced by Confucianism. Its doctrines included the civil service examination system, the dominance of a "mandarin" class of governors, and the widespread notion of the "Mandate of Heaven."

The Indian influence, however, created a way of life in Cambodia, Thailand, and to some extent, Laos. As early as the first century A.D. the "Indianized" kingdom of Funan emerged in the Mekong delta. This kingdom spread its sphere of influence to include all of southern Indochina and was dominant until the sixth century. A smaller state was formed around the city of Hue, to the north of Funan. This was the state of Champa. Champa, however, was compelled to yield to the rule of the Dai Viet. When Funan ultimately succumbed in the tenth century, the entire southern extension of Indochina came under the rule of the Cambodian Khmers. Similar to Funan, the Khmer kingdom was Indian-oriented and differed markedly in performance and outlook from its Vietnamese neighbors.

The collapse of the Khmers in the thirteenth century was the direct result of Thai penetration. In time, the Thais established their own dominion over the region. This was also the period that signalled the passage of the Lao people into the region. In A.D. 1353, they founded the state of Lan Xang, the "land of a million elephants." This empire lasted until the seventeenth century but never developed, as the people were content with their primitive existence. As did the Dai Viet, Lan Xang also recognized the preeminence of China and paid tribute in order to maintain their quasi-independence. Indochina was never really unified. Dynastic and cultural rivalries even prevented the integration of Vietnam. Laos suffered a similar fate, while the Khmers of Cambodia struggled to sustain their individuality despite repeated Annamese and Thai attacks.

The Thais were in some ways more fortunate than the people of Indochina. Originating in the Yunnan province of China, they were forced to vacate after the Mongolians invaded and conquered their territory in A.D. 1253. The Thais moved westward across northern Burma, with one group entering Assam in India. The great majority, however, proceeded down the river valleys of the Mekong and the Menam Chao Phraya. The group occupying the Menam Chao Phraya were identified as *Thai*. The group that entered the Burmese region were called *Shans*. The third element of the great migration were named *Lao*. All the groups developed similar, but separate languages. The Thai movement south was slowed by Khmer resistance, but could not be halted. The advanced culture of the Khmers, however, made a lasting impression on the Thais, who adopted Buddhism as they consolidated their conquests.

Ayuthia, established by the Thais, was situated in the lower part of the Menam Chao Phraya valley, and became the most influential Thai state. At one point this kingdom extended from Malaya to the Tenasserim coastal region of Burma. Ayuthia was subjected to attacks both from other Thai states and Cambodia. It repelled all invaders until a Burmese strike into its heartland forced it to yield independent status for a brief period. By 1583, however, the Thais had built a powerful kindgom. During the early seventeenth century, Thailand, or Siam as it was then known, received worldwide attention as one of the more successful Buddhist states. Such publicity served as a magnet for European traders and missionaries. Other Europeans were recruited to serve in advisory capacities within the Thai government.

The reigning dynasty in Thailand was founded by King Rama I (1782-1809). It was during his rule that Bangkok became the capital, and the foundation for modern Thailand was laid. It was, however, Rama IV (King Mongkut of *King and I* fame) who managed to keep Thailand from being overwhelmed by its immediate neighbors, and most important, by European colonialism.

The Thai successes against the Khmers may have influenced the Dai Viet kingdom, which pressed southward in the fourteenth century under the Le Dynasty. Champa was absorbed, but efforts at incorporating the Mekong delta region were thwarted by internal rivalries. The powerful Nguyen and Trinh families competed for dominance, and in 1672 the country was divided somewhere near the seventeenth parallel. This was to be the same dividing line separating contemporary north from south Vietnam. In theory, the Dai Viet kingdom was unified under one emperor. In practice, however, the Trinh family ruled the northern half from Hanoi, and the Nguyen clan controlled the southern portion from Hue. The vacuum created by the fall of the Khmer kingdom enabled the Nguyen family to extend its influence into the Mekong delta. As a result all of coastal Indochina came under Vietnamese influence.

After a brief period of stability, peasant unrest climaxed in the Tay-son Rebellion, which forced both the Trinh and Nguyen families to be overthrown. The Tay-son was a rural-based family on the northeastern edge of the tribal Montagnard plateau who were determined to destroy the reigning dynasties. They are considered the first of Vietnam's rulers to try and impose a military dictatorship on the country. After a bloody civil war, coastal Indochina was divided into three parts governed by the Tay-son, but they too were destined to reign for only a brief period. Nguyen Anh, a prince from the former ruling family, obtained the help of a French missionary organization that recruited French adventurers. With this support, Nguyen Anh reconquered the Mekong delta region and established Saigon as the capital. After this victory, he received additional French assistance and soon was capable of attacking both Hue and Hanoi.

By 1802, Nguyen Anh had conquered both cities and proclaimed himself Emperor Gia-Long of a unified Vietnam.

The Gia-Long dynasty emulated the government of the Ch'ing dynasty in China. Confucianism was reinforced, and the politico-administrative structure was a replica of the bureaucratic system prevailing in China. Although the French were instrumental in the establishment of the Gia-Long dynasty, Nguyen Anh and his immediate successors wished to avoid European dominance. The Gia-Long administration persecuted Vietnamese who had been converted to Christianity, and French attempts to protect them were frustrated. It was partly for these reasons and fear of European influence that French and other European overtures for cementing diplomatic ties and promoting trade were rejected. The French were especially incensed with this treatment. Under the pretext of protecting persecuted Christian missionaries, with Spanish aid, they attacked the Vietnamese. In 1859 they eventually seized Saigon and began their mastery over Indochina.

THE FRENCH IN INDOCHINA

In the last quarter of the nineteenth century, European imperialism had spread to all parts of the world. The French government saw Indochina a region rich in resources, one that would enable France to compete with the other great western empires. What had begun as a punitive expedition was soon transformed into a concentrated effort to dominate continental Southeast Asia. In 1874, the French forced the Vietnamese emperor to cede all of the southern Mekong delta region, the area known as Cochinchina. Unsatisfied, in 1883 they launched a more concerted drive to seize control of Annam and Tonkin. They occupied Hanoi after sharp but minor resistance, declaring both Annam and Tonkin under French rule. The Chinese refused to recognize the French action in Tonkin. As a result, France successfully waged war on China (1883-1885), and neutralized the challenge to its authority. With China no longer an obstacle, and encountering no difficulties from other European states, France continued to spread its control. By 1887, Cambodia had become part of the French Indochinese Union. Laos was included in the Union in 1893.

The French had given little thought to the land, its people, and how Indochina was to be administered. Although the French boasted about their "civilizing mission," this latin version of the Anglo-Saxon "White Man's Burden" had little substance. Their main concern was the conversion of the Vietnamese, and to a lesser extent the Cambodians, to Catholicism. Although French culture and language were adopted by the Vietnamese, Cambodian, and Laotian elites, the broader population was largely unexposed. Colonial administration centered on the French bureaucrats

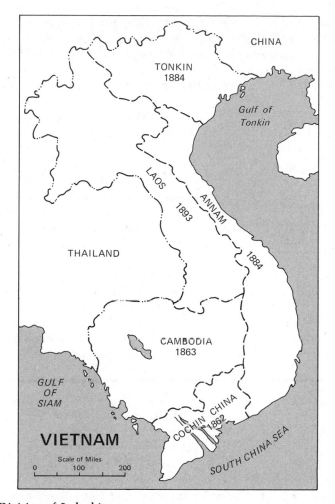

French Division of Indochina

Source: Harvey H. Smith et al., *Area Handbook for Vietnam* (Washington, D.C.: U.S. *Government Printing Office, 1967), p. 47.*

and their Vietnamese counterparts. Indochina was nominally controlled from Paris through an appointed French governor-general. The governor-general, however, served in Indochina for short periods, and the everyday work was the responsibility of career bureaucrats.

The French Indochinese Union was divided into five administrative areas: Cochinchina, Annam, Tonkin, Cambodia, and Laos. The heaviest French influence was felt in Cochinchina. This area divided into provinces, led by administrators who served the governor of Cochinchina. The governor's immediate superior was the governor-general. Tonkin and An-

nam appeared less under the influence of the French, given the preservation of their Confucianist mandarin systems. There was no question,
however, concerning ultimate French political authority. Laos was treated
as Tonkin and Annam, while Cambodia's system bore similarities to
Cochinchina's administration. Although there were differences in administering the Indochinese states, there was no difference in French policy
concerning the purpose of each colony. Indochina was expected to provide
natural resources and food for France. The economic benefits derived
from the region's commodities were to enhance French power.

Cochinchina was primarily jungle, and was sparsely populated when
the French arrived. After assessing the region's potential, French engi-
neers built a network of irrigation and drainage systems. These turned the
rich delta land into a granary of wet-rice cultivation. Developed lands
were sold to wealthy French speculators and members of the Vietnamese
gentry, who employed large numbers of landless peasants to cultivate their
estates. As a result, Cochinchina saw the emergence of a plantation
system, while in Annam and Tonkin the small independent cultivator
remained dominant. The French also endeavored to develop the rubber
industry in Indochina, and they were forced to transfer workers from
Tonkin in the north to Cochinchina in the south. These workers came to
the rubber plantations as indentured servants for a limited period. Although France's immediate economic interests were enhanced, the dislocation and resulting instability in Vietnamese society suggested growing
socio-political problems for the future.

Ignoring the socio-political situation, private French investors sought
to maximize their investments in Indochina. The Bank de l'Indochine
promised investors a striking return on their capital. Chinese and Vietnamese entrepreneurs were encouraged to invest in the development of
Indochina, as were the French citizenry. The French came to dominate
the rubber, mining, and manufacturing industries. The Chinese monopolized the rice trade and general commerce, and some Vietnamese became
oppressive absentee landlords. The Vietnamese peasants found the French
system of taxation a heavy burden. Between 80 and 90 percent of the
population depended upon the land for their livelihoods and small holdings in Tonkin and Annam were insufficient to provide for the individual
cultivator-family. The imposition of a regular tax took no account of lean
years, and caused greater impoverishment to the agrarian population. In
addition, the centralized administrative system, erected to facilitate the
collection of taxes, undermined the Vietnamese communal structure. This
structure was based on the village as a cooperative, self-contained unit.
The culmination of these acts added to the insecurity and dislocation of
the peasantry.

French colonialism developed an indigenous elite, educated in

French schools and familiar with French culture and manners. This elite became the new authority among the general population, at the expense of local leadership. The Vietnamese village remained, but could no longer provide for the well-being of its inhabitants. Many villagers drifted to urban centers and adopted a way of life they found degrading. In their efforts to build a profitable enterprise, the French consciously widened the gap between the prosperous few and the impoverished multitude. They altered the socio-political order which gave stability to a tradition-bound people, and developed on urban proletariat whose growing appetites they could not satisfy.

Unlike the Vietnamese sectors of the French Indochinese Union, Cambodia was given little economic attention. Law and order were maintained, but development of the country's resources was generally ignored. The relatively few Frenchmen in Cambodia enabled the country to maintain its traditional life-style. This advantage was offset by the fact that the colonial power posted Vietnamese in the country. The Cambodians and Vietnamese had been historic adversaries and this arrangement proved abrasive to both the Cambodian elite and general population. The Cambodians resented requirements to channel trade through Saigon, and the taxing of Cambodians to pay for the government in Vietnam. Beyond these difficulties, however, the Cambodians were in a position to retain their individuality. The French did not impose western educational institutions on the country. Traditional Buddhist schools remained intact, and only Cambodian leaders learned the ways of their European overlords. France, however, developed a military strategy that emphasized the maintenance of Cambodia as a buffer between Vietnam and Thailand. The Cambodians were secure in the knowledge that the French would keep traditional foes from invading their land.

Preservation of the monarchy and retention of traditional Buddhist beliefs provided Cambodia with stability and cohesiveness. This was in vivid contrast to the events reshaping Vietnamese society. Laos received less attention from the French than Cambodia. Both countries were perceived in a purely defensive context. The basic strategy was to protect the Vietnamese coastal region from assault by neighboring Thailand and China. As in Cambodia, the French employed Vietnamese administrators in Laos, but maintained traditional governmental structures. Laos remained largely undeveloped, but tin was extracted, and opium cultivation was encouraged among the hill tribes. The French supported the Lao royal family in Luang Prabang, and the average Laotian continued to display reverence to the monarchy. The French presence in Indochina had little effect on Laotian or Cambodian society. When they departed in the early 1950s, both countries remained much the way they were before they were found by the French in the last quarter of the nineteenth century.

WORLD WAR II:
CATALYST FOR CHANGE

Understanding the results of French influence on Vietnamese society, it is not surprising that they resorted to revolutionary devices in an effort to force the Europeans from Indochina. Traditionally dynamic, and having been exposed to western education and ideas, they found subordination to French authority anathema. Numerous underground movements arose in the early part of the twentieth century. Some had their bases in China, beyond French control. When the French gave no indication of peacefully transferring power to indigenous hands, these movements resorted to violence. Early efforts at mobilizing elements of the peasant population were crushed by the French. The extreme measures employed and the heavy loss of life stiffened resistance and expanded the revolutionary cadres. The traditional secret societies of East Asia kept the revolutionary fires burning. It was at this time that Vietnamese nationalism was developed.

Prior to the outbreak of World War I, the Manchu dynasty in China collapsed, and the monarchy was abolished. The Chinese revolution had a profound influence on Vietnamese revolutionaries, who felt the Chinese republican model could be duplicated in Vietnam. Vietnamese society had been so deeply undermined by the French that drastic socio-economic and political reforms were needed to restore the country's identity. It was toward the building of a new national consciousness that the Vietnamese movement was restructured. Organization was accelerated when the Vietnamese, who had fought with French forces in Europe during World War I, returned to their own country. They believed in the principle of self-determination and found continuing servitude intolerable. By 1925 a leader had emerged from the many revolutionary movements. Ho Chi Minh organized the Association of Vietnamese Revolutionary Youth, the forerunner of the Indochinese Communist Party, formally established in 1930. Ho Chi Minh started with a relatively small party. His driving personality and selfless devotion, however, began to attract adherents.

The principal revolutionary group of the period was the Vietnam Quoc Dan Dang (the Vietnamese Nationalist Party), which resembled the Kuomintang in China. This party encouraged violence and assassination. Despite numerous attempts to overthrow the French, the Vietnam Quoc Dan Dang was unable to precipitate a popular uprising. Their ranks were thoroughly disrupted by the French, and their leaders were killed or arrested. The movement ceased to function, although it was revived briefly during World War II.

The destruction of the Vietnam Quoc Dan Dang left Ho Chi Minh and the Communist Party as the remaining popular political group. First organized along decentralized lines, efforts were made to establish "soviets" or peasant councils, especially in the northern segment of the country. Its widespread, secret organization managed to survive repeated endeavors by the French to root it out and crush it. Internal problems, however, weakened the Communists. It was not until the outbreak of World War II and the coming of the Japanese to Indochina that they could regain their momentum.

Japan defeated the Vichy French government in July, 1941, and gained control over Indochina. Curiously, the French were allowed to continue in a governing capacity. The Japanese wanted to be free to exploit the region's resources, while conserving their own manpower. The French were prepared to comply with Japanese terms to avoid a renewal of the fighting, but especially as they were left to run the administration of the country. This arrangement endured for most of the war. In March, 1945, however, the French showed signs of becoming more aggressive. The Japanese had suffered grievous losses elsewhere in the Pacific and were being forced into retreat from their Pacific strongholds to defend their home islands. Fearing a link-up between the Allies and the French in Indochina, the Japanese assumed the direct administration of the colony.

As the French administered Indochina for the Japanese, Ho Chi Minh was developing a widespread organization with the help of the Nationalist Chinese. A nationalist coalition was formed to defeat the Japanese. This coalition was called the Vietnam Independence League, or Viet Minh. Ho Chi Minh became the Secretary-General of the organization. The Chinese nationalists grew suspicious of Communist leadership in the League. They arrested Ho Chi Minh and organized another group called the Vietnam Revolutionary League. It was this party that the Allies made contact with and assisted in a campaign to free Indochina from Japanese control. When initial efforts of the Vietnam Revolutionary League proved fruitless, Ho Chi Minh was released from prison and sent into Vietnam to encourage Viet Minh support of the war effort. At this time, Ho Chi Minh was recognized as the dominant nationalist leader in Indochina. Between 1943 and 1945, the Viet Minh expanded their organization and became the dominant influence in the rural areas of Tonkin.

When the Japanese took control of Indochina in March, 1945, they installed Emperor Bao Dai as titular head of an independent nation. True authority, however, remained in Japanese hands. The Viet Minh refused to recognize the Bao Dai regime, and with the French neutralized, consolidated control over North Vietnam. Japanese troops had not occupied the northern sector of Vietnam. This allowed the Viet Minh to take direct control of the region. When the Japanese surrendered to the Allies in August, 1945, the Viet Minh occupied Hanoi and declared it their capital.

Bao Dai was pressured to abdicate, and in yielding, became the supreme political advisor to the new government. This, however, was a purely ceremonial office. On September 2, 1945, the Viet Minh established the Democratic Republic of Vietnam under the leadership of Ho Chi Minh. Only in the Cochinchina segment of Vietnam, did the Viet Minh have difficulty establishing control. Groups were dispatched to the region in a campaign to incorporate this vital territory. However, events happening thousands of miles from Indochina were to have a fateful effect on the effort to integrate Vietnam under an indigenous government.

The victorious powers in World War II picked the Nationalist Chinese and British to replace the Japanese in Indochina. The Chinese controlled the northern part of the country to the sixteenth parallel, and the British occupied the southern half. The main objective was to disarm the Japanese armies in their respective regions. They were also to provide transitional administration. The British occupied Saigon on September 12, 1945. The general in charge of the operation exceeded his immediate authority by preventing expression of differing viewpoints and imposing martial law on the country. Ten days after their occupation of Saigon, the British secretly armed the French troops, which they had freed from Japanese captivity. Fresh contingents of French troops were flown into Saigon, and on September 23, 1945, France reestablished its rule over Cochinchina. The Vietnamese would not again succumb to French colonialism, and a ferocious struggle ensued. This was briefly abated by Allied attempts to arrange a ceasefire. The French returned to southern Vietnam in time to destroy the Committee of the South, a Vietnamese nationalist organization that had successfully resisted Communist Viet Minh penetration. The French destruction of the nationalist movement and the growing hatred for the Europeans swelled the ranks of Communist organizers in the south. Two important Buddhist organizations, the Cao Dai and Hoa Hao, however, refused to join the Viet Minh coalition against the French. Thus the region was left in a condition of unresolved conflict.

To make the movement more acceptable to the general Vietnamese population, Ho Chi Minh dissolved the Indochinese Communist Party. He adjusted his policies to reflect Nationalist Chinese ideology, which tended to support other Vietnamese parties. Flexibility paid off. In elections for the National Assembly in 1946, the Viet Minh remained the dominant political organization in the country. By the spring of 1946, the Chinese were making preparations to evacuate Vietnam. The Viet Minh and other parties in the coalition government of the Democratic Republic of Vietnam reached an accord with the French. France agreed to recognize Vietnam as a "free state" within the broader French Indochinese Federation. It also received the Democratic Republic of Vietnam's agreement to a plan for the holding of a referendum on unification of the country, as well as the withdrawal of French forces. Meanwhile, the Vietnamese consented to the movement of French armies into the north to replace the Chinese. It was clear that Ho Chi Minh, instrumental in negotiating the agreement, did not want to engage the French in battle. It is safe to assume that Ho believed the collapse of the Axis powers and the termination of World War II would guarantee independence for Vietnam. Nonetheless, the agreement met with severe criticism. Radical elements in the Viet Minh argued that too many concessions had been granted the French, perpetuating their rule. The French were also discontent, however, and actions were taken to sabotage the agreement.

Conferences were held to implement the accord but resulted in further dissension. The French would not comply with the Vietnamese interpretation of the agreement, and Ho Chi Minh could not concede more ground without losing control of his disquieted movement. Expectations for a unified Vietnam were dashed by French recognition of a separate status for Cochinchina. The French decision to further their private interests in Indochina produced an armed clash. The center of fighting occurred in the northern city of Haiphong. After a ceasefire was arranged, the French navy was ordered on a punitive mission, and the Vietnamese section of Haiphong was shelled and set ablaze. Thousands of the inhabitants were reported killed in the attack. In the closing days of 1946, the French endeavored to disarm the Viet Minh. They were met by a defiant people, and the war for Indochina commenced.

LAOS, CAMBODIA, AND THAILAND:
WORLD WAR II

The French had minimal involvement in Laos, and prior to World War II, were primarily interested in controlling fiscal administration and abolishing slavery. The French gave some consideration to annexing Laos with Annam, but Lao agitation prevented this move. The Lao made it clear they wanted to avoid Vietnamese and Thai incursions into their territory. As long as the French satisfied this desire, they had little difficulty in administering the country. When France surrendered to Nazi Germany in June, 1940, the Japanese were moving toward the borders of Indochina. A Treaty of Friendship had been negotiated by Thailand and Japan, and under its terms Thailand was allowed to occupy the Laotian cities of Luang Prabang and Champassak, west of the Mekong River. By July, 1941, all of Indochina was under Japanese control. Although the Lao were basically unaffected, the realization that the French could no longer protect them modified their perceptions of the Europeans.

In August, 1945, the French took advantage of the confusion caused by the Japanese surrender. French rule was reestablished in Laos, including those territories seized earlier by the Thais. A declaration of Laotian independence, instigated by the Japanese, was ignored as the French protectorate was given official sanction by King Sisavang Vong. A group led by Prince Phetsarath organized the Lao Issara (Free Lao) and formed their own government. King Sisavang Vong refused to recognize this government, and he was ordered deposed by the Japanese. The King then relented his opposition, accepted the constitution of the Lao Issara, and was in turn reinstated and proclaimed king of all Laos. The French would not recognize these maneuvers, and they quickly defeated the Lao Issara contingents. Remaining factions ironically joined both Viet Minh and Thai groups and Prince Phetsarath set up a government in exile across the border in Thailand.

The French seized Vientiane and the royal capital of Luang Probang, retaining King Sisavang Vong. In the absence of the most educated leaders, the French installed a new government and employed the services of Prince Souvanna Phouma, a younger half-brother of Phetsarath. Another half-brother, Prince Souphanouvong, remained unreconciled. As leader of the Lao Issara army, he slipped through the French lines to join forces with the Viet Minh. The Franco-Laotian Convention of 1949 brought the dissolution of the Lao Issara. Laos was given independence as an Associate State of the French Union. Most of the exiled leaders, with the exception of Prince Phetsarath, returned to take assignments in the new government. With the French-Viet Minh war in a crucial stage, Laos announced its full independence on October 22, 1953. The country was declared a parliamentary democracy and the king became the titular head of state.

Although Laos sought to avoid the war that engaged the Viet Minh and the French, they found themselves hopelessly involved. Laos was compelled to organize an army, which the French eagerly financed, trained, and equipped with assistance from the United States. The principal threat to the new sovereign status of Laos was not the Viet Minh, but Prince Souphanouvong's movement of dissident Laotians, the Pathet Lao. The Pathet Lao asked all Laotians to support their efforts. They claimed to represent the true government of Laos, condemning the Vientiane government as dependent on the French and Americans. After limited success, the Pathet Lao were joined by the Viet Minh. The war that began in and around Haiphong was spreading to include much of Indochina.

The Franco-Cambodian Treaty of 1863 had given the French control over Cambodia's foreign affairs and the right to defend the country from both foreign and domestic enemies. In fact, the French assumed political and economic control over Cambodia. King Norodom was retained as a symbol of authority, and the Cambodian social structure was largely untouched. Cambodia, however, remained an integral part of the French Indochinese Union. King Norodom died in 1904, and was succeeded by his brother Sisowoth. He, in turn, was followed by his son in 1927. On Sisowoth's son's death in 1941, the son of his oldest daughter succeeded to the throne. Thus, Prince Norodom Sihanouk, the great-grandson of Norodom became King of Cambodia. Sihanouk himself acknowledged that he obtained the throne because the French believed he was more malleable than other aspirants. Sihanouk played the role prepared for him by his French overlords, but waited for the opportunity to assert Cambodia's independence.

The Cambodians and Thais were traditional foes. With the outbreak of World War II Thai forces, encouraged by the Japanese, attacked the French. France agreed to a treaty in May, 1941, that ceded a number of Cambodia's western provinces to Thailand. The French presence in Cambodia was dramatically altered in March, 1945, when the Japanese took charge of the colonial administration. The Japanese persuaded the Cambodians to declare their independence within the Japanese Greater East Asia Co-Prosperity Sphere. King Sihanouk complied on March 12, 1945. The Japanese collapse, however, brought the French back to Phnom Penh in late September, 1945. They arrested many of the country's leaders on the grounds they were Japanese collaborators.

King Sihanouk was treated with respect, given his royal status. He was asked to develop a new relationship with the French and his reply was determined and straightforward. A new relationship could be reached, only if the French recognized Cambodia as an independent country. On January 7, 1946, the French recognized Cambodia as an "autonomous" kingdom within the French Union. The Cambodians viewed this as a temporary arrangement pending further negotiations. By 1949, with the French consumed in a struggle with the Viet Minh, the Cambodians pressured the French into transferring more power to the Sihanouk government, but the more radical elements within Cambodia were not appeased and armed themselves for a possible campaign against the Europeans. Fearing loss of support, King Sihanouk left Cambodia for a speaking tour in Europe and the United States. During this tour, he developed a reputation for denouncing the French. Instead of returning to Cambodia, Sihanouk went to Bangkok, the capital of Thailand, and threatened not to return until the French gave full independence to his people. Sihanouk later left Thailand and took a position in Cambodia's border region, where resistance strategy was contemplated. The French, already preoccupied in Vietnam, wanted no part of the worsening situation and on July 4, 1953, the French announced their intention to remove forces from Cambodia. On November 9, Cambodia became fully independent.

Thailand was spared the full impact of European colonialism because of its geographic location. France and Great Britain were keen rivals in the latter part of the nineteenth century. By 1890, the two empires were in direct confrontation in upper Burma and Laos. At this time, there was no clearly defined frontier between the two empires. In order to reduce suspicion, it was agreed to establish Thailand, then known as Siam, as a buffer between their respective colonial holdings. In 1893, Thailand, without being consulted, was neutralized by the two powers. The Thais were annoyed but relieved, as their independence seemed assured. The Anglo-French accord, however, did not dissuade the European states from seizing Thai territory. Between 1902 and 1909, Thailand was forced to yield control over Siem Reap and Luang Prabang to France, and Kelantan and Trengganu to Great Britain.

The reign of Rama VI (1910-1925) was without incident, despite opposition to his monarchy. It was during his reign that Thailand decided to enter World War I on the side of the Allies and sent a small detachment to Europe. In return for this service, the fiscal control exerted over Thailand was withdrawn, and the country was identified an equal in the community of nations. Absolute monarchy in Thailand was beginning to crumble, however, and finally came to an end with Rama VII (1925-1935). On June 24, 1932, high ranking officers in the Thai army and civilian bureaucracy carried out a bloodless coup, which toppled the old dynasty. Thailand's first constitution was created a few months later. A new constitutional monarchy was created, with a Supreme Council comprising important princes, princely bureaucrats, and military figures. The revolution was not a popular or radical movement, and Thailand would still be governed by members of the aristocratic elite. Nonetheless, the 1932 revolution heralded the beginning of a slow, developmental process.

Thailand was officially neutral during World War II, but did conspire with the Japanese to undermine the French position in Indochina. At the close of the war, Thailand's relative period of tranquility ended. The country became unavoidably involved in the mounting conflict in Indochina.

THE FRENCH COLLAPSE

Driven from Hanoi, the Viet Minh established their headquarters in the jungles and caves of Tonkin and Annam. By December, 1946, the decision was made by Ho Chi Minh to wage an extended war, irrespective of the cost. Ho was confident he had the support of the vast majority of Vietnamese. Ho Chi Minh concluded that only the complete withdrawal of French troops and administration would satisfy his demands. The war against the French was to last eight and a half years. It produced extremely heavy casualties, but never did the Viet Minh give any indication that they would stop short of their goal. The French attitude was less resolute. Initially confident in their capacity to subdue their Asian colony, they began to question the purpose of their mission as the toll of dead and wounded grew.

The French scored quick victories against the Viet Minh in the early stages of the conflict. The major cities and towns were cleared of the enemy, and the road between Haiphong and Hanoi was opened for traffic. The Viet Minh had challenged the French armies in a conventional posture. They soon realized that their fight had to be pursued along other lines. As the Viet Minh developed their guerrilla war tactics, the French lost the initiative. The jungles provided camouflage, and Ho's hit-and-run attacks made it virtually impossible for the French to strike back. French armor proved useless in the dense vegetation of Vietnam, and most forays into the jungles were without results. By 1950, the Viet Minh was firmly in control of the countryside, with the French confined to the large cities.

The French worked feverishly to draw popular support away from the Viet Minh. They negotiated with non-Communist Vietnamese, and in June, 1949, they called upon Emperor Bao Dai to head a quasi-independent state of Vietnam within the French Union. Prominent Vietnamese nationalists, however, refused to accept the agreement on the grounds that the new government would remain under French influence. While the French were making diligent efforts to erect a political defense against the Viet Minh, Ho Chi Minh was purging the moderates and nationalists from his coalition. The Indochinese Communist Party, which Ho reluctantly dissolved in 1945, was revitalized in 1951 under a new name, the Dang Lao Dong Vietnam, or the Worker's Party of Vietnam. By this date the Chinese Communists had consolidated their hold over China and were concerned with developments in Vietnam. Ho's government was recognized by Mao Tse-tung as the only legitimate government of Vietnam, and the Soviet Union and other Communist states followed this lead. By 1950, the Chinese were sending military supplies southward. The French appealed to the United States for assistance and Washington dispatched a stream of weapons, which the French desperately needed to contain a Vietnamese assault on their principal defense lines. Through 1952, the two sides fought numerous battles, neither gaining an advantage over the other.

France continued to press its political offensive and entered into agreements with both Cambodia and Laos. Linked with Vietnam, the three countries became the Associated States of Indochina and were promptly recognized by the United States, Great Britain, and approximately thirty other nations. The first United States economic mission to the new government of Bao Dai began its work in May, 1950, and within a year the United States became Vietnam's chief external supplier. But this did little to reduce the appeal of the Viet Minh. The continued presence of the French in Indochina only reinforced Ho's already widespread support.

The fighting grew more intense as weapons from China, the Soviet Union, and the United States were given to the combatants. The circumstances of the war also thrust them into the forefront of the Cold War as the United States and Soviet Union supported opposing sides in what soon appeared to be a clash of ideologies. By 1953, the Viet Minh had been provided with sufficient quantities of heavy artillery to bring the fortified positions of the French under direct fire. The conflict had suddenly taken on a new dimension. No longer content to hit and run, the Viet Minh mobilized for a major attack on the French army. The French gave the appearance of being confident, but the years of fruitless struggle had taken a toll on the army's morale. Toward the end of 1953, the French were surrounded by the Viet Minh at their Dien Bien Phu stronghold. A decisive battle was fought and won by the forces of Ho Chi Minh. Dien Bien Phu was surrendered on May 7, 1954. After French pleas to the United States and Great Britain for direct military intervention went unheeded, Paris declared its willingness to end the war and begin negotiations.

The United States, Great Britain, the Soviet Union, and France called for a Geneva Conference in order to bring an end to the war in Indochina. This conference met in April, 1954, and shortly after the session was convened, a joint Franco-Vietnamese announcement declared Vietnam to be sovereign. During May, the conference addressed itself to the question of Indochina's independence and unity with representatives from both the Communist and Nationalist Vietnamese in attendance. Other countries participating in the deliberations were Laos, Cambodia, and Communist China. The negotiations, which brought French involvement in Indochina to an end, were completed on July 20, 1954. The Viet Minh agreed to a provisional military demarcation line, drawn roughly along the seventeenth parallel. The French consented to pull all forces out of the region to the north of the line, and the Viet Minh agreed to do the same in the south. Three hundred days were specified to permit the free movement of people from north to south, and vice versa. No new forces could be brought into Vietnam except on a replacement basis. The Geneva Agreement also provided for an independent Laos and Cambodia, although further details were to be treated in separate documents. Finally, an International Control Commission, comprised of representatives from India, Canada, and Poland, was directed to supervise the implementation of the agreement. The agreement also planned for general elections in both the northern and southern regions of Vietnam by July, 1956.

The Geneva Agreement was opposed by the Vietnamese nationalists, who had formed the State of Vietnam (to be distinguished from Ho Chi Minh's Democratic Republic of Vietnam). They refused to sign the armistice. Their Prime Minister, Ngo Dinh Diem, condemned the partitioning of the country and called for the United Nations to administer the whole country until general elections could be held. Diem also argued against the French capacity to agree to hold elections without consulting his government. (The French were to withdraw from the remainder of Vietnam after the elections had been completed, and a final decision on unification rendered.) The United States was also a dissenting participant at Geneva. The United States acknowledged the truce agreement but refused to sign the final declaration. The American representative assured the concerned parties that it would not disturb the provisions of the agreement, but that it would consider any other nation's violation of the understanding as a threat to international peace. The United States stated it would continue to support efforts aimed at the reunification of Vietnam, but that it would also uphold the principle of the people's right to determine their own future. In this context, the United States welcomed the holding of general elections under the auspices of the United Nations.

THE AFTERMATH OF GENEVA

Ho Chi Minh's party, the Dang Lao Dong Vietnam, formed a government for the entire region north of the seventeenth parallel. North Vietnam was more heavily industrialized than the south, but deficient in agriculture. The war had destroyed much of the region's productive capacity, and reconstruction taxed the organizational ability of Ho's regime. In 1955, the country was given a three-year plan for economic development, and land distribution, which had been started earlier, was accelerated. The landlord class was purged along with the cosmopolitan elements in the cities. Thousands are alleged to have been executed, while several hundred thousand refugees fled to the south. The new regime tolerated nothing less than total obedience. The entire population was mobilized for the purpose of building the state.

Ho's and his aides' perception of conditions in South Vietnam focused on the problem of multi-factional strife. They did not believe a government could be established in the south that could command the loyalty of its disparate population. They anticipated an easy victory at the polls in 1956, and hence the eventual unification of Vietnam under their leadership. When the North Vietnamese raised the subject of the elections in the spring of 1956, however, the Premier of South Vietnam, Ngo Dinh Diem, insisted he was not bound by the terms of the Geneva Agreement insofar as his government had not signed the accords. He also stated that the North had violated the agreement on numerous occasions, an observation that was vehemently supported by the United States. Indeed, the United States had concluded quite independently that free elections were impossible given the Lao Dong's total control over the people above the seventeenth parallel, and its clandestine activities in the south. The elections were never held, and the line separating North and South Vietnam became an international frontier separating two hostile states. North and South sought to absorb each other.

Deprived of a victory at the polls, Ho reactivated his guerrilla organization, which had remained underground in the South after the 1954 Geneva conference. Between 1956 and 1959, the North Vietnamese restructured this force, recruiting men and women into small military cadres. These units were trained and equipped for a protracted effort and they were sent into battle to undermine the Saigon government's authority. In 1959, a new military phase began as the Viet Cong or South Vietnamese insurgents, under direction from Hanoi, launched their campaign to capture the South's countryside. In 1960, in North Vietnam, the Lao Dong convened its Third National Congress and publicly declared its intention to liberate South Vietnam from the United States and Ngo Dinh Diem.

The future of South Vietnam appeared to rest on the ability and popularity of Ngo Dinh Diem. As a fervent nationalist Diem could not be accused of pro-French proclivities. He was, however, a Catholic in a predominantly Buddhist society. His staunch anti-communist attitude made him suspicious of those espousing creeds different from his own. Moreover, Diem took over the government in the south, but vast areas were under the control of militant Buddhist groups, such as the Cao Dai and Hoa Hao. In Saigon the police were dominated by a politico-religious sect called the Binh Xuyen who were notorious for their criminal activities. His government was deficient in administrative and technical skills, and even the army was of questionable loyalty. The hundreds of thousands of refugees fleeing the north complicated the work of constructing a coherent political and administrative system. It was not surprising that the North Vietnamese should conclude that the South Vietnamese government would collapse under its great burden. But the North Vietnamese did not anticipate the tenacity with which Diem and his chief aides would strive to impose a highly centralized, authoritative system in South Vietnam. Nor had the North Vietnamese counted on the volume and nature of American support. As already noted, the United States came to see the struggle in Vietnam in ideological terms and it was determined to prevent the spread of what it perceived as international communism.

Diem endeavored to absorb the various sects and their private armies. When they resisted, he adopted strenuous tactics, which ultimately brought the issue of their autonomy to the surface. A United Front of all nationalist forces was organized to force Diem from power. Emperor Bao Dai was pressured to dismiss Diem, but the royal personage was without power. When fighting erupted between the Front and Diem's loyal forces, the French and Americans were on opposite sides. The French wanted Diem ousted, but the Americans chose not to heed this advice. Extensive fighting destroyed a major portion of Saigon, but the Diem government slowly established power and eased the Binh Xuyen from its powerful position. Diem then sent his army against the Hoa Hao, which had taken up arms against the government. The Hoa Hao were eventually crushed. The other important Buddhist sect, the Cao Dai, decided it would be foolish to challenge Diem's growing power and they removed themselves from the political arena. In the meantime, Diem had conducted a referendum calling upon the people to choose between himself and Bao Dai. Diem's success compelled Bao Dai to abdicate, and Ngo Dinh Diem became the President of the sovereign Republic of Vietnam. The French occupation of Vietnam south of the seventeenth parallel drew to a close and by the winter of 1956, there were two governments in Vietnam; each controlled half the country, and both claimed to represent all the Vietnamese people. Yet another significant development was the growing American presence in South Vietnam, which seemed to portend a protracted United States involvement in Indochina.

LAOS, CAMBODIA, AND THAILAND:
POST-GENEVA

From 1953 the Viet Minh were actively pursuing military advantages in Laos. Joining with the Pathet Lao Communists, the two forces virtually severed Laos in half, but stopped short of seizing the principal cities of Vientiane and Luang Prabang. When the Geneva Conference was convened in July, 1954, Laos was *de facto* a partitioned country, and the accords took notice of this reality. All foreign troops were ordered to withdraw from Laos. Pathet Lao forces were directed to occupy the two northern border provinces, and a national army comprising all Lao factions was planned. The Royal government in Luang Prabang was supposed to hold sovereignty over the country until elections were held to achieve a formal reunification of the country. As in Vietnam, an International Commission for Supervision and Control, composed of representatives from Poland, India, and Canada, was established to oversee the implementation of the agreement. A similar arrangement was developed for Cambodia, and the French and Viet Minh pledged to withdraw their forces from the country. Cambodia, however, insisted upon reserving the right to permit American troops to be stationed on its territory, vehemently insisting on its sovereign status. It is important to recall that the United States refused to become a signatory to the Geneva Agreement. That same year, the United States organized the Southeast Asia Treaty Organization (SEATO), which in a separate protocol appeared to guarantee the independence and territorial integrity of South Vietnam, Cambodia, and Laos. Thus, the Geneva Conference signalled the end of French dominance in Indochina, but it did not rule out the possibility of continuing major power involvement. The Indochinese states had achieved considerable independence given the French departure, but internal questions were far from resolved. Now the United States, China, and the Soviet Union were left to play a more direct role in shaping the area's destiny.

Cambodia was by far the more settled of the Indochinese countries. A Constitution had been put into force as early as 1947, and a Cambodian parliament was convened in 1948. Although political factions threatened the political experiment, King Sihanouk tried to act as arbiter. The King's major opposition, however, came from the radical Khmer Issarak (Free Cambodia), which later became the Cambodian Democrat Party. Given the party's capacity to impede the work of the government. King Sihanouk eventually dissolved the Parliament and between 1949 and 1951, he ruled Cambodia by decree. In new elections conducted in 1951, the Democrats again won a majority, and King Sihanouk once more announced he was assuming full powers. Although the King's acts were in violation of the Constitution, the Cambodian population did not contest his authority. A pattern of rule known as the *Royal Mandate* (1951-1953) was imposed on the country, and Cambodia was generally stable. It was during this period that the Geneva Conference was held and King Sihanouk earned the respect of his subjects by obtaining major concessions from the French. In February, 1955, Sihanouk allowed the Cambodians to express their opinion on the handling of the state's affairs. When the referendum was completed the King had received 99.8 percent approval. Shortly thereafter he abdicated the throne and declared his intention to become a political leader. It was after this abdication that Sihanouk took the title of Prince, and has since been addressed as Prince Sihanouk.

Sihanouk created the Sangkum party, or People's Socialist Community. In time he gained ground over the political opposition, which heretofore had perceived him as an instrument of the French. Sihanouk's dedication to the cause of the Cambodian peasantry, his efforts in behalf of Cambodian reconstruction, and his staunch nationalist posture vis-à-vis the French and other foreign elements, raised him to new heights of popularity. In national elections held in September, 1955, Prince Sihanouk's Sangkum won every seat in the ninety-one member National Assembly. Even the more radical segments of the opposition were recruited into the new political system. Sihanouk understood the task of building a viable nation lay before him. He was active in all spheres of national activity, organizing youth movements, overseeing the training of administrators and technicians, and assisting in programs to socialize the tribal hill peoples. Sihanouk recognized that Cambodia's resources for full scale economic development were meager, and he was not adverse to receiving financial and material assistance from the United States and even France. Indeed, the latter was instrumental in building the port of Sihanoukville, which altered Cambodia's traditional dependence on Saigon and the Vietnamese. Prince Sihanouk was determined to maintain Cambodia's independence. He labored tirelessly to keep the civil wars in Vietnam and Laos from sweeping over his country. His neutrality, however, was seldom respected by his neighbors or those who came from other lands to fight in Indochina.

Laos had difficulty from the start in normalizing a governmental system. The International Control Commission proved ineffective in mediating between the government and the Pathet Lao. Disputes arose over the correct interpretation of the Geneva Accords. The Royal government wanted the integration of Pathet Lao forces within the Lao army before other issues were considered. The Pathet Lao, led by Prince Souphanouvong, called for political integration as a first step. When elections were held in December, 1955, the Pathet Lao boycotted them, but 80 percent of the voters turned out anyway. In August, 1956, Prince Souvanna Phouma was called upon to form the new Lao government. Souphanouvong then consented to join with him in a government of National Union. This arrangement was short-lived. The Pathet Lao's political organization, the Neo Lao Hak Xat, was believed by some moderate and conservative members of the Royal government to be gaining control over the decision-making process. Thus, an anti-Communist group called the Committee for the Defense of National Interests was assembled, which eventually forced Souvanna Phouma from office and drove the Pathet Lao from the government.

The leader of the Committee was a colonel (soon to be elevated to the rank of general) in the Royal army named Phoumi Nosavan. The Royal government, however, came under the leadership of Phoui Sananikone. It was in his name that Prince Souphanouvong was arrested along with most of the members of the Neo Lao Hak Xat in the National Assembly. The Pathet Lao army retreated into the back country and from there prepared for a renewal of hostilities. The Communists accused the Royal government of falling under the influence of the United States. When Sananikone attempted to purge some members of the Committee from his government, the Lao army, under Nosavan's leadership, forced him from power. As expected, General Nosavan created a government more to his liking, but it too did not last very long. In August, 1960, a group led by a young paratrooper named Kong Le seized Vientiane, and Souvanna Phouma was returned as Premier of the Lao government. By this time, Prince Souphanouvong and many of his supporters had escaped from prison to join forces in the more remote provinces. Souvanna Phouma wished to avoid an intensification of the conflict and called for still another coalition government. General Nosavan was brought into Phouma's Cabinet, but he continued to advocate ideas of his own. He pushed for a revolutionary committee, which Prince Boun Oum agreed to head. After Souvanna Phouma and Prince Souphanouvong agreed to form a government, both Boun Oum and Nosavan were invited to join. The military officers that they represented, however, refused to accept such an arrangement. Prince Souvanna Phouma was forced to flee to Cambodia, as General Nosavan again seized control of Vientiane. The new King, Savang Vatthana, was urged by the military to call upon Boun Oum to form a new government. General Nosavan became Deputy Prime Minister, as well as Minister of Defense. Moreover, the new Boun Oum government was quickly recognized by the United States and neighboring Thailand.

Kong Le believed in the possibility of drawing the Royal Lao army and the Pathet Lao into a unified force. He formed a leftist government in the Plain of Jars with Souvana Phouma's support. This government was quickly recognized by the Communist states, as well as India. The lines between the two factions were clearly drawn. In the winter of 1961, Kong Le's troops, along with the Pathet Lao, mounted a significant offensive with assistance provided by the Soviet Union via Hanoi. The conservative forces under General Nosavan were compelled to retreat. The United States, fearing an intensification of the fighting and the possibility of its spreading throughout Indochina and into Thailand, agreed to convene an international conference. The three princes, Souvanna Phouma, Souphanouvong, and Boun Oum, were flown to Switzerland where a tentative agreement was arrived at. When difficulties emerged the princes met again in Cambodia, where it was finally declared that Souvanna Phouma would form a new government. Eventually, the United States withdrew its support from Boun Oum, and General Nosavan was forced to seek asylum in Thailand. A government of National Union was organized with Prince Souphanouvong as the Deputy Prime Minister. All foreign troops were ordered out of Laos. A unified army and police force were forecast. By this time, however, the conflict between North and South Vietnam was gaining in intensity. Laos could not remain isolated from that struggle because the principal supply routes to insurgents in the South were roads built through the Laotian jungle, better known as the Ho Chi Minh Trail.

After World War II and up through the Geneva Accords in 1954, Thailand enjoyed comparative tranquility. But the success of the Viet Minh in defeating the French required a reappraisal of the country's overall security. Hence, Thailand joined the Southeast Asia Treaty Organization and permitted the alliance's headquarters to be established in Bangkok. The Thais expected the United States to provide for their defense. They viewed the situation across the Mekong border in Laos with considerable concern. North Vietnamese forces were known to be operating in Laos. By 1955 there were signs that small cadres had moved into the more remote northern provinces of Thailand, as well as along their northern border with Malaysia. The government initiated a program to prevent the Communists from recruiting ethnic and religious groups that had been suppressed by the Thai majority. It was obvious, however, the insurgents could only be contained, not eliminated.

Thailand has long been a political autocracy. The general population has been passive, politics being reserved for elites. Succession, therefore, was more likely to be expressed in the form of a coup than through any predictable or electoral process. The coup d'état of 1932 gave the military a dominant role in the political life of the nation. Although experiments with constitutions, political parties, and elected parliaments had been attempted, they made little impression on the Thai population. Thus, with a growing security problem along its eastern frontier, Thai leaders felt justified in taking strong measures to ensure the country's independence. In 1958, Field Marshal Sarit Thanarat assumed control of the Thai government and promptly banned all political activities. Martial law was imposed on the country and remained in effect through the 1960s. Marshal Sarit died in 1963, but his successor, Thanom Kittikachorn, continued Sarit's policies despite a declared intention to permit the formation of political parties. When this issue was aired, the Kittikachorn government reminded the petitioners of the war raging in Indochina, as well as the insurgency within their own country. Although successful in dampening the desire for partisan politics, it was apparent that Thai society had passed into a transitional stage: the demand for some form of participatory politics could not be ignored indefinitely.

THE SECOND INDOCHINESE WAR

Unlike the remainder of Indochina, the North Vietnamese set about, relatively unhindered, the tasks of consolidating their political system. Similar to most Communist states, the North Vietnam Constitution did not mention the Lao Dong, or Communist Party. Nevertheless, the government and the entire administrative apparatus came under the control of the party. Ho Chi Minh was recognized as President of the country, head of government, Supreme Commander of the Armed Forces, Chairman of the National Defense Council, and Chairman of the Central Committee of the Lao Dong. He also dominated the party's Politburo. Although the 1960 Constitution replaced the 1946 Constitution, there was no mistaking the absence of any limitations on the operations of government in either document. In North Vietnam, the Constitution was not a defense against arbitrary power but rather a description of basic structures and how they functioned. It was a document whose central purpose was instructional. The masses were to be exposed to specific values related to their obligations to state and society. In this regard, the 1960 Constitution followed a path laid down earlier in the Constitution of the Chinese People's Republic. North Vietnam was declared a people's democracy, in which laborers and peasants combined their energies under the leadership of the working-class. The Constitution was emphatic about the need to reunify Vietnam, a goal which was envisaged with the defeat of "United States imperialism."

Although the Constitution describes the National Assembly as the highest organ in the state, there is no reference to legislative supremacy. In fact, the executive and legislative institutions are not clearly delineated. It can be assumed that whatever powers they possess are treated as a collective whole. Most important is the fact that the Lao Dong party is absolutely powerful, and that no organ of government can function without first receiving its sanction. Similar to all constitutions, the North Vietnamese Constitution lists numerous fundamental rights, such as freedom of speech and assembly and freedom from arbitrary arrest. Citizens are permitted to vote at the age of 18 and run for public office at 21. In the economic sphere, the Constitution speaks of several forms of ownership during the transition to socialism; "state ownership" involves all the people; "cooperative ownership" refers to the collective ownership of the working masses; and "private ownership" which permits certain forms of national capitalism. The right to inherit property is also guaranteed, and citizens may petition the government for a redress of grievances. All citizens are declared equal before the law, and women are given the same status and economic rewards as men. Article 38 takes note of the liberal nature of these fundamental rights and asserts that no person is permitted "to use democratic freedoms to the detriment of the interests of the state and of the people."

The National Assembly of North Vietnam had more than 400 members, including representatives from the region south of the seventeenth parallel. They were elected by universal suffrage for four-year terms by secret ballot. The Assembly not only was supposed to pass laws, it also could amend the Constitution, elect the president and vice-president, the president of the People's Supreme Court, and the chief prosecutor of that court. The Assembly, however, usually met only twice a year. Its actual powers were pre-empted by the executive arm of the Lao Dong, the Politburo. It was also through the Lao Dong apparatus that the president and Council of Ministers performed their tasks. The president of the Republic was constitutionally the chief executive officer. He worked through a Council of Ministers that was often described as the Government or State Council. Unlike the Assembly, the Council of Ministers operated continuously and oversaw the work of the national bureaucracy. (See Figures 6-1 and 6-2.) Essentially, the identical constitution and system were adopted on July 2, 1976, for the Unified People's Republic of Vietnam. The National Assembly now consists of 492 members.

Mass participation in governing the society is made possible through

**THE FORMAL GOVERNMENTAL STRUCTURE OF NORTH VIETNAM
PRIOR TO REUNIFICATION IN 1976**

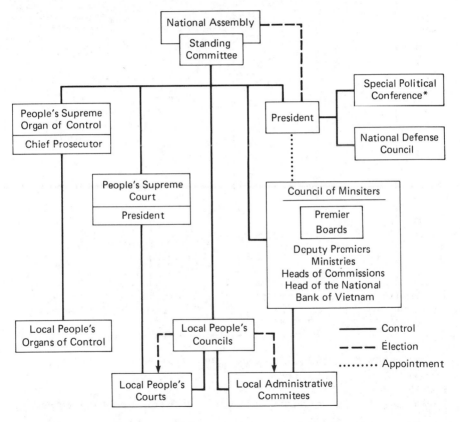

*Convened when necessary by the President. The first conference was held in March 1964.

FIGURE 6-1
The formal governmental structure of North Vietnam prior to reunification in 1976.
Source: Harvey H. Smith et al., *Area Handbook of North Vietnam*, Washington, D.C.: U.S. Government Printing Office, 1967, p. 168.

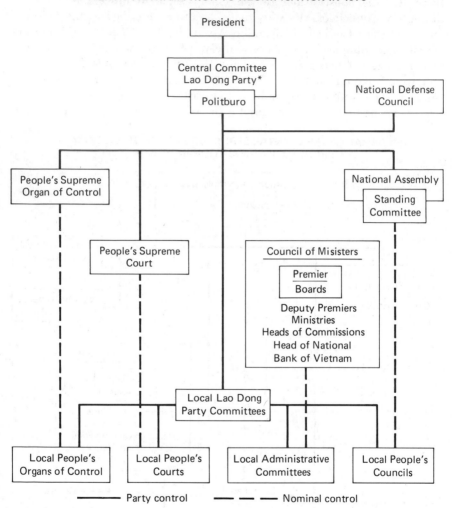

FUNCTIONING OF THE GOVERNMENTAL SYSTEM
OF NORTH VIETNAM PRIOR TO REUNIFICATION IN 1976

*Lao Dong Party is an extraconstitutional body, the principal members of which also
occupy all key government positions.

FIGURE 6-2
**Functioning of the governmental system of North Vietnam prior to reunification
in 1976.**
Source: Harvey et al., *Area Handbook of North Vietnam,* p. 168.

the People's Organs of control. Constitutionally responsible to the National Assembly, in practice they appear to be independent of all government agencies and answer only to their own immediate superiors in the

Lao Dong. The People's Organs scrutinize the work of the bureaucracies and generally aim at maintaining a high degree of public awareness among officials at all levels. Corruption and administrative malpractices or inefficiencies are particular concerns of these bodies, and unproductive officials are publicly criticized.

The People's Organs of Control are to be distinguished from local government units, which operate as administrative extensions of the central government and Lao Dong. These bodies are identified as People's Councils. The People's Council is divided into representative organs and administrative or executive committees. The country is divided into provinces and districts. Municipal areas are identified by cities or towns, and they in turn are subdivided into wards. In the rural areas, the districts are subdivided into villages and hamlets. People's Councils and administrative committees are found in every division and subdivision. They are elected by the local population for three-year terms in the provinces and for two-year terms in the lesser territorial units. Membership varies according to population. Thus the villages and hamlets have the smaller number of representatives and so-called *minority autonomous* (self-governing) regions have the largest. The People's Councils execute government edicts, plan development projects, check expenditures, and maintain law and order. Decisions taken at local levels, however, are subject to challenge from higher administrative offices, and orders can be reversed or revised without consulting the lower body.

The administrative committee of the People's Council is the most influential. It is responsible for the day-to-day requirements of local government. These bodies are directly controlled and hence influenced by the Lao Dong, which ratifies its membership. They direct the work of the lower bodies and are connected in an intricate network of higher organs to the Council of Ministers of the Republic.

In the final analysis, however, North Vietnam and now all Vietnam, has always been governed by a small elite element whose principal base of operations is the Lao Dong party. Since Ho Chi Minh's death in 1969, no single personality has been established as the supreme ruler of the country. The following list identifies the prominent leaders of the Lao Dong party before the country was unified in 1976:

Name	*Position*
Le Duan	First Secretary of the Lao Dong party.
Truong Chinh	Chairman, National Assembly
Pham Van Dong	Premier
Pham Hung	A Deputy Premier
Vo Nguyen Giap	Defense Minister, Commander in Chief of the North Vietnamese army.
Le Duc Tho	Chief of the party's organization department

Name	Position
Nguyen Chi Thanh	A senior general
Nguyen Duy Trinh	Minister of Foreign Affairs
Tran Quoc Hoan	Minister of Public Security
Van Tien Dung	Chief of the General Staff of the North Vietnamese army.

Ho Chi Minh, even in death, remains a symbol of Vietnamese unity. For the time being his successors are content to remain in the background. As members of the Politburo, they are responsible for keeping the state apparatus running smoothly. They have been known to be divided on important issues, however. In the late 1960s, factions developed among the key figures, with Le Duan and Pham Van Dong on one side and Vo Nguyen Giap and Truong Chinh on the other. They were divided over preferences in the Sino-Soviet dispute, as well as over military tactics being employed in South Vietnam. Subsequent events, however, have shown that the North Vietnamese leaders are capable of moderating their differences, thus sustaining their unified administration.

The political picture of South Vietnam in the 1960s did not compare with the organized discipline of the North. Ngo Dinh Diem was the undisputed leader in South Vietnam from the time of the Geneva Conference until November, 1963. But after initial victories over dissident sects and warring factions, his regime began to suffer. Diem's insistence on developing a personal dictatorship and his suspicions concerning all those around him save his intimate family members were factors contributing to his decline. In addition, the widespread corruption and inefficiency of the government bureaucracy, and its hesitation to implement social and economic reforms prevented any genuine mobilization of popular support. By this time the United States was heavily committed to the survival of South Vietnam as an independent state. However, the United States could do nothing to make the Diem administration more palatable to the South Vietnamese people.

South Vietnam was, in theory, a constitutional democracy, borrowing from both the French and American experiences. The system of government was described as parliamentary, but real power was concentrated in the presidency. Although powers were distributed among the executive, legislative, and judicial branches, nothing prevented Diem from interfering and pre-empting their prerogatives. By the same token, Diem made a sham of the electoral process. His success at the polls was not a true test of his public support.

Diem gained the confidence of the Americans because he was a sophisticated, somewhat westernized Roman Catholic. Also, he was completely committed to the fight against communism in Indochina. He brought to his office intellectual skills and a reputation for incorruptible behavior. What the Americans did not realize was that Diem could not adapt to the changing conditions in Vietnam. He was to be the last of the notable Confucians, a mandarin who demanded obedience and unquestioning loyalty. His paternalistic instincts and his aloof, scholarly manner were more suited to the past, not the turbulent era into which Southeast Asia had been plunged. Diem confused the immediacy of the threat to South Vietnam with his own personal well-being. The more resistance he met, the more tyrannical his response. Diem emerged from the same northern province in Annam as Ho Chi Minh and had served in the Annamese government as early as 1932. He became a dedicated anti-Communist after the death of his elder brother at the hands of the Viet Minh in 1945. As head of state in South Vietnam, Diem tended to rely on his co-religionists rather than the majority Buddhist community, which he felt could not be firm in the face of the Communist advance.

Diem was momentarily successful in isolating his rivals. But in the course of this activity, he placed inordinate powers in the hands of family members. His brother Nhu built and ran the secret police, while his brothers and sister-in-law, the wife of Nhu, occupied key posts in the administration. Diem's tactics did more to divide the population of South Vietnam than unite them. Confronted with a well-organized Communist threat, Diem felt compelled to develop a political organization, which, like that of his adversary, would tolerate no opposition. But Diem did not have the time nor the conditions to successfully challenge the Communists. His determination to produce a viable system often alienated many of those who might have buttressed his endeavor. Instead of trying to reconcile disparate groups and sects, he destroyed the very societal foundation that could withstand Ho's forces. Disaffected groups were either driven into the arms of the Viet Cong and North Vietnamese, or so hopelessly disillusioned that they ceased to benefit the regime or add to the strength of the South Vietnamese state.

By 1959 the North Vietnamese were ready to continue their conquest of the South. The land reforms in the North had caused severe unrest. Only after the countryside had been pacified could Ho Chi Minh consider launching a protracted guerrilla war in the South. The first step was to mobilize agents of the Viet Minh who had gone underground after the Geneva Conference. These cadres were reactivated, and terror seized the country-side as village headmen and government officials were brutally murdered or kidnapped. In time, the rural areas became bases from which pressure was applied to the larger towns and cities. Efforts to counter this threat to South Vietnam were unsuccessful, and the South Vietnamese Army (ARVN) revealed weaknesses that the supply of modern weapons could not cure.

The inability of South Vietnam's military to cope with the Communist attack was interpreted by the Diem government as another example of enemy penetration. Thus the regime became increasingly repressive, and at the same time, more unpopular. When members of the army sought to air their grievances, they were silenced. Buddhist monks who sought to petition the government to adopt more humane policies were arrested and often tortured. The political opposition was judged to be in violation of the law. What was left of the constitutional process was systematically dismantled. The people of South Vietnam could find little distinction between the terror of the Communists and the oppression of the secret police, or *Can Lao*. Although Diem was not directly involved in the excesses of his police, he bore responsibility for their acts. When Buddhist monks began to set themselves afire in Hue, and popular unrest against Catholic domination produced mass demonstrations, which were indiscriminately fired upon by the police, the Diem edifice was seriously undermined. On November 1, 1963, in an effort to prevent the Diem government from making a more forceful attack on the Buddhist associations, General Duong Van Minh (Big Minh) seized the government. Diem and his brother Nhu were murdered. The deaths of these leaders, however, did not bring calm to events in South Vietnam. Groups, heretofore suppressed by the regime, resurfaced to claim their lost privileges.

Big Minh could not contend with the variety of demands placed upon him. He was soon replaced by other members of the armed forces. This was a period of significant instability in which the Communists were able to consolidate control over much of the countryside. It was in this general situation that the United States, under the leadership of President Lyndon Baines Johnson, decided to make a maximum effort in South Vietnam.

The Tonkin Gulf incident, in which it is alleged North Vietnamese torpedo boats attacked American destroyers in international waters, caused a crisis in the United States. The President called upon the United States Senate to pass a resolution condemning the act and authorizing him to make an appropriate response. The Senate complied with the request and the United States' commitment to South Vietnam escalated dramatically. Under John F. Kennedy, the United States had committed less than twenty thousand troops, mainly comprised of special forces and logistical supply elements. Now the air force and navy were ordered to play a major role, and regular army and Marine Corps personnel were ordered into the field. Eventually, the United States was to send more than one-half million frontline forces to Vietnam. Additional numbers were on ships in the marginal seas off Southeast Asia and in adjoining countries, especially in Thailand. With such a commitment of American personnel, weapons, and other assistance, it was quite natural for the United States to take particular interest in South Vietnam's troubled domestic politics.

The United States government had gambled on Diem establishing a meaningful alternative to Ho Chi Minh's Communist system. Diem's failure highlighted the difficulties of trying to create a popular counter-force and government among the disparate people of South Vietnam. Between 1964 and early 1965, efforts were made to restore a semblance of civilian government to South Vietnam. General Nguyen Khanh organized a coalition of all political groups, but it soon collapsed. Tran Van Huong and Phan Huy Quat, civilians, formed governments but they too were unsuccessful in moderating differences among the competing sects. Finally, the military took full power. In February, 1965, American aircraft bombed North Vietnamese targets for the first time, marking a dramatic expansion of the theater of war. By this date, the Viet Cong had extended control over most of South Vietnam, north of Saigon. United States authorities had concluded that only a massive air campaign against the Ho Chi Minh Trail supply routes, military staging areas, and industrial capacity could prevent the eventual collapse of all South Vietnam. Connected with this military program and of importance, therefore, was the establishment of a strong, authoritative government in Saigon.

On June 9, 1965, Air Marshal Nguyen Cao Ky became the Prime Minister of South Vietnam, and Lieutenant General Nguyen Van Thieu assumed the presidency. Ky was the more dominant personality at the outset, but he apparently was too flamboyant for the Americans, who preferred the more reserved Thieu. Thus, with the help of his brother officers in the army, and apparently with the concurrence of the United States, General Thieu gained primary control over the political process in Saigon. In a drive to win legitimacy for their administration, the military leaders organized a Constituent Assembly for the purpose of drafting a new presidential constitution. The Assembly labored from September, 1966, until March, 1967, when the new law of the land was completed. The Constitution was promulgated on April 1, 1967. In September, 1967, elections were conducted to give the Constitution full force. Ky was forced to accept second place on a ballot with Thieu, who was elected the country's president. Ky dutifully accepted the powerless role of vice-president. The Armed Forces Council of South Vietnam shuddered at the thought of Thieu and Ky running against one another and splitting the armed forces, hence Ky's capitulation despite his political ambitions.

On the positive side, the general elections were the first of their kind in South Vietnam. They were judged to be relatively free, except for the pressure exerted by the government bureaucrats who were charged with getting people to the polls. It was important for the South Vietnamese government to demonstrate that they could hold open and free elections despite the war raging within. It was hoped a sizeable turnout would also prove that the majority of South Vietnamese were anti-Communist. Almost five million voters cast their ballots, which seemed to indicate that the majority of the South's population was firmly under government control. Moreover, the fairness of the elections can be gauged from the fact that the Thieu-Ky ticket received only 34.8 percent of the votes cast, far smaller than any of the earlier predictions. The leading runner-up was the civilian politician, Truong Dinh Dzu, a Saigon lawyer who received 17.2 percent of the ballots. Dzu had campaigned on a peace platform and had directed severe criticism at the military establishment. Numerous other candidates divided the remainder of the votes.

Overall, the elections reiterated the fragmented nature of South Vietnam's politics and society. However, the elections brought at least a modicum of legitimacy to South Vietnam's government, moving the country ever so slightly in the direction of realizing a political life. The many different opinions that were represented in the Assembly suggested a significant amount of political vitality. Combined with the voter turnout, this seemed to imply a growing belief in South Vietnam's future. The negative factor was the awareness that the majority of Vietnamese wanted little to do with military regimes, but were too divided among themselves to prevent the military's domination. Clearly, President Thieu and his military advisors could not overlook the need to maintain a firm hand in the face of what they perceived to be a growing subversive threat. It was this fear that caused the government to have the runner-up candidate, Truong Dinh Dzu, arrested. American fears that the military leaders would utilize their new powers to completely crush the opposition were justified in the ensuing months.

It was the enormous American commitment to South Vietnam that prevented the country from falling to the insurgents. Indeed, it was the relative success of the American effort that enabled the country to stabilize its political situation and to conduct a business-as-usual approach to government. But there was at least as much suspicion of Americans as there was gratitude. Those in government were uncertain about their future, given past American actions which forced the ouster of Diem and which to the South Vietnamese appeared to be highly contradictory. Those outside the government were convinced that the United States was concerned with establishing a regime that served its interests. All American attempts to reduce factionalism in South Vietnam were doomed to failure. But the real test of American resolve in Indochina came just five months after the Thieu government took office.

The National Liberation Front, or *Viet Cong*, supported by a massive force from North Vietnam, launched the greatest military offensive in the long history of warfare in Indochina. The timing for the attack was the Buddhist New Year, and the campaign was quickly called the *Tet Offensive*. Starting on January 29, 1968, virtually all major towns and cities, including Saigon, came under attack. The fighting was ferocious and often hand-to-hand. The Communists sought to demonstrate, contrary to predictions by the American commander in South Vietnam, General William Westmoreland, that the North was capable of carrying the fight into every region of South Vietnam. Casualties on both sides in the Tet Offensive were extremely high. Property damage was extensive. In Hue, the ancient capital, little remained standing after three weeks of savage encounters. The Tet Offensive, as later events were to show, was the United States' Dien Bien Phu. The Americans had not been militarily defeated. On the contrary, American forces had taken a heavy toll of the enemy, and all territory had been regained. But there was a growing realization in the United States that the Vietnam war could not be won on the battlefield; a political solution, no matter how elusive, had to be found.

President Thieu had reason to mistrust his American ally. But being completely dependent on the United States, he was compelled to acquiesce to most policies laid down by the United States government. Thieu was embittered by President Johnson's decision to order a partial end to the bombing of North Vietnam. Thieu opposed the talks that began in Paris in May, 1968, between representatives of the North Vietnamese and American governments. In October, 1968, the bombing of the North ceased completely. By March, 1969, the National Liberation Front had been permitted to join the Paris deliberations. Reluctantly, Thieu also sent a delegation to France, and the peace conference began in earnest. In June, 1969, the Viet Cong declared the establishment of a Provisional Revolutionary Government of South Vietnam. It was accorded diplomatic recognition as the only lawful government of South Vietnam by other Communist countries and so-called neutral states, which included Cambodia.

In January, 1969, President Richard M. Nixon succeeded Johnson in the White House. He promptly appointed Henry Kissinger to be his advisor on national security affairs. Nixon had campaigned for the presidency on a platform that called for withdrawal of American forces from Vietnam and terminating the war with "honor." But with Kissinger assisting him, the American President was also determined to leave Vietnam in a strong position from which to defend its independence. Therefore, the United States took a less conciliatory position in Paris and increased pressure on the North Vietnamese and Viet Cong. North Vietnam was again brought under air attack. For the first time, American strategic bombers (B-52s) were ordered to bomb targets north of the seventeenth parallel. A surprising extension of the war came when Nixon ordered American troops into Cambodia in May, 1970.

Prince Sihanouk had struggled against mounting pressure to keep Cambodia out of the war in Vietnam. He knew the Cambodian border was being used as a sanctuary for Viet Cong and North Vietnamese contingents. He was well aware that American aircraft had bombed these areas in an attempt to curtail guerrilla forays into South Vietnam. Nevertheless, he insisted on his country's neutrality, an attitude that worked to safeguard Cambodia's population. Internally, Sihanouk was faced with a growing insurgency in the form of Khmer Rouge, or Cambodian Communists, who sought a change in the country's aristocratic system. The Prince could not yield to the Khmer Rouge, but he was aware of a need to develop flexibility on social and economic issues. Until 1966, Prince Sihanouk had no difficulty in determining the makeup of the National Assembly. His Sangkum (see page 270) dominated the political process, and there were no real attempts to challenge, let alone displace it. But Prince Sihanouk noted the rising Communist sentiment and hence organized a *contre-gouvernement*, or "shadow cabinet," comprised of opposition elements. This unusual step was followed by another: the Prince provided the opposition with a physical plant in Phnom Penh from which it could publish a newspaper. The opposition thus availed itself of the opportunity to level heavy criticism against the government.

The Cambodian government was astounded at what the Prince had done. When they proceeded to criticize his actions, Sihanouk promptly dismissed the government and once more assumed dictatorial powers. The key to Sihanouk's conflict with Cambodian officialdom was the Vietnam war. The Prince wanted Cambodia to remain neutral no matter the consequences. His fear was that any involvement, no matter how limited or indirect, would render Cambodia a battleground, ultimately destroying its territorial integrity. Cambodian neutrality, therefore, implied the participation of differing political elements in the country's political, social, and economic life. Moreover, Sihanouk's reasoning involved his perception of the American role in Indochina. He was convinced that the United States would eventually tire of its assignment in Vietnam and withdraw its forces. In such circumstances, Sihanouk was prepared to come to terms with his Communist opposition and neighbors.

Cambodia's conservative leaders did not agree with Prince Sihanouk. They could not imagine that Cambodian neutrality could be preserved when the country was already being utilized by the warring camps. It was their conviction that Cambodia should acknowledge that their interests were linked with the American presence. In 1967 these leaders began to insist on Cambodian support for American policies in Southeast Asia. Sihanouk, however, was steadfast in his convictions. He refused to grant the conservatives their wishes, arguing that Cambodia could not defend itself against both the Khmer Rouge from within, and the Vietnamese from without. But the problem of how to deal with the spreading insurgency in Cambodia did not lend itself to simple solutions. The Khmer

Rouge were not content with the regions under their control. Their stated aim was to overthrow the aristocratic element that dominated the socio-political and economic life of the country. Toward this objective they began a terror campaign. The government's response was a more resolute stand against the guerrillas, and even Sihanouk was powerless to prevent their clashing. In March, 1970, a series of anti-Communist demonstrations rocked the major municipalities in Cambodia. Prince Sihanouk was in France at the time, and he was asked to speak out publicly against the Viet Cong, who were using Cambodian territory from which to launch attacks against the Saigon government. Sihanouk refused to heed this advice and threatened those members of the Cambodian government, who he believed were undermining the country's neutrality, with dismissal.

The Cambodian National Assembly and Council of the Kingdom met in joint session. They concluded that the Prince would not change his position. The assembled leaders decided to strip Prince Sihanouk of his powers. They hastily assembled a new government under the leadership of General Lon Nol and Sirik Matak. Cheng Heng, the aging President of the National Assembly was made acting head of state. Prince Sihanouk left France for Peking via Moscow. No longer able to play the role of a neutral, Sihanouk called upon the Cambodians to oppose the new regime. He vowed to return to his country after it had been liberated by popular forces. Shortly after this sequence of events, American and South Viet-namese troops swept across the frontier into Cambodia. Although there was no indication that the Lon Nol government had been consulted prior to this move, it was clear that his government supported the campaign to destroy the Viet Cong sanctuaries. Although the Americans remained in Cambodia for only a brief period, there was no retreating from the course that had been set in motion. Cambodia was now considered a belligerent in what had suddenly become a large scale Indochinese war.

On October 9, 1970, the monarchy was dissolved, and Cambodia became a Republic. All royal titles were dropped: however, the rulers of Cambodia continued to represent the same conservative elements that had traditionally governed the country. Little did they know at the time that the course they had taken was irreversible and that on their passing, the new Communist governors of Cambodia would not have to agonize over the best course to follow in ridding Southeast Asia of its oldest monarchy—the conservatives had already accomplished this task.

Unlike Cambodia, Laos could never claim to be neutral in the Vietnam war. Although Souvanna Phouma tried to keep Laos from being overrun by Pathet Lao forces, and coalition governments which included the leftists had been agreed to, all the major belligerents in the Viet-namese conflict used Laos for their particular purposes. The North Viet-namese built trails, tunnels, underground stations, and munitions depots in eastern Laos. This infrastructure became very important to the North Vietnamese war effort. For its part, the United States was actively involved in organizing the tribal people, which played a principal role in stemming the Pathet Lao advance. American aircraft also rained down thousands of tons of bombs on Laos in an effort to slow down the war supplies and reinforcements that moved down the Ho Chi Minh Trail. Thus the Souvanna Phouma government never functioned as a meaningful institution. Laos's economy was wrecked by the war, and the country was dependent on American aid. As a result of this dependency, the Pathet Lao intensified their activities in 1968 and again in 1970. All Souvanna Phouma could do was complain to the International Control Commission, which was itself divided along ideological lines and powerless to exert any influence.

In 1971, emboldened by the Cambodian incursion the year before, South Vietnamese forces were sent across the border into Laos for the purpose of cutting off the Ho Chi Minh Trail. Although the Americans provided logistical support, no United States troops took part in the campaign. When the South Vietnamese force met with stiff opposition, the troops panicked. The campaign ended in disaster with the Americans attempting to rescue what remnants remained of the invading army. The foray into Laos was supposedly a test of a much heralded United States policy called *Vietnamization*. The term implied the training and equipping of an expanded South Vietnamese army, which could adequately defend South Vietnam when the Americans withdrew. Apart from the humiliating defeat visited upon the South Vietnamese, the thrust into Laos only tended to widen the war to the outer limits of Indochina. By mid-1971, it was fairly obvious that once the Americans departed Indochina, only a military solution would determine the political future of the region.

THE PARIS ACCORDS OF 1973

By 1971 the Americans were beginning to leave Vietnam in significant numbers. Despite examples to the contrary, there were many official United States declarations about the success of the Vietnamization program. It was argued the South Vietnamese could defend themselves as long as the United States continued to supply the country with arms and economic assistance. Indeed, many military observers had concluded that the war in the South was over and that only scattered Viet Cong action in remote areas could be anticipated. But this sanguine perception was not shared by those who viewed the political scene. In fact, the future of the South Vietnam political system was cause for much concern. Thieu had grown more aloof and autocratic. Comparisons were being made between his behavior and that of Ngo Dinh Diem prior to his overthrow and murder. Like Diem, Thieu insisted on concentrating power in his own hands. Even Nguyen Cao Ky was forced from Thieu's government and into an opposition posture. Thieu's support was drawn from the army, the Catholics, and the Americans, and the latter were now very problematical given the rising disdain for the South Vietnam government in the United States. American dissatisfaction with Thieu multiplied when the Vietnamese President forced opposing candidates off the ballot in the 1971 elections. Challenges had developed from both Nguyen Cao Ky and Duong Van Minh. Each man was attractive to different segments of South Vietnamese society. But Thieu feared a loss of personal prestige, even if he thought he had sufficient support to carry the campaign. Therefore, both candidates were persuaded to withdraw their names from contention. Thieu ran unopposed in the 1971 election but his "victory" did little to bolster his appeal among the people of South Vietnam.

By 1972, it was clear that the Americans intended to pull all combat forces out of Vietnam. The future and survival of an independent South Vietnam was more than ever the responsibility of the Thieu government, the South Vietnamese military, and the polyglot South Vietnamese society. At the same time the discussions between the major contenders continued in Paris. When the United States sensed that the North Vietnamese were stalling to delay a final settlement, President Nixon ordered an intensification of the bombing in the northern cities, the mining of Vietnam's principal rivers and harbors, and a selective blockade along the Indochinese coastline. Although it was never determined if these acts were instrumental in breaking the deadlock, negotiations were resumed in earnest. On January 27, 1973, the United States, the North Vietnamese, representatives of the Viet Cong, and the South Vietnam government put their signatures to an "Agreement on Ending the War and Restoring Peace in Vietnam." A separate protocol was signed with regard to the hostilities in Laos, but none of the agreements applied to Cambodia, which now became a main theater of conflict.

The Paris Accords did not end the war, although President Nixon described the agreement as "peace with honor." The United States agreed to pull all its forces out of the Indochinese peninsula. The seventeenth parallel was again identified as the dividing line between North and South Vietnam, although those areas of South Vietnam occupied by the North, or falling under the control of the Viet Cong, were to be left undisturbed. No new forces were to be introduced into South Vietnam, but provision was made for the replacement of troops by the North Vietnamese. The agreement also stipulated that no new arms could be brought into the country; however, replacements for consumed supplies were sanctioned. The South Vietnamese government was especially displeased with the agreement. All that had been done, they argued, was to permit the United States to withdraw its forces without being fired upon. The treaty in no way terminated the hostilities, nor were the clauses concerned with troop deployment and weapons shipments enforceable. There was no doubt that the war would continue.

Although Henry Kissinger and Le Duc Tho, the principal negotiators at Paris, were to receive the Nobel Peace Prize for their work, the war in fact proceeded to take its frightful toll. The South Vietnam government lost tens of thousands of frontline forces during 1973 and 1974. The peace settlement had done little more than usher in a new military phase. President Thieu felt more isolated than ever. His fears were manifested in the tactics employed by his police establishment. Thousands of political prisoners and leaders from various walks of life were suspected of dissident behavior and imprisoned. For example, in September, 1973, a number of important labor leaders were tried and found guilty by a military court on charges that they were working with the Communists to subvert the South Vietnamese labor movement. Many labor leaders did not survive their imprisonment long enough to stand trial. The government called the death of one prominent personality a suicide after he had "confessed" to Communist affiliations. Informed reports insisted, however, that he was tortured and killed by the government police.[1]

Such incidents symbolize the Thieu government's deep insecurity in the face of the American withdrawal. Thieu and his supporters knew the Indochina War had entered a crucial political phase, and that strong efforts were needed to win the support of his fragmented society. But the regime was on the horns of a dilemma. There seemed to be no way of separating subversive acts from those of the "loyal" opposition. The Thieu administration, therefore, behaved as though every demonstration of political discontent was connected with the Communist program of total victory. Although harshly criticized by outsiders, especially the Americans, the South Vietnam regime became more oppressive. Like Diem before him, Thieu concluded that only a highly centralized political system could save the country. In the waning months of 1973, the President ordered his loyal followers to organize a new political party, which was promptly given the name Democracy Party. Thieu envisaged a one-party state for South Vietnam under his continuing leadership. In January, 1974, he called upon the National Assembly to amend the Constitution to enable him to serve a third term. But these maneuvers did little to change the reality that South Vietnam was divided against itself and that no degree of military repression could ensure popular unity.

[1]Information provided the authors by informants now residing in the United States. Also appeared in *The New York Times*, September 4, 1973.

THE FINAL PHASE

While the South Vietnamese army gave the appearance of being able to hold the enemy to limited gains in the remote regions of South Vietnam, the war in Cambodia increased in tempo. All hopes of arriving at a partial peace settlement with the Khmer Rouge were dashed, as the insurgents opened a drive aimed at overthrowing the Lon Nol government in Phnom Penh. The Cambodian army, expanded by Lon Nol after Sihanouk's fall, had never amounted to more than a ragtag outfit. Men and boys had been recruited to serve in the front lines, but they were poorly trained and badly led. Their pay was meager, and they never were provided with adequate clothing or nourishment. Yet it was this force that was thrown into the principal battles with the Khmer Rouge. The result was a heavy loss of life, which began to weaken the armed forces. This situation contrasted with the elite members of Cambodian society, who spent their days in the business-as-usual atmosphere of the capital. Members of the elite families did not have to confront the Khmer Rouge. They could purchase draft exemptions, educational certificates, and even visas with which to leave the country. In addition, corruption at all levels, including the highest military ranks, made the running of government as well as the pursuit of the war a frustrating exercise. Truckloads of artillery rounds and other supplies simply vanished on their way to government military bases. American aid was paying the salaries of 100,000 nonexistent Cambodian soldiers, the money being pocketed by unscrupulous army commanders. Indeed, even the enemy was capable of taking advantage of the black market, and much of what the United States forwarded to Cambodia for its defense ultimately wound up in the hands of the Khmer Rouge. Thus, while the poor were being mobilized to fight for Cambodia's freedom, wealthy Cambodians were going about their customary routines oblivious to the world around them. A report in *The New York Times* of March 16, 1975, gave this account.

> While ministers ride to and from their air conditioned villas in chauffered Mercedes, hungry begrimed refugees, crushed by food prices that have risen more than a 1000 percent since the war began, hunker beside their sidewalk leantos stirring the garbage in the gutter in search of a scrap of something salvageable.
>
> The wounded fill the hospitals wall-to-wall. When soldier amputees recover and emerge, they begin their new lives as beggars along with the thousands of other war cripples and malnourished children who now swarm along Phnom Penh's boulevards.
>
> War widows stand weeping outside government offices because they cannot cut through the bureaucracy. That is, they don't have the bribe money necessary to get the pensions due them. At the same time, some army commanders personally collect and keep the death benefits of soldiers killed

in their units. This money, one year's salary, is supposed to go to the family of the dead soldier.

But the commander produces fake relatives, paying them a small amount for the masquerade while keeping the bulk of the money for himself.

"They don't deserve to win the war," a Western diplomat said here the other day. "The communists may be no better and I've no love for them, but this side has treated its people so badly and so corruptly that it has forfeited all right to govern them."[2]

As the insurgents began to surround Phnom Penh, even the elite were forced to face the issue of the country's inevitable fall. An American airlift was organized to keep the Lon Nol regime afloat, but it was too late to save the discredited government. Troops abandoned their stations and flooded into the capital, as the rich tried to make their way out of the country. As Lon Nol prepared to leave Cambodia for refuge in the United States, Cambodia's fall was only days away. While attention had been riveted on Cambodia, the key drama returned to the battlefields of Vietnam. The combined forces of the North Vietnamese and Viet Cong launched a major attack in the northern provinces of South Vietnam. After a stiff resistance, the Thieu army crumbled and was forced southward. At that moment the Communists opened a major offensive, described by some to be larger than the Tet Offensive of 1968, and much of western South Vietnam came quickly under the control of the North. In quick offensives in March and April, 1975, South Vietnam was severed in half. The main force of the South Vietnamese army was cut off without its weapons and supplies. From the beginning of the campaign, a frightened South Vietnamese population took to the roads in a feverish attempt to reach safety from the battles. But the South Vietnamese army had lost its will, and as commanders abandoned their troops, the once vaunted force threw away their arms, tore off their uniforms, and joined the civilian population as they journeyed to Saigon.

South Vietnam's collapse was sudden and total. Panic seized everyone, and under the circumstances even a defense line north of Saigon endured for only a few days. President Thieu was in no position to rally his forces or the South Vietnamese population. Pressure was placed upon him to resign so that others might negotiate a settlement with the victors. Thieu pleaded with the United States government to come to his assistance. The Paris Accords had been interpreted as requiring the United States to reconsider its options, given a renewal of the hostilities. But Washington was hesitant. The fighting had never stopped between North and South, and at one point the South Vietnamese army had sought to expand its areas of military control. Now, with Saigon itself under seige,

[2]*The New York Times,* March 16, 1975.

Thieu accused his American allies for his army's debacle. It was argued that the United States had not delivered on older promises, and that this inaction had destroyed the morale of his forces. But despite explanations for the South Vietnamese collapse, it was obvious that South Vietnam was doomed.

Like Lon Nol, Nguyen Van Thieu was forced to resign his office and was soon on a plane, which took him to exile in Taiwan. Thieu's departure had been a major condition imposed by the North Vietnamese for terminating the hostilities. It was hoped the Communists would settle for a government of reconciliation, but with their troops in enormous numbers encircling Saigon, they were in no mood to accept anything less than unconditional surrender. Duong Van Minh (Big Minh) became the last ruler of the Republic of South Vietnam, and he assumed the awesome burden of transferring power to the Viet Cong and their North Vietnamese supporters. A few days earlier the Cambodian government had surrendered to the Khmer Rouge. For the first time in three decades Indochina ceased to be at war.

Laos, the scene of so many earlier battles, had been spared this last great bloodletting. The 1973 Accords reestablished a coalition government under Prince Souvanna Phouma and his half brother Prince Souphanouvong. From the outset there was no mistaking the Pathet Lao intention to remain in and dominate the government. American and Thai forces were withdrawn from Laos under terms of the agreement, and the Royal Laotian army was soon infiltrated by cadres of the Pathet Lao, which transformed it into a united force. Those tribal elements that had assisted the American effort in Laos were forced to take refuge in Thailand or were overrun by the reinforced Pathet Lao. Between mid-1973 and the spring offensive of 1975, which toppled the Thieu regime, the North Vietnamese with Pathet Lao assistance had transformed the Ho Chi Minh Trail into a four-lane gravel-surfaced highway. It was this network and others extending down from North Vietnam that enabled the Communists to mount their successful drive on the South.

THE VIEW FROM THAILAND

Thailand's destiny has seemingly been intertwined with that of Indochina's. This fact became apparent with the decision of the United States to withdraw its forces from Indochina and possibly all Southeast Asia. Despite gestures toward constitutionalism, Thailand has been under military influence since 1932. Although the monarchy held a prominent position in the thinking of the Thai people, the military-bureaucracy dominated the decision-making process. This control was reinforced by the

American presence, the overriding concern with national security, and Thailand's role in the Southeast Asia Treaty Organization. The war in Indochina threatened Thailand's defenses. The country's anti-Communist leaders put their faith in American power and United States determination to prevent the Communists from controlling all of Southeast Asia. The war in Indochina had been a long and costly one, however. When American patience as well as resolve were exhausted, the United States settled for a dignified withdrawal. The anti-Communist governments were informed that they would be supplied with necessary armaments and economic assistance. They would have to defend themselves, however, and this meant correcting their internal problems. If they were reasonably strong from within, their collective self-defense would be enhanced. Without domestic unity, however, no amount of American aid could perpetuate their control.

It is against this background that the collapse of the military-dominated Kittikachorn government must be viewed. On October 14, 1973, Thanom Kittikachorn was pressured into resigning his office and ordered to leave the country with General Prapass, who had been the real power in the government. The Thai King, Phumiphol Adulet, appointed Sanya Thammasak, the Dean of Thammasat University in Bangkok, to be the new Prime Minister. Thammasak promised a new constitution and general elections. The uprising that swept Kittikachorn and Prapass from power was violent, with the student population in Bangkok playing a primary role. The violent events were also without precedent in Thailand. Coups and revolutions are not unknown, but were confined to factional elites. This time, however, Thailand experienced something akin to a popular revolt.

The Thai students taking part in the demonstrations that toppled Kittikachorn were not identified with the Communist insurgents on the country's eastern frontier, but they were politically left of center. Few students saw anything worthwhile in Thailand's association with the Southeast Asia Treaty Organization. Most were convinced that American presence merely added to their own dilemmas. This same element condemned Thailand's role as a satellite of the United States, advancing the argument that Thailand should protect itself by dealing directly with the Chinese and the Vietnamese. But for such negotiations to prove successful, it would first be necessary to urge the United States to withdraw its forces from the country. This view was expressed sharply by the Secretary General of the Thai National Student Center, the most important student organ in the country. Thailand's security, he insisted, could only be assured when the country no longer relied on either economic or military assistance from the United States.

Another reason for the direct attack on the United States was the general opinion that Thai constitutionalism had been sacrificed to military power, that the Americans promoted military preparedness with little concern for the country's overall well-being. The new Thammasak Cabinet reduced the military from seven to three offices. Of the thirteen deputy ministers, however, two were generals, one an admiral, and three were police generals. In addition, General Kris Sivara, who had played a crucial role in the events leading up to the Kittikachorn resignation, was appointed Director for the Maintenance of Peace and Order. At the same time, efforts were underway to improve the morale in the armed forces. Air Chief Marshal Dawee announced that the post of Supreme Commander of the Armed Forces would be abolished. Also the Supreme Commander Headquarters would be changed to a Department of Joint Chiefs of Staff headed by a Chief of Staff, who would act as a military advisor to the Defense Minister. By and large, attention was given to redistributing the personalized institutions with which successive Thai military leaders had dominated the country.

On December 11, 1973, the King appointed a national convention to choose a new National Assembly. Later that month the new 299 member Assembly was chosen from among a list of civil servants, university teachers, former politicians, military officers, and journalists. Only thirty-six officers were from the armed forces compared with the one hundred that sat in the previous Assembly. Late February, 1974, the National Assembly began discussions on a new constitution. On October 5, 1974, a document was approved by a vote of 280-6. The Constitution provided for a bicameral legislature with a lower house of 300 members and an upper house or Senate totalling 100 members. The lower house is elected on the basis of direct adult franchise, but the Senate is appointed by the King. The King, however, voiced opposition to that segment of the Constitution that stipulated the president of the Privy Council would countersign the King's order selecting the senators. The monarch argued that since the King alone chose the president of the Privy Council, the provision is contrary to the principle that the King is above politics in a democratic system. The Constitution outlined other powers in which the King was empowered to dissolve the Assembly, to nominate high civil and military officials, and in an emergency, to proclaim martial law for thirty days without the Assembly's approval.

Thailand remained in a state of considerable turbulence throughout 1974. There were hundreds of strikes in a country where trade unions and strikes were previously illegal and where wages were pitifully low. So widespread were the disturbances that the country was paralyzed when Bangkok's port, the international aerodome, electric service, and oil supplies all struck simultaneously. Insofar as the workers' demands were modest, the strikes were eventually cancelled and the country returned to normal activity, however.

In January, 1975, elections were held for Thailand's parliament under the new Constitution to replace the interim government that had held power after the fall of Kittikachorn. Of the 269 seats in the lower house, the moderate Democrats won the largest number, 72, but this was far from the majority required. A coalition was organized under the leadership of the Democrat Seni Pramoj, who attempted to bring the four major conservative organizations into his government. These were the Social Justice, the Thai Nation, the Social Agrarian, and the Social Nationalist parties. The new senate was appointed on January 26, 1975.

Seni Pramoj was formally elected Premier on February 13, and headed an all-civilian Cabinet comprising the Democrats, the Social Agrarians, and non-party members. The new Thai leader announced he would try to bring permanent democratic rule to the country. He would seek to combine the mild socialism of his party with the policies of the smaller parties that supported him. But the Seni government was destined to have a very short life. On March 6, his government fell on a no-confidence motion by a vote of 152-111. The debate that brought down his government centered on his call for the withdrawal of United States forces from Thailand within eighteen months. Seni's plan was regarded as an attempt to muster left-wing support to counter opposition to his regime by a group of rightists and military-backed parties. Seni's successor was his brother Kukrit Pramoj, leader of the conservative Social Justice Party, who formed a new Cabinet of twenty-seven members. Kukrit's coalition, similar to his brother's, was formed from slightly less than a majority in the National Assembly, hence the inherent weakness of their governments. Thai parties have proliferated, and no party or leader has emerged who can organize a working majority. Real power remains with those in the opposition who, although unable to mobilize sufficient support to form their own government, can prevent another government from functioning over an extended period.

Thailand still confronted an insurgency in its remote eastern provinces, as well as a growing border dispute with Laos. Thailand has long patrolled the Mekong River using small gunboats to intercept smugglers and to control piracy. The border is especially important given the passage of supplies to the insurgents in Thailand. In November, 1975, the Laotians open fired on Thai gunboats. More incidents of this nature could precipitate a larger conflict that the Thai government wishes to avoid. It is in this context that Kukrit Pramoj visited the People's Republic of China and developed amicable relations with the revolutionary government in Phnom Penh. On June 1, 1976, the Thai government announced it had reached a settlement on demarcating its border with Cambodia and that the two countries had agreed to exchange ambassadors. It was obvious that Thailand had to find new ways to protect itself, as well as assure domestic tranquility.

Thailand, comparatively speaking, had been a tranquil country during the long Indochinese war, but it was certainly affected by that conflict. The rigidity of the Thai political system, its emphasis on paternalistic authoritarianism, sustained the country at a time of upheaval. But new challenges lay ahead, and the return to civilian and parliamentary government did not herald a smooth transition to popular rule. The military had been compelled to step aside in October 1973. However, the new political format was untested and clearly incomplete. Coalition government, the multitude of opposition parties, and a disenchanted congeries of youthful intellectuals were a poor mixture for stable, progressive politics. Kukrit Pramoj's frustration was apparent when on January 12, 1976 he called upon the Thai King to dissolve the parliament and call for new elections. The Prime Minister acknowledged that he could not keep the eight parties of his coalition government together. Moreover, the twenty-two parties that were represented in the parliament insured that paralysis of government programs. No way could be found to satisfy everyone, and no single group was powerful enough to even manage a minimum of government responsibilities. Furthermore, efforts at limiting the number of political parties went unfulfilled.

The election of the new parliament was slated for April, 1976, but Thai society had been fractured and polarized. The campaign therefore was one of the bloodiest conducted in any Asian country. Terrorist groups of both the left and right plotted against the country's leadership, as well as each other. The leftist National Student Center, for example, was attacked and a number of student leaders killed. In March the young, American-educated Secretary General of Thailand's Socialist Party was assassinated. An ultra-conservative organization, the nationalist Navapol, which suddenly appeared on the scene, also assaulted the leftist New Force Party offices in Bangkok and did considerable damage to the premises. Isolated acts of violence in and around the capital city were commonplace. In the circumstances, it was somewhat remarkable that the elections could be held at all. There was considerable fear, however, that if the elections could not be held, the military would once again intervene in Thai affairs.

Thirty-nine political parties contested the April elections, one less than the previous year. Approximately 2,300 candidates were seeking the 279 seats in the parliament. But when the vote was tallied it was apparent that one party was beginning to gain the favor of the voting public. Seni Pramoj, Kukrit's brother, had led his Democratic Party to a striking victory by carrying all the seats from Bangkok and by gaining support among the peasantry. Although far from achieving a majority position, it was clear his party was the most successful of those in contention, and he was called upon to form a new four-party coalition government. Seni, of course, had headed a Thai government for a short period in 1975 and that episode was not to be ignored.

The new Prime Minister pleaded with his countrymen to support a reform program that would give the nation stability and strength to meet the challenges both within and outside the country. His apparent success in gaining the support of 206 of the 279 members of parliament signified the concern that the parliamentarians had of Thailand's future. Seni's program called for land to the landless, a ceiling on essential commodities, jobs for the urban poor, and perhaps most important, a pledge to the student population that the American military bases would be completely closed down. The latter problem continued to trouble the Thai government as the United States sought to maintain at least one military base for intelligence gathering purposes. The Thais were on record, however, as demanding the total departure of American military personnel and Prime Minister Seni Pramoj was in the difficult position of having to insist that his order stand. All American installations were thus closed by July 20, 1976, although 270 American military advisers were to remain in the country. Thailand still looked to the United States for military assistance, and there was no indication that the country was pulling out of SEATO, but the American presence was a constant threat to the Thailand's stability.

THE NEW INDOCHINA

The decisive victory achieved by the combined force of Viet Cong and North Vietnamese troops seemed to forecast the future shape of political events. The government that first established itself in Saigon bore the designation Provisional Revolutionary Government. Its leader Huynh Tan Phat, however, was not the real ruler of South Vietnam. Genuine power appeared to reside in Pham Hung, a member of the North Vietnamese Politburo. It was Hung who controlled the Central Office of South Vietnam through the long years of war and although he had no title in the South Vietnam government, he is the most distinguished North Vietnamese official to be associated with the take-over in the South. Policy execution, however, is neither a function of the Provisional Revolutionary Government, its cabinet, or the central administration. This task had been pre-empted by the Military Management Committee, which was headed by Tran Van Tra, a senior member of the Viet Cong military. Military Management Committees also existed in every other major city in South Vietnam and efforts were being made to integrate them into a coherent framework of administration. These committees, of course, were temporary and were to be replaced as North Vietnam prepared a larger program of incorporation. Past experience suggests strenuous programs will be implemented to reduce the military role in political decision-making.

The reports of civilian and military goods being shipped to North Vietnam can be interpreted as an attempt to reduce the military capacity of the South, prior to imposing a new political system on the country. Further indications in November, 1975, led to the conclusion that the line dividing the two Vietnams would be dissolved. Reunification has been the stated policy of the Vietnamese Communists from the earliest days of their movement. There was no reason to believe that that objective would now be ignored in favor of an independent South Vietnam, which originally was a result of intervention by the big powers.

It came as no surprise when on November 9, 1975, both the North and South Vietnamese governments announced they would move toward unification early in 1976. Elections would be held to form a single government. A National Assembly would represent the entire country, and it would select all the state organs. It was the North Vietnamese Prime Minister, Pham Van Dong, who revealed the plan, and he noted the South Vietnamese authorities had concurred with the arrangements. There was no hint of any dissatisfaction from South Vietnam. Indeed, following the announcement, spokesmen for the South Vietnamese Buddhist, Catholic, professional, and student organizations all reiterated their support for the proposal.

And, as forecast, on July 2, 1976 North and South Vietnam were officialy reunited; more than three decades of persistence, sacrifice and determination had resulted in triumph. Ho Chi Minh did not live to see the culmination of his dream, but his colleagues who had fought with him through many campaigns were on the scene to receive the plaudits of the people. Indeed, these same North Vietnamese leaders now governed all Vietnam. Only one position in the top circle was left for a South Vietnamese representative. This was Dr. Nguyen Huu Tho, President of the Provisional Revolutionary Government in South Vietnam, who was made one of the two vice-presidents in the new united government. The other vice-president was Nguyen Luong Bang, North Vietnam's vice-president since 1969. The president of the *new* Vietnam was also the North's former President, Ton Duc Thang, the eighty-eight year old father-figure who succeeded Ho Chi Minh, but who remained a ceremonial officer. Real power resided in the traditional elite. Pham Van Dong continued as Prime Minister, Truong Chinh was Chairman of the Standing Committee of the 492-member National Assembly and the recognized chief ideologist in the country, while the military hero Nguyen Vo Giap, remained as Deputy Prime Minister and Defense Minister. No change was forecast in the Lao Dong, Vietnam's Communist Party, and Le Duan retained the important post of First Secretary of the organization. Moreover, except for the reunification of the country, there was little tampering with the established political structure that had carried North Vietnam through decades of conflict and tribulation. Now that Vietnam was one country, it was the southern region that was called upon to learn the ways and routines of the north. Rectification campaigns were pressed in all sections of the south and the heavy hand of the regime was felt chiefly among the Buddhist sects, and especially the resisting Hoa Hao, whose ranks were decimated as an estimated twenty thousand devotees were rounded up and imprisoned or placed in labor brigades. The *new* government of Vietnam showed no interest in opposition groups of any character.

Laos also was prepared for dramatic changes. The two-level government created in 1973 lacked coherence in light of the collapse of the South Vietnamese Republic. Laos was the last country in the region to contain even a hint of non-communist government, hence it was only a matter of time before the consequences of the North Vietnamese and Cambodian Communist victories forced a change in the pattern of Laotian rule. Prince Souvanna Phouma was powerless as the American military mission was withdrawn and the Agency for International Development (USAID) was forced to terminate its program. The Pathet Lao ministers not only took charge of the government, they also absorbed the Royal Lao army and instigated a series of student demonstrations, which made any semblance of coalition government impossible. In the meantime, Pathet Lao cadres quietly, but effectively, went about the work of displacing the Vientiane government's limited control in the provinces. There was no opposition to this maneuver, but upwards of 100,000 of the estimated three million population of Laos are reported to have fled into neighboring Thailand. Wherever the Pathet Lao spread their influence, indoctrination "schools" were formed to re-educate the population in the ways of their new masters. Dissent, obviously, is not to be tolerated. Another striking example of the changes occurring in Laos was the replacement of American assistance with that provided by the Soviet Union. In late 1975, more than 1,500 Soviet technicians were operating in Laos alone, much to the concern of the Chinese who appear to fear Russian encirclement in Southeast Asia.

By October 12, 1975, on the Laotian thirtieth year of "independence," it was clear the Communists were firmly in control of the country. Even Vientiane was completely under their leadership. Communist officials from the various parts of Indochina joined with the Laotians to celebrate the event. North Vietnam sent Truong Chinh, a key member of its Politburo; Tan Phat, the then President of the Provisional Revolutionary government represented South Vietnam; and Ieng Sary, the Cambodian Foreign Minister and a Deputy Premier, came from Cambodia. The principal speech was given by Kaysone Phomvihan, the Secretary General of the Phak Paksason Lao, or Lao People's Party—the Communist Party of Laos. He bitterly attacked Thailand and warned that country to cease "provocations" along the Thai-Laotian border. The Communist chief in Laos accused Thailand of seeking to sabotage the Laotian government.

Pathet Lao operations against Thailand are linked with North Vietnamese intentions. The number of troops sent by North Vietnam into the Laotian panhandle on the Thai frontier are of growing concern. In this regard, the flow of weapons to Thai insurgents has been greatly accelerated. The interests of Laos are different from those of the North Vietnamese in Thailand. For example, the Laotians are dependent on Thai supplies of rice, meat, vegetables, and oil. Laotian belligerence toward Thailand can possibly be interpreted as a sign of North Vietnamese dominance over Laotian decision-making.

Prince Souvanna Phouma began to fade from public view as the Communists consolidated their hold on the country. Elections were forecast for April, 1976, and the Prince had indicated he would step aside at that time. But events were already moving far beyond his influence. On November 3, 1975, the Laotian People's Congress, now firmly in Communist hands, voted for the abolition of Laos' six hundred year old monarchy and created the new People's Democratic Republic of Laos. King Savang Vatthana was compelled to abdicate his throne, and Prince Souvanna Phouma was removed as Premier after thirteen years in office. His new role was described as an advisor to the government, and the former King was called the Supreme Advisor. The President of the Laotian Republic was Prince Souphanouvong, but his position was only ceremonial. Although the titular leader of the Pathet Lao over the years, real power lay with younger men, particularly with the head of the Lao People's Party, Kaysone Phomvihan and his top assistant. Neuhak Phoumsavan. Kaysone Phomvihan become the Republic's first Prime Minister. Only fifty-five years old, he has been closely identified with the North Vietnamese. It was at their urging that he organized the Lao People's Party. Thus the future of Laos, like that of South Vietnam, will be heavily influenced by the North Vietnamese. As unification proceeds with South Vietnam, it is likely that some form of federation with Laos will also be arrived at. Where their political systems are concerned, the Communist parties clearly intend to form the base of all future governments in Indochina.

Cambodia is also a fully communized state. However, this country's historical aloofness and conflict with the Vietnamese suggests a more concerted effort to maintain an independent status. Whether this is possible appears to depend on the new leaders of Cambodia. Prince Norodom Sihanouk received considerable satisfaction from the overthrow of his nemesis Lon Nol, but the Prince has always known that he would never again wield power in Cambodia. Cambodian leadership at first was in the

hands of three deputy premiers. They included Ieng Sary, Khieu Samphan, and Son Sen. The latter held the important defense post and was a
key personality of the triumvirate. The first Prime Minister was the aging
and infirm Penn Nouth who was given no more than figurehead status.

There is sufficient evidence to conclude that Cambodia is the most
unstable country in Indochina. The ferocity of the struggle against the
Lon Nol government, the discontinuities in the government, the contradictions within the Communist Party in Cambodia, and their desire to
maintain the unique Cambodian experience have caused a display of
radical savagery unlike any other of the Indochinese states. The Khmer
Rouge's demand for revenge resulted in the summary execution of Premier Lon Boret who replaced Lon Nol, even though the former wished to
terminate the civil war and submit to the victorious Cambodian leftists.
Virtually the entire high command of the enemy military establishment,
including Sirik Matak, were also killed without trial. Sirik Matak was a
cousin of Prince Norodom Sihanouk and had helped to engineer the coup
against him in 1970. Other government officials throughout the former
administration were similarly treated. But perhaps the most dramatic
demonstration of Khmer Rouge harshness was the forcible ouster of the
great majority of Phnom Penh's inhabitants. A city of 500,000 was reduced
to a tenth of its original size as people were herded into the Cambodian
back woods, where thousands are believed to have died from starvation
and unattended ailments and wounds. Moreover, numerous Buddhist
shrines were closed, and most of the monks forced to join the general
population in the exodus from the city.

Cambodia in late 1975 was administered by revolutionary committees whose leaders had been selected by the Communist leadership. The
committees are military in nature and are charged with the distribution of
food and providing for the rudimentary needs of the dislocated population. Only they could issue permits for people to move freely throughout
the country. The war literally destroyed the economy of the country, but
there were reports of Chinese assistance in rebuilding and running basic
industries. Efforts were also being made to produce a rice crop, but the
country could not ignore a continuing dependence on the outer world.

Cambodia's internal bloodletting did not end with the victory of the
Khmer Rouge. The new regime is determined to submerge the country's
urban elite in a rural sea and the dislocation caused by these maneuvers
has perpetuated the suffering of the general population. There is clearly
no organized opposition remaining within the country, but the current
rulers must contend with their own factions while cautiously seeking to
interpret the intentions of their neighbors, especially in Vietnam.

On January 5, 1976, Cambodians were given a new constitution. It is
a brief document, containing only twenty-one articles. The constitution

establishes a legislative assembly consisting of 150 farmer-peasants, 50 factory workers and 50 members of the armed forces. The Assembly is publicized as being the chief organ of state, deciding on domestic as well as external policy. All members of the Assembly are to serve five year terms. They are also authorized to select members for the high judicial tribunal. Fundamental rights are written into the document such as the right to work and follow the religion of one's choice, providing it did not interfere with the operations of the state. With a view to Cambodia's immediate past, the Constitution spells out that no foreign bases will be permitted on Cambodian soil.

The Constitution could hardly obscure the stringent conditions existing in Cambodia. The entire society has been mobilized for national purpose, and Cambodians are ordered to labor without pay. Hence those not cultivating the land are forced to barter for their needs, itself a difficult matter insofar as all private ownership has been barred. For the great majority who work on the land, however, the acquisition of food is no real problem. The regime is well aware of the need to feed its population, lest it become desperate. Despite their monopoly of power and the brutal means employed in avenging the old order, the new leaders of Cambodia know they must encourage cooperation. This also helps to explain the elections for the National People's Assembly which was held on March 20, 1976. None of the key Cambodian leaders were elected to the Assembly, suggesting that the Constitution which endows the body with significant powers, cannot be taken seriously; in fact it could only hold one session each year. As in other Communist states, the legislative institution seems destined to follow the dictates of the high party leadership. All the same, the holding of the election and the convening of the assembly, reinforced the notion that Cambodian life was being stabilized after an extended period of turbulence.

The consolidation and rationalization of the Cambodian government was more obvious in April, 1976 when Prince Sihanouk who had been described as the honorary Chief of State and Penn Nouth, the symbolic Prime Minister retired from political life. Khieu Samphan assumed the new title of Chairman of the State Presidium and thus became Cambodia's formal head of state. Tol Saut, an unknown rubber plantation worker was named the country's new Prime Minister. Speculation on Tol Saut's elevation centered on his probable role in the Khmer Rouge military during the civil war. Supporting Tol Saut in the central cabinet was the familiar Ieng Sary who continued as Deputy Prime Minister responsible for foreign affairs, and Son Sen, Deputy Prime Minister for defense.

A more obscure personality who was beginning to draw attention in the Cambodian hierarchy was Saloth Sar, the Secretary General of the Cambodian Communist Party. Indeed, the view was being expressed that

Soloth Sar was the ultimate power in the new Communist state. He is little known in the outside world, but is believed to be about fifty years of age and a former school teacher who had passed some time in France. If Cambodia in any way resembled the other Indochinese states, it was in the Communist Party structure that was slowly taking shape. In these circumstances it would not be surprising to see the leader of the country's Communist Party assume the dominant decision-making role.

RECOMMENDED READING

North Vietnam

Burchett, Wilfred G., *Vietnam North*. New York: International Publishers, 1967.

Cameron, Allan W., *Indochina: Prospects After "the End"*. Washington, D.C.: American Enterprise Institute, 1976.

Duncanson, Dennis J., *Government and Revolution in Vietnam*. New York: Oxford University Press, 1968.

Fall, Bernard B., *The Viet-Minh Regime*. New York: Institute of Pacific Relations, 1956.

Fishel, Wesley R., ed., *Vietnam: Anatomy of a Conflict*. Itasca, Illinois: Peacock Publishers, 1968.

Ho Chi Minh, *Against U.S. Aggression for National Salvation*. Hanoi: Foreign Languages Publishing House, 1967.

Hoang, Van Chi, *From Colonialism to Communism*. New York: Praeger, 1964.

Honey, P. J., *Communism in North Vietnam*. Cambridge, Mass.: M.I.T. Press, 1963.

——————— , *North Vietnam Today*. New York: Praeger, 1962.

Huyen, N. Khac, *Vision Accomplished? The Enigma of Hi Chi Minh*. New York: Macmillan, 1971.

Lake, Anthony ed., *The Legacy of Vietnam*. New York: New York University Press, 1976.

Langer, Paul F., and Joseph J. Zasloff, *North Vietnam and the Pathet Lao*. Cambridge, Mass.: Harvard University Press, 1970.

Le, Duan, *The Vietnamese Revolution*. New York: International Publishers, 1971.

McAlister, John T., Jr., *Vietnam, The Origins of Revolution*. New York: Knopf, 1969.

——————— , and Paul Mus, *The Vietnamese and Their Revolution*. New York: Harper & Row, 1970.

Maneli, Mieczyslaw, *War of the Vanquished*. New York: Harper & Row, 1971.

Neumann-Hoditz, Reinhold, *Portrait of Ho Chi Minh*. Hamburg: Herder and Herder, 1971.

Pike, Douglas, *Viet Cong*. Cambridge, Mass.: M.I.T. Press, 1966.

Salzburg, Joseph S., *Vietnam: Beyond The War*. Hicksville, N. Y.: Exposition Press, 1976.

Trager, Frank N., *Why Viet Nam?* New York: Praeger, 1966.

Turner, Robert F., *Vietnamese Communism: Its Origins and Developments.* Stanford: Hoover Institution Press, 1975.

South Vietnam

Asian Survey, *Vietnam's Postwar Development: A Symposium, Asian Survey* Vol. XI, No. 4 (April 1971).

Bouscaren, Anthony T., *The Last of the Mandarins: Diem of Vietnam.* Pittsburgh, Pa.: Duquesne University Press, 1965.

Buttinger, Joseph, *Vietnam: A Political History.* New York: Praeger, 1968.

Cameron, Allan W., *Viet-Nam Crisis: A Documentary History.* Ithaca, N.Y.: Cornell University Press, 1971.

Critchfield, Richard, *The Long Charade.* New York: Harcourt Brace Jovanovich, 1968.

Dang, Nghiem, *Viet-nam Politics and Public Administration.* Honolulu: East-West Center Press, 1966.

Fall, Bernard B., *The Two Vietnams: A Political and Military Analysis.* New York: Praeger, 1967.

Fitzgerald, Frances, *Fire in the Lake.* Boston: Little, Brown, 1972.

Goodman, Allen E., *Politics in War.* Cambridge, Mass.: Harvard University Press, 1973.

Hammer, Ellen, *Vietnam Yesterday and Today.* New York: Holt, Rinehart & Winston, 1965.

Honey, P. J., *Genesis of a Tragedy: The Historical Background to the Vietnam War.* London: Ernest Benn Limited, 1968.

Kahin, George M., and John W. Lewis, *The United States in Vietnam.* New York: Dial Press, 1967.

Lindholm, Richard W., *Viet-nam: The First Five Years.* Lansing, Mich.: Michigan State University Press, 1959.

Marr, David G., *Vietnamese Anticolonialism, 1885-1925.* Berkeley: University of California Press, 1971.

Monroe, Malcolm, *The Means Is the End in Vietnam.* White Plains, N.Y.: Murlagan Press, 1968.

Murti, B. S. N., *Vietnam Divided.* New York: Asia Publishing House, 1964.

Penniman, Howard R., *Elections in South Vietnam.* Washington, D.C.: American Enterprise Institute for Public Policy Research, 1972.

Scigliano, Robert, *South Vietnam: Nation Under Stress.* Boston, Mass.: Houghton Mifflin, 1963.

Smith, Ralph, *Viet-nam and the West.* Ithaca, N.Y.: Cornell University Press, 1971.

Sobel, Lester A., ed., *South Vietnam: U.S.-Communist Confrontation in Southeast Asia.* New York: Facts On File, Inc. 1967.

Laos

Adams, Nina S., and Alfred W. McCoy, *Laos: War and Revolution.* New York: Harper & Row, 1970.

Burchett, Wilfred G., *The Second Indochina War: Cambodia and Laos*. New York: International Publishers, 1970.

Champassak, Sisouk Na, *Storm Over Laos: A Contemporary History*. New York: Praeger, 1961.

Dommen, Arthur J., *Conflict in Laos: The Politics of Neutralization*. New York: Praeger, 1971.

LeBar, Frank M., and Adrienne Suddard, *Laos: Its People, Its Society, Its Culture*. New Haven, Conn.: Human Relations Area Files Press, 1960.

Toye, Hugh, *Laos: Buffer State or Battleground*. New York: Oxford University Press, 1968.

Viravong, Saha Sila, *History of Laos*. New York: Paragon Book Reprint Corp., 1964.

Zasloff, Joseph J., *The Pathet Lao*. Lexington, Mass.: Lexington Books, 1973.

——————— and Allen E. Goodman, *Indochina in Conflict: A Political Assessment*. Lexington, Mass.: Raytheon/Heath, 1972.

Cambodia

Armstrong, John P., *Sihanouk Speaks*. New York: Walker, 1964.

Caldwell, Malcolm, and Lek Tan, *Cambodia in the Southeast Asian War*. New York: Monthly Review Press, 1973.

Herz, Martin F., *A Short History of Cambodia*. New York: Praeger, 1958.

Leifer, Michael, *Cambodia: The Search for Security*. New York: Praeger, 1967.

Munson, Frederick P. et al., *Area Handbook for Cambodia*. Washington, D.C.: U.S. Government Printing Office, 1968.

Osborn, Milton, *The French Presence in Cochinchina and Cambodia: Rule and Response (1859-1905)*. Ithaca, N.Y.: Cornell University Press, 1969.

——————— *Politics and Power in Cambodia*. Hong Kong: Dai Nippon Printing Co., (Hong Kong) Ltd., 1973.

Simon, Sheldon W., *War and Politics in Cambodia: A Communications Analysis*. Durham, N.C.: Duke University Press, 1974.

Steinberg, David J. et. at., *Cambodia: Its People, Its Society, Its Culture*. New Haven: Human Relations Area Files Press, 1959.

Williams, Maslyn, *The Land In Between: The Cambodian Dilemma*. New York: William Morrow, 1970.

Thailand

Bennett, Alan, *Thailand—The Ambiguous Domino*. London: Current Affairs Research Services Centre, 1969.

Blanchard, Wendell, *Thailand: Its People, Its Society, Its Culture*. New Haven, Conn.: Human Relations Area Files, Inc. 1968.

Darling, Frank C., *Thailand and the United States*. Washington D.C.: Public Affairs Press, 1965.

Henderson, John W. (co-author), *Area Handbook for Thailand*. Washington, D.C.: U.S. Government Printing Office, 1971.

Landon, Kenneth Perry, *Siam In Transition*. New York: Greenwood Press, 1968.

Pye, Lucien W., *Southeast Asian Political Systems*. Englewood Cliffs, N.J.: Prentice-Hall, 1967.

Riggs, Fred W., *Thailand: The Modernization of a Bureaucratic Polity*. Honolulu: East-West Center Press, 1966.

Siffin, William J., *The Thai Bureaucracy: Institutional Change and Development*. Honolulu: East-West Center Press, 1966.

Sutton, Joseph L., ed., *Problems of Politics and Administration in Thailand*. Bloomington, Ind.: Institute of Training for Public Service, 1962.

Wilson, David A., *Politics in Thailand*. Ithaca, N.Y.: Cornell University Press, 1962.

_____ *The United States and the Future of Thailand*. New York: Praeger, 1970.

Wit, Daniel, *Thailand: Another Vietnam*. New York: Scribner's, 1968.

A village in Laos

Cambodian market

The Thai skyline

Classic Thai dancers

Manila by the sea

Household chores in the rural Philippines

A family dwelling in the Philippines

Chapter Seven

Indonesia and the Philippines: The Politics of Stability

Indonesia and the Philippines are archipelago states comprising thousands of islands spread over vast distances of the Southwest Pacific. Of the two, Indonesia has the longer recorded history, but both countries are destined to play important roles in contemporary Asia. Each came under the influence of the Europeans: the Dutch occupied Indonesia and the Spanish seized the Philippines. During the late nineteenth century, the United States defeated Spain in a brief encounter and eventually came to absorb the Philippine islands. Whereas Dutch rule in Indonesia did little to prepare the islands for self-government, the Americans were determined to make the Philippines a model of democratic processes in Asia. World War II proved to be the catalyst for change in both countries, but the alacrity with which the United States transferred power to indigenous Filipinos contrasts with the grudging withdrawal of the Dutch from Indonesia. The eventual independence of the two states did not terminate their problems and their development as nations has been an uncertain and often violent experience. Democratic goals were the stated objectives of both nations. But the difficulties encountered in perpetuating political experiments whose roots lay outside the region caused them to seek methods closer to the traditions of their respective cultures. Neither country has been involved in a significant international conflict since the end of World War II. Internal developments, however, have produced sustained guerrilla or civil warfare, and neither is truly at peace with itself. This chapter traces the course pursued by these states as they seek to unify their disparate peoples and political systems.

310

INDONESIA

Indonesia comprises more than three thousand islands that stretch over a distance almost the size of the continental United States. The major islands are Java, Andalas or Sumatra, Sulawesi (formerly Celebes), and Kalimantan (formerly Borneo). Other islands of note are Bali, Western Irian, the Moluccas, and Lesser Sundas. Indonesia lies within eleven degrees of the equator, and the climates of all the islands are roughly the same. Due to their proximity to the sea and the equator, the atmosphere is usually humid and warm. Only in higher elevations can Indonesians seek relief from their tropical climate. Rainfall is heavy throughout the country, and some areas receive over one hundred inches a year. Caught between two monsoon flows, Indonesia has long been known for its tropical agricultural products, such as spices, indigo, rubber, tea, quinine, copra, sisal, palm oil, and sugar. In recent years, petroleum has been discovered, and extensive fields are being developed by joint Indonesian and foreign companies. Indonesia's natural resources provide it with a potential for greatness, long recognized by other nations.

By population, Indonesia is the fifth largest country in the world. Approximately one hundred and twenty-eight million people live in the archipelago. But Java alone is estimated to have in excess of eighty million. Thus, while Java is considered the most densely populated area on earth, Indonesia as a whole is very sparsely inhabited. Given the concentration of population in Java, it is no wonder that this island tends to influence the others. Non-Javans, quite expectedly, harbor grievances against this dominance of their affairs, but they have not succeeded in lessening its encroachment. Approximately 90 percent of Indonesia's population are Muslims. In fact, Indonesia is the world's largest Muslim nation. Nevertheless, Islam has had to adapt itself to older Buddhist and Hindu cultures, especially in eastern and central Java. Some argue that Islamic tradition has been diluted by the need to adjust to local customs and mystical rituals. Irrespective of this synthesis, there is no mistaking the Islamic character of Indonesian society.

The remains of Java man inform us that one of the earliest traces of human evolution occurred in Indonesia. Little, however, is known about the region until the first century, A.D., when Chinese Han chronicles speak of trade missions between China and a kingdom in northern Sumatra. The Indians also are known to have traded with Indonesia in this same period, and it was commerce that linked ancient China, India, and Indonesia with Greece and Rome. The advent of trade brought with it cultural exchanges. Both Hinduism and Buddhism spread into the major islands of the Indonesian archipelago, and by the fifth century, Hindu

Brahmin priests were exploiting local festivals and practices to exert considerable influence over the Indonesian population. Between the ninth and the fourteenth centuries, the Hindu kingdoms of Shrivijaya and Majapahit dominated the region, extending their influence to the Philippines and Malay peninsula.

Shrivijaya was a commercial crossroads between Europe, the Middle East, India, and China, but Majapahit, which was established in 1293, gave an indelible character to the Indonesian state. The one outstanding leader of the period, a *patih* (prime minister) named Gajah Mada, is said to be the last person able to unify Indonesia until the coming of Sukarno in the mid-twentieth century. Upon Gajah Mada's death in 1389, Majapahit began to disintegrate, and civil strife made it possible for alien forces to penetrate the islands. Chinese settlers became more numerous, and Java began paying tribute to the court in China. Islam also spread over the area, as earlier Arab settlements in Sumatra began to expand their influence. By the sixteenth century Majapahit had crumbled, and Muslim states sprang up all over the archipelago. Indonesia became the central way station on the spice trade route between India and China. Islam therefore replaced Hinduism, just as it had overwhelmed Buddhism centuries before. It is notable that Islam, like Hinduism, moved into Indonesia peacefully. The carriers of the new faith and culture were mainly interested in commerce. They were joined by missionaries who eventually won the confidence and support of the people. The first Islamic stronghold was developed in Sumatra, where it remained somewhat localized until the sixteenth and seventeenth centuries. At that time it met with stiff competition from the Christian Portuguese and later the Dutch. In addition to trade ventures, the Portuguese assumed the responsibility of zealously proselytizing their religion. However, the Muslim Javans maintained general control over the primary trade routes and market centers. Due to this power they managed to maintain their religious integrity, despite Portuguese attempts to convert them.

Although the Portuguese found a foothold in the Indonesian archipelago, it was the Dutch who achieved the greater success. The Dutch arrived in the area in 1596, signed a treaty of friendship with one of the Javan states and laid the groundwork for a significant influx of their countrymen. Unlike the Portuguese, the Dutch were less interested in religious questions and focused on the region's great material resources, which they hoped to exploit. The Portuguese sought to drive the Dutch out but were impeded by Great Britain's blockade of Lisbon. Meanwhile, the Dutch ingratiated themselves with the Indonesians, who came to see them as an ally against the Portuguese. The Dutch took Malacca from the Portuguese in 1640, a step toward Dutch dominance in the area that was to become the Dutch East Indies. The Dutch understood that Java was the key to their future, and it was only in the middle of the eighteenth century, that their writ was extended over most of that island. A Dutch East India Company was set up after the initial penetration of the islands. The consolidation of Dutch rule gave the Company the added responsibility of governing a distant colony.

Colonial Relationships

Pre-colonial Indonesian politics took on the form of monarchy, with strong overtones of religious influence. Hinduism and Buddhism had influenced the relationship between ruler and ruled, and kingship was sanctioned as a part of the forces of nature. Society was sustained in a tenuous equilibrium as long as obedience was given the divine ruler. The latter's spiritual powers enabled him to communicate with the unknown to maintain the essential harmony between humans and their environment. The more practical aspects of Islam did not alter this fundamental belief in supernatural forces and how they affected the governance of society. To some extent, however, religious beliefs are separate from customary behavior. Indeed, it is argued that *adat*, or custom, is far more instrumental in determining Indonesian behavior than *agama*, or religion. This may explain why Islam is practiced differently in Indonesia than in the Middle East or South Asia.

Adat, the law of social custom, is vital to an understanding of Indonesian society. As an indigenous development, adat is the most significant unifying factor among the people of Indonesia. Each locality creates its own adat, which is a reflection of their activities and aspirations. Mostly, it is supposed to produce harmony through cooperative endeavors, and *gotong royong*, or mutual aid, has been an age-old principle guiding the operation of village communities. Family elders make up the village council, and all power devolves upon them. A modified aspect of adat was exploited by the Dutch who pressed their "culture system" in order to squeeze higher yields from the village cultivators. But even contemporary Indonesia is moved by the dictates of the customary order, and no government can be successful without giving special importance to adat.

The Dutch established their rule over a foundation already engineered by centuries of socio-religious experience. The Kingdom of Mataram in Java gave the Europeans a political edifice from which to claim hegemony over the region. Mataram was governed by an authoritarian system, and the leaders of the Dutch East India Company saw no reason to liberalize that experience. Instead, they recruited indigenous administrators and sought to reinforce an already creditable bureaucratic apparatus. This system not only proved to be successful, it also was economical.

The elites in power when the Dutch arrived were little disturbed and, in fact, their privileged status was further enhanced. What the Dutch insisted upon was unquestioning loyalty. The Dutch system placed the greatest burden on the peasantry. They were compelled to work for harsh local masters who wished to remain in the good graces of the Europeans. The coercive nature of the system undermined the cooperative principles so long in vogue in Javan and Sumatran villages and widened the gulf between the peasants and their aristocratic overlords. Any attempt to break the shackles of servitude would bring out the Dutch police, which was always ready to go to the assistance of landlord-administrators in distress.

Along with the indigenous aristocracy, the Dutch also promoted Chinese enterprises in their East Indies possession. The Dutch had a more favorable perception of the Chinese than of the Indonesians. The Chinese were viewed as industrious and highly motivated, whereas the Indonesians were considered listless, lethargic, and backward. The Dutch East India Company never employed a large staff, and they saw their objectives enhanced by allowing the Chinese to play a larger role in the archipelago. The Indonesians had heretofore confined the activities of the Chinese merchants and traders to intermediary roles, and there was considerable suspicion between the two communities. The Dutch provoked these sentiments of displeasure by providing the Chinese with economic opportunities in Indonesia. They also precipitated a greater migration of Chinese to the East Indies, where they were permitted to obtain extensive tracts of land, displacing the natives. In time, the Chinese took over much of the colony's commerce and taxing prerogatives, and even Java's privileged middle-class of entrepreneurs was reduced to penury. The landed aristocracy, however, was sustained.

The Dutch East India Company collapsed in 1798, due to corrupt activities, and the East Indies came under the direct control of the Netherlands government. The British held sway over the region between 1811 and 1816, as a consequence of the Napoleonic Wars raging in Europe. But the Dutch regained control thereafter. The Netherlands did little to change the structure or methods of ruling developed by the Company, and the uncertainties created by the decision to abandon the Company prompted some disenchanted Indonesians to pursue a revolutionary course. The 1825-1830 rebellion in central Java forced the Dutch government to establish its own policy for the colony. The result was the *cultivation system*, which was sustained in one form or another until 1919.

The cultivation system required the Indonesian peasant to utilize one fifth of his land for a crop determined by the government to have export potential. Thus land normally used for rice cultivation was to be set aside for cash-crop purposes under government control. Although the Netherlands administration promised that taxes would not have to be paid and that the peasant would otherwise be free to work his lands, the actual practice was quite different. The cultivators soon found themselves giving more than half of their holdings to government control. The time spent in these efforts to support the government made them little more than indentured slaves. To make the system work, the Dutch turned again to the rural aristocracy, who seized the opportunity to expand their power. Even the Chinese were shunned in order to strengthen the appeal of the indigenous elite, and this elite accepted the cultivation system with considerable enthusiasm. The government of the Netherlands had done little to alter the performance of the East India Company, which it had succeeded. Moreover, they had created a system of indigenous landlords who merely reinforced the authoritarian character of political relationships in the archipelago.

By 1877, the cultivation system had outlived its usefulness and began to decline in importance. The Dutch had spread their administration beyond Java and Sumatra into the Celebes, Borneo, and many of the smaller islands. The islands outside Java were important for their mining resources and other commodities, which required heavy capital investment. In order to attract the needed money, a more liberal economic system was developed, and foreign companies were induced to invest in the East Indies. This free trade policy, however, affected agricultural programs in Java, and as a result, non-Indonesians were prevented from purchasing arable land. Nevertheless, the astounding growth of Java's population, coupled with diminishing farmland, intensified the problem of administering the colony. Peasants were forced to migrate to the metropolitan areas, where they became dependent on government rather than on family or local leaders. In the cities, these displaced Indonesians were faced with the prevalance of Chinese who monopolized economic life. They also faced a Dutch bureaucracy that was less able to win their confidence than had been the traditional power elite in the villages.

Indonesian Nationalism

Demand for social and political change in Indonesia grew after World War I. By that time Indonesia had a small group urging modernization, some of whom had been exposed to western education. The most effective segment of so-called modernists was the Serekat Islam (United Islam), which appealed to the peasant masses by calling for a Muslim renaissance. The movement's dramatic success in mobilizing a broad section of the Javan peasantry frightened the Dutch who responded with repressive tactics to reduce the group's activities. Forced to retreat from the countryside, the Serekat Islam ceased to be a popular movement. The

Indonesian Communist Party had its beginning at about this time, and although it sought to fill the vacuum left by the Serekat Islam, the Dutch had no difficulty in reducing it to impotence, forcing it underground. The Dutch colonial government proved to be a formidable institution. Given the support it received from native aristocrats and the Chinese, no popular movement could generate sufficient leverage to challenge Dutch power.

The Dutch neutralized the aristocracy, prevented the growth of an Indonesian middle-class, and kept the majority of peasants dependent on traditional elites. The emerging nationalist leaders were the few who had been exposed to western education or modern Islamic ideas. This handful of enlightened individuals articulated the dissatisfaction of a larger community that could not otherwise express itself. The claim that Indonesians should have greater control over their destiny and should participate in decision-making could only be pressed by this group. Dutch educational policies upheld a general colonial policy aimed at maintaining the Indonesians in a servile capacity. The Dutch believed without education there could be no articulate dissent, and the status quo would remain intact. The Dutch did little to alter the conventional habits of the Indonesians, but they also did virtually nothing to prepare them for self-government. Moreover, the absence of Indonesian socio-economic mobility gave credence to the Leninist-Marxian axiom that imperialism, colonialism, capitalism, and bourgeois behavior were synonymous. If there was a middle-class in Indonesia, it was comprised of Europeans and Chinese. To the small group of dissident Indonesian leaders these foreigners were considered parasites. It was inevitable, therefore, that the Indonesian nationalist movement became radicalized.

World War II precipitated a major change in Indonesian power relationships. The colonial administrative structure developed by the Dutch was obscured by the Japanese seizure of the East Indies. The Japanese were regarded as liberators by those holding strong grievances against the Dutch. But the new conquerors were little interested in furthering the interests of the Indonesians. Nevertheless, the Japanese were determined to destroy Dutch authority, which also involved breaking the back of the indigenous aristocracy. A campaign of anti-Dutch propaganda was spread among the peasant masses. Indonesian nationalists, heretofore prevented from working in the villages, were given opportunities to weaken the rural power structure. In this way, Indonesian nationalism crystallized into a mass movement.

Java became the primary base for the Indonesian national movement. In Sumatra, where another Japanese command held sway, there was less inclination and relatively no need to encourage the Indonesian nationalists. The other islands came under Japanese naval control, and no purpose was served by allowing the Indonesians to heighten their political identity. Java was different because both Dutch power and the Indonesian population were concentrated there. The other islands were important for material resources, but the thinly spread population was no problem for the occupying force. Java, however, had to be controlled, and a scheme was developed to share some powers with the indigenous anti-Dutch elite. As a consequence, the Javans developed a political consciousness, which could not be duplicated elsewhere in the archipelago. It was also in these circumstances that Sukarno emerged as a spokesman and then the leader of the Indonesian nationalist movement.

The Japanese occupation gave the Indonesian leaders an entry into government they did not enjoy under the Dutch. Moreover, when the Japanese were put on the defensive in 1943-1944, they were compelled to lean heavily on these Indonesians. The Japanese hoped to secure their loyalty so they could continue tapping the resources of the region without tying down their troops in occupation duties. Thus, toward the end of 1944, the Japanese government declared its intention to give Indonesia its full independence. In the following year, some important governmental posts were given to Indonesians in the Javan government. A lesser proportion were provided opportunities in the Sumatran administration. This was the first exposure to high-level government decision-making for the nationalists, and the exposure proved very valuable. The Japanese also organized a small Indonesian army (Peta), which they placed under indigenous command. The military force was only armed as a token gesture, its stated mission being internal security. Nevertheless the Peta did form the nucleus for a revolutionary Indonesian army. This army was called upon to fight the Japanese, the British, and finally the Dutch before the country acquired its full independence.

Sukarno led the Japanese-sponsored assembly of religious, ethnic, and social groups, which was convened in Madura on Java in March, 1945. Sukarno took the initiative in attempting to bridge differences between the religious and secular factions in the nationalist movement. His five principles, or *Pantasila*, were enunciated there for the first time and quickly were adopted as the philosophical foundation for the Indonesian national revolution. The five principles were: nationalism, humanitarianism, representative government, social justice, and belief in God (with emphasis on religious freedom). Sukarno expressed the view that a free Indonesia should include all the islands of the Dutch East Indies. He stressed Indonesia's desire to work on an international level with other nations. The concepts of representative government and social justice were broad enough to provide all groups with a voice, as well as the means, to satisfy their aspirations. The emphasis on religious freedom was meant to neutralize the Muslim nationalists, simultaneously emphasizing Indonesia's monotheistic character.

On August 7, 1945, the Japanese proclaimed the creation of an All-Indonesian Independence Preparatory Committee and made Sukarno its chairman. The Sumatran leader, Mohammad Hatta, was named vice-chairman. There were eighteen representatives on the Committee: 11 from Java, 2 from Sumatra, 2 from the Celebes, and one each from the Lesser Sundas, the Moluccas and the Indonesian Chinese community. But the imminent defeat of Japan short-circuited these efforts to transfer power to the Indonesians. Tokyo was about to surrender to American forces as the Japanese in Indonesia were ordered to await the landing of an Allied force, which would accept their formal capitulation. Fearing a situation that would ruin their chance for independence, Sukarno and Hatta declared Indonesia's full independence on August 17, 1945, and fighting erupted between the Japanese and the Indonesian Peta. Sukarno wanted control of the key cities in Java and Sumatra before the Allied landings. In the outer islands of the archipelago, Austrialian troops had moved ashore meeting no resistance, and the Dutch colonial administration was instantly restored. Sukarno was determined that similar developments would not occur in Java and Sumatra.

Troops under British command arrived in Java and Sumatra approximately six weeks after Indonesia had been declared independent by Sukarno. They found a coherent, if somewhat primitive administration, totally manned by Indonesians. The British forces had been instructed to return political authority to the Dutch, but the Sukarno regime would not yield. Fighting erupted between the Indonesians and the Allied occupation army, and the latter even called upon Japanese contingents to assist them in putting down the resistance. The British had not anticipated the dimensions of the problem, and their small force was hardly in a position, or indeed willing, to ignite a major conflict. The British prepared to leave Indonesia by the end of 1946 and urged the Dutch to come to terms with their erstwhile subjects. The result was the Linggadjati Agreement, which was entered into by the Netherlands and Sukarno's government. The Agreement called for the *de facto* independence of Java and Sumatra and the protection of Dutch economic investments. A larger federation of Indonesia was envisaged, which would be linked in a Netherlands-Indonesian Union by 1949. The Dutch, however, soon revealed that they only sought to buy time with the treaty. They consolidated their hold on the islands previously occupied by the Australians, while the British returned to the Dutch the administration of the principal port cities on Java and Sumatra. A Dutch army was hastily assembled, and in July, 1947, major fighting broke out in clear violation of the Linggadjati Agreement. After initial battlefield successes, the Dutch were pressured by the United States and the United Nations to sign yet another agreement with the Indonesians. The Renville Agreement called for a ceasefire in place and the later holding of a plebiscite to determine the future rulers of the islands. The Dutch never intended to uphold this agreement either, knowing they could not count upon the votes of their Indonesian subjects. As a consequence of Dutch ruthlessness and duplicity, the ranks of the Indonesian Communist Party (PKI) began to swell. The Communists claimed they could better insure Indonesia's independence, and differences between this group and Sukarno's Indonesian Nationalist Party (PNI) produced a series of skirmishes. Sukarno fought the Communists and the Dutch simultaneously, but there were no decisive battles. The Dutch finally concluded that continuing the struggle was futile, and on November 2, 1949, they were ready to recognize Indonesia's independence in return for guarantees protecting their economic interests. With the Dutch no longer a concern, Sukarno had little difficulty in bringing the Communists under his influence.

Sovereign Indonesia

Indonesia received a new constitution in 1950, which replaced the 1945 document and nullified many of the pledges made to the Dutch. The Sukarno government wanted to establish a unitary state in order to control the outlying islands. Under the original arrangement, the outer islands were loosely incorporated in a federation, which seemed to serve Dutch financial interests more than those of the new republic. Indonesian nationalism could not develop with such a plan, hence Sukarno's abrogation of the old constitution. The new constitution seemed to emphasize the centralization of power in Java. But instead of providing the president with dominant powers, as had been the case with the earlier constitution, this one concentrated authority in the parliament. Also the central cabinet was made responsible to the parliament. The shift from the presidential to a parliamentary system was prompted by a desire to win the confidence of the outer islands. If they were expected to give up their autonomy, gestures had to be made to reduce Java's influence. Unity, it was noted, could only emerge from mutual trust. But regardless of the rationale for the change, the most immediate effect was the proliferation of political parties, causing increased political squabbling. Political instability was a crushing problem, as cabinets were tenuous coalitions with extremely short life-spans. Moreover, elections were repeatedly postponed, and when they were finally held in 1955, the Indonesian electorate refused to give any party more than 25 percent of the vote.

Sukarno stood above the parties, but he gave lip-service to the Nationalist Indonesian Party (PNI) and it became the strongest political organization in the country. The PNI was followed by the Masjumi, a modernist Islamic party, the Nahdatul Ulama, a more traditional Islamic

organization, the Indonesian Communist Party (PKI), and finally the Socialist Party led by the nationalist poet-philosopher Sutan Sjahrir. Sjahrir
had proven to be the most expressive voice of Indonesian independence
against the Dutch, but his disaffection from Sukarno eliminated him from
key leadership positions. By and large, Sukarno sought to isolate all the
nationalist leaders. His perception of Indonesia's future left little room for
compromise and political brokering. From the outset, Sukarno insisted on
a paternalistic style. In time he solidified the myth that he was the
embodiment of the Indonesian nation, its indispensable leader. The numerous political parties and the parliamentary process, therefore, were
nuisances to be overcome. As President of the Indonesian republic, Sukarno did his utmost to undermine these institutions and strangle the
procedures laid down in the 1950 Constitution. He never accepted the
view that the executive was a ceremonial figure and used every opportunity to complicate the work of the cabinet. Thus, the country's political
instability was aggravated, not ameliorated, by his manipulative, flamboyant performance. But for all Sukarno's extraconstitutional behavior, he did
not lose the support of the overwhelming portion of Indonesians. To them
he was the father of the nation, the most consistent nationalist, and an
infallible leader. The Indonesians demanded a charismatic leader, and
Sukarno was only too eager to satisfy their desire.

Sukarno's preeminence, however, meant that sophisticated political
institutions would be difficult to secure. Moreover, Indonesians had only
limited experience in day-to-day administration, hence the government
bureaucracy could not yet fill the vacuum left by the Dutch colonial
administration. Political disorder combined with bureaucratic ineptness
and corruption. Sukarno exploited this political and administrative instability to neutralize the opposition. The Masjumi party and the Darul Islam
army, both of which wanted to establish an Islamic state in Indonesia,
were thwarted by Sukarno's determined political and military action.
Although the latter formed a strong guerrilla force, they were deemed less
important than the Masjumi, which was the strongest party outside Java,
and hence most effective in articulating anti-Javan sentiment. But the
collapse of the Darul Islam and the weakening of the Masjumi strengthened the Communist PKI and the army. Sukarno was forced into a
delicate balancing act in which he had to placate the leftists, as well as
their chief nemesis, the Indonesian armed forces.

The Crisis of 1957-1958

While political, military, and bureaucratic leaders poorly managed
Indonesian government, the country's economy worsened. Socio-economic
dislocation was a hardship on the general population, but the government

and political factions seemed indifferent to the problem. When Vice-president Mohammad Hatta implored Sukarno to promote a reconciliation between the Muslim groups and limit his dependence on the Communists, relations between the two men deteriorated. In December, 1956, Hatta offered his resignation as vice-president following a series of abortive coups, which were responses to rampant government corruption. Regionalism, however, was becoming even more worrisome. The heavy hand of the Javans was felt in all the outer islands. Their monopoly over vital political, military, and economic posts proved abrasive. Development projects promised by the central government were ignored. Indeed, even salaries earmarked for the armed forces based on islands outside Java failed to reach their proper recipients.

In 1957, a rebellion broke out on Sumatra, which was allegedly promoted by the Masjumi party. Sukarno perceived a mortal threat to Indonesian unity, his prize objective. He mobilized his forces to crush the movement before it spread to other islands. The Masjumi, on the other hand, had concluded that Sukarno was determined to eliminate all parties that he could not personally manage. His speech on November 10, 1956 had been interpreted as a declaration of war on dissident political organizations. It was also at that time that President Sukarno voiced the view that Indonesia required a form of democracy that was more in harmony with its political and social ethos. He had alluded to "guided democracy," but his opposition knew this meant a personal dictatorship and the termination of their activities. Moreover, the Masjumi claimed Hatta's departure from the vice-president's office implied the end of balanced representation for non-Javans. As civil war raged in Sumatra, it was obvious the rebellious elements were divided; yet the government could do little more than contain the fighting. Sukarno made the most of the situation. He declared his intention to build an entirely new political system, one that would be free of western influence and more in keeping with Indonesian custom. The remedy he prescribed was a modification of Indonesian communal life with particular emphasis on functional cooperation. The plan also envisaged bringing the Communists into the government.

Sukarno had the support of the PNI, the Communist Party (PKI), and the Nahdatul Ulama. The Masjumi, however, refused to go along. They sided with Hatta, who believed the inclusion of the Communists in the government was a poorly disguised Trojan Horse tactic. The PKI would be given an excellent opportunity to bore from within and eventually to seize control of the government. As the war in Sumatra intensified, Sukarno called for, and received, emergency powers, which permitted him to declare martial law throughout the country. The cabinet resigned, leaving Sukarno and the army with absolute power. Indonesia's brief parliamentary experience had come to an inglorious close.

Guided Democracy

The rebellion in Sumatra was eventually brought under control, but Sukarno had no intention of reverting to the now defunct political system. Moreover, a good portion of his opposition had been destroyed, and the way was clear to promote the more disciplined, albeit limited, "guided democracy." Sukarno assumed the Indonesians wanted harmony, not dissonance. His new order was predicated on delivering that harmony, even if it meant the elimination of all his critics. Sukarno believed Indonesians needed direction not options, purpose not promises, consensus not controversy, and guided democracy was judged the only vehicle for those objectives. In 1945, Sukarno argued in favor of a strong presidential system. Outwardly accepting the parliamentary constitution in 1950, he never intended to submit to its restrictive provisions. Now that the parliamentary system was discredited and the 1950 constitution abandoned, he could disassociate himself from it. Sukarno could not ignore Indonesia's right to build a democratic system, but he was convinced that democracy could only have meaning in the context of strong leadership.

Sukarno was also impressed with the Chinese Communist experience, which enabled a poor people not only to restore their pride, but to mount a prodigious economic program. Sukarno decided to model many aspects of his country's development upon the Chinese example. Social mobilization, for instance, was at the heart of Chinese development effort: this method harnessed the energy of many millions for state-building projects. The Indonesian President wished to follow such a campaign. Sukarno was determined to play a role similar to that played by Mao Tse-tung in China. To do this, it was necessary for all political factions to unite into one all-inclusive organization. Sukarno desired the creation of a National Front, which would consist of functional groups rather than political parties. He insisted that the peasantry, labor, students, and army had no need of politics and should be organized by the government into programs for action. Development could only be achieved when energies were directed into productive channels. Political activity, on the other hand, was wasteful and of no genuine utility in an emerging nation. The army, under the leadership of General A. H. Nasution, was sympathetic with Sukarno's plan to liquidate the political parties, especially because it was considered a device for controlling the growth of the PKI. But the struggle between the army high command and the Indonesian Communist Party also prevented Sukarno's guided democracy plan from being fully implemented.

Indonesia's political parties were without the formal trappings of a parliament, but they continued to organize. Thus some continued to operate openly, as did the Communists, while others went underground.

The National Front of functional groups that Sukarno strove to develop was postponed. Sukarno found himself in a struggle to satisfy both the army and the PKI. The latter had now become the largest Asian Communist party outside of Communist China. Moreover, the United States had been implicated in the Sumatran rebellion and a rift developed between the two countries. Dutch economic interests were also taken over by the government, and the Europeans were forced to leave the country. Sukarno now looked toward China and the Soviet Union, both of which became Indonesia's chief suppliers of military hardware. This dependence on the two Communist states not only improved the image of the PKI, it also affected the high command in the Indonesian army. The PKI was prepared to use Sukarno, but they were not ready to dilute their long-range objectives to undermine the traditional power elite. Sukarno's Political Manifesto (Manipol) outlining "basic democracy" was adopted by the PKI, but they tried to convince the Indonesian President that others were trying to destroy it. This was the Communist explanation for the continuation of bureaucratic corruption and ineffectiveness, despite the President's reform program. Guided democracy, it was stressed, could be successful only after the destruction of vested interests, both foreign and domestic. The PKI made a convincing presentation, and their improved political leverage was revealed in their capacity to use the President as a buffer between themselves and the army.

Sukarno prevented the army from moving against the PKI. He also refused to ban the PKI's operations. Sukarno, in fact, sought to reduce the army's prestige by taking credit for the suppression of the Sumatran and the Celebes insurrections. He claimed even greater fame when the Dutch were finally pressured into giving up West New Guinea (now West Irian) in 1962. The army was made the target for growing criticism, especially from those groups that felt it was too deeply involved in political decision-making. Overall, the PKI fared better than the army in the early 1960s. This was demonstrated by the 1963-1964 confrontation with Malaysia over northern Borneo.

The army high command allegedly advised Sukarno against the plan to seize northern Borneo, which the British, not the Dutch, had colonized. In departing the regions, the British made it possible for two of the three political entities in northern Borneo to join the Malaysian Federation. The third group wished to maintain independence. The Indonesian confrontation with Malaysia, therefore, was also considered an indirect attack on Great Britain, and the English reinforced the Malaysian command. Sukarno, however, was overconfident due to a victory in West Irian, and he refused to heed the advice of his army leaders. In addition, he was encouraged by the PKI to use aggressive action against the Malaysians. If Sukarno was successful, the Malaysian state would be prey for continuing

Communist encroachment, and the Indonesian President would be the Third World's outstanding leader. If unsuccessful, the Indonesian army would have to bear maximum responsibility, and changes would be forced on its high command. Either way the Communists could not fail to improve their position. Thus the confrontation with Malaysia proceeded despite a disastrous impact on Indonesia's economy. The Indonesian army was ill-prepared for a prolonged struggle. When forced to retreat, they were confronted with the displeasure of Sukarno and the PKI.

Sukarno was the victim of his own rhetoric. Guided democracy was lost in an avalanche of slogans and symbols. National planning was transformed into "guided economy," and the nominated assembly, hand-picked by Sukarno in 1960, was called by the classical Indonesian expression of Gotong Royong (Mutual Aid). The Indonesian President identified his party under the principle of NASAKOM, which translated into the unity of nationalists, religious groups, and Communists. Sukarno publicized his programs without discriminating between important and trivial issues. Presidential speeches were given special sanctity and labeled to fit the occasion. Among these were: the "Message of the People's Suffering" and the "Threefold Command of the People." Special festival days were arranged, such as National Awakening Day and Electricity and Gas Day. He called for the institution of a Prosperity Command, which was to utilize students as developmental workers and technicians in the impoverished rural areas. Simultaneously he ordered the construction of stadiums and hotels to facilitate the Asian Olympics in Djakarta, later renamed "Games of the New Emerging Forces." Sukarno hoped to weave these diverse activities into a national ideology. The acronym USDEK seemed to sum it all up. It stood for five ideas: the 1945 constitution, socialism *à la* Indonesia, guided democracy, guided economy, and Indonesian pride. Thus the Sukarno ideology was usually abbreviated as Manipol-USDEK. Although the media and all government officials were required to repeat the phrase, no amount of repetition could obscure the fact that the country was badly run and that the continuing struggle between the PKI and the army now involved the President.

Sukarno's Fall

Sukarno had been designated president for life, but events were beginning to overtake him. He had permitted himself considerable flexibility in dealing with his diverse polity, but he was increasingly compelled to support one side against the other. Because the President had been drifting to the left, a movement was organized called the "Body for the Preservation of Sukarnoism" (BPS). Its primary purpose was to promote a non-communist Indonesian socialism. BPS had the active support of the army high command, as well as a majority of the non-communist political parties that had continued to function. Sukarno's reaction to the formation of the BPS was sudden and decisive. He ordered the BPS banned, and in January, 1965, announced he would not be disturbed by a Communist Party take-over, as long as the Indonesian state remained unified. The months that followed were tense and uncertain, as the opposing sides maneuvered for a showdown.

On the night of September 30, 1965, six of Indonesia's senior army generals were murdered by followers of an order called the *Gestapu* (Gerakan September Tiga Puluh or the September 30 Movement). The commander of Sukarno's palace guard, Lieutenant Colonel Untung, led the movement and justified his acts by insisting that the generals were plotting to overthrow Sukarno. General Nasution had been marked for death but had escaped to rally his loyal troops. Joined by General Suharto (who had not been targeted by Gestapu), they led a successful counter-attack and soon crushed the revolt. Sukarno was placed under house arrest, while the perpetrators of the murders were summarily executed. Perhaps more significant, however, was the opportunity that the coup and counter-coup afforded for anti-communist forces in the country to be unleashed. The PKI was judged the real power behind the Gestapu, and orders went out to seize their leaders and close down all Communist Party operations. In the ensuing weeks and months virtually all Indonesian Communist leaders were executed. Their party offices were destroyed, and party workers were imprisoned or set upon by troops and citizens, alike. Once begun, the violence was not halted until several hundred thousand persons were killed. Many of the victims were not Communists, but people who were simply disliked by their neighbors. For example, anti-Chinese sentiment exploded during the chaos, and this minority paid a high price in human lives. When the killing had run its course, the PKI was neutralized as an effective political force. Its survivors moved underground to reorganize their forces.

Sukarno was still officially in office in the winter of 1966, and in a display of determination, he ordered the dismissal of General Nasution from his post as Defense Minister. The army up to this time did not want to remove Sukarno, given the popular support that he continued to enjoy. Moreover, the army did not relish taking full responsibility for the government's failures. These, it was argued, could more easily be blamed on Sukarno. But Sukarno's act of defiance in dismissing Nasution was directed at the army. The army high command knew that the Indonesians could be swayed and the army discredited by events, if decisive action was not taken. Thus on March 11, 1966, the President was forced to sign an order providing General Suharto with the necessary powers to restore the country's equilibrium. Sukarno was now little more than a symbol. After he had devoted so much effort to the creation of symbols, it was ironic that he became one himself.

General Suharto had the responsibility for "de-Sukarnoizing" Indonesian policy and performance. He ordered an end to the confrontation with Malaysia and directed Indonesia to rejoin the United Nations, which Sukarno had quit earlier. Suharto avoided demands calling for Sukarno's trial, but he did yield to the call of the People's Consultative Assembly and moved Sukarno out of the president's palace. He also agreed to become Indonesia's acting president pending national elections. By March 27, 1968, Sukarno had been effectively isolated and was officially replaced by General Suharto. Sukarno was confined to a remote village in Java until his death several years later.

The New Indonesia

Two months after assuming the presidency, President Suharto broadened his government to include a number of civilian ministers. The anticipated elections were postponed in order to give the new government time to restructure its operations and clarify its policies. Moreover, Suharto no longer held the view that he needed the elections to legitimize his rule. The People's Consultative Assembly, like the cabinet, was enlarged and only those loyal to the regime were permitted to retain their seats. Suharto's foreign policy meshed with his economic policy in that new efforts were launched to attract foreign capital. Relations between Indonesia and the United States improved immediately, and the latter country sought to aid the former's shaky economy. Concessions were given to foreign companies, and the mining of metals, the cutting of timber, and especially the drilling for petroleum proceeded at a rapid pace. On the domestic front, the government moved against black marketeers and smugglers, pressed charges against tax evaders, sought to reduce corruption within the bureaucracy, and managed to bring the prices of basic commodities under strict controls. Although agriculture continued to be a problem for the regime, Indonesia began to amass considerable wealth as a result of the exploitation of its oil reserves. In conjunction with the state-owned oil company, known as Pertamina, foreign companies, such as the Union Oil Company of California, made the petroleum industry a lucrative enterprise. These petrodollars were easily converted into needed manufactures and foodstuffs.

President Suharto stressed his determination to revive the 1945 presidential constitution. His satisfaction with that constitution signalled his desire to control the legislature and the country's political parties. In the latter case, the Masjumi religious party, which had been banned in 1960, was given permission to reform, and was again active as the Parmusi

(Partai Muslimin Indonesia). Suharto even went so far as to select the Parmusi's leader. President Suharto's actions have been interpreted as a desire to court the Muslim organizations in the country. In a nation of more than one hundred million Muslims, this is not an aberrant maneuver. His predecessor had stressed radical secularism to the point of utter disaster. Suharto sought a more moderate approach, but he is still openly opposed to the establishment of an Islamic state. Nevertheless, he will cater to this segment of the population with the hope of winning their confidence, particularly in the outer islands, where the possibility of separatist movements remains great. Suharto's performance is also important in preventing the PKI from reasserting its influence, especially in those non-Javan territories.

The elections held under Suharto's leadership in 1971 tell much about the current political system in Indonesia. First, the 1971 general elections were the first since 1955, and only the second since the country had gained its independence. Second, many of the same political parties that participated in the earlier election took part in the 1971 affair. There were very real differences between the two elections, however. For instance, the principal organizations in the 1955 elections were the Indonesian Nationalist Party (PNI), which was closely identified with Sukarno; the Indonesian Communist Party (PKI); the modernist Masjumi; and the more traditional Nahdatul Ulama. In the 1971 elections the PKI was not permitted to run candidates, and the PNI bore the stigmas of Sukarno and their alleged involvement in the Gestapu plot. The Masjumi, as already noted, had returned as the Parmusi, but its internal organization was in considerable disarray. Only the Nahdatul Ulama was generally intact, but its platform and influence were limited in both content and geography. Two other Muslim parties took to the field in the 1971 campaign. They were the Partai Serikat Islam Indonesia (PSII), and the Pergerakan Tarbiah Islamijah, better known as Perti or the Islamic Education Movement. In March, 1970, all the Islamic parties announced they would coalesce into one group for the purpose of winning the election. This grouping of religious parties was more the result of Suharto's initiative than the parties themselves. The Indonesian President wanted the election process simplified, and he believed that by separating the parties into religious, nationalist, or secular groups the people would better understand their choices and alternatives.

Suharto, however, was skeptical about the utility of the established political parties. Although he refrained from ridding Indonesia of these organizations, he was preoccupied with his predecessor's idea: the concept of apolitical functional groups acquiring representation in the legislature. Now, Suharto felt, was the moment to give the idea institutional expression. The end result of the Suharto government's deliberations was the *golkar* (golongan karya), or functional groups. These functional groups were divided into seven categories, or *kino* (kolompok induk organisasi), and all came under a central joint secretariat, which was called the *Sekber Golkar*. Although it was free of conventional politics, the Sekber Golkar was given the status of a political party in order to run candidates in the 1971 election. Thus the Sekber Gokar had all the outward signs of a political party. They were given an easily identifiable political symbol. Each group, or kino (meaning labor, peasants, army, women, intelligentsia), was given a leader by the government, usually an ex-military officer. Moreover, the entire Sekber Golkar came under the Ministry of Interior, which was also led by a high army officer. Suharto had realized Sukarno's dream, but there was an important difference. Sukarno had wanted to keep the functional groups independent of the army; Suharto preferred the integration of the two bodies. It could be said that Suharto had militarized the political process, while the military had become more politicized.

The Sekber Golkar is a unique institution. It has emerged from the Indonesian cultural setting and attempts to provide a coherent response to the nation's manifold problems. It addresses itself to the unity of the country without raising the emotional issues of race, ethnicity, regionalism, and religion. It seeks to satisfy the aspirations of a diverse people by stressing positive accomplishments. The Sekber Golkar is a heterogenous arrangement that cuts across ideological frontiers and historical legacies. But all the customs and values of Indonesian society are operative in the organization. It stresses authoritarian organization, and military discipline. It accepts Suharto as the ultimate leader, and it is his leadership that members of the Golkar credit with the creation of harmony in the country. There is also recognition that the functional groups interact in a productive and mutually beneficial manner, and the consensus is achieved through joint deliberation. The Golkar's seven-point working program, the Sapta-Krida, is as follows:

1. promotion of political stability;
2. economic stability;
3. security stability, including the problem of subversion;
4. development;
5. public welfare;
6. measures to improve the state apparatus; and
7. general elections.

In its own right, the Sekber Golkar had considerable importance in the context of Indonesian political history. But the Suharto administration supported the group's campaign in such a way as to assure a victory in the

1971 elections. Government officials were ordered to make strenuous efforts to win the "confidence" of the voting public. Moreover, funds were drawn from the public treasury in order to purchase votes considered doubtful or destined for the more conventional political parties. Local officials also were ordered to pressure voters in their districts to cast ballots for Golkar candidates. Whether this frantic and illegal behavior was necessary is impossible to gauge, but the Suharto government did manage to come away with an overwhelming victory. Unfortunately, the election could not be considered a true test of the functional groups' strength in a competitive political situation. In addition, the regime did not aid its legitimacy, and this important purpose was lost. This may also explain why the 1976 elections were postponed until 1977.

TABLE 7-1.
Election Results of 1971

Party	Seats
Sekber Golkar	227
Nahdatul Ulama	58
Parmusi	24
PNI	20
PSII	10
Parkindo	7
Partai Katolik	3
Perti	2

An evaluation of the election results suggests that the Sekber Golkar ruined the established political parties. The legislative experience of the remaining parties must be confined to minor acts. It is doubtful that they can play the role of the "loyal" opposition, given the monopoly of voting power by the government's party. The fact that the political parties are oppressed, and that the public knows the elections were conducted in a flagrantly unprincipled manner, does not help the cause of Indonesian democracy. The protests of the PNI and Nahdatul Ulama are bound to be heard. When political parties conclude that the system is stacked against them, they more often than not adopt extra-legal tactics. Indonesia's politics will most likely continue to be fought in the streets rather than in a forum with established rules and procedures.

Suharto is not oblivious to the problems inherent in governing a country as complex as Indonesia. He has ruled for more than a decade, and the country has enjoyed relative political stability. In part, this is due to his vigilance and the demands he makes on his subordinates. Suharto is Indonesia's principal leader. His re-election to another five year term in March, 1973, was without opposition in the People's Consultative Assembly. His goal to improve the political system has led to the fusion of the four Islamic parties into a single organization called the Partai Persatuan Pemhangunan. The five non-Muslim parties (the Indonesian Nationalist Party, the Christian Party (Parkindo), the Catholic Party (Partai Katolik), Murba, and Ipki) have also been united into one group, Partai Demokrasi Indonesia or Indonesian Democratic Party. The elimination of the old parties subordinates the two new political organizations to the Sekber Golkar and, importantly, seems to reduce the number of issues between them. It certainly provides the government with greater overall control.

As a result of the political "simplification," the 460-member House of the People's Congress, or central legislature, showed the following breakdown:

Golkar (functional groups)	261
Development Unity Party (Muslim)	94
Indonesian Democratic Party (non-Muslim)	30
Armed Forces (appointed by the president)	75

Suharto has also organized a National Board of Political Stabilization and National Security, which he chairs. It is comprised of eleven members who are selected from among his cabinet ministers and gives President Suharto an inner council directly concerned with the maintenance of the regime's authority. The creation of such a body, however, suggests that Indonesia is far from tranquil, and that the government must maintain absolute control over the political and military centers to sustain the surface calm.

Suharto was disturbed, as well as embarrassed, when Japanese Premier Kakuei Tanaka visited Djakarta in January, 1974. The Japanese Premier's presence became the pretext for intense student rioting. More than a dozen students died in the disorder, while more than one hundred were injured and several hundred arrested. Hundreds of Japanese-made vehicles were also destroyed. The government instituted a curfew in the major cities of Java and banned all demonstrations. But students in Bandung defied the order and demonstrated to condemn the imprisoning of their counterparts in the capital. The students did not limit their attack to Japanese symbols, however, as Chinese merchants, who have always been accused of questionable business practices, were also set upon. In an effort to ward off a major race war, Suharto ordered all foreign holdings in the country (most of which were owned by Chinese) to be shared jointly with Indonesians, who were to be given at least 51 percent control. But underlying these actions was Suharto's sense of having been failed by his subordinates. Years of relative stability made it possible for a number of highly placed Indonesian officials to aggrandize themselves. This provided the opposition with leverage to mobilize support against his regime. Suharto's decision to dismiss four of his top aides and abolish the post of personal presidential assistant demonstrated his intention to delegate less authority in areas of vital concern. The President also ordered the release of 1,300 political prisoners in November, 1975, and his government contemplates releasing an additional 35,000 of the almost 50,000 that were arrested in the aftermath of the abortive 1965 coup in an effort to improve the regime's image.

Indonesia and the Future

Suharto must contend with basically the identical problems that confronted Sukarno. Indonesia therefore will be governed with firmness and resolve. Despite some sign of democratic procedure, the political system will remain authoritarian and highly personalized. Differences in style between Suharto and Sukarno are obvious. Suharto will maintain a low profile, insist on complete loyalty, and attempt to neutralize all movements aimed at altering the military-bureaucratic process. He will avoid antagonizing the armed forces and will defer to them in any conflict with political groups. Suharto would like to depoliticize Indonesia, but he knows this is impossible. Nonetheless, he will not hesitate to use coercive methods or employ violence if threatened with clandestine acts. He is constantly on guard against subversive elements, and orders have been given to the armed forces to execute guerrillas and terrorists without trial if necessary. Suharto is concerned about the volatile student population, which is the only organized group capable of openly demonstrating its dissatisfaction with his regime. Suharto does not want to alienate the students, and he has given them a voice in the Golkar. Nevertheless, the Gerakan Mahasiswa Nasional Indonesia, a student organization formerly affiliated with Sukarno's PNI, declared itself independent when the political parties were fused into simplified groupings in 1973. It is these students who periodically disturb public peace. The forcible handling of student rioters has contained the fighting. But the government fears the students are filtering into more remote locations on Java and throughout the outer islands, where they are undergoing intensive political indoctrination and receiving guerrilla training by small cadres of the underground PKI. Moreover, there is sufficient evidence that the Chinese Communists are supplying these subversive bands with weapons and ammunition. The latter problem has produced something of a split in the Indonesian high command, with the more anti-communist officers insisting on the removal of any official, military, or civilian, who favors Peking.

At the same time, the communization of Indochina has caused Indonesia to reconsider its foreign policy options. United States support for Indonesia has been fulsome since Sukarno's fall, but the American withdrawal from Southeast Asia leaves many questions unanswered. Indonesia's domestic condition is inextricably a part of its posture in foreign policy, and it cannot afford to worsen relations with the large Communist states. On the other hand, Indonesia has invited heavy American investment and looks to the United States for much of its military requirements. But 1978 has been set for a massive demilitarization with defense expenditures limited to 3 percent of the budget. Army strength is supposed to be reduced by 30 percent, from 300,000 to 200,000 soldiers. Naval and air force strength has already been reported reduced from 70,000 to 30,000. Indonesian officials explain this reduction with the view that Indonesia plans no aggression and is solely concerned with countering subversion, infiltration, and insurgency within the archipelago. Indonesia's foreign policy therefore is predicated on peaceful cooperation with its neighbors in Malaysia, the Philippines, and Australia. It has also developed intimate relations with India and shows every indication of normalizing relations with Vietnam. Given its ability to engender goodwill among these countries, it hopes to placate China, while inducing the United States (through attractive oil concessions) to support Indonesia in case of increased Soviet or Chinese pressures. It was a curious coincidence that crack troops of the Indonesian armed forces were poised for an invasion of Portuguese Timor as President Gerald Ford was stopping in Djakarta on his way back to the United States from Peking in December, 1975. Indonesian fears that Timor was coming under Communist control is said to have precipitated the action. President Ford insisted he had not been informed of the Indonesian invasion. But the incident highlighted the tension with which Indonesia views any overt changes in the status quo of the region. There was the fear that Communist control of Timor could provide communist dissidents with a base from which to escalate their struggle against the Suharto regime. Thus despite United Nations calls for the Indonesians to withdraw their troops from eastern Timor, the Suharto government moved to annex it. A 28-member East Timor People's Assembly was hastily organized by the Indonesians and they quickly approved joining the Indonesian Federation. By June 24, 1976 all of Timor was brought within the Indonesian union. Moreover, Indonesia's immediate neighbors did not interfere with these maneuvers. On the contrary, at a summit meeting of the Association of Southeast Asian Nations, (ASEAN) held in Bali in February 1976, the five nations comprising the organization, Indonesia, Thailand, Malaysia, Singapore and the Philippines, signed a treaty of amity and cooperation and for the first time established a fully operative secretariat and high council of ministers that is charged with resolving all political disputes between the member-states.

Indonesia has been reasonably stable, but recurring dilemmas are symptoms of an inability to resolve hard issues. Indonesia is improving its economic position, but it is still seriously short of dedicated, nationally motivated, professional administrators. Its political parties are ineffective vehicles for development. In general, the country remains divided. The army, which remains the key to the country's stability, contains, but cannot solve, persistent national problems.

THE PHILIPPINES

To the north of Indonesia lies the Philippines, some seven thousand islands stretching from north to south for more than one thousand miles. Total land area is 115,600 square miles, approximately the size of Italy or the state of Arizona. The climate of the Philippines is much like Indonesia. Its tropical position and archipelagic character ensure warm and uniform temperatures throughout the year. Rainfall is plentiful, particularly during the sultry summer and winter monsoon seasons. November is the month of highest precipitation, and April shows the least rainfall. The topography of the Philippines varies from island to island, but virtually all are covered by forests and jungle vegetation. The two largest islands are Luzon in the north and Mindanao in the south. Together they constitute about 70 percent of the total land area and contain the overwhelming majority of the population. Only 740 of the many thousands of islands are large enough to support human habitations, and most of these are small and isolated from the mainstream of Philippine activity. The people of the Philippines speak nine different languages, though Tagalog, the Luzon dialect, has been given official status. Nevertheless, one-third of the population speaks English, and American and Spanish influences affect most aspects of Filipino political, economic, and social life. The prominence of Luzon, similar to the significance of Java to Indonesia, poses serious problems of national integration. Moreover, the inability to develop a coherent Philippine culture and the concentration of power in Luzon further exacerbates this unstable society.

Nurtured by the United States as a democratic republic, after independence, the Philippines experimented with political structures and institutions associated with western democracies. In the first twenty-five years following World War II, elections were held at regular intervals. Although violence has been a part of the scene, political parties have been active, and changes of government took place along constitutional lines. The Philippines gave the appearance of being one of the few working democracies among the developing nations of Asia. The imposition of martial law in 1972, however, shattered its democratic image.

The veneer of political stability in the Philippines crumbled when the patronizing influence of the United States was withdrawn. The Philippines had achieved political independence, but there were no accompanying social and economic revolutions. Thus the political institutions and practices inherited from the Americans could not enable the country to cope with widespread public dissatisfaction. The Philippines must be examined as any other developing nation, and it reveals many of the same problems described in Indonesia and other new Asian states.

Historical Background

Today the Phillippine islands contain approximately forty million people, but the islands were sparsely populated until modern times. The first inhabitants may have been the ancestors of the Negritos, a pygmy-like people with Negroid characteristics, who are found today in the remote uplands of Luzon and some of the other islands. How these people arrived in the region is not known, but fossil remains and stone tools date the original inhabitants of the islands back some 25,000 years. The theory persists that the Negritos wandered into the area across land bridges, speculated to have connected the Philippines with lands to the south and west. More important migrations were to come much later when people from east China and Taiwan moved into the islands between 4000 and 2000 B.C. They were followed by still larger groups from Malaya and Indonesia around 300 to 200 B.C. The vast majority of Filipinos today are of Malayan ancestry. Virtually nothing is known about the people of the Philippines until the Spaniards settled in the islands. Although recent discoveries of primitive Filipino habitations may pre-date the arrival of the Malays, it is the latter that the Europeans came in contact with. These descendents of the early inhabitants were hunters and itinerant cultivators whose principal concern centered on their rice culture. There is little to even suggest that they were also concerned with progress because they did not leave behind any great monuments, temples or legends as did the other people of Southeast Asia. By the same token, whatever governmental structure they erected is judged to be of a fragmented and rudimentary nature.

Isolated from the main events of Southeast Asia, the Malayan immigrants focused their attention on the local community, or *barangay*, a term used to describe the crude boats that carried them to the islands. They were unaffected by the Indian influence in Southeast Asia, nor did Hindu culture reach the inhabitants of the Philippines. Moreover, no empires bothered to extend control over the archipelago. Even Chinese influence was peripheral and of a commercial nature. Arab traders did manage to spread Islam in Mindanao and some smaller adjacent islands in the south.

The Spaniards, however, were the first to have a significant impact on the indigenous population; they also sought to unify the Philippines.

The Spaniards found their way to Southeast Asia by sailing around the South American continent. The first circumnavigation of the world was attempted by Magellan who reached the Philippine islands in 1521. Magellan was killed by the islands' inhabitants but his ship, the *Vittoria*, continued its voyage, and the Spanish survivors finally returned to Spain after passing around the Cape of Good Hope. The tales told by Magellan's crew excited others to launch new missions. The Spaniards eventually returned to the Philippines and established a permanent settlement in 1565. Meeting no resistance, the Spanish laid claim to the islands by right of discovery. The Philippines, it was stated, was a group of scattered islands without semblance of political unity, hence Spain justified its incorporating the colony within the realm.

Spanish Rule

Spanish rule over the Philippines meant the islands would become a part of greater Southeast Asia. The years of isolation were at an end. European rivalry pitted Spanish forces against the Dutch, and even the British were involved for a time. Manila, the capital of the Philippines, was occupied by the British for a brief period from 1762 to 1764. But Great Britain soon recognized Spanish dominance in the islands. The Spanish consolidated their conquests and promoted trade through Manila, creating elaborate commerical arrangements with the Chinese. As a result, many Chinese traders settled in Manila and other ports of the Philippines. The Philippines, however, were linked more significantly with New Spain, which had been developed in North and Central America. For example, Mexican silver flowed out of New Spain into the commercial center of Manila, and from there it was easily distributed throughout East Asia.

The Philippine islands were governed as a province of Spain from that country's Mexican possession until 1815. When Spain was pressured by indigenous revolts and the European powers to give up its colony in Spanish America, the administrative system which had been developed in Mexico was transferred to the Phillippines. The chief Spanish authority in the Philippines was the governor-general, who had been appointed by and represented the Crown. The overall system can best be described as feudal. Royal fiefs (*encomiendas*) came under the control of Spanish aristocrats who had also been appointed by the king. Each encomienda included a number of barangay villages that were controlled by traditional village headmen (cacuques). The *cacuques* were local estate owners in their own right, and their alliance with the Spanish aristocrats worked a special hardship upon the peasantry, who were forced to pay heavy taxes, as well as provide labor for the local chief. Thus the peasants were tied directly to their village superior, or patron, who offered protection from outsiders and was responsible for local law and order. The villagers served their patrons with considerable faithfulness. In time, a social network of obligations, duties, and services was developed, which endured under American rule. This socio-economic arrangement introduced by the Spanish is an integral feature of Philippine interpersonal relations to the present time.

The Spaniards had no inclination toward social or political reform, and their rule was authoritative and in many instances, oppressive. They were interested, however, in spreading Christianity, and the conversion of the Filipinos became a primary undertaking. The Spaniards intended to make the Philippines a center for Christian missionary activity in Asia. Under the leadership of King Philip II, Spain assumed the role of converting the peoples of the Orient to Christianity. The political record of Spain in the Philippines was influenced by the religious mission that consumed the Spanish authorities. From 1578 to 1609, the missionary enterprise made considerable headway. The Filipinos lacked a sophisticated culture of their own, and the missionaries found them to be easy converts. The missionaries proved to be adept at winning the confidence of the indigenous population, especially in Luzon and the other northern islands. Instead of displacing local customs and traditions, they emphasized accomodation, and the Filipinos sensed they had little to lose and much to gain from the conversion. The success of Spanish missionary efforts can be observed in the fact that 80 percent of the population of the Philippines today profess the Catholic faith.

The Catholic Church came to play an eminent role in the Philippines, and it had the reputation of being the largest landholder in the country. The Church's governing structure was a facsimile of the Spanish administrative system, and the Bishop of Manila was by law the second most powerful political figure in the islands. In the outlying areas, the church administrative system was often more important than the government apparatus. There, local clergy became the chief means of communication between the villagers and the Spanish authorities.

All was far from quiet in the Philippines, however, and popular dissatisfaction often degenerated into open rebellions. Economic grievances, such as forced labor, cacuque exactions, tribute payment requirements, or loss of land, were the principal causes of violence. The local nature of the rebellions made it possible to contain them with limited means. By the time the United States appeared on the scene, however, there were indications of broader, more organized resistance. Newspapers, such as *El Ciario de Manila* and *El Commercio*, were established in 1848 and 1850, respectively. They published articles criticizing Spanish rule, despite the colonial administration's threats and efforts to shut them down. Moreover, the conversion of the Filipinos to Christianity brought many natives into the clergy. The indigenous clergy, along with the Filipino commercial and landed elite, which had taken advantage of the opportunities to obtain a western education, resented the Spanish refusal to treat them as equals. Lines were becoming more clearly drawn between the Spanish colonizers and their erstwhile indigenous supporters. The latter groups "nationalized" the grievances against the Spanish and ultimately undermined Spain's control of the islands.

The Spanish were reluctant to part with their privileged social and economic positions. Even the Spanish friars came under attack as symbols of Spanish arrogance. Therefore when Spain was defeated in the Spanish-American War of 1898, the entire European system had been repudiated. The people of the Philippines sensed their independence was at hand. It was clear the Filipinos wanted to be free of colonialism. But the Filipinos were yet to see their dream realized. The Americans came ashore with a view to freeing the Philippines from Spanish rule, but they were not yet convinced they could turn the affairs of the islands over to indigenous rulers. The United States occupation of the Philippines was not without incident. Filipino nationalists continued their fight with the Americans, and for three years struggled to achieve their goal. The United States, however, was determined to crush the resistance, and its superior forces eventually destroyed the nationalists.

The Philippines as an American Colony

The United States had no clear colonial design for the Philippines. Some ultra-patriots with expansionist interests, however, as well as missionary groups, blatantly publicized the United States *Manifest Destiny*. This doctrine advocated the formal annexation of the islands. Overall, the American government was hard-pressed to justify its occupation of the Philippines. In order to separate the United States' action from that of the European states, it publicly declared its intention to prepare the Filipinos for eventual self-government. But first the Spanish legacy of abuse and exploitation was to be reformed, and programs were to be initiated, aimed at avoiding a new era of colonialism.

American tutelage of the Filipinos was conceived in moral terms. Particular emphasis was given to an American-style education, and the English language was made the medium of instruction; this also facilitated the utilization of American textbooks and the learning of American values. In the political area, the development of political parties was given a prominence not found in any of the European-dominated colonies. The Americans also called for the liquidation of friar landholdings, an increasing source of discontent among the Philippine tenant farmers. This reform went a considerable distance toward separating clerical influence in government.

The pattern of American rule in the Philippines was established by Commissioner William Howard Taft between 1901 and 1904. Taft later became Secretary of War in the Cabinet of President Theodore Roosevelt, and was himself elected President in 1909. During Taft's administration of the Philippines, the Filipinos were given a voice in the government. The first local elections for village and municipal consultative bodies were held in 1903, and the first elections for the Philippine Assembly followed in 1907. It was stated American policy that the Filipinos were to gradually assume all key responsibilities connected with operations of government. When the Jones Act was passed in 1916, the United States promised the Philippines independence as soon as a stable government could be established. American educational and political reforms, however, did not affect the traditional pattern of landholding or entrepreneurial control. Indigenous power remained in the hands of the wealthy who took advantage of every opportunity to increase their strength. Moreover, given the American willingness to grant independence to the Philippines, Filipino nationalist movements lost their vitality, and were markedly ineffective. Although their agitation was intended to pry greater political concessions from the Americans, they would have preferred a more forceful campaign. The Philippine population could not be mobilized for struggle, and they followed those leaders who urged moderation and patience rather than revolutionary change.

With the Tydings-McDuffie Act of 1934, the United States government authorized the Philippines to convene a constituent assembly to draft a constitution as a prelude to full independence. The Americans laid down general guidelines for the constitution, which prescribed a republican system of government and a democratic orientation that would guarantee fundamental rights. It also provided for the position of a High Commissioner who would act as the representative of the American president until the country became completely independent. The Tydings-McDuffie Act specified a ten-year interim between the adoption of the constitution and the date of the Philippines' independence. The Filipino Constituent Assembly completed a draft constitution in February, 1935, and it was submitted to President Franklin D. Roosevelt for approval. The Philippine electorate ratified the document on May 14, 1935. Although still under American tutelage, the Filipinos put the constitution into effect and elected Manuel L. Quezon as their first president. Full independence for the Philippines was scheduled for July 4, 1946, but during the interim period, the country was drawn into World War II when the Japanese invaded the islands. Japanese forces occupied the Philippines from 1942 to

1945. The Filipinos showed remarkable strength in resisting Japanese control, and many Filipinos joined the Hukbalahap Movement, the Anti-Japanese People's Liberation Army, in order to fight the invaders.

The *Huk*, or People's Army, was organized by Luis Taruc. Initially an anti-Japanese guerrilla resistance movement, it soon developed Communist sympathies. The movement attracted Philippine Communists, in addition to discontented and impoverished peasants. The Huk did not lay down their arms when the Japanese surrendered. The Huks fiercely attacked the big landlords, hoping to seize their feudal holdings. Areas that came under Huk control experienced quick land reform, as well as commune-like governments.

The Huks thrived after the war, and their movement spread over vast areas of Luzon, ultimately posing a threat to the government in Manila. As a result of their popularity, Taruc and six other Huks were elected to the Philippine Congress in 1946. But President Manuel Roxas denied them their congressional seats. Roxas maintained that the Huks were in armed revolt against the state. He also did not wish to antagonize the Philippine landlords or the United States, principal targets of the Huks.

Denied the right to participate in government or to claim compensation for their anti-Japanese resistance activities, the Huks returned to the jungle, and resumed their war against the Philippine government. Taruc insisted the Huk struggle was directed against corruption in government and the exploitation of the peasants, and his movement had considerable appeal. Economic dislocation also swelled Huk ranks as the country experienced ruinous inflation. At the height of their power, the Huks ruled over more than 500,000 people, mostly in central Luzon. The government in Manila could not tolerate this, and a plan was conceived to destroy the movement. An extensive military campaign led by Ramon Magsaysay, the Minister of Defense and later president from 1953 to 1957, aided by material and advisors from the United States, finally succeeded in dislodging the Huks. Once Huk military power was broken, the government proposed amnesty for all those wishing to return to peaceful pursuits. Many captured Huks were relocated, largely in Mindanao, where they were given areas to farm. Taruc surrendered in 1954, but many of his followers continued to fight from their remote jungle hideaways.

Political Developments in the Philippines

The United States transferred power peacefully to the Philippines. The basic structure of government had already been established in the 1935 constitution. Though influenced by American political practices, the Constitution was a product of Filipino leaders, particularly Manuel L.

Quezon, who was the most powerful political figure during the 1935 to 1951 period. He valued democracy, but he was no civil libertarian. He believed in the paramountcy of the state and he stressed the building of a strong, centralized government that could meet the challenges of development, ensure national integration, and also provide for the welfare of the people.

The 1935 constitution prescribed a presidential system similar to the United States, but it did not emphasize federalism or "states' rights." All local governments were considered agencies of the national government and were given power through legislative act, not by constitutional right.

Under the 1935 constitution, the presidency is the most powerful office. Originally, the president was given one six-year term, but a 1940 amendment changed this to two four-year terms with the maximum number of years in office limited to eight years. The president controls patronage through his extensive power of appointment. These appointments include the director of the Central Bank, the municipal treasurer, health officers, and even law clerks. The president is also deemed the chief administrator and can control the allocation of government funds. The power to suspend *habeas corpus* or declare martial law is given the president as commander-in-chief of the armed forces.

Given the power of the president, the legislature, or Congress, is ineffective as an independent law-making body. The president determines what is an important measure and worthy of immediate congressional attention. The president may veto any bill, and a two-thirds majority in both houses of Congress is required to override. The 1935 constitution provided for only one house, but in the amended 1940 version, a two-house legislature was adopted. In the senate, or upper house, senators were elected at large for six-year terms. In the lower chamber, or House of Representatives, congressmen were elected by districts for four-year terms. The judiciary was supposed to be independent, but all judges are presidential appointees and serve during good behavior until the age of seventy. As in the United States, the Philippine Supreme Court is the highest judicial body in the land.

Socio-Political Relationships

American colonial rule paved the way for independence and a comparatively democratic system of government. It did little, however, to modify a traditional social and economic power structure that was based on large landholdings. While the Americans ruled the Philippines, politicians, administrators, businessmen, lawyers, and technocrats all came from this class of the *principalia*, a recognizably Spanish legacy. These same people have been in power since independence, and are often related by blood and marriage. Their presence remains ubiquitous, and no government has really attempted to act against their interests.

The traditional Philippine society is family-centered. The family is the basic unit of social organization and the main instrument for transmitting cultural values. For each relationship within the family, there is a superior and inferior role to be played. Respect is expected of younger family members by elder ones. Filipinos base their power on many things, but whoever has the most power is expected to help his family.

When one is talking about the Philippine family, one is talking about a family consisting of godparents, grandparents, and sponsors for marriages, in addition to the nuclear family members. The system is also one of bilateral kinship in which both sides of the family carry equal influence. This so-called family becomes extremely large and almost amorphous. The politicians want to become part of these families in order to gain more support. However, other family members expect something in return for bringing them to the politician, who grants them a favor in return for some future favor. This bargaining process, indigenous to the family, has transcended its traditional role and must now be seen in the context of the national political system.

It has often been said that Philippine democracy was founded on this bargaining culture. The Filipinos see all relationships as a matter of power; when doing a favor for another, a credit is created which is payable on demand. The Philippine language is highly manipulative, and the use of a mediator in sensitive negotiations is a common practice. The typical Filipino personalizes his ties to the political system and uses his vote as a *quid pro quo*, if he is skillful in exploiting his relationship with those in positions of power. Power is expected to be exercised in the interests of the family. Benefits acquired through the wielding of legitimate power are socially accepted. The Philippine people do not distinguish between the role and the individual. For example, an administrator is expected to treat different persons in different ways according to their relationship to the administrator.

The Filipino politician understands this reciprocal type of relationship and knows that if he helps the people, the people will, in turn, help him. As it is often assumed that politicians are involved in furthering their own interests, those who claim their activities are taken in the national interest are looked upon with suspicion. With no national interests to strive for and with the poorly defined roles of politicians, the bargaining process of the Philippine political system is open to corruption.

In view of the traditional forms of association and the highly personalized nature of Filipino relationships, most interests are represented through a system of personal loyalties and obligations. Institutional groups are of less importance than in other countries. Philippine businessmen tend to work with their own congressman to promote certain special interests. The large companies, such as the sugar and tobacco blocs, wield significant informal power and influence over both provincial and national politicians.

Thus far the Philippines has been free from conflict between institutional groups, such as the military, bureaucracy and politicians. Group membership is very often overlapping and the groups become subordinate to the political system. There are, however, some groups that do play an important role in Philippine politics. Interest groups that do exist operate within the political system through such means as contribution of funds and recruitment of candidates. One of the most prominent interest groups is the Catholic Church. With more than 80 percent of the population Catholic, the role of the Church has remained one of major significance. The Church supports organized groups such as the Catholic Lawyers Guild and the Catholic Women's League. Each has supporters in the legislature, considered to be the Church's representatives, and they take public stands on various issues.

Bureaucratic interests are actively supported by the efforts of individual bureaucrats who lobby directly in the legislature for their particular bureau. Business interests are represented by associations such as the Philippine Chamber of Commerce and the Chamber of Industries of the Philippines. These groups use financial support to political parties to ensure their interests, but have not directly influenced any considerable amount of legislation. Labor groups have had a history of disunity and have pursued only limited interests in the political system. Students and intellectuals, alienated from the whole process of development, have also been politically vocal. The Communists have been underground since the Huk insurgency movement, but remain active. And the Muslim population in the southern islands have organized dissident political movements.

Philippine political parties have tended to become dominated by one person and are run in a very authoritative fashion, but their organizations are far from disciplined. Strong localism in the Philippines has militated against the creation of a tightly organized national party. A national party is, therefore, a coalition of small, local personal parties and factions.

Although political parties have not functioned since the imposition of martial law in 1972, prior to that event there were two major political parties in the Philippines. The Nacionalista party was formed in 1907, as an independence organization. During the early stages of the electoral dominance of the Nacionalista, factionalism temporarily split the party and a power struggle ensued between Sergio Osmena and Manuel Quezon. Following Quezon's attack on Osmena, who was then Speaker of the House and the party leader, the two factions were reunited and formed a coalition government. A two-party system did not develop until a permanent Nacionalista party split occurred in 1946. Elections and parties had been dominated by the wealthy provincial landowners. The peasants and urban middle-class were not represented and they turned to radical peasant movements and minor opposition parties. Following the conclusion of World War II, political fighting developed between Manuel Roxas and President Osmena of the Nacionalista party. The left faction of the Nacionalista split from the major party in order to form the Liberal Party and supported the candidacy of Roxas. In the election of 1946, Roxas was elected president, and the Liberal Party was established as the second major Philippine political party.

Although there was the appearance of a two-party system, it was almost impossible to find any party identification. The party system suffered from the strong hand played by the president, and as there were no basic differences in ideology between the two parties, no gain could be achieved by opposing the president. Following each election there was considerable switching of party allegiances. The result was a relatively low level of party unity or voter loyalty. Moveover, because parties generally consisted of factions and coalitions, the opposition was often formed within the administration's own party.

Parties were generally less important than the followings of individual political personalities. The key politicians benefited the party by their acquisition of influence, power base, or ability to deliver patronage. With no single interest group dominating a party, these individual politicians tended to amass sizeable public support, but they also were accused of corrupt practices. National politicians were therefore dependent on the local party leadership and sought their assistance in winning an election in their own districts. The local parties also provided information on the candidates to the voters who otherwise were unaware of their choices. Voters have had little awareness of legislation, but they have developed a personal commitment to specific individuals.

Land Reform

Land reform has been promised, but remains little more than campaign rhetoric. There have been many legislative proposals over the years, but the final bills have always been too compromised to be meaningful. The conservative, landed interests are strong, and they have blocked genuine land reform legislation. Even the minor reform law that was approved has not yet been implemented. The stability observed in the Philippines is really a form of inertia caused by tradition and feudal social patterns. The democracy operative in the Philippines involves a consensus among the ruling elites that frequent changes in the government would not affect their privileged status.

The Filipino masses live in villages (*barrios*) unaffected by national politics. These villages contain four-fifths of the Philippine population, and they are largely apathetic toward government. The peasants are more concerned with the numerous fiestas that take place. They are an easy-going people, but they live in poverty.

President Magsaysay was alert to the peasant problem. In 1955, he succeeded in getting legislation passed that would have broken up the big estates and redistributed land among the peasants. The utility of the bill was later questioned even by those favoring the reform. Most economic experts saw the necessity of dividing the biggest holdings and eliminating absentee landlords. But they also argued that the large Filipino family would cause further fragmentation, and hence the country would be left with a multitude of uneconomic holdings. Finally, nothing came of the legislation.

Another bill already enacted into law is the Agricultural Tenancy Law. Under this law, the tenant-farmer was to be given the legal means (through an Agrarian Court, if necessary) to obtain a more equitable share of the harvest (70 percent instead of the customary 50 percent of what he grew). It also provided for security of tenure and the option to become a lessee tenant. What kept the law from being properly implemented was the usual combination of red tape, bureaucratic inefficiency, or outright corruption. The law was also too complex for the timid farmer, nor did he have a tenant organization that could help him. All that was left to him was the village political structure, which favored the landlords and local politicians.

Magsaysay possessed charisma, he was an inspirational leader, but a poor administrator. After he died in a plane crash, his successor, Carlos P. Garcia, showed none of his positive qualities and far more negative traits. The Philippine administration foundered until Diosdado Macapagal assumed the presidency.

Macapagal called himself the "poor man's" candidate. Once in office he tried to push for land reform; he also created a new Rice and Corn Administration, which aimed at controlling retail prices by eliminating unnecessary middlemen. The Rice and Corn Administration was also supposed to make it easier for peasant farmers to obtain credit and hence cut down on corrupt practices that brought ruin to many small farmers. President Macapagal was responsible for the Barrio Charter Act, which was enacted in 1959, and supposedly provided for decentralized administration. The barrios were called upon to elect their own councils, each to be headed by a barrio lieutenant and each council was given limited powers to raise and collect local taxes and to use 10 percent of all land taxes for local use. President Macapagal's grand design was his Five Year Integrated Socio-Economic Program, which was to cost 6.5 billion dollars through the year 1967, with a third of the money coming from foreign aid. At the same time, both public and private investment was supposed to pump 12.7 billion dollars into the economy. The multi-dimensional development plan was meant to aid agricultural productivity and, consequently, to raise the purchasing power of the farmers and generate rapid industrial development.

Unfortunately, all these well-intentioned plans were stillborn, as the Philippine bureaucracy delayed their implementation. Macapagal's program was also impeded by the Philippine Supreme Court and by mid-term, he was so embroiled in political controversy that he could no longer press his advantage. His critics proceeded to condemn him for being "all talk and no performance" and his re-election bid in 1965 was unsuccessful. After his defeat, he accused the Congress of non-support and for sabotaging his economic and administrative reforms.

Emergency Rule

The Philippines lacked substantial indigenous political tradition. Once colonized, the Filipinos accepted the West readily and proved more receptive of western values than other peoples in Southeast Asia. During their period of colonial servitude, an educated Filipino elite became reasonably experienced in running western institutions. Moreover, the adoption of an educational system fashioned after the American prototype seemed to guarantee a constant flow of trained western-oriented persons. The Filipinos also enjoyed an extended period of preparation for self-government; independence was achieved peacefully, and their relationship with the United States was amicable. None of these positive developments, however, deterred the Filipinos from abusing their constitution or engaging in corrupt activities. Nor did it prevent President Ferdinand Marcos from declaring emergency rule and then martial law in 1972.

Marcos was elected president of the Philippines in 1965. He was a national hero who had fought against the Japanese in World War II. He was also relatively young and energetic, and no ordinary politician. He won the presidency by defeating President Macapagal whose Liberal Party waged a fierce election campaign highlighted by numerous political murders. Marcos won by 630,000 votes from a total of seven and one-half million. He was re-elected in 1969, and his margin of victory was one of the greatest in Philippine history. Marcos received approximately 60 percent of the votes cast. Since 1946 no Filipino president had been re-elected. Constitutional performance was sustained, but personal ambition and shifting coalitions were still the prominent theme in Philippine politics. Marcos had been head of the Liberal Party, but just before the 1965 election he broke with Macapagal, and engineered his nomination from the opposition Nacionalista party. As noted above, party discipline has never been uppermost in Philippine political culture. Personality has always dominated, and favors must be returned. The more hotly contested an election, the more promises made. After the 1969 election, Marcos found himself burdened with more promises than he could honor.

During his first term in office the government built new schools, constructed roads through remote areas, and promoted industrial growth. Also the International Rice Research Institute was finally successful with its new rice seed project, and rice production in the Philippines increased. The Philippines went from a rice deficit of 300,000 tons to a surplus in 1968. Nevertheless, after his re-election, Marcos faced many problems. The country was plunged into a financial crisis. Inflation was spiralling, and consumer prices soared. Large segments of the literate population were unemployed or under-employed, and inefficient industries sapped the vitality of the hard-pressed economy. Severe typhoon floods also added to government dilemmas. Thus when students began demonstrating against Marcos, his party, and government, the administration was moved to strike back. Marcos and his wife were pelted with stones, bottles, and placards by demonstrating students as they left the Congress after delivering the state of the nation address. The police arrested a significant number, and Marcos let it be known his government would not tolerate such behavior.

Shortly thereafter, tension between the indigenous Muslim population and Christian settlers in Mindanao flared into open conflict. The immediate issue centered on control of land, but the conflict quickly assumed aspects of a religious struggle. The Marcos administration did not show any mercy to the Muslims, and the government dispatched a large security force that took a heavy toll on the community. Marcos also faced a renewed Communist threat. Terrorist acts were traced to the New People's army, a military arm of the reestablished Communist Party of the Philippines, identified as Maoist descendents of the Huk.

The martial law declaration came on the morning of September 23, 1972. The particular incident cited for the action was the unsuccessful ambush of the Defense Secretary's car. Marcos took note of the violence and growing disorder in the country, and his administration moved to stifle all opposition. Communication with the world outside was temporarily halted. Newspaper and radio operations were suspended. Hundreds of persons were arrested including the opposition leaders. The government acted to prevent illegal traffic in firearms and banned all private security guards and armies. Marcos followed up the martial law decree with a publicized plan to build a "New Society" in the Philippines. The government seized basic industries and transportation; the prices of food staples were fixed, and an announcement was made forecasting extensive land reforms. The government declared war on inefficiency and corruption, and deviants were threatened with harsh treatment. But President Marcos had also put an end to old "democratic practices" in the Philippines—an era had quickly drawn to a close.

The New Constitution

Before the declaration of martial law, a constitutional convention had been convened in June, 1971, to rewrite the basic charter. Serious questions had been raised about the system of government inherited from the Americans. Criticism was directed at the amount of power concentrated in the presidency, and a reduction in presidential authority and a devolution of power to local government was forecast. Some speakers called for limiting presidential tenure to one six-year term. Others proposed a parliamentary system for the Philippines. Concerted attacks were directed at special economic interests and the privileges granted Americans. The general view prevailed that the country was still too dependent on the United States. The convention brought to the surface a whole series of complex issues without any possibility of their immediate resolution. The constitutional convention was unable to complete its work within the year allotted for that purpose. By July, 1972, however, a plan began to emerge and on July 7, the convention decided by a vote of 150 to 120 to change the governmental structure from a presidential to a parliamentary system.

In a parliamentary system, Marcos would not be limited to two consecutive terms. As leader of the majority party, he could remain prime minister for as long as his party maintained a majority in Congress. Thus despite the move away from the strong presidential system, Marcos saw considerable merit in the new arrangement. Curiously, while Marcos stood to gain from the constitutional change, he did not mastermind the switch. The constitutional convention drew support from the students and intelligentsia, the President's more severe critics. Marcos, however, had come to see himself as an indispensable leader, and he was determined to shape all situations in a way that would add to his authority.

The convention approved and signed the new Constitution in October, 1972. Martial law had already been in force several weeks. Marcos intended to utilize his emergency presidential powers to administer the plebiscite on the Constitution and conduct elections for the National Assembly. But there was indecision among the ruling elite as to when the time would be appropriate. A plebiscite on the new Constitution had been scheduled for January 13, 1973, but this date was considered inopportune, and it was postponed indefinitely.

Increasing hostility toward the government, Muslim-Christian clashes in Mindanao, and acts of indiscriminate violence had caused Marcos to conclude that the military establishment, not the political institutions, was the best safeguard against political sedition and anarchy. Instead of appealing to the sophisticated elements, Marcos turned toward the mobilization of the peasantry. Moreover, People's Assemblies were set up throughout the country, and they were asked to approve the new Constitution. All citizens over the age of 15 constituted an assembly in each barangay, and the government reported that 95 percent of the assemblies had cast ballots approving the new system. A People's Congress consisting of 4,600 delegates and chosen from among the members of the People's Assemblies and other civic groups was organized to formally ratify the new Constitution. But their acceptance of the new Constitution did not terminate martial law. The interim National Assembly, which was to elect an interim president and prime minister under the new Constitution, was indefinitely suspended. This action also meant elections for the permanent National Assembly would be held in abeyance. Meanwhile, Marcos drew upon the president's powers under the 1935 constitution and those of prime minister under the new Constitution. The Filipino politician had assumed dictatorial powers, and justification for his behavior is observed in his comment that "traditional democratic processes" have no place in the new Philippines and "old ways and habits are to be purged."[1]

The Uncertain Future

After experimenting with a form of democracy for approximately twenty-five years, the Philippines succumbed to the forces and problems that afflict many states of contemporary Asia. Martial law is associated with unbridled conflict and political decay. As an instrument of last resort, martial law will not be lifted until the government feels more secure. In the Philippines this not only translates into popular confidence in government, it also means the neutralization of all opposition to Ferdinand Marcos.

When Ferdinand E. Marcos imposed martial law on the Filipino people he insisted it was only an expedient device, prompted by the breakdown of law and order. That was several years ago. In the years of virtual dictatorship, Marcos with the help of the military and bureaucracy, has disassembled the political system which the country inherited from the United States. Fundamental rights have been indefinitely suspended and all the trappings of a free society removed. Moreover, the Filipino President is determined to fashion a new system which will insure his preeminent status. On January 12, 1976, the President declared that the Philippine National Assembly would be drastically modified to conform to the

[1]*The New York Times*, January 11, 1973.

more traditional ways of the Filipino peasantry. Sounding much like a voice out of Asia's immediate past, he seemed to stress some form of "basic" or "guided" democracy that would be closer to the genius of the Filipino population. In 1972, before the declaration of martial law, the Philippines were given a new constitution which called for the election of parliamentarians from among the members of the constitutional convention. Marcos now also wanted those individuals drawn from local councils and youth groups that were dependent on him for their positions.

Such changes in the political structure were not promoted without resistance. Former President Diosdado Macapagal, who had chaired the constitutional convention, criticized the Marcos plan and called for the reinstatement of traditional parliamentary government, and in April 1976, went further in calling upon the country's leaders and armed forces to terminate Marcos' "lawless dicatorship."[2] Macapagal later sought refuge in the American embassy in Manila but the United States, fearing reprisals against its installations in the islands, declared it could not honor the request for asylum. Macapagal was perhaps the most prominent Filipino seeking the end of Marcos' rule, but there were many thousands more who sought the same objective. In January 1976 a wave of labor strikes swept over the Philippines. Students demonstrated and courted arrest and thousands of slum-dwellers in Manila protested the order of the President's wife, Imelda Marcos, who had called for the demolition of whole neighborhoods. Imelda had been made governor of metropolitan Manila by Marcos in November 1975. Some opposition leaders were already referring to Mrs. Marcos as the Philippines new vice-president.

The President's response to his opposition has been direct and ruthless. Thousands of people have been arrested, including members of the clergy as well as intellectuals and laborers. Approximately 4,000 Filipinos are alleged to be in custody without charges being brought against them. President Marcos has been able to describe most of his opposition as leftist and sympathetic to communism. But the adding of such dedicated anti-communists as Macapagal to the opposition ranks gives that claim an air of gross unreality.

Democracy is not dead in the Philippines, but it has been seriously undermined. Filipinos are accustomed to competitive politics, and they demand the right to choose, as well as oppose, their leaders. President Marcos is criticized for weakening democracy in the country. The conservatism of his administration incites mistrust from those who demand change. Members of the intelligentsia have concluded that present conditions are linked with traditional superior-inferior relationships that are slowly being broken down. The more that vested interests seek to prevent

[2]*The New York Times*, April 2, 1976 and April 13, 1976.

change, the greater the likelihood of a clash with an embittered and exploited class.

Martial law is designed to de-politicize a politically turbulent Philippine society. It aims at promoting political stability; but genuine stability requires something more than punitive action. As a consequence of martial law, the military and police establishments have been enlarged and strengthened, and they will play a ubiquitous role in national decision-making. President Marcos sustains an intimate relationship with the country's military leaders, but he must reckon with their perceptions of the Philippines' needs as well as their own ambitions. He certainly must be alert to the pitfalls into which Sukarno tumbled, if he is to avoid an ignominious demise.

After the question of how long can President Marcos maintain control over the military is posed, the next query is whether he can also continue to satisfy the business community, the landlords, and the Church. Will these traditionally strong groups remain quiescent? If so, for how long? Perhaps the answer lies in how Marcos will organize his "New Society" program. National austerity may promote development, but are the critical pressure groups willing to sacrifice their personal and parochial interests for the larger society? Marcos demands sacrifices from the general population, but his attentive public will be looking for a model in the President's own performance.

President Marcos must reestablish his legitimacy just as the Philippines has begun to question its national identity. Both appear to be in search of greater national purpose. The success of one is dependent on the other. The Philippines will survive without Marcos, but the course set for it by present leaders will influence the behavior of all its future governments.

RECOMMENDED READINGS

Indonesia

Brackman, Arnold C., *The Communist Collapse in Indonesia*. New York: Norton, 1969.

Dahm, Bernhard, *History of Indonesia in the Twentieth Century*. New York: Praeger, 1971.

Feith, Herbert, *The Decline of Constitutional Democracy in Indonesia*. Ithaca, N.Y.: Cornell University Press, 1962.

Grant, Bruce, *Indonesia*. London: Cambridge University Press, 1964.

Henderson, John W., *Area Handbook for Indonesia*. Washington, D.C.: U.S. Government Printing Office, 1970.

Hoadley, J. Stephen, *The Military in the Politics of Southeast Asia*. Cambridge, Mass.: Schenkman, 1975.

Holt, Claire, ed., *Culture and Politics in Indonesia*. Ithaca, N.Y.: Cornell University Press, 1972.

Hughes, John, *Indonesian Upheaval*. New York: McKay, 1967.

Jones, Howard Palfrey, *Indonesia: The Possible Dream*. New York: Harcourt Brace Jovanovich, 1971.

Kahin, George McT., ed., *Government and Politics of Southeast Asia*. Ithaca, N.Y.: Cornell University Press, 1959.

_____ , ed., *Major Governments of Asia*, (2nd ed.). Ithaca, N.Y.: Cornell University Press, 1963.

Legge, J. D., *Sukarno: A Political Biography*. New York: Praeger, 1972.

McAlister, John T., Jr., ed., *Southeast Asia: The Politics of National Integration*. New York: Random House, 1973.

Mortimer, Tex, *Indonesian Communism under Sukarno: Ideology and Politics in Indonesia, 1959-1965*. Ithaca, N.Y.: Cornell University Press, 1974.

Pauker, Guy J., *Indonesia in 1966: The Year of Transition*. Santa Monica, Calif.: Rand Corp., 1967.

Pye, Lucian W., *Southeast Asia's Political Systems* (2nd ed.). Englewood Cliffs, N.J.: Prentice-Hall, 1974.

Reinhardt, Jon M., *Foreign Policy and National Integration: The Case of Indonesia*. New Haven, Conn.: Yale University Southeast Asia Studies, 1971.

Sloan, Stephen, *A Study in Political Violence: The Indonesian Experience*. Skokie, Ill.: Rand McNally, 1971.

Van Der Kroef, J. M., *Indonesia in the Modern World*. Bandung, Indonesia: Masa Baru, 1954.

_____ , *Indonesia after Sukarno*. Vancouver, Canada: University of British Columbia Press, 1971.

Waddell, J. R. E., *An Introduction to Southeast Asian Politics*. New York: Wiley, 1972.

The Philippines

Abueva, J. V., and R. P. DeGuzman, *Foundations and Dynamics of Filipino Government and Politics*. Manila: Bookmark, 1969.

Aruego, Jose R., *Philippine Government in Action*. Manila: University Publishing Company, 1964.

Averch, Harvey A., et al., *The Matrix of Policy in the Phillippines*. Princeton: Princeton University Press, 1971.

Chaffee, Frederic H., et al., *Area Handbook for the Philippines*. Washington, D.C.: Government Printing Office, 1969.

Corpuz, O. D., *The Philippines*. Englewood Cliffs, N.J.: Prentice-Hall, 1965.

Golay, Frank H., ed., *The United States and the Philippines*. Englewood Cliffs, N.J.: Prentice-Hall, 1966.

Gordan, Bernhard K., *The Dimensions of Conflict in Southeast Asia*. Englewood Cliffs, N.J.: Prentice-Hall, 1966.

Grossholtz, Jean, "Philippines 1973: Whither Marcos?," *Asian Survey*, XIV, 1 (January 1974), 101-12.

——————, *Politics in the Philippines*. Boston: Little, Brown, 1964.

Hall, D. G. E., *A History of Southeast Asia*. New York: Macmillan, 1964.

Hayden, Ralston, *The Philippines*. New York: Macmillan, 1942.

Kahin, George McT., ed., *Government and Politics of Southeast Asia*. Ithaca, N.Y.: Cornell University Press, 1959.

Lande, Carl H., *Leaders, Factions and Parties: The Structure of Philippine Politics*. New Haven, Conn.: Yale Southeast Asia Studies Monograph Series, No. 6, 1965.

——————, *Voting in the Philippines; A Structural Analysis*. Report to the Agency for International Development, 1971.

Lightfoot, Keith, *The Philippines*. New York: Praeger, 1974.

Manglapus, Raul S., *Philippines: The Silenced Democracy*. Maryknoll, N.Y.: Orbis Books, 1976.

McAlister, John T., Jr., ed., *Southeast Asia: The Politics of National Integration*. N.Y.: Random House, 1973.

Shaplen, Robert, *Time Out of Hand*. New York: Harper & Row, 1969.

Smith, Robert Aura, *Philippine Freedom, 1946-1958*. New York: Columbia University Press, 1958.

Starner, Frances Lucille, *Magsaysay and the Philippine Peasantry*. Berkeley: University of California Press, 1961.

Pye, Lucian W., *Southeast Asia's Political Systems* (2nd ed.). Englewood Cliffs, N.J.: Prentice-Hall, 1974.

Taruc, L., *Born of the People*. New York: International Publishers, 1953.

Taylor, George R., *The Philippines and the United States*. New York: Praeger, 1964.

Waddell, J. R. E., *An Introduction to Southeast Asian Politics*. New York: Wiley, 1972.

Wernstedt, Frederick L., and J. E. Spencer, *The Philippine Island World*. Berkeley: University of California Press, 1967.

Chapter Eight

Korea:
The Politics of
a Divided Nation

Korea has been a divided land ever since it was liberated by the Allied Powers in World War II. Before the liberation, Korea was under Japanese colonial rule. Japan's surrender invited the occupation by the Soviet Red Army north of the thirty-eighth parallel, and the occupation of American troops to the south. It was originally a temporary division. But since the establishment of two separate governments in the north and south, the division has produced one of the most impassable boundaries in the world. It has also influenced subsequent patterns of development in the Korean peninsula. The Korean War was fought because of it, and the two wartime foes of North and South Korea remain as mutually antithetical as ever. Korea remains a danger spot in East Asia.

THE LAND AND THE PEOPLE

Korea is also known as *Chosen*, the Land of the Morning Calm, but a quick glance at the map is enough to give a disquieting feeling about the country. Geopolitically, Korea has been a troubled land throughout its history. Sandwiched between the overpowering presence of China and the Soviet Union to the north and Japan to the south, Korea has been a critical spot of international rivalry. Before Korea became a Japanese colony in 1910, two wars, the first Sino-Japanese War (1894-1895) and the Russo-Japanese War (1904-1905), were fought over Korea.

The Korean peninsula, approximately 85,000 square miles in size, occupies 900 miles from north to south and about 240 miles from east to west. Korea is situated in the northeast corner of the Asian mainland,

353

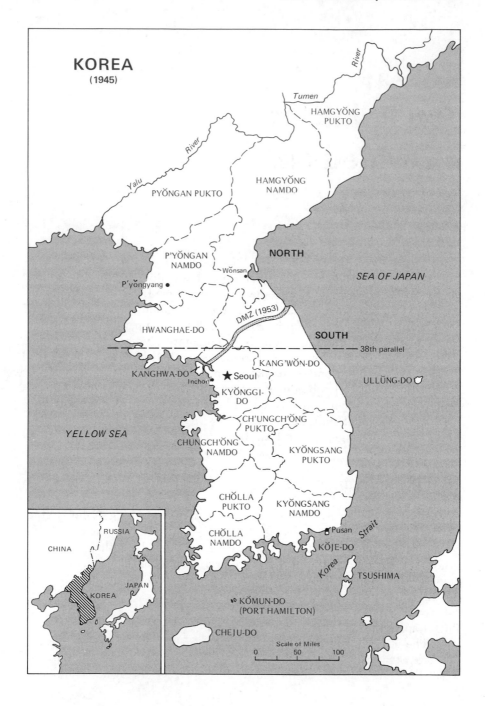

land, bordering Manchuria and Siberia in the north and pointing to Japan in the south.

As the land of the morning calm, *Chosen* more readily describes her scenic beauty. Climatically the area belongs to the temperate zone, similar to the New England area of the United States. Korea's numerous hills, mountains, and rivers are among the world's most scenic. Only about 20 percent of the land is arable, but the land is fertile and is adapted to rice cultivation with plentiful summer rainfall.

In the primitive stage of its development, the Korean peninsula was undoubtedly conducive to the self-sustaining life of the people. When the first Korean people settled in the peninsula, however, is not known. According to Korean mythology, the first kingdom of *Tangun* was set up in the twenty-fifth year of the Emperor Yao of China, which corresponds to 2332 B.C. It was in the province of Pyongan, North Korea.

In the beginning the Korean peninsula seems to have been inhabited by the same nomadic tribes found in Manchuria and far north in Asia. Later, the Tung-i people from the eastern coast of China also migrated to Korea. The physical features of Koreans are related to the Mongoloid people. Linguistically, Korean belongs to the Altaic language family.

The history of Korea has been closely woven into the political vicissitudes of China. Particularly during the Chinese Han dynasty, the Emperor Wu-ti conquered and colonized the northern part of the penin-sula. Four provinces under Chinese control were then set up. These provinces were later consolidated under the Kokuryo tribe in A.D. 313. Also at that time, two tribal kingdoms, Silla and Pakje, emerged in the south. Thus began the period of three kingdoms in Korean history. In 677, these three kingdoms were united under Silla. Korea as a unified kingdom dates from this period. Silla rule lasted until 918 when it was followed by the Koryo dynasty (918-1392). The last dynasty was the Yi dynasty (1392-1910). Japan colonized Korea in 1910.

Since Silla's unification of the country to more or less present-day geographical boundaries, Korea experienced only two dynastic changes until 1910. This is a remarkable record of political continuity and stability, contributing to the homogeneous makeup of the Korean people. Given political stability, the Korean people thrived, and their indigenous contri-butions to civilization have been numerous. One such contribution is the invention of a unique writing system (alphabet) of 28 letters, which was commissioned by King Sejong the Great of the Yi dynasty and promul-gated in 1443, as *Hunminjongum* (Right Letters to educate the People), *hangul* in short. The Korean people were, however, never far from the threatening presence of the powers in the north, and, to some extent, China served to legitimize existing order in the peninsula.

THE YI DYNASTY

The Yi dynasty was the last Korean dynasty and did much to mold the behavior pattern of modern Korea. During this period, the governmental authority was centralized, discarding the semblance of feudalism that had existed during the preceding Koryo dynasty. Officials were recruited through the Chinese Confucian examination system. Confucianism was given royal support and eventually became the prevailing code of behavior for rulers and ruled alike.

The Chu Hsi school of Confucianism was the governing creed of the Yi dynasty. As in Confucian China, one's role in both the family and the society was ordered by position in a hierarchy. In the family system of patriarchy, it was the father who was sovereign. Likewise, in the paternalistic Korean society, it was the ruler and his *yangban* ruling class that were sovereign in relationship with the masses. There was not much chance for the masses to cross class boundaries, despite the official examination policies. Education in the Chinese classics was encouraged, but it was not likely for a commoner to pass the examination for scholar-official recruitment.

The government of the Yi dynasty was, in theory, an absolute monarchy, as in traditional China. All civil and military appointments, down to the lowest level of administrative organization, were supposedly made with the monarch's sanction. Appointees were chosen from those who succeeded in the competitive examinations based on the Chinese classics or military arts. Emphasis was, however, on civilian supremacy. In the government hierarchy, the military was given lower ranking than the civilian officials. Very often the Department of War was headed by a scholar-official.

In practice, however, the Yi government lacked machinery for effective centralization. All authority was supposed to emanate from the monarch, but local autonomy was encouraged. The government welfare function was minimal, though it collected heavy taxes. The people, 85 percent agrarian, were poor, ignorant, and politically inactive. They provided for themselves whatever services they needed, while developing strong localism.

As was true with every new dynastic rule, the Yi dynasty saw prosperity and, during its first two centuries, engineered several periods of brilliant political and cultural development. These periods were, however, dominated by the ruling class, and mass participation was only through service to the ruling strata of society. The farmers produced for the *yangban*-landlords. The artisans' employment was for those who could afford it and, in the case of traditional Korea, they were again the ruling class. There were merchants, but they were generally traveling salesmen, carrying goods on their backs or on pack-horses from one fair to another. Korea was lacking in shops, stores, and wealthy merchants, unlike China and particularly Japan during their first steps toward modernization. Then, too, all artistic expressions were monopolized by the ruling class.

The progressive era of the Yi dynasty, following the founding of the new dynasty, soon saw its zenith of development. Then followed the problems of monarchical succession, corruption in the hereditary ruling class, and factional power politics within the court. In the end, the country was unable to meet any outside challenge. Most destructive of the Yi dynastic rule were two Japanese invasions (1592-1598) under Hideyoshi, and the Manchu domination over the peninsula following their invasions in 1627 and 1636. The Yi dynasty never fully recovered from these invasions. The country, therefore, generally mantained itself by the force of inertia, as a tributary state of China, within the protective wall of self-imposed isolation until 1876, when Meiji Japan imposed a treaty upon the peninsular kingdom.

JAPANESE DOMINATION

Japanese domination over Korea, culminating with the Treaty of Annexation in 1910, occurred in several waves. "Conquer Korea" was already a battle cry of many chauvinistic Japanese, following the Meiji restoration. Largely made up of anti-government, disgruntled samurai (warriors), they were irritated by Korea's pretense of superiority. Japan wanted a treaty relationship with Korea, which was rejected. Modern Japan was kept away by the Yi government as a threat to its policy of isolation. No Japanesee conquest of Korea took place at the time, but the Japanese government pressed for the opening of Korea and a closer relationship with the peninsular kingdom. Finally, Japan broke Korea's wall of isolation by force in 1876. Japan launched a naval demonstration of power against the Kangwha forts near Seoul to persuade the Korean government to cooperate.

Korea, by the treaty of 1876 and later conventions, opened her ports and concluded trade and fishing agreements. Korea was also severed from her traditional protective relationship with China. Korea was to be an independent nation capable of dealing directly with Japan. Chinese influence in Korea was still dominant, however. In order to counterbalance the unfettered inroad of Japanese influence in Korea, a series of treaties were negotiated, at Chinese insistence, between Korea and interested western powers. Treaties were signed with the United States in 1882, Germany and England in 1883, Russia and Italy in 1884, and France in 1886. Suddenly Korea found itself on the international scene, unprepared. Korea was increasingly entangled in the surrounding international rivalry. First, Japan and China struggled for power. Later, Russia joined the rivalry.

Closely connected to these international developments was Korea's inability to bring about transformations in society to meet changing needs. The government in Seoul was weak and ineffective. No revolutionary leadership was forthcoming. Instead, the leadership was divided into many factions supported by different foreign powers.

The Yi political system of some 500 years left Korean society moribund at the end. Reformers, like the Independence Club Movement headed by some western-educated, new leaders of Korea, were few in number and without any mass base. They were not able to revitalize the country. There was no new class resourceful enough to meet the challenge of a new era and to present effective opposition to the pernicious conservative elements. Korea's political system lacked resilience. Moreover, the existence of strong traditionalism precluded the possibility of any revolution and the Tonghak Movement was no solution. The Tonghak began as a religious movement to save the country. In the teachings of its founder Ch'oe Che-u (1824-1864), the Tonghak (Eastern Learning), against So-hak (Western Learning), unified Confucianism, Buddhism, Taoism, and Christianity. The government suppressed it, and Ch'oe was executed. But his teachings spread among the peasants and many dissatisfied segments of the society. The followers of the Tonghak rebelled against the government in 1894. They wanted to reform the government and drive out the Japanese and westerners. Japanese and Chinese troops intervened in support of the government. The rebellion was put down, but Japanese aggressiveness gave them the upper hand in Korean affairs. The Japanese and Chinese troops in Korea finally clashed during the first Sino-Japanese War (1894-1895). When Russian influence increased in Korea, Japan also fought Russia in the Russo-Japanese War (1904-1905). In the end, the Yi government was forced to sign Korea's independence over to Japan and some nationalistic resistance movements were ineffective in deterring Japanese control.

Japan ruled Korea as part of Japan's imperial system. Koreans were suppressed politically and exploited socio-economically. The traditional relationship between ruler and ruled was unaltered, with Japanese officials replacing the traditional Korean ruling class. Systematic efforts were made to assimilate the Korean people into the Japanese political system as second class subjects.

In Korea, the Japanese colonial government developed a modern educational system and built port facilities, transportation and communication networks, and industrial and commercial establishments. The mineral resources of Korea, found largely in the north, provided an important source of industrial raw materials, and the Japanese carried out extensive exploitation. But these developments did not contribute to the growth of Korea as a nation.

Throughout Japanese rule in Korea, the Korean people harbored strong anti-Japanese feelings. The Korean people never regarded their conquerors as superiors, and a great deal of animosity existed between the two people. The first ten years of rule by Japan, which lasted until the famous Independence Movement of 1919, did nothing to alleviate the mutual distrust.

A coincidence of two events triggered this nation-wide peaceful demonstration for independence on March 1, 1919: American President Woodrow Wilson's promise of self-determination for the colonial people at the end of World War I and the death of the old Korean Emperor, Yi Hyong. The Movement was secretly organized by Korean students in Japan, along with Korean Christian and other religious leaders. The March 1 date was selected because the people started to gather in Seoul to observe the funeral of the dead Emperor, set for March 2.

March 1 arrived. The Korean people were to show their determination for independence. The thirty-three leaders of the Movement gathered in a Seoul restaurant and read Korea's declaration for independence. Then their followers took charge in reading the declaration to the crowds in Seoul and in other places throughout the country. Independence, however, did not follow. The leaders had already surrendered themselves to the Japanese authorities. The demonstrations continued and Japanese authorities suppressed them without mercy. There was no foreign intervention on behalf of demonstrating Koreans.

Through the March, 1919 Independence Movement, Koreans showed their nationalistic desire for independence. Also throughout the movement, Japan showed determination to stay in Korea. Japan would never allow another independence movement to develop. After 1919, the Japanese administration in Korea took every precaution to suppress Korean political activities.

Following the Independence Movement, Korean students and political leaders, however, did not cease their nationalistic activities. The Korean Provisional Government was organized in Shanghai, China, in 1919, coalescing many groups and leaders and carrying out their clandestine activities in Korea and abroad. The Korean Communist Party was organized in Seoul, in 1925. They and other militant groups fought Japanese forces along the Korea-Manchuria border. None of these activities were effective in overthrowing the Japanese colonial regime or in uniting the masses into an effective resistance. Japan's control instruments were too overpowering for them. Most of the Korean people felt helpless, and many were forced to join Japanese imperial expansion into Manchuria and China.

LIBERATION AND DIVISION

The Japanese surrender to the U. S. and its allies on August 15, 1945, was unexpected by the Korean people. There were days of wild celebration. The Japanese administration was quickly discredited. The Red Army of the Soviet Union was present to accept Japanese surrender north of the thirty-eighth parallel. American troops arrived in Korea south of the dividing line a month later. Thus, the ill-fated line was drawn between North and South Korea.

> "The 38th Parallel was picked up by a tired meeting on a hot night in Potsdam" [where the Potsdam Conference was held in 1945], said a State Department official last week. "It's a line that makes no political, geographical, economic or military sense. But the Russians and Americans at the meeting couldn't agree on who should occupy what. Finally a general suggested the 38th parallel. And that was that."[1]

In this same vein, Mr. James Byrnes, then Secretary of State, later revealed that the thirty-eighth parallel plan of division originated with the other Allied military leaders and was accepted by the Soviet Union.

As stated above, the bi-zonal division of Korea by the thirty-eighth parallel had no particular purpose, except convenience for the occupying troops. Korea had been a unified country from the establishment of the first Silla state during the seventh century. Even Japanese rule in Korea had retained this unity. There were no political factions in Korea at that time to justify dividing the land. Geographically, too, the thirty-eighth parallel is an artificial boundary that roughly divides the peninsula into half, and there is no natural boundary corresponding to the division. Economically, the north and the south were complementary, and the division was devastating at the outset. Each found itself crippled for economical sustenance. Militarily, the division was also misconceived. Russian military aid to the United States in defeating Japan was minimal. There was no longer a powerful Japanese Kwantung Army in Manchuria to resist occupation. The Soviet Union declared war against Japan on August 8, and on August 15, when Japan surrendered, the Soviet Red Army was already in North Korea, swiftly moving southward, without meeting resistance from the Japanese troops.

Confusion in Transition

Before the war's end, the Soviet troops had already overrun much of North Korea by force. In the south, however, the discredited Japanese

---

[1]*Time*, LVI, 1 (July 3, 1950), pp. 14-15.

administration was still maintaining order together with the Korean Committee of Preparation for Independence, while awaiting American arrival. In the north, the Japanese sabotaged mines and factories in the path of the approaching enemy and fled to the south in large numbers. Many Christians and non-Communist Koreans also fled to the south creating refugee problems. The Japanese, in the south, had been carrying out a hurried, yet orderly evacuation. When the American forces landed in Korea, the Japanese assumed an attitude of guileless cooperation. In the north, the Soviet authorities had no Japanese administration to deal with and did not hesitate to support the local People's Committee, organized by Koreans in sympathy with the Soviet system. Yet in the south, the American authorities had to deal with the Japanese administration, plus the various Korean political groups that had mushroomed in the interval between Japan's surrender and their late arrival.

The Soviet authorities were more single-minded about their role in North Korea than the American authorities were in South Korea. They brought with them Kim Il-song, then thirty-three years old, and some 30,000 Soviet-Koreans. They encouraged local Communists to organize and carry out land reform. The Communist Party was quickly rebuilt led by Kim Il-song.

Uncertainty, however, was characteristic of the American authorities. The U.S. 24th Corps, fresh from the Okinawa campaign, was hurriedly dispatched to Korea to accept the Japanese surrender. General Hodge, Commander of the Corps, was instructed to deal with the Japanese Governor-General in Seoul to effect the transfer of authority. He was not to deal with any Korean political group. He refused to recognize any Korean group as the legitimate heir of the Japanese administration. He ignored the Korean Committee of Preparation for Independence, which had been reorganized as the People's Republic to welcome the arrival of American authorities. General Hodge had no definite guidelines, and he refused to make any permanent commitment concerning the future of the country.

In December, 1945, the foreign ministers of the United States, the Soviet Union, and the United Kingdom met in Moscow to clarify the meaning of the "in due course" clause of the Cairo Declaration. During the war, President Franklin D. Roosevelt, Prime Minister Winston Churchill, and Generalissimo Ch'iang Kai-shek met in Cairo. Their declaration stated "mindful of the enslavement of the people of Korea, [we] are determined that in due course Korea shall become free and independent." Joseph Stalin of the Soviet Union was not present at the meeting, but he endorsed it later. As clarified in the Moscow Agreement, the "due course" meant a period of tutelage for Korean independence and a four-power trusteeship over Korea was proposed. The four powers included the

United States, the USSR, Great Britain, and China. The U.S.-USSR occupation authorities were to consult the Korean people in setting up a provisional government.

The Koreans violently opposed the Moscow Agreement. The Korean people feared colonialism under the big powers. Song Chin-wu, a rightist leader, was believed to have endorsed trusteeship. He was assassinated in his sleep. Syngman Rhee and Kim Koo, two of the Korean Provisional Government leaders, organized an anti-trusteeship committee, instigating nation-wide demonstrations and work stoppages. Both the left and the right factions joined this nationalist expression. Suddenly in January, 1946, the leftist elements, apparently persuaded by the Soviet authorities, came out in support of the Moscow Agreement.

The first Joint U.S.-USSR Commission opened in Seoul in March, 1946, but adjourned on May 6, without having reached a conclusion. It met again on May 22, but was unable to make any progress in setting up a provisional government. The Soviet Union insisted that only those Korean groups supporting the Moscow Agreement should be consulted, thus excluding most of the rightist groups. The United States did not agree and the United States was forced to transfer the impasse to the United Nations.

On November 14, 1946, the General Assembly of the United Nations approved, against the objections of the Soviet Union, the formation of a United Nations Temporary Commission in Korea (UNTCOK) to facilitate Korean independence. An election for all of Korea was to be held no later than March 31, 1948.

UNTCOK opened its first sessions in Seoul on January 29, 1948. Leftist elements opposed its work. The Soviet Union refused to cooperate and did not permit entry of UNTCOK into North Korea. UNTCOK was then advised by United Nations headquarters to interpret the original resolutions to mean holding elections in such parts of Korea as were accessible to it. UNTCOK was forced to sponsor the creation of the Republic of Korea only in South Korea and elections were held there on May 10, 1948. The representatives thus elected met as a National Assembly on May 31 and they were charged with drafting and adopting a new constitution. The government of the Republic of Korea was inaugurated on August 15. Counter to these developments, the Soviet Union created its own North Korean regime, the Democratic People's Republic of Korea, on September 9. The two Koreas were born in the atmosphere of the cold war. The Korean war broke out less than two years after the establishment of the two governments. By then both American and Soviet troops had been withdrawn. On June 25, 1950, North Korean forces launched a well-planned attack against South Korea and virtually overran the southern half of the peninsula in the initial weeks of the war. Only massive

American intervention, sanctioned by the United Nations, saved South Korea from total absorption by North Korean forces.

SOUTH KOREA

The division of the country and the subsequent war between North and South caused the emergence of two different patterns of development in Korea. The Korean War ended in a stalemate, which reaffirmed the division of the country. Neither side was able to generate a national liberation war. Instead, each pursued its own course of development.

The Constitutional System

The Republic of Korea, supported by the United States, was born with the blessing of the United Nations. A western style democratic constitution was drafted and put into effect. Its original form, however, which called for indirect election of the president, lasted for a short time only. The constitution has become a major political issue and has often been amended. From 1948 to 1975, the Republic of Korea has had four new constitutions and four different republics.

The First Republican constitution (1948-1960) was drawn up in less than a month, in July, 1948, to meet the deadline of August 15, 1948, the date set for proclamation of the Republic of Korea. Thereafter, almost each session of the National Assembly fought over the constitution. Should there be a presidential system or a cabinet system? An American type of presidential system or a Fourth French Republican type? Which basic framework of government was to be instituted became the most crucial issue of party politics. The opposition Democratic Party, which had been unable to replace Syngman Rhee as president, tried to make Rhee's office merely titular. They hoped to obtain a majority in the National Assembly and thus the premiership by placing their party head in a foremost position, under a cabinet form of government. For the general public, the point of this dispute was immaterial.

The constitution was amended in 1952, and again in 1954, in order to provide for an unlimited term of office for Rhee. But the negative evaluation of Rhee's autocratic rule continued. Abuses of power and police brutality were often reported. The national economy was in a constant depression. Then, in the 1960 elections, widespread election rigging was reported. Students demonstrated and were joined by the general populace. The situation got out of hand when the police were unable to control the crowds. The military was called in to enforce martial law, but they refused to fire on the demonstrators.

Rhee was forced to resign his office, and a "caretaker government" was instituted by men who were designated by Rhee before his resignation. During this interim period, a new constitution was set up. The presidency had been changed from a popularly elected office with broad executive power to a more formal office with election by the National Assembly. The new constitution provided for a cabinet system of government and elections were held in July, 1960. The Democratic Party, as opposed to the former Liberal Party of Rhee, won a majority of seats in the National Assembly.

The Democratic Party, however, failed to provide leadership and bring order to the country. The party was split into two factions: a progressive and an old guard faction. The compromise between the two gave Chang Myon, head of the progressives, the position of prime minister, and Yun Po-son, head of the old guard, the presidency.

There were other causes for the failure of the Second Republic. Chang's government was weak. Chang had no charisma and his leadership was only mediocre compared with Rhee's. Chang also shouldered paradoxical demands. The people, particularly students, were proud of their achievement in bringing down the Rhee regime. They demanded that all the ills of the country be quickly solved. Demonstrations were daily occurrences. Students agitated for negotiation with the North. Communist infiltration was feared. As a result of these developments a military coup headed by Major General Park Chung Hee overthrew Chang's Second Republic, on May 16, 1961.

The coup ushered in military rule in South Korea. The military junta of thirty men was made up mostly of generals and colonels representing an oversized army of 600,000 men. They dissolved the National Assembly, prohibited all political activities, and pledged a strong anti-communist stand and a stronger tie with the United States. Also promised were efforts to eradicate corruption and social evils, rejuvenate the national spirit, and develop a self-supporting economy. Once their missions were accomplished, they announced that they would turn over the government to conscientious civilians.

The key junta leaders, headed by General Park, however, never returned to the barracks. Instead, they took off their uniforms and filled the key positions in government. They created a political party (the Democratic Republican Party) as a device to give themselves decision-making positions. They created a third republic and drew up their own constitution. The elections for the president and the National Assembly were held in October, and November, 1963, respectively. The creation of Korea's Third Republic was formally announced in December.

The junta would have liked to have foregone these formalities, ruling the country under their own dictatorial arrangements in the name of the

Supreme Council for National Reconstruction. They entertained their own vision for the future of the country, i.e., an administrative state of technicians and administrators. Political dissent was to be suppressed and various austerity measures were to be forced on the people. The junta was faced with too much opposition, however.

The opposition came from many sources, and the junta became factionalized as their military backing began to slip. They were hard put to legitimize their rule. Their puritanical measures were found impractical under age-old, corruptive societal influences. The politicians were agitating for a return to civilian rule. American pressure to resume civilian control was also evident.

The third constitution expressed many of the same goals as the two earlier ones. It inherited all the western constitutional principles, particularly those of the United States. It conscientiously attempted to remedy the weaknesses of the earlier constitutions. Intermeshed in these efforts were the junta's distrust of politicians and their assumption of responsibility for the country's future guidance. The third constitution prescribed a presidential system with the principle of separation of powers and a system of checks and balances. The president was limited to two consecutive terms. Candidates for elective offices were to be nominated by their parties.

The third constitution provided for a highly centralized system dominated by the executive branch. Traditionally, the judiciary was never an independent body. The one-house legislature worked as long as it was dominated by the disciplined ruling party. The legislative power over the purse strings was greatly curtailed as the constitution stipulated:

> [The] Executive shall formulate the budget [and] The National Assembly shall, without the consent of the Executive, neither increase the sum of any item of expenditure nor create new items of expenditure in the budget submitted by the Executive. (Arts. 50-52, 53).

The Executive could also introduce any bill along with the members of the National Assembly.

The term, *the State*, has a special meaning in the third constitution. It means an independent executive body. It is the State that is to guarantee fundamental rights of the people (Art. 8). It is "the State" that is to guarantee "independence and political impartiality of education" (Art. 27-24). It is also "the State" that is to regulate, coordinate, and promote economic activities (Art. 11-2).

This constitution was amended in 1969, to permit President Park to run again in 1971, for his third term. It was again amended in 1972, to underwrite a lifetime presidency for him. As a matter of fact, a whole new constitution, subsequently called the *Yushin* (Revitalization) Constitution, was created in 1972—thus, South Korea experienced a fourth constitution and a fourth republic.

The Fourth Constitution

The new Constitution was drawn up in secrecy. No public criticism was allowed upon its promulgation, although the government conducted an extensive campaign for the education of the masses. Ultimately, the document was approved in a national referendum held on November 21, 1972. The country was then under martial law. The government reported that 91.9 percent of the voters participated in the referendum, and 91.5 percent of them voted for approval of the new Constitution.

Timing for the creation of the Fourth Republic was most propitious. As stated in the preamble of the Constitution, it was to prepare the country for negotiations with North Korea toward an eventual, peaceful reunification. The two Koreas had initiated a dialogue in response to the changing international relations surrounding the Korean peninsula. For instance, President Nixon's historic visit to Peking in February, 1972, emphasized detente. Japanese Premier Tanaka then made his official visit to Peking in September. The two Koreas could have been persuaded by the allied powers to lessen their mutual tensions and negotiate a reunification formula.

Given the attractiveness of the reunification issue, opposition to the new Constitution was silenced. In the new Constitution, however, President Park amassed enormous personal power. The whole Constitution of the Fourth Republic revolves around the changes in the office of the president and its relationship to the other branches of government.

Comparing the constitutions of the Third and Fourth Republics, almost no change is found in the provisions dealing with the courts, election management, local government, and the economy. It is still an executive-dominant, highly centralized system. The chapter on "Rights and Duties of Citizens" in the Fourth Constitution, however, shows significant modification from that of the Third Constitution. As the following chart shows, the Fourth Constitution displays significant modification in areas of freedom of speech, press, assembly, association and collective bargaining, and collective action by workers.

The Third Constitution	*The Fourth Constitution*
Art. 18 (1) All citizens shall enjoy freedom of speech and press and freedom of assembly and association.	Art. 18 No citizen shall be subject to restriction of freedom of speech and press, or freedom of assembly and association, except as provided by law.

The Third Constitution	*The Fourth Constitution*

(2) License censorship in regard to speech and press or permit of assembly and association shall not be recognized. However, censorship in regard to motion pictures and dramatic plays may be authorized for the maintenance of public morality and social ethics.

(3) The standard for publication installations of newspaper press may be prescribed by law.

(4) Regulation of the time and place of outdoor assembly may be determined in accordance with the provisions of law.

(5) The press or publication shall not impugn the personal honour or rights of an individual, nor shall it infringe upon public morality and social ethics.

Art. 29   (1) Workers shall have the right of independent association, collective bargaining and collective action for the purpose of improving their working conditions.

(2) The right to association, collective bargaining and collective action shall not be accorded to the workers who are public officials except for those authorized by the provisions of law.

Art. 29   (1) The right to association, collective bargaining and collective action of workers shall be guaranteed within the scope defined by law.

(2) The right to association, collective bargaining, and collective action shall not be accorded to workers who are public officials, except for those authorized by the provisions of law.

(3) The right to collective action may be either restricted or may not be recognized in accordance with the provisions of law for public officials and workers engaged in state, local autonomous governments, state-run enterprises, public utility businesses, and enterprises which have serious influence on the national economy.

Art. 32   (1) All liberties and rights of citizens may be restricted by law only in cases deemed necessary for the maintenance of order and public welfare. In case of such re-

Art. 32   (2) Laws which restrict liberties and rights of citizens shall be enacted only when necessary for the maintenance of national security, order and public welfare.

The Third Constitution	*The Fourth Constitution*
striction, the essential substances of liberties and rights shall not be infringed.	

What is missing in the Fourth Constitution, furthermore, is an effort to encourage the institutional growth of political parties. In the Fourth Constitution, as in the Third, a plural party system is guaranteed, but candidates to elective office, unlike the Third Constitution, now need not have endorsement by duly recognized political parties. Candidates for president and for the National Assembly may run as independents, the very practice which President Park and his military revolutionaries feared in 1961, and attempted to remedy. The Fourth Constitution, in short, denies the need for political parties.

The National Conference for Unification is new in the Fourth Constitution. Defined as "a national organization based on the collective will of the people as a whole to pursue peaceful unification of the fatherland" (Art. 35), it is charged with the election of the president. But it is, as previously stated, to be a nonpartisan body; candidates are debarred from membership in political parties (Art. 37, Sec. 3). It is furthermore a huge body of not less than 2,000 nor more than 5,000 members (for the first National Conference elected on December 15, 1972, the size was set at 2,359 members), directly elected by the voters for a three-year term; the president of the Republic serves as chairman. Its other functions include: approving a list of one-third of the members of the National Assembly, to be appointed by the President for a three-year term (the other members of the National Assembly are directly elected by the voters for a six-year term); and approval of constitutional amendments proposed by the National Assembly.

During the transition from the Third to the Fourth Constitution, President Park, as the incumbent president, assumed chairmanship of the newly elected National Conference, and was elected the first president of the Fourth Republic on December 23, 1972. His term of office is now six years, compared to the previous four-year term, and it is now constitutionally unlimited.

As the Chairman of the National Conference, and as the President of the Fourth Republic of Korea, President Park has placed himself above the regular branches of government. Electorally, he is responsible only to the National Conference, and his extensive powers are almost unchecked. To be noted in this connection is Article 43, which states:

1. The President shall be the head of the State and represent the State vis-à-vis foreign states.

THE GOVERNMENT OF THE REPUBLIC OF KOREA (1972 –   )

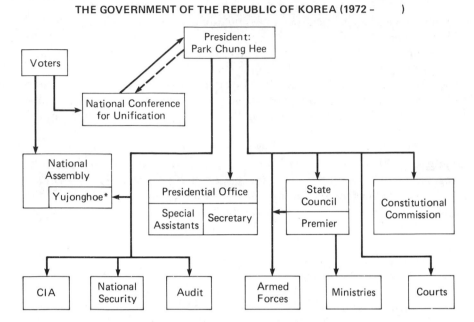

*Members appointed by the president.

— — — — (actual control)

FIGURE 8-1
The Government of the Republic of Korea (1972-   )

2. The President shall have the duty to safeguard the independence, territorial integrity and continuity of the State, as well as the Constitution.

3. The President shall have the duty to pursue sincerely the peaceful unification of the fatherland.

The President of the Fourth Republic has all the powers he had in the Third Republic and more. His emergency power is broader, and the exercise of it is less hampered by civil rights provisions in this Constitution. He can furthermore "submit important policies of State to national referendum in case he deems it necessary," thus bypassing the regular legislative process (Art. 49). He can propose constitutional amendments for approval by the voters (Art. 124, Sec. 1). Each legislative session is now constitutionally limited to ninety days, and the president can even dissolve the Assembly before the maturation of its six-year term.

The president's extensive appointment powers include: the appointment of the prime minister and the members of the State Council; other cabinet level and political positions including one-third of the members of the National Assembly, as previously mentioned; the chief justice and the other judges of the Supreme Court; members of the Constitution Committee, newly provided to decide upon the constitutionality of a law; and members of the Central Election Management Committee. No checks on these appointments are provided, except for the appointment of the prime minister and the chief justice of the Supreme Court, which require approval by the National Assembly.

The one-house National Assembly and the Supreme Court are constituted much weaker in the Fourth Republic than in the Third. Regarding local self-government, the Fourth Constitution states specifically that "Local assemblies under the present Constitution shall not be formed until the unification of the fatherland has been achieved" (Supplementary Art. 10).

The Political Processes and Dynamics

It is in the name of national security that President Park has been able to amass undisputed power. He has also had a remarkable record of economic development during his administration. Under his administration, the first Five Year Plan (1962-1966) was successfully implemented with the annual average rate of growth of real GNP at 8.3 percent. For the second Five Year Plan (1967-1971), the growth rate was 11.4 percent. Emphasis in these plans was placed on industrial development and construction of infrastructure. Production of manufactured goods for export was encouraged. With the initiation of the Third Five Plan (1972-1976), increasing attention was given to rural development plans, and the New Community Movement (*saemaul undong*) has been gaining momentum. This movement which was initiated in 1972 was designed to mobilize the masses for "self-help and community development."[2] Since 1963, South Korea's per capita GNP had increased five times and stood at more than 500 dollars in 1975.

After a rather slow start, compared with development in the north, South Korea's recent gains are regarded as spectacular. The Park administration has also successfully concluded a treaty with Japan in 1965 for the normalization of relations between the two countries. It was accomplished amidst a great deal of domestic opposition, but it has paid off for President Park's development scheme. Japan has become a significant source of development loans and an important trade partner. It was also under the

[2]President's special message, Republic of Korea, October 17, 1972. *Dong-a Ilbo* (Seoul), October 17, 1972.

administration of President Park that South Korean troops were dispatched to Vietnam in response to the American call for help. The Koreans fought bravely, and the people have shown much pride in the fighting capability of their troops.

Perhaps the greatest asset of the Park administration is its record of political stability in the face of considerable opposition. Political experiments continue in South Korea, however. Economic development and social modernization create new political forces in the country. Thus far, they have been silenced, and have not been integrated into the total political process. The forces of democracy and traditional authoritarian centralism have motivated the people in many different directions.

Seoul is the capital city, a huge metropolis of some seven million people. The majority of the Korean people, however, still live in a rural setting: a small village surrounded by rice paddies. No village is, however, completely isolated in this densely populated society. Modern highways run through many areas. During the Japanese period and since the liberation, modern communications media and transportation networks have been developed. The Korean people are 70 percent literate.

The village has dominant kinship groups. They have, however, been increasingly penetrated by the national bureaucracy which runs the provinces and their local administrative units, such as *myon* (county) and *ri* (village).

The possession of power is treated as a monopoly and is applied totally. Korea lacks viable horizontal organizations. Interest groups are organized by the leaders for their own purposes, and many functional, professional, and occupational organizations are penetrated by the government. These groups then either promote the personal ambitions of the leaders or serve functionary purposes for the government programs. Labor strikes are often branded as communistic. Students and intellectuals are closely watched. Villagers are still politically malleable and mobilized by the village leaders and the government. The urban population is more articulate, but they feel powerless and are too busy making a living to advocate a cause.

Opposition parties have never been known to flourish in a coercive system. In Korea, however, attempts to maintain the facade of democracy necessitate the existence of an opposition party. Once established and institutionalized, that party may develop into a viable interest group and provide a greater variety of inputs to the state management system. The major opposition party to the ruling Democratic-Republican Party of President Park is the New Democratic Party. It is a cadre party of old-time professional politicians, local notables, and leading figures in the military and civilian bureaucracy. They have joined the opposition because of their professed anti-government stands. The opposition caters to urban, student, and intellectual interests, but exists primarily at the mercy of the government. It remains ideologically sterile and has failed to recruit new members. Instead, it has displayed a tendency toward intra-party rivalry between leaders on the basis of personality differences rather than on programs and policies.

The Democratic-Republican Party (DRP) was organized in 1962, as a modern political party. South Korea has suffered from the multiplicity of political parties. Since the liberation, all the political parties that have ever existed number some five hundred, including all the minor parties. Parties have come and gone. The leaders of the DRP intended it to be a permanent party, with headquarters and local organizations manned by trained and paid party cadres. It was created to be the major government device for political recruitment and policy input. These original intents have not been fulfilled, however. They have been modified due to internal factional strife. Above all, it has not received the support that it needed from President Park, who minimizes party politics in his "administrative state." He wishes to remain above party politics. To President Park, his DRP is a useful instrument for electoral success, but it does not fit his vision of administrative polity. For decision-making, President Park's chief advisors are found, not in his party, but in his presidential secretariat and cabinet manned by highly trained administrators and professionals.

The Significance of The 1971 Elections

The last elections under President Park's third constitution were held in 1971. The presidential election was held on April 27, and President Park won a controversial third term with 51.2 percent of the total votes cast. His major contender was Kim Tae-jun of the New Democratic Party (NDP). A young, dynamic campaigner, Kim Tae-jun polled 43.6 percent of the votes. There were five other presidential aspirants competing in the election, but altogether they pulled only 1.4 percent of the votes. For the National Assembly election, held on May 25, Park's DRP candidates won 86 seats from the 153 single member electoral districts and 27 additional seats from the party list, on the basis of total votes received. The NDP won 65 and 24 seats, respectively. The other party candidates won only in two districts, and no party list candidates were elected.

The most critical issue of the elections was the accusation that Park and his DRP have been in power too long. Park's re-election was unquestioned, however. His image is that of a sincere man dedicated to the modernization of the country, a fact that even his political opponents admit. This is especially important in a country that had long suffered from a lack of political morality.

The DRP's election strategy called for, at least on the surface, a fair and quiet election. Park, however, was forced to actively campaign. The oppostion NDP seemed well-united behind its presidential candidate. He repeatedly challenged Park's third term and denounced corruption in the high official government circles. As the tempo of the election heightened, however, Kim was increasingly identified with the Cholla province (southwest) area, where he was regarded as a favorite son. Park's geographic identification was with the Kyongsang (southeast) area.

The Cholla region has been known as Korea's rice bowl, but this agrarian center of the country has traditionally been depressed. Kim, as a favorite son of Cholla, became the rallying point of the Cholla people. Kim as a dynamic and youthful candidate captured the support of urban Koreans and those who felt alienated from the mainstream of development. Park's winning margin in the populous Kyongsang area, however, surpassed his earlier records, despite a large defection by the people of the two Kyongsang urban centers of Taegu and Pusan. In other areas, Park fared well. The DRP's massive cell organizations numbering some 260,000 and its overall mobilization of enormous resources also contributed to Park's success.

Park's reelection in 1971 was easily predicted, but the Korean voters were most unpredictable in the National Assembly election. The opposition NDP defied predictions and fared much better than anticipated. Many reasons can be cited for the DRP loss. The NDP candidates could protect the constitution and restrain the DRP-dominated Assembly from another constitutional amendment making Park a life-time president, a precedent disparagingly remembered by the people in the case of President Syngman Rhee of the First Republic. The NDP, as the major opposition party, was united and was able to concentrate on electable personalities as its district candidates. It benefited from what amounted to a two-party contest in most of the districts.

The 1971 Assembly election helped accentuate a growing anti-government trend in the rapidly growing urban areas. It also reflected popular disenchantment with old-time politicians and the DRP. The capital city of Seoul traditionally voted anti-government, and despite the DRP's intensive effort to woo Seoul voters, only one DRP candidate was elected from a total of nineteen Seoul electoral districts. The DRP candidates also suffered a major defeat in many urban centers, where its presidential candidate, Park, won. The DRP also experienced less support in the rural areas.

Interestingly, only 39.2 percent of the incumbent assemblymen (60 members) were reelected. Among the others elected were 75 first-time members (49.0 percent) and 16 former assemblymen (11.8 percent).

The above electoral experiences show a growing sophistication among the Korean voters about elections, which often defies professional

A glimpse of Seoul, Korea

A government building in South Korea

A scene of thriving modern Korean industry

The Korean countryside

guesses. The Korean voters supported the 1969 constitutional amendment and Park's third term as president much more strongly than they did the DRP candidates for the Assembly. They showed a strong mood of protest against the Park regime, without rejecting Park as president. At the same time, they readily rejected many of the DRP's incumbent candidates for the Assembly.

The creation of the Fourth Republic in 1972 was to deter such electoral trends and deemphasize electoral politics. Emphasis now is on administrative decision-making and the forced modernization of the country. The trend is toward authoritarianism under the personal leadership of President Park.

The Mixed Military-Civilian Regime

One notable feature of Park's military regime was the junta leaders' realization that they were not qualified to govern the country by themselves. Thus, in pursuit of their goals, they consciously co-opted the people they needed. As soon as the coup was successful, coup leaders brought many senior officers from the powerful armed forces into the junta government. They also recruited civilian and academic professionals *en masse*, as advisors and councilors. The CIA (Central Intelligence Agency modeled after that of the United States) and other intelligence networks were quickly developed to counteract any activity subversive to their powers.

This *brain-trust* is a trademark of the Park regime. Many academicians and other professionals have been recruited. The Park regime has had strong military support and, unlike the previous regimes of President Rhee and Premier Chang, a large number of retired military officers have been recruited into influential government positions. More than the military, however, has constituted the backbone of stability in the Park regime. Political acumen has produced a sophisticated political balance of power in the government and the society at large. The Park regime also has been mindful of representation for various geographical areas and influential groups in the country.

Many modernizing elites were brought into decision-making positions by the Park regime. Recent studies show these elites (1) have middle- and lower-middle social status; (2) generally are less traditional in their values; (3) predominantly Christian or have no religion; (4) usually western-educated and have a knowledge of the western legal system; (5) largely middle economic level; and (6) overwhelmingly westernized in attitudes and beliefs.[3] They are technicians and administrators, however.

[3]For instance, see Chan Kwon, "Social Backgrounds of the Emergent Political Leadership of Korea, 1948-60," *Koreana Quarterly* (Seoul), 12, 1-2 (Spring-Summer 1970), pp. 41-63.

Their preoccupations deal in problem-solving and they respect their leader who is unchallenged in the exercise of power. Park rewards and punishes his followers, at will, through his patronage system.

The balance sheet of political development of Park's military-civilian regime shows a mixed pattern. Political stability has been emphasized as a prerequisite for social and economic development. The mobilized masses, resulting from social and economic development, have not been integrated into the decision-making process. Instead, they have been subjected to increasing manipulation and repression by the government.

Korean development defies simple categorization. Leadership skills in meeting crises and in adapting to both internal and external changes are highly developed, but political power is not shared. The mobilized masses are, on the other hand, pragmatic in orientation, and votes are often traded for immediate gains. The students and intellectuals are either co-opted or remain powerless and cynical. There are no institutional checks on the arbitrary exercise of power. There are no groups that could effectively articulate the interests of the people, other than those considered useful to the powerholders. Indeed, elections are held periodically. Interest groups and political parties are present. Government structures and functions are very much differentiated, and social and economic changes are visible. All of these, however, have not changed the traditional pattern of interaction between ruler and ruled.

NORTH KOREA

Kim Il-song's undisputed leadership rapidly filled the post-war political vacuum in North Korea. His leadership has provided for more unity and stability than has been the case in the South. With the backing of Soviet occupation authorities, combined with smart political maneuvering, a one-time young guerrilla fighter along the Manchurian-Korean border has successfully eliminated his political rivals. He has set up a Communist state, initially patterned after the Soviet Union. Ever since his assumption of power, however, Kim has tried to dispel the image of indebtedness and subservience to the Soviet Union. In official North Korean history, he is described as a nationalist leader of the Korean revolutionary movement.

Kim Il-song, when he was brought to Korea by the Soviet occupation forces, together with some 30,000 Soviet Koreans, held the rank of major, and in his bid for power, the Soviets were quick to neutralize opposition factions. Many landlords and Christian followers had already evacuated voluntarily in the face of Soviet occupation. The few who remained were quickly culled from the positions they had previously enjoyed. Simultaneously, land redistribution eliminated the possibility of a wealthy class to oppose him. At the time, however, there were several power groups with

which Kim had to contend. The non-Communist nationalists were organized around a well-known Christian leader, Cho Man-sik. Likewise, there
were those returnees from China who together with the Chinese Communists fought the Japanese in China before 1945, the so-called Yenan
faction. The domestic Communists constituted yet another power group.

On October 10, 1945, the Soviet command called a meeting of the
leaders of all the provincial branches of the Communist Party of the North
to form a "North Korean Branch" of the Korean Communist Party. Kim
was then made First Secretary. In December, when the North Korean
Communist Party was created, Kim became its chairman. The party was
reorganized in July, 1946, to placate an organized challenge by returnees
from China who felt threatened by Kim's rapid rise to power and organized as the New People's Party. The North Korean Communist Party
merged with the New People's Party. But given a sizeable following that
the latter had, particularly among North Korean intellectuals, Kim was
forced to yield the chairmanship to Kim Tu-bong, leader of the New
People's Party, a well-known Korean literary scholar, and prominent figure
in the 1919 *Manse* uprisings. The leadership of the new party, the North
Korean Workers' Party, then consisted of Kim Tu-bong (chairman), Kim
Il-song and Chu Yong-ha (vice-chairmen), Ch'oe Ch'ang-ik, and Ho Ka-
ui. The leadership attempted to balance different Communist factions in
North Korea. Kim Tu-bong and Ch'oe Ch'ang-ik represented the Yenan
faction; Ch'oe Ch'ang-ik, the domestic Communists; and Ho Ka-ui, the
Soviet Koreans. It was an unstable situation momentarily held together by
the strong hand of Soviet authorities. When the Democratic People's
Republic was created in September, 1948, Kim Il-song was made premier.
Kim eventually assumed the position of chairman of the party, when the
North Korean Workers' Party was merged with the South Korean
Workers' Party in June, 1949. Thus he had completed the various maneuvers to place himself at the helm of the regime. Competition for power,
however, continued through the Korean War period. By March, 1953, Kim
purged from the party and from positions of power Mu Chong (the
military leader of the Yenan faction), Kim Il (one of Kim Il-song's comrades as a guerrilla fighter and the vice-minister of defense), and Kim Yol
(the Sovietflkorean commander of the rear areas). Then, in 1953, Pak
Hon-yohg, the leader of the South Korean faction, was changed with a
plan to oust Kim Il-song and was later executed.

Kim was not satisfied with these purges. In each step of his absolute
control of power, he continued to purge his erstwhile followers who stood
for the old policy. His most trusted followers were his Manchurian-Korean
comrades but even they were unsafe from purge at any sign of defection
from Kim's established lines. By the time of the Fourth Party Congress of
1961, however, Kim's consolidation of power over the party and the

society was complete. He was then able to announce that the party had been purged of dissident factions, the army solidified under his leadership, the economy totally socialized, the working-class enlarged, and the people resocialized by his ideology.

The Constitutional System

With the proclamation of the Democratic People's Republic of Korea on September 9, 1948, the constitution, which had been drawn up as early as November, 1947, was put into effect. The constitution legitimized the existing system, modeled after the Soviet system. Pyongyang was made the capital city of North Korea, a city with a population of some one million people.

According to the constitution, the people are sovereign, and they elect their representatives to manage the affairs of state. The highest organ of government is the Supreme People's Assembly, which consists of delegates elected for a four-year term. Its impressive array of powers include: to approve or amend the constitution; to formulate the basic guidelines for both domestic and foreign policies; to elect a Presidium while the Assembly is not in session; to approve the state economic plans and the state budgets; to establish or alter provincial and local administrative divisions; to grant amnesties; to elect a Supreme Court; and to appoint the Procurate-General. The Assembly, however, seldom exercises these powers independently. It is freely subjected to the will of the party and Kim Il-song. The Assembly is a large body of approximately 500 delegates. It meets infrequently and then only for two to six days. The primary function of the Assembly like in the PRC and other Communist states is to legitimize the decisions made elsewhere by the party and the Cabinet.

The Presidium is the permanent executive body of the Assembly, and its chairman, theoretically elected by the Assembly, acts as the titular head of state. The Presidium is empowered to convene the Assembly, to interpret the constitution and laws, to promulgate the laws adopted by the Assembly, as well as supervising daily activities of the executive and judicial branches. It also appoints and dismisses cabinet members upon the recommendation of the premier, ratifies and revokes treaties, and appoints or recalls envoys abroad.

The Cabinet is a major center of government authority in North Korea. Kim Il-song headed the Cabinet as premier until 1972, when he was named president under the new Constitution. The various Cabinet posts have been manned by some of the more powerful figures of the party.

In North Korea, the relationship between the national, provincial, and local governments is unitary as in the PRC, and the whole system is highly centralized. The constitution states that the local organs of state power in provinces, cities, counties, towns, villages, and workers' settlements are the respective people's assemblies. They are empowered to exercise state power in their political subdivisions. These assemblies are furthermore composed of the deputies periodically elected by the voters.

These local organs are not autonomous bodies. The constitution specifically provides that the people's committee at upper levels can repeal and change the resolutions passed by the people's assembly at lower levels.

The 1972 revisions of the constitution were to elevate Kim Il-song to his supreme leadership role, unfettered by any institutional constraints. Not only in the actual exercise of power but also structurally, he was to be supreme. Earlier, as previously noted, the chairman of the Presidium of the Supreme People's Assembly performed the functions of head of state. Kim Il-song's monopoly of power is unexcelled anywhere within the Communist world. Kim Il-song, as the newly provided President, is the head of state and represents the state power of the Democratic People's Republic of Korea. He is above the government and the party. He is almost a sacred personage in North Korea.

The reorganization of government under the new Constitution pro-

THE GOVERNMENT OF THE DEMOCRATIC PEOPLE'S
REPUBLIC OF KOREA (1972 –   )

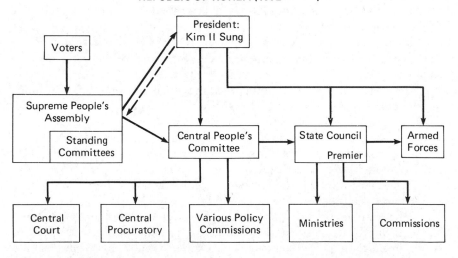

– – – – – (actual control)

FIGURE 8-2
The Government of the Democratic People's Republic of Korea (1972-   )

vided for the Central People's Committee and the Central Administrative Council, in place of the old Cabinet directly under the president. The Presidium of the Assembly was kept, but was also placed under the president. Kim, as the president, is head of the party. The president is not merely the chief executive, he is also the chief policy-maker and the chief justice. He is, at the same time, commander of the armed forces and the beloved chief of the people.

The Personality Cult of Kim Il-song

Kim Il-song is grand *suryong* (leader) of North Korea. His leadership is unquestioned. His words, written as well as spoken, are widely propagated. Kim's personality cult is practiced with unusual thoroughness.

The following, from the *Pyongyang Times*, is vividly descriptive of the degree to which Kim's personality cult is practiced in North Korea.

> Placed respectfully on the platform was a portrait of Comrade Kim Il-song, the greatest Leader of our Party and forty million Korean people, peerless patriot, national hero, ever-victorious iron-willed, brilliant commander and one of the outstanding leaders of the world Communist and working class movements. At the time when they were quietly awaiting the appearance of Comrade Kim Il-song, the respected and beloved Leader, the hearts of the entire attendants of the meeting were beating high with the unbounded reverence for, and trust in, and burning loyalty to the great and sagacious Leader who has confidently led our revolution along the road of victory for over forty years, personally ploughing rough its thorny bushes, taking upon himself the destiny of the fatherland and the nation, and the high honour and pride of being his revolutionary soldiers.

The report continues:

> At nine A.M., the respected and beloved Leader Comrade Kim Il-song, General Secretary of the Central Committee of the Workers' Party of Korea and the Premier of the Cabinet of the Democratic People's Republic of Korea, mounted the platform. At the movement the entire attendants of the meeting rose from their seats all at once and enthusiastically welcomed the respected and beloved Leader with the loud shout "long live Comrade Kim Il-song" and prolonged thunderous applause that shook the hall. Amid the shouts of *Manse* (hurrah) and prolonged applause, women labor innovators presented to Comrade Kim Il-song, the respected and beloved Leader, a basket of fragrant flowers carrying the feeling of unbounded adoration of the attendants of the meeting and the entire local industrial workers of the country.[4]

[4]*The Pyongyang Times*, March 2, 1970, cited in Yang Ho-min, "The Personality Cult of Kim Il-song as a Strategy for National Unification," in *Report of International Conference on the Problems of Korean Unification*, August 24-29, 1970 (Asiatic Research Center: Korea University, 1971), pp. 908-9.

The above scene is almost ritualistic in North Korea. The popular admiration of the supreme leader is ubiquitous. Kim is believed to be the most patriotic and outstanding leader, the legitimate successor of national independence movements, the legitimate political leader of both Koreas, and the only creative and determined leader of a truly independent Korean nation, free from foreign interference.

Kim's words and deeds are guidelines for all party members, workers, peasants, students, and office workers. For example, in February, 1960, Kim went to the Kangso County organization, and from there to the Ch'ongsan-li (village) organization and its component work teams. He was setting up an example—learn from the masses. Party workers were encouraged to learn from the masses for their works and in their promotion of the "cultural revolution" to remold the masses into the behavior patterns and ideology of the new society. This is the so-called "Ch'ongsan-li method." Kim's personal example is a widely used textbook. As Kim does, so does the rest of the population.

The Selected Works of Kim Il-Sung were first published in 1955. As they study the works of Kim Il-song, the people are armed with the unitary ideas of the party. During 1968 and 1969, two million copies of his writings were reported published with party funds, and they were distributed to all party members. Between the Fourth and Fifth Party Congresses (1961-1970), about thirty-nine million copies of them were reported published. Their translations have appeared in many languages. Their interpretations and analyses have been published in millions of copies. Kim's biography, *Brief History of the Revolutionary Activities of Comrade Kim Il-Sung*, is a required reading thoroughout the North Korean school system, party training schools, and special "leader study centers," found in various industries and communes.

The effects of Kim Il-song's personality cult serve to place him above the political milieu, as well as legitimize his personal control over the party and the government. Kim's leadership, therefore, is considered infallible.

Despite his personality cult, Kim's leadership is far from perfect. He has purged many leaders for many of the same faults that he himself exhibits. He is reputed to live well and maintain several villas for his personal use. To a large degree, nepotism is characteristic of his rule. Most importantly, serious errors in judgment, to which he has freely admitted, would have been sufficient reason for dismissal if they had occurred on lower levels. Kim's lack of accountability is the single most weighty effect of his cult. Whether this dictatorial system will persist after Kim is open to debate. Kim's position gives him powers to determine his own successor. To some extent, therefore, the effects of the personality cult of Kim Il-song may last beyond his death.

In the frenzy of his cult in 1967, Kim purged several of his Manchurian-Korean comrades. About one hundred party members at the upper level were reported removed. Their places have been taken over by a new generation of leaders more loyal to Kim. Several members of Kim's family, including his immediate family members, his brothers, and father-in-law have risen to important positions of power. Even Kim's genealogy has been revised to read:

> The family of Comrade Kim Il-song is a patriotic and revolutionary family that has fought from generation to generation for the independence of the country and the freedom and liberation of the people against foreign aggressors.[5]

Listed and illustrated as patriots are Kim's great-grandfather, grandfather, father, mother, uncle, brothers, and cousins. Kim's birthplace is a national shrine in North Korea. Kim's most likely successor is his son, Kim Chong-il.

The Chuch'e Ideology and the Workers' Party

Chuch'e means being one's own master, independent and guided by one's needs and available resources. It is the opposite of Confucianism, in which dependence on a ruler is fostered. From the time it was first expounded in 1955, before a group of Korean Workers' Party agitation and propaganda workers, the term has gradually become the trademark of Kim Il-song and the guiding spirit of the North Korean regime. Thus, in the new North Korean Constitution of 1972, the Chuch'e principle was given a distinct place in history: "The Democratic People's Republic of Korea is guided in its activity by the Chuch'e idea of the Workers' Party of Korea, which is a creative adaption of Marxism-Leninism to our country's reality."

By Kim's own admission, the idea of Chuch'e is not new. Kim, however, gave a special emphasis to it. Also significant is the time of its pronouncement. North Korea was then in the midst of recovering from damages incurred during the Korean War. North Korea had to rely on aid from its Communist allies, creating a fear of the loss of national identity by absorption into the Communist bloc.

Internationally, Chuch'e means solving the problem of reunification of the Korean people independently. It means expelling foreign "aggressors." The Korean people must follow the dictates of Kim Il-song, the supreme leader, in order to secure these goals.

[5]The Party History Institute of the Central Committee of the Workers' Party of Korea, ed., *Brief History of the Revolutionary Activities of Comrade Kim Il-Sung* (Pyongyang, Foreign Languages Publishing House, 1969), pp. 3-7.

The Workers' Party is Kim's organizational arm, an elite body of one and a half million members. It is organized hierarchically throughout the state system and controls and supervises the government and the people. Very often the personnel of government and the party overlap, and this is considered to be a natural career progression as men are shifted from party positions to government posts and vice versa.

According to the party constitution, the National Party Congress is "the highest decision-making organ of the Party," and is to convene every four years. The National Party Congress elects the Central Committee to direct the affairs of the party during the intervals between congresses. The Central Committee then elects its Standing Committee. During the Fourth Party Congress held in 1961, this Standing Committee was replaced by a newly created Political Committee (Politburo). Then at the Party Representative Conference in October, 1966, a Presidium (standing Committee) of the Political Committee was created Since the Fifth Congress of November, 1970, however, no reference has been made to this highest decision-making body.

The Party Congress also elects a Party Secretariat. The Party Secretariat was abolished in 1966 for some unknown reason. It was then revived in 1970, with Kim Il-song as General-Secretary. It has ten other secretaries. The Secretariat, as a collective body, supervises the thirteen party executive departments, which in turn supervise the government departments.

The bulk of organizational efforts are concentrated on mass organizations. These mass organizations are the mechanistic arm of a philosophy that seeks to make the North Korean a champion of the cause of the party and revolution. The training of the youth along ideological lines, therefore, receives top priority. The educational system also is based upon this policy and serves as an extension to the various youth organizations. The concept of "truth" is presented as an absolute, while any attempt to question objectively the party's goals is looked upon as subversive. The Young Pioneers and the Socialist Working Youth League are the two major youth groups, and together they form a united and somewhat monolithic Communist front.

In the vast youth-oriented literature, love of party, leader, and revolution receives the most attention. Ideology, in this context, takes on the attributes of faith, a faith so all encompassing that the individual should be prepared to exercise any sacrifice to further party priorities. A further emphasis for the youth is the inculcation of a militaristic, revolutionary mood in the young, as physical defenders of the revolution. Finally, the advance of productivity for the state becomes yet another ideological imperative for the youth.

Although the greatest emphasis of socialization is directed to the young, women and workers also receive considerable attention. The Korean Democratic Women's League serves a dual function. In one way, its role is to increase the productivity of the women's labor force, yet it also aims at the politicization of women through special interest programs, such as child care and hygiene. The mass occupational organizations have assumed major proportions, as well. The Korean Agricultural Workers Federation (KAWF) encompasses workers, technicians, and administrative personnel engaged in agriculture and other rural pursuits. The KAWF has responsibility for education along political and technical lines for all farm workers. In the industrial area, the General Federation of Korean Trade Unions serves basically the same function as does KAWF in the rural setting.

In North Korea, local government is seen as an instrument of mass mobilization. The administrative and bureaucratic functions of the government at the local level are carried out by "administrative cadres" whose function is designed to maintain close contact with the people, as well as promulgating the party line. The class line of ideological loyalty to the chuch'e movement is seen to merge with the mass line of administrative competence.

Party membership is viewed as a combination of privilege and responsibility. It involves study, discipline, and the necessity of serving as a teacher to the masses.

THE PATTERNS OF DEVELOPMENT

Kim's total mobilization of people has meant regimentation of society along military lines. The people are organized into production units. Personal desires are subordinated to collective needs. Instead of more food and consumer goods, Kim has called for more austerity and patriotic demonstrations.

North Korea recovered from the war with the aid of the Soviet Union, Communist China, and other Communist bloc nations. Reconstruction was part of the long-term plan of development. Although the credibility of official figures is in question, by the end of the Three-Year Plan (1954-1956), North Korea had regained its pre-war status. The five-year plan (1957-1961) involved the collectivization of agriculture in 1958, and the initiation of the *Cho'llima* Movement, an equivalent of Communist China's "Great Leap Forward." The Cho'llima was a concerted effort to mobilize the masses for "socialism," economic self-sufficiency, and independence. The movement, however, had the unfortunate effect of unbalancing the economy, but has been modified in recent years to produce real benefits.

If 1958 figures are used as a base to compare North and South Korea in terms of national income, the North Korean figures over the ten-year period from 1953 to 1962 are impressive. The average annual growth rate was 22.1 percent, compared with 3.6 percent for South Korea. However, South Korea made great strides in economic development in the 1960s, growing at a rate of 10.2 percent in the 1963-1973 period, whereas North Korea suffered a slow-down. The growth rate of North Korea during the same period was estimated at 6.5 percent. The earlier advantages of Soviet style planning in North Korea were not without adverse effects.

The North Korean economy is in need of major readjustment. With an increasingly independent economic and political posture, foreign aid has been reduced. As an industrializing nation, North Korea needs trading partners, but is faced with growing isolation. Furthermore, North Korea suffers from labor shortages and has been relatively unsuccessful in wooing Koreans back from Japan. Other problems resulting from the Stalinistic emphasis on heavy industrial development involved the sacrifice of development in other economic sectors, especially light industry and agriculture. The North Korean population has been compelled to accept a lower standard of living than their counterparts in the South. The ideologically-motivated development program has been pressed at the expense of quality, effectiveness, and an awareness of inter-relationships between sectors of the economy. It has also been executed without properly trained personnel. The result is constant breakdowns and inefficiency. Relentless pressure to mobilize human capital for greater production and longer hours of work is countered by deficiencies and lack of bold, local initiatives.

Readjustment in the North Korean pattern of development involves improving the lot of the people. It means promoting balanced development in light and heavy industries, as well as agriculture. Such a redirection of priorities seems to have been the objective of the Seven-Year Plan (1961-1967). But Kim postponed the completion date of the plan for three years. The goals of the Seven-Year Plan were not met, and further planning efforts have been difficult.

In summary, we have seen abnormal patterns of development in both North and South Korea. Except for the short but costly interlude of the Korean War, the two Koreas have been forced to co-exist despite a strong urge, on both sides, for reunification. Neither side has been able to generate a Vietnamese-type guerrilla war in the other half. Instead, each side has sought to become a showcase of development for its sponsoring power.

In North Korea, an imported Soviet-type government had initial success in achieving political stability and generating economic development. Increasingly, however, political stability is maintained by silencing the opposition, further regimenting the society, and exploiting the personality cult of Kim Il-song. Moreover, the Sino-Soviet rift has created new problems. Kim treads a tightrope between the dangers of "revisionism" in the Soviet Union and "extremism" in Communist China.

THE PROBLEM OF REUNIFICATION

For the two Koreas, the major political problem remains the reunification of the country. Korea has suffered from the politics of the Cold War, and it may be that detente among the big powers would help Korean reunification. Partly in reaction to changes in the international scene, character-ized by a personal visit to Peking by President Nixon early in 1972, the two Koreas have begun official discussions for peaceful reunification.

On August 15, 1970, President Park of South Korea, in his speech commemorating the twenty-fifth anniversary of Korean liberation, called upon the North Korean government to renounce force and join South Korea in a peaceful contest for economic and social development. North Korea's initial reaction was to reject it as empty rhetoric. Then the South Korean Red Cross Society proposed a meeting with its North Korean counterpart for a humanitarian project aimed at reuniting the families separated by the division of the country. Surprisingly, North Korea readily agreed, and their first meeting was held on August 20, 1971, at Panmun-jom, along the demilitarized zone, thus initiating the subsequent round of talks. More dramatic was an announcement in Seoul and in Pyongyong on July 4, 1972, about the secret meetings of representatives to discuss Korean reunification. The announcement stated that they had agreed to set up a North-South Coordinating Committee to prevent armed clashes, facilitate exchanges, expedite the Red Cross talks, and settle the unification problem. Subsequently the Committee met with great fanfare, only to be stalemated and suspended from further meeting. The first plenary meet-ings of the Committee were held in Seoul on November 30, and Decem-ber 1, 1972. Altogether three such meetings were held alternately in Seoul and Pyongyang, before their suspension by the August 28, 1973 announce-ment on Radio Pyongyang that North Korea was "unilaterally leaving the table." In order to resume the dialogue, North Korea demanded that South Korea:

1. Replace the head of its Committee delegation, Lee Hu Rak, who, as Director of South Korea's CIA, was implicated in the Tokyo kidnapping of self-exiled opposition leader, Kim Tae-jun.
2. Renounce its new foreign policy statement for peace and unification, which assumed the existence of two Koreas.
3. Stop "punishing" Communists by legalizing their activities and releas-ing all Communists serving prison terms.

4. Reorganize the Committee for wider participation of individuals, social organizations, and political parties.

The causes for the deadlock were, of course, more deeply rooted than those stated in the Pyongyang announcement. Each regime had different perceptions about the dialogue. To North Korea, the dialogue may have been to probe into the durability of the South Korean system. South Korea was believed to be a corrupt, chaotic, and stagnant country on the verge of collapse. North Korea perhaps also wanted to convince the United States to withdraw its military presence from the peninsula. North Korea insisted on removal of American troops from South Korea and on the resolution of basic political problems dealing with reunification. To South Korea, the dialogue was perhaps to show North Korea the progress made in recent years. It was also to prevent North Korea's possible military onslaught and continued subversive attempts.

Since the announcement of the so-called Nixon Doctrine in 1969, South Korea has shown a grave concern over what seemed to be America's return to isolationism. America's military interest in South Korea has been waning. South Korea has become uncertain about America's commitment to its defense, in case of another war provoked by North Korea. The dialogue gave time to South Korea to become stronger militarily and economically. Indeed, against North Korea's advocacy of resolving critical political questions first, South Korea advocated a gradual, step-by-step approach, starting with the resolution of non-political and humanitarian problems, such as the reunion of divided families.

The North-South dialogue was an interlude. Through it, they discovered irreconcilable differences wrought by the Cold War animosity of more than twenty-five years. The dialogue was a mutually self-reinforcing experience, with each hardening its intractable position against the other. The big power detente in the 1970s has not resolved their differences.

In the North, the Communist system of Kim Il-song rules supreme. In the South, the civil-military regime headed by President Park Chung Hee thrives on anti-Communism and fear of a North Korean threat. Neither side has been able to generate a national liberation war against the other. Each has proven its own viability. Each has developed its own vested interests. North Korea is determined to see a united Communist state of Korea, whereas South Korea is uncompromising in its anti-Communist North Korean stance.

As has often been pointed out, the two Koreas share many things in common. What deters their reunification, however, are leadership differences. Historically, Korea was for a long time a unified country. Geographically, the Korean peninsula is well-defined and the North-South division is artificial. Ethnically, the Korean people are primarily of one group and speak the same language. Economically, the two Koreas are complementary in many areas. Politically, they show many similarities and share the same traditional political culture and authoritarian outlook. The Korean people are, furthermore, strongly desirous of reunification of their artificially divided land.

The critical problem of Korean reunification is leadership. The leaders of both Koreas must be willing to sacrifice their personal powers and transcend their parochial interests. They must also be convinced that they are compatible and that their actions toward reunification would not involve wholesale destruction of their power.

RECOMMENDED READINGS

Berger, Carl, *The Korea Knot: A Military-Political History*. Philadelphia: University of Pennsylvania Press, 1967.

Cho, Soon-Sung, *Korea in World Politics, 1940-1950*. Berkeley, Calif.: University of California Press, 1967.

Chung, Joseph S. II., *North Korean Economy: Structure and Development*. Stanford, Calif.: Hoover Institution, 1972.

Chung, Kyung-Cho, *Korea: The Third Republic*. New York: Macmillan, 1970.

Cole, David C., and Princeton N. Lyman, *Korean Development: The Interplay of Politics and Economics*. Cambridge, Mass.: Harvard University Press, 1971.

Conroy, Hilary, *The Japanese Seizure of Korea*. Philadelphia: University of Pennsylvania Press, 1961.

Dallet, Charles, *Traditional Korea*. New Haven, Conn.: Human Relations Area Files, 1954.

Grajdanzev, Andrew J., *Modern Korea: Her Economic and Social Development Under the Japanese*. New York: Institute of Pacific Relations, 1944.

Hahm, Pyong-Choon, *The Korean Political Tradition and Law*. Seoul: Hollym, 1967.

Han, Sungjoo, *The Failure of Democracy in South Korea*. Berkeley, Calif.: University of California Press, 1974.

Henderson, Gregory, *Korea: The Politics of the Vortex*. Cambridge, Mass.: Harvard University Press, 1968.

Hong, Sung-Chick, *The Intellectual and Modernization: A Study of Korean Attitudes*. Seoul: Korea University Press, 1967.

Kim, C. I. Eugene, "Korea at the Crossroads: The Birth of the Fourth Republic," *Pacific Affairs*, Vol. 46, No. 2 (Summer 1973), 211-31.

——————, and Han-Kyo Kim. *Korea and the Politics of Imperialism, 1876-1910*. Berkeley, Calif.: University of California Press, 1967.

——————, and Young-Whan Kihl, eds., *Parties and Electoral Politics in Korea*. Silver Spring, Md.: Research Institute on Korean Affairs, 1975.

Kim, Ilpyong J., *Communist Politics in North Korea*. New York: Praeger, 1967.

Kim, Joungwon A., *Divided Korea: The Politics of Development, 1945-1972*. Cambridge, Mass.: East Asian Research Center, Harvard University, 1975.

Kim, Kwang-Bong., *The Korea-Japan Treaty Crisis and the Instability of the Korean Political System.* New York: Praeger, 1971.

Kim, Se-Jin, *The Politics of Military Revolution in Korea.* Chapel Hill, N.C.: University of North Carolina Press, 1971.

——————, and Chang-Hyun Cho, eds., *Government and Politics of Korea.* Silver Spring, Md.: Research Institute on Korean Affairs, 1972.

Koh, Byung-Chul, *The Foreign Policy of North Korea.* New York: Praeger, 1969.

Lee, Chong-Sik, *The Politics of Korean Nationalism.* Berkeley, Calif.: University of California Press, 1963.

Lee, Hahn-Been, *Time, Change and Administration.* Honolulu: East West Center Press, 1967.

Li, Yuk-Sa, ed., *Juche: The Speeches and Writings of Kim Il Sung.* New York: Grossman, 1972.

McCune, George M., *Korea Today.* Cambridge, Mass.: Harvard University Press, 1950.

Meade, E. Grant, *American Military Government in Korea.* New York: Columbia University Press, 1951.

Nelson, Melvin Frederick, *Korea and the Old Orders in Eastern Asia.* Baton Rouge: Louisiana State University Press, 1945.

Oh, John K. C., *Korea: Democracy on Trial.* Ithaca, N.Y.: Cornell University Press, 1968.

Oliver, Robert, *Syngman Rhee: The Man Behind the Myth.* New York: Dodd, Mead, 1954.

Osgood, Cornelius, *The Koreans and Their Culture.* New York: Ronald Press, 1951.

Paige, Glenn D., *The Korean People's Democratic Republic.* Stanford, Calif.: Hoover Institution, 1968.

Park, Chung Hee, *Our Nation's Path: Ideology of Social Reconstruction.* Seoul: Dong-a Publishing Co., 1962.

Reeves, W. David, *The Republic of Korea.* London: Oxford University Press, 1963.

Scalapino, Robert A., and Chong-Sik Lee. *Communism in Korea,* 2 vols. Berkeley, Calif.: University of California Press, 1972.

Suh, Dae-Sook, *The Korean Communist Movement, 1918-1948.* Princeton, N.J.: Princeton University Press, 1968.

Wright, Edward Reynolds, ed., *Korean Politics in Transition.* Seattle, Wash.: University of Washington Press, 1975.

Index